LEARNING TO BE A WINNER

Whether you're a beginner or a sophisticated, on-the-go gambler, this authoritative guide is a must if you want to improve your skills and gain the winning edge. Up-to-date and comprehensive, it covers the most popular games played today, both at home and in the casino, including poker, rummy, bridge, pinochle, hearts, blackjack, craps, baccarat, roulette, backgammon, and chess among others. Valuable as a reference for checking rules, this book also gives the insights and strategies you need to obtain the best possible odds for yourself—no matter what the gamble.

THE NEW AMERICAN
GUIDE TO GAMBLING AND GAMES

EDWIN SILBERSTANG brings to his expertise in this field a novelist's writing skill, a lawyer's precision, and an ex-intelligence officer's concern with significant detail. Among his previously published works on the subject of gambling are *The Winner's Guide to Casino Gambling* (available in both Plume and Signet editions), *How to Gamble and Win*, *Winning Poker Strategy*, and *Winning Casino Craps*. A former resident of New York, he now lives in Studio City, California, and travels frequently to the gambling capitals of the world.

THE NEW AMERICAN
GUIDE TO GAMBLING
AND GAMES

Edwin Silberstang

A PLUME BOOK

NEW AMERICAN LIBRARY

NEW YORK AND SCARBOROUGH, ONTARIO

TO

Julian & Allan

NAL BOOKS ARE AVAILABLE AT QUANTITY DISCOUNTS WHEN USED TO
PROMOTE PRODUCTS OR SERVICES. FOR INFORMATION PLEASE WRITE
TO PREMIUM MARKETING DIVISION, NEW AMERICAN LIBRARY,
1633 BROADWAY, NEW YORK, NEW YORK 10019.

 PLUME TRADEMARK REG. U.S. PAT. OFF. AND FOREIGN COUNTRIES
REG. TRADEMARK—MARCA REGISTRADA
HECHO EN HARRISONBURG, VA., U.S.A.

SIGNET, SIGNET CLASSIC, MENTOR, ONYX, PLUME, MERIDIAN and
NAL BOOKS are published *in the United States* by NAL PENGUIN INC.,
1633 Broadway, New York, New York 10019, *in Canada* by The
New American Library of Canada Limited, 81 Mack Avenue,
Scarborough, Ontario M1L 1M8

Library of Congress Cataloging-in-Publication Data

Silberstang, Edwin, 1930–
    The new American guide to gambling and games.

    Includes index.
    1. Games.   2. Gambling.   3. Gambling systems.
1. Title.
GV1301.S52   1987   795   87-5713
ISBN 0-452-26007-8

First Plume Printing, September, 1987

1 2 3 4 5 6 7 8 9

PRINTED IN THE UNITED STATES OF AMERICA

Contents

Author's Preface

The theme of the book is adventure and boldness. The games in this book lend themselves to adventure, for each is exciting in its own way, and each is a challenge.

Too often, we give up the true adventure of life to immerse ourselves instead in dreams and fantasies, allying our lives with the destinies of sports, TV or movie personalities. How much more satisfying to accept the challenge that life offers, and that games, which are an integral part of life, also offer!

In order to be bold, we must be serenely confident of our skill and knowledge. We must act when the opportunity presents itself; when the odds, whether in life or games, are in our favor. Otherwise, there is nothing but regret, certainly not joy or fortune. So, for those who desire this adventure, who want to test their skill, their talent and their luck in a variety of interesting games, this book is written.

"Chance favors the well prepared."

Introduction

The games discussed in this book fall into three major categories: games of chance; games of skill; and games involving both chance and skill.

First we have the games of pure chance. In this group we deal with the basic table games played in American and Caribbean casinos—craps, roulette, and baccarat. All three games deal with random probability; there is no skill needed to play them. By skill we mean the ability of the player, by his own knowledge and grasp of the game, to affect the final outcome. A player cannot do this in craps, roulette, or baccarat. The only possible skill involved in craps is knowing the most effective bets. This essentially means making those bets whose odds are least unfavorable to the player. There are absolutely no favorable bets in any of these games.

Since the last edition of this work, baccarat and its European counterpart, chemin de fer, have been added to this book, and these games are covered in full. The European version of roulette has also been added. Thus the reader can gamble at these games intelligently no matter where he or she is in the world.

But they remain games of pure chance, which eliminate the factor of past performance. Each new event in any of these games is completely independent of any previous or future event. For example, if ten passes in a row were thrown in a game of craps (assuming that the dice are honest), the eleventh roll would still be at the same odds on the front line—approximately 1.40 percent in favor of the house—for each roll is independent of any other roll and is not affected by the past.

The same is true of roulette. If fifteen reds came up in a row, the sixteenth spin of the wheel would still be favorable to the house by 5.26 percent (assuming a double zero) and the odds for or against another red coming up would not be affected at all by what had happened previously. Many systems are based on continuous rolls of dice or spins of the roulette wheel, as affected by past performance, but all such systems are futile, being based on an erroneous premise.

To play these games of pure chance, all a player must bring to the game is a basic knowledge of the best bets; that is, bets least favorable to the house. Knowing this, he knows most of what is involved.

Blackjack, as played in a casino or private game, is another money game. Again we have skill and luck combined. In the casino game, which is covered here much more extensively than the private game, all possible skill is necessary to win, since it is built up as an unfavorable game by the gambling bosses. If the skill is not learned, the odds remain with the house at all times. Unless he has full knowledge of the odds and adjusts his bets accordingly, unless all the options open to the player are mastered and taken advantage of, the average player has little chance of winning.

The second category of games is those of pure skill. The typical game of skill, and indeed the most popular and complex game yet devised by the mind of western man, is chess. Unlike games of pure chance, chess is not a gambling game; the pleasure is in the game itself, in winning and in playing well. It provides enormous challenge, for although any game of skill can theoretically be played perfectly, no man has a perfect mind. Yet the best minds continue to search for perfection, and, of all the games, the search is most challenging in chess.

Here there is no luck at all involved. The game is open to view, each player has an equal number of moves, and nothing is really unknown. Theoretically, the better player should beat the less skillful player, all other factors being equal.

In the third category are most of the games presented in this book. They are games involving not only skill, but chance as well. Practically all of them are card games. In some, like bridge, the skillful aspect of the game far outweighs the element of luck involved. In a game like knock rummy, the opposite may be said to be true. Other card games fall somewhere in between.

Bridge, since it is so skillful a game, tends to be less of a gambling game. It has been my experience in the study of these games that the more skillful the game, the less the desire to gamble on it. The pleasure is in the playing, and the reward is a win as a result of best play. While bridge is certainly not as skillful a game as chess, since there is an element of luck involved by the mere dealing of different hands and the placement of key cards in these hands (an unknown factor), it is skillful enough to be enjoyed without stakes.

Some games, such as poker, are difficult to classify in terms of skill and luck. Because poker can only be enjoyed when playing for stakes, the element of skill tends to be downgraded. However, it cannot be totally ignored, for almost certainly, over the course of time, a skilled player will beat an unskilled player in poker. What skill is involved? In the normal game for limited stakes, the skill is in staying in or going out, calling bets, or raising them, gauging the odds against drawing certain cards. There are other skill factors involved, but these are the essential ones. However, when the game of poker moves into higher stakes or unlimited stakes, the psychological aspect comes to the fore, and the whole character of the game changes. Not only must the ordinary skills be present, but the opponent's mind, his thoughts and actions, must be weighed. Otherwise, no matter how skilled the player, he will be at a disadvantage. Since signals and emphasis on bids are restricted in bridge, while in poker all kinds of inferences may attach to any move or bet, the psychological factor of poker far outweighs that of bridge. Often the test of skill in bridge is in having an exact knowledge of the odds involved in breaks of suits, etc. This knowledge is also essential in poker, but the bet itself, which is not present in bridge, also has overtones which must be considered.

Thus, bridge and poker each have their adherents. For the conservative player, bridge might be better. For the daring player, high-stakes poker cannot be praised too highly.

Other games involve a balance of skill and luck. Auction pinochle is a very skillful game, but not so skillful that it can be played without stakes. Many times in pinochle the hands are conceded. This rarely happens in bridge. It does not enjoy the enormous popularity of contract bridge because, although it has partnership aspects, it is not, like bridge, a purely partnership game. Also, it cannot be played as a duplicate game, a factor which enables bridge to surmount most of the elements of luck attached to is as a rubber game. Pinochle is much like rubber bridge. Duplicate bridge is much like chess.

We have not dealt with duplicate bridge here, other than to outline its basic rules and importance. Without duplicate bridge, contract bridge would certainly not enjoy its enormous popularity. Playing it, any partnership or team of four can aspire to championship status, and the result of good play is expressed in master points. Partners playing duplicate bridge can know their own strength in relation to the other players; they can compete in national and international tournaments. Except for chess, there is no other nonathletic game, played on an international scale, with so many world class players.

Gin rummy is a game of luck and skill which is often enjoyed as a social game. There has been some effort to make it into a competitive game, much in the manner of duplicate bridge, and indeed some tournaments have been held, particularly in Las Vegas. It is not a more skillful game than pinochle, and one of the reasons that pinochle is only good when played for stakes, while gin rummy can be played socially, is that in pinochle there is an auction and active bidding. Without money being involved, the bidding would have no limit, since there would be nothing to lose.

This is not to say that all these games cannot be played socially. Certainly they can. When I speak of them as being money games, I mean that the enjoyment of these games is enhanced by stakes. Not all games are so improved. Certainly chess would not benefit as a money game, since the tension and excitement are already there.

Blackjack, as played in a casino or in a private game, is another money game. Again we have skill and luck combined. In the casino game, which is covered here much more extensively than the private game, all possible skill is necessary to win, since it is built up as an unfavorable game by the gambling bosses. If the skill is not learned, the odds remain with the house at all times. Unless he has full knowledge of the odds and adjusts his bets accordingly, unless all the options open to the player are mastered and taken advantage of, the average player has little chance of winning.

Blackjack and poker are the only card games discussed in this book that are recommended for play in casino. Poker is a game of skill, and if the house rake isn't too great—that is, doesn't exceed 5 percent—a skillful player can make a living as a professional in the game. In this book, we'll discuss most of the poker variations played in the Nevada casinos, such as seven-card stud, high-low split, draw, and Texas Hold 'Em.

Because of their popularity, I've included chapters on horse racing and sports event betting. Horse racing, for all the millions bet on it, is a much misunderstood gambling situation, and I have endeavored to show the possibilities of confronting it on its own terms. Otherwise, any random play bucks about about an 18 percent service charge. Sports events betting has become a major way of life for many gamblers, who bet on football, baseball, and basketball both in the casinos and illegally with bookmakers.

I've excluded the pure sucker games offered in the casinos, such as slot machines, keno, chuck-a-luck, and the big six wheel. The house edge is too great, and it would be foolish for any serious player to attempt to win these games.

Slot machines will pay back anywhere from 96 percent to 60 percent in the more greedy casinos. The payoffs have grown steadily to the point that a lucky player can win over a million dollars with the pull of a handle. From nickel games, the slots now allow players to bet a dollar at a time, and some machines swallow up three to five dollars a pull, which really adds up. Of course, the suckers have stars in their eyes, dreaming of the million-dollar payoffs.

Keno has become a popular casino game, and many of the lounges that featured singers and small groups of musicians have given way to this game. The house edge is at least 30 percent no matter what bet you make, and keno likewise has been left out of this book.

I've updated the book since its last printing, bringing it into line with the 1980s, introducing some new games and considerably expanding discussion of others. As mentioned in the original and subsequent editions, all the games presented in this book have interested me, and quite a bit of enjoyment can be had sampling them. Some will appeal more than others to particular individuals, but there is enough skill, chance, and excitement in all of them to find an audience among those who want to test their skill, their luck, or themselves.

Above all, this book will make you a winner.

THE NEW AMERICAN
GUIDE TO GAMBLING
AND GAMES

I

Shuffling Cutting & Dealing

♠ ♥ ♦ ♣

Introduction

One of the best protections against being cheated, or put to a disadvantage by improper mixing of the cards or poor dealing, is a knowledge of correct shuffling, cutting, and dealing methods.

Shuffling

In my experience with card players, I have noticed that approximately 50 percent of those I have played with didn't know how to properly shuffle a deck of cards. They were so sloppy, in fact, that all an opponent had to do was watch carefully and he could keep track of one or two cards in the deck. This is a terrible disadvantage to the shuffler. Avoid any disadvantage; avoid being cheated. Learn to shuffle correctly.

One of the major faults of shufflers is that they know only one method of shuffling and use it exclusively. Or, if they vary their methods, they do so only in the last mixing of the cards, which does little to break the concentration of an opponent who has seen cards during the shuffle. A dealer should vary the "riffle shuffle" with the "overhand shuffle," mixing the cards extensively with both methods. He should also cut the cards in the suggested way during the shuffle. In this way he will minimize, if not entirely eliminate, any advantage the opponent might gain from improperly mixed cards.

Overhand Shuffle

Most players, when thinking of shuffling, think there is but one method. There are, in fact, two techniques. The first is known as the overhand shuffle.

3

To accomplish this shuffle, hold the deck of cards comfortably in the left hand (or right hand, if you're left-handed), so that the bottom card is against the palm and four fingers (not the thumb) and the back of the top card is in view. The thumb should be on the top of the deck, and the other fingers on the bottom of the deck. With the right hand, grasp the deck from beneath so that the right thumb is against the bottom edge of the deck (not the lengthwise edge) and some of the other fingers against the top edge. Now, lift the cards with the right hand so the left thumb pulls off a few cards at a time (see illustration). Keep dropping the remainder of the deck on the

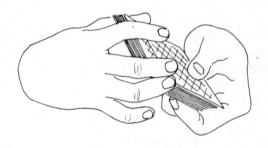

Overhand shuffle

cards that remain in the left hand, until all the cards are taken off the deck, and a new deck now forms in the left hand. That, in essence, is the overhand shuffle.

What this shuffle does is break up the deck into small packets of five or ten cards and mix them up to some degree. Some players rely on this shuffle alone, but it will not really divide melds or sequences sufficiently. To do this, the riffle shuffle must be employed.

Riffle Shuffle

Split the deck of cards into two equal or almost equal piles and put them on the table so that the cards are resting face down. The smaller edges of each pack should face each other, rather than the two longer ones. Now, with the middle phalanx of the index finger of each hand pressing against the top of each pile, grasp the piles so that the thumb knuckles face each other and almost touch, while the other three fingers of each hand grasp the

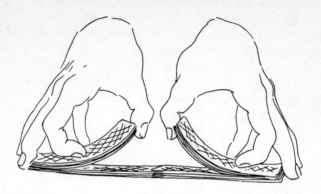

Riffle shuffle

far edge of the cards (see illustration). Press up with the thumbs so that the cards arch against the index-finger phalanxes, and keeping tension in the cards, slowly release the tension with the thumbs so that the bottom cards snap down, card by card, one from the right pile and one from the left pile, overlapping by approximately a quarter of an inch. After all the cards are released in this manner, the two piles should interlock at their inner edges. Now, lift up the thumbs and remove the index fingers and, with the three remaining fingers in each hand, push the two piles into one.

It all sounds very complicated, but it's quite easy to learn and anyone with normal dexterity can do it gracefully and well.

When shuffling a deck of cards, mix up the overhand with the riffle shuffle. Do the overhand twice, the riffle shuffle twice, the overhand once,

Cutting while shuffling

the riffle twice, then the overhand twice and riffle once. By this time the cards should be fairly well mixed. Alternate from the above ratios, too, so that there is no fixed way that you shuffle the cards. After a couple of overhand and riffle shuffles, take the pack, put it flat on the table, remove the middle portion (see illustration) and put this portion on the top, and continue with the shuffles. This kind of cut breaks the pattern of the cards, so that anyone trying to follow a particular card will lose his way. Do it a couple of times during the shuffling.

Avoiding Exposure of Bottom Card

When using the overhand shuffle, it is important to remember that the cards should be held perpendicular to your body. The bottom of the deck should be parallel to the floor. In this way, no one can see the faces of the cards as you shuffle them. Also, your hands should be just a couple of inches off the table, to further eliminate anyone's possible view of the card faces.

When using the riffle shuffle, do not lift the cards off the table, but press them together at the end of the shuffle while they are flat on the table. Again, don't let anyone see the bottom of the deck or all your shuffling will have been in vain.

If you watch the other players shuffling, you will immediately notice how badly they mix the cards and how, with keen observance, it is not difficult to see the cards on the bottom as they are shuffled. Don't be sloppy. Practice till perfect. It is easy to learn and will save you a lot of money, believe me.

Cutting

Cutting is a very simple proposition. Simply take a portion of the deck and put it to one side, so that two piles are formed. Then the dealer puts the part not removed on the top of the removed part. Make sure he doesn't simply put the removed part back on top.

Never cut the cards in the same place twice. Try not to cut them in the middle all the time. If the deck seems to divide naturally so that you seem to be lifting the cards at a certain point all the time, check to be sure that the cards aren't crimped. (See *Cheating at Cards*.)

If possible, cut the cards occasionally by the method illustrated. Simply pick up the middle portion of the deck, put it on top, then cut in the regular

Cutting

fashion. That simple maneuver should disrupt any predetermined examination of the cards.

Dealing

Dealing is just as important as shuffling. Each card should point downward as it is slid off the top of the deck; the whole deck should be pointing this way, so that the front edge is at a slight angle to the table. As each card is slid off, it should be held by the right thumb and forefinger and carried as long a distance as possible before being released in the direction of the player. Don't throw it across, and don't reach him with it. He should have to gather it in by extending his arm.

The point of all this is that nobody should see any of the cards dealt to anyone else. Deal in the way suggested and no one will.

After you finish dealing, or after any round of dealing, put the stock or unused portion of the deck face down on the table, so that the bottom card cannot be seen. Again, giving away this advantage by a sloppy deal is sealing your doom. Be careful.

All of the foregoing is quite easy to master. With just a little time and effort you will be a competent and safe dealer and, most important, you won't be giving away information that would make you a loser before you began.

II

Poker

♠ ♥ ♦ ♣

Introduction

Poker is the great American card game. It originated in the United States, and its advocates have spread its popularity around the world.

Although it is played in some gambling casinos, it is basically a private game. It is played by people of all ages as a money game, and the stakes involved may be pennies or thousands of dollars. Either way, it is exciting to play, fascinating to learn, and involves more than good card sense. To play well one must take into consideration the psychology of the opposition and must count on one's own skill, knowledge, and courage.

There are literally dozens of variations of poker, but the basic games are covered in this book. A good poker player will find that he can accommodate himself to any variation of the game, for the strategy remains basically the same.

The question is often asked: Is poker a game of luck or a game of skill? The question is easily answered. A merely lucky player will never be a consistent winner at poker; a skillful player will. Anyone who sits down at a poker table thinking the game requires only luck will be disappointed, both in his performance and in the adventure of the game, for it is one of the most exciting games when played at its best. And, in addition, it can be rewarding financially—two very good reasons for learning to play well.

How the Game Is Played

The Dealer
In all poker games, a dealer gives out the cards to the players on all

rounds of play. In private games and in the California poker rooms, the dealer is one of the participants, whereas in the Nevada casinos, the house supplies a dealer, and the players never get to deal the cards.

In all private games and in the California parlors, each player gets a turn dealing the cards, and he or she deals to all participants, including himself or herself. Each player deals once in rotation, and the deal moves around the table in clockwise fashion.

In those poker games, such as draw and Hold 'Em, where position is important, the deal has value, since the dealer acts and bets last. In the stud games, it is merely a chore.

The dealer must shuffle the cards before they are first dealt out, and after a game is complete, the cards must be reshuffled by the new dealer. After they are thoroughly shuffled, they're given to the player on the dealer's right to be cut. If this player refuses, any other player can cut the cards. Then they're restacked by the dealer, and the deal commences. In all first rounds of poker, the cards are dealt one at a time, face down, till each player gets a card. In five-card stud, the second card will be dealt face up, but again, each player will get one card in turn. In seven-card stud, the first two cards are dealt face down, and the third face up.

In draw poker, all five cards will be dealt face down, and on the next round of play, a group of cards will be given to each player remaining in contention, according to the player's needs. For example, a player may request three cards, and will get all three at once. Draw poker's second round of play is the exception to the rule that all players get one card at a time.

In five- and seven-card stud, all subsequent rounds of play require each player, in turn, to get one card at a time from the dealer.

The dealer calls the game. In stud poker, where cards are open on the table, he or she announces the high or low hand (depending upon the game) and makes certain that the right player makes the first bet, and that all other bets are made in sequence and for the right amount.

In all poker games, the dealer gets the last card dealt, and always deals the first card to the player on his or her left, so that the deal is clockwise.

The Ante

The ante is defined as money placed into the pot prior to the deal of the cards in order to enhance, or "sweeten," the pot. When antes are required, all players must contribute their share if they intend to play that next game of poker.

Once in the pot, the ante cannot be withdrawn, even if players subsequently fold their cards and go out. Antes may be waived in home games such as seven-card stud when there's a great deal of action, but in draw poker and five-card stud, they usually are mandatory. In the Nevada casinos and California clubs, they are almost always required.

Antes may be divided into three categories: low, normal, and high. A normal ante would be 50¢ in a $5-$10 game, or $1 in a $10-$20 one. In other words, a normal ante is 10 percent of the low range on the betting scale. Any ante lower than 10 percent is a low ante, while one in excess of 10 percent could be considered a high ante.

In high-ante games, there is more fast play, that is, raising and betting at the outset on the first round, because it is to the players' benefit to "steal the ante." In low-ante games, the game is slower for the most part, for the antes are too small to be worth "stealing."

Betting Limits

Most poker games have at least a double-tiered limit, with the higher limit double the lower. For example, there is $1-$2 poker, $3-$6, $5-$10, and so forth.

In draw poker, the higher limit prevails after the players have drawn cards to improve their hands. In stud poker, the higher limit is in force on an open pair or in a later betting round. In private games, the players set the limits prior to actual play, and decide when the higher limits will prevail. In casino and club games, the rules are stricter, and are usually printed for all to see.

Betting limits will remain in force in a casino game at a particular table. For instance, if you sit down at a $5-$10 game, that is going to be the limit while that game is played. In private games, however, the limits can be raised or lowered with the consent of the players remaining in the game. Sometimes, after a few hours of play, the losers have departed, or want to get even, and so the game may be changed to incorporate higher limits.

Most games are table-stakes games, and this is almost the universal case in casinos and clubs. Table stakes mean the amount of cash and chips on the table in front of the player. For example, if, during a round of play, the player has run out of money on the table, he cannot then take more money from his pocket to bet with. He can no longer make any bets while that game is going on, but after it is over, he can then replenish his table stakes. Suppose that, on the second round of betting in seven-card stud, a player runs out of table money. What happens? He is still in the game, but all other bets are segregated, and he cannot share in any of the pot made up of bets after he has run out of money. Even if he has the best cards of all the players, he only wins the pot made up of his own money and that of others before he went dry. The second-best hand would win the remainder of the pot with the segregated funds in it.

Betting Rounds

The number of rounds depends upon the particular game played. In draw poker, there are two rounds of play, prior to the draw and after. There are at least two rounds of betting in all poker games, and sometimes many more.

In seven-card stud there are five rounds, while in Texas Hold 'Em and five-card stud there are four rounds altogether.

Who Bets First

Betting first, or "bringing it in" in poker parlance, plays an important role in the game. It is always to the advantage of a player to bet late or last; then he or she can act more intelligently, having seen what has preceded him. On the opening round of play in draw poker, there are two separate situations going on: who acts first and who bets first. In a game like Jackpots, in which only a hand containing at least jacks may open, the player to the dealer's left acts first, but he may not bet first if he doesn't hold the requisite strength. Suppose we assign this player position one. He must pass if he doesn't have jacks, and it may go around to player number five before the pot is opened.

In private stud games, where each player holds his own cards and doesn't use community cards, the general rule is that in high games, high card brings it in on the opening round, and in low games, low card opens the betting.

In casino games, to promote more action, the rule is reversed. In high games, the low card is forced to bet and stay in, and in low games, the high card must open the betting. What if two players have identical cards, such as 6s? Then the suits are taken into consideration in a casino game, because the dealer is in a fixed seat. Clubs, diamonds, hearts, and then spades, in ascending order, force the action. A 6 of clubs is the lowest 6; a 6 of spades the highest.

In private games, when two players have identically ranked cards, the player closest to the dealer's left opens first.

Checking, Calling, and Raising

The above are the three options open to the player during most betting rounds. On the first round of betting, where a player is forced to make a first bet by position, such as in Texas Hold 'Em, or by the value of his open card, such as in most stud games, after this initial bet is made, all other players must make a bet equal to that bet, known as "calling the bet," or may raise the bet or reraise a previous raise. No one may check after an initial bet, without being forced to throw away his or her cards and stay out of play for all subsequent rounds of this individual game.

Let's illustrate this: Player A must open, player B calls the bet by making an equal bet, Players C, D, and E, who don't wish to bet, fold or throw away their cards and are out of the game, Player F raises the bet, and Player G reraises. Player H folds his cards, and now Player A, to stay in, must make a bet equal to the reraise, and in order to stay in, Player F must make a bet equal to the reraise also. Either player can again reraise, and then those remaining in the game would have to again equal the amount raised or fold.

After the initial round of betting, and on all subsequent rounds, the game reverts to high hand betting first in high games, and low hand betting first in low games, whether the game is played privately or in a casino.

On subsequent rounds, the player who is to bet first can check or pass, without throwing away his hand, but if there is a subsequent bet or raise, he must match it to stay in the game. A complete betting round may be checked by all players without a single bet being made, and then another card will be dealt. But once a bet is made on any round, including the first, players cannot check their hands and stay in the game.

There is a concept called "check and raise," which may be allowed in private games and is usually the rule in casino games. Normally, after a player checks his hand, he cannot then raise a previous bet, but is limited to calling all subsequent bets and raises on that round. However, if check and raise is permitted, a player can come back and raise a previous bet even if he first checked his hand.

The Showdown

At some point in any game of poker, all the bets are in, all raises have been called, and the players are now ready to decide who won the pot. In order to do this, players show their cards and the best hand will win—in high poker the highest-valued hand, and in low poker the lowest-valued hand.

The first one to show a hand is the player who was last called. For example, if there are three players remaining in the game on the final round in a stud game, and Player A had bet, Player B had called, and Player C had raised, and both Player A and Player B had *called the raise*, then Player C must show his or her cards first. Suppose Player C had shown a single pair of aces as his best hand. Player A, who goes next, has only a pair of kings, an inferior hand in this game of five-card stud, high, and so he can concede without showing his cards. Player B has 6s and 2s, a superior hand, and shows this, and claims and in fact wins the pot.

If two players with the best hands have identical hands, then it is a standoff, and they split the pot. For instance, if in the previous example Player C and Player B both had straights led by a jack (J 10 9 8 7) it would be a tie and they would split the pot. But if Player A had a flush, which beats a straight, he would win the pot, and the tie hands, being second, wouldn't count.

There is a version of poker, known as high-low, in which the pot is split between the high and low hands; this version will be explained fully in its own section.

The Rake

The rake may be defined as money taken out of a pot by the person or house running the game, as his or its fee for so running the game.

In private games, there is usually no rake, for the game is not run as a business, but in casinos, since the house supplies both a dealer and table, it wants not only to be reimbursed for expenses but show a profit as well. Thus the rake.

The general rule in casinos is this: The smaller the stakes played for, the higher the percentage of the rake. In $1-$4 games in Las Vegas, the rake can be 10 percent. In the $5-$10 games, it will be about 5 percent, and by the time you're in the $30-$60 games, the rake will be just a tiny percentage of the total pot.

Some casinos will post signs announcing the rake on all games. For example, the rake might be either 5 percent of the pot or $2.50, whichever is less, in a $5-$10 game. With a big pot, the $2.50 taken out by the dealer will be a small fraction of the pot, much less than 5 percent.

The reader should be aware of the rake in any club or casino game he or she plays in. Never play where the rake is more than 5 percent, for you'll be just spinning your wheels, playing for the house, not for yourself.

In some casinos and clubs, an hourly fee is charged instead of a rake. This is particularly true in the California club poker games, where the house supplies no dealer, just the table and cards. Each half hour, an employee collects a fee from the participants at the tables. The fee varies and is in proportion to the size of the game being played. A $20-$40 table will be charged more per hour than a $5-$10 table. Generally, these fees are not burdensome and are fair to the players.

A Basic Strategy for Winning at Poker

There are five maxims of poker that a good player must know and play by. The first is the most important:

1. *Only the best hand on the showdown wins; and only the holder of that hand collects the pot.*

What this means is that there is no payoff in poker for second and third best. This statement may seem obvious, but many weak players, contributing money hand after losing hand, have forgotten its simple truth.

Whether you are in a nickel-and-dime game, or in a pot-limit game where hundreds of dollars may be involved in a single bet, the same rule applies: If you don't have the best hand at the showdown, you're not going to win the pot.

Suppose you are involved in a game of five-card stud. The stakes are high, and at this moment there is $400 in the pot. The betting has been heavy up to this point, and all the players except you and your opponent have dropped out. The cards stand as follows:

You hold 8 8 8, one 8 being a hole card. Your opponent holds ? K K, the ? being his hole card.

You are dealt a 10, making your hand 8 8 8 10; and your opponent, who is a strong player, is dealt a deuce. He now holds ? K K 2. It's his bet.

Without any hesitation he bets $100. You know that he figures you for three 8s. Why should he bet $100 into three 8s, unless he has three kings or is bluffing?

From the play of the cards, you know there are still one king, one 8, two 10s, and two 2s still in the deck. Since you will be dealt just one more card, you will have to buy an 8 or 10 to beat those three kings. You study the hands and take your time. Your opponent sits opposite you serenely. The serenity of a bluffer? Perhaps.

You figure rapidly. A little more than half the deck has been used up, leaving approximately twenty-four cards. It's going to cost you $100 to try and get that remaining 8 or one of the 10s.

Your opponent sits calmly and stares at your face, waiting for your move. You study the cards and calculate your chances. And therein lies the drama of the game of poker. Judgment. Psychology. Courage. All on the line.

You look over at his cards. He could be bluffing with only two kings, but it's going to cost you that hundred to see whether he is.

In this situation, remember the first rule—*only the best hand on the showdown wins; and only the holder of that hand collects the pot.* After the last card is dealt, will you have the best hand? The odds are against it. You turn over the cards and fold the hand, conceding the pot.

The hundred dollars is still yours. If you had bet it, you would have added to a five-hundred-dollar pot, at a payoff of five to one. Were your chances of winning that good?

Well, there were only three chances of improving your hand, and twenty-one chances of not improving it. And you had to improve the hand to win. At best, the odds were seven to one against you. With the payoff merely five to one, it would have been a bad bet even if your opponent didn't draw another card, but he also had three chances to improve his hand.

If he had been dealt a king, you could not have won; if he had drawn a 2 and you a 10, he would still have won; and if neither of you improved your hand, which is the most likely of the possibilities, he would win.

The second maxim comes readily to mind as a result of that play.

2. *Don't throw good money after bad.*

Understanding this rule involves acceptance of the fact that the money in the pot, no matter how much you have contributed to it, is not your money. It belongs to the pot and only belongs to you if you win.

If, in the game just discussed, you put eighty dollars into the pot prior to the last bet, forget about it. The only thing that matters is the hundred dollars that you still have and that is all you must think about.

The same rule holds true at the racetrack, at the crap table, in any betting situation. The bet in the cashier's hand, or on the dice table, doesn't belong to you anymore. More importantly, if you add to the bet, it is not going to change the odds in your favor at all.

Save your money for the next pot, when perhaps you'll have the three kings, and your weary opponent with three jacks will have to make the hard decision of calling or folding.

3. *Calculate the odds against you, and if the return is greater than the odds, make the bet.*

This rule generally applies to the last two bets in stud poker or, in draw poker, the bet before the draw. For instance, in draw poker, the odds against drawing one card and making a flush are approximately nine to two (nine chances in forty-seven). If there is ten dollars in the pot and your bet is two dollars, fine—you're getting five to one on a nine-to-two bet. But if you must make a two-dollar bet and there's only six dollars in the pot, six to two is three to one, a sucker's bet. Fold your four flush.

Conversely, if the odds are in your favor, bet as heavily as you can. This statement, however, is subject to other considerations, discussed in other sections of this chapter.

4. *At the start of play, stay in only with cards that can win.*

This will be explained more thoroughly in the later discussion of each of the games of poker. For example, in seven-card stud, where three cards are dealt before the first bet, if you don't have three of a suit, three to a straight, a low pair with a picture card or ace, or a high pair, why stay in? Why contribute to someone else's pot? Poker is not a charitable exercise; it's a game of skill, and you must play and bet accordingly.

The final rule:

5. *Study your opposition and adjust your game accordingly.*

This rule should not be interpreted to mean you should play poorly against poor players and better against better players. It means nothing of the kind. The worst mistake you can make is to play below your strength at any time. It would be just as foolish as for a professional golfer to alter his swing because he is in a foursome with amateurs. When you reduce your skill you become sloppy, and there is a danger that you will lose it permanently and thus lose that edge that makes you a winner.

Therefore, even if you're playing against your maiden aunts in a penny-ante game, play as carefully as you would in a pot-limit game. Playing this way, often and at your best, will improve your game.

In any game of poker you're in, the first thing you must do (after determining that there are no cheats in the game and that the cards are not crooked, which will be dealt with in a subsequent chapter) is judge the quality of your opposition. This can be done fairly easily once you become a strong player and recognize good play.

For instance, in a game of draw poker, a player sitting third or fourth calls a bet, and then, after a raise, sees that raise also. He draws two cards and, on the first bet after the draw, folds his hand and drops out. You can be sure he's weak. He probably had one of the following hands: A pair with a kicker, a three-card flush or a three-card straight. Seeing a raise with a weak pair is the sign of a poor player. Holding a three-card flush or three-card straight under any circumstances shows him to be a very weak player.

Now let us suppose that despite his poor playing, this player is only a moderate loser. Never, never bluff him in this situation. If he is willing to absorb raises with three-card flushes when he is holding decent cards, it's next to impossible to get him out of the game. The best strategy: You don't have to respect the quality of his play, but you must respect the fact that he falls in love with his cards and, like a jealous lover, is reluctant to let go.

On the other hand, a poor player who is losing heavily may lose his nerve completely, and without the proper judgment based on knowledge of the odds, he may fall for a bluff at the appropriate time.

If you have been playing a strong game, you probably have been in the game holding only good cards, and when you make a big bet against a weak player who has very few chips left, he must figure you for good cards. The pair of queens he has nurtured up to the last card can look very small to him when he sees that big bet.

It is far easier to bluff a good player, because he probably has already judged that you are a strong player and thus will respect your bet. In the hundred-dollar betting situation discussed previously, your opponent may have had only two kings, but it is better to be bluffed occasionally than make reckless and foolish bets. Even the best players get bluffed at times; it's part of the game.

There will be other rules of strategy discussed in subsequent sections, beginning with draw poker. But if these five basic ones are studied and absorbed, you will be well on your way to becoming a strong player. Remember them and use them. They will make you a winner.

Rank of the Hands in Poker

First, the rank of the cards: Ace is highest, followed by king, queen, jack, 10, 9, 8, 7, 6, 5, 4, 3, and 2 (the lowest). As stated earlier, in all games of poker the best hand wins at the showdown. To determine that best hand, however, a player must know the relative rank of all poker hands.

Probably the two most frequently asked questions concern the rank of the hands when 1) there is a wild card in the game; 2) a player is unsure about the relative value of a straight and a flush. Before going any further, let's put these two questions to rest.

1) Where there is a wild card, five of a kind (K K K K WC) is the best hand. (WC stands for wild card.)

2) A flush is always higher than a straight.

As to the relative rank of low hands, see sections on lowball and high-low. We are examining only the best, or high, hands in this section. Following is a list of them in descending order:

Royal Flush: This is the highest-ranking of all hands. It consists of five cards of the same suit in sequence, from the ace to the 10. Thus ♦A ♦K ♦Q ♦J ♦10 is a royal flush. Should two players have a royal flush, the pot would be split.

In poker, unless there is a definite agreement among the players prior to the game that certain suits will take precedence in case of tie hands, suits have no intrinsic value. A royal flush in spades is not superior to one in diamonds.

Straight Flush: Consists of five cards in the same suit, in sequence. ♥K ♥Q ♥J ♥10 ♥9 or ♣5 ♣4 ♣3 ♣2 ♣A is a straight flush. In a straight flush, the ace would be the lowest card. If the ace were the highest card, the five-card sequence would then qualify as a royal flush. A hand such as ♠4 ♠3 ♠2 ♠A ♠K would not be a straight flush, but merely an ace-high flush, reading ♠A ♠K ♠4 ♠3 ♠2.

Four of a Kind: Any four cards of equal rank, one from each of the four suits, qualifies as a four-of-a-kind hand. For example, four kings, four 7s, four 9s. The fifth card accompanying such a hand has no value, since there are no ties between four-of-a-kind hands. The hand with the highest-ranked cards would win.

Full House: Basically, a full house consists of two sets of cards—three of a kind together with a pair. 6 6 6 A A is an example of a full house. All five cards must be utilized, and only cards of the same rank, rather than sequenced cards, are used. Thus A K Q 6 6 is not a full house. In determining the relative value of full houses, the highest-valued three-of-a-kind set wins. For example, 8 8 8 2 2 would beat 7 7 7 A A, and K K K 3 3 would beat Q Q Q J J. When calling out the hand at the showdown, the usual method is to announce the three of a kind first. Thus 8 8 8 2 2 would be called "Eights full." As in four-of-a-kind hands, there are no ties among competing full houses.

Flush: Any five cards from the same suit, not in sequence, constitutes a flush. An example is ♠K ♠J ♠6 ♠5 ♠4, which would be called a "king-high flush." If all five cards in the same suit were in sequence, the hand would increase in value to that of a straight flush. Another example of a flush is ♣7 ♣6 ♣5 ♣4 ♣2. This would be called a "7-high flush." Since two players may each have a flush, the highest-ranking card in the flush determines the best hand. An ace-high flush beats a king-high flush. Should both players have, for example, a queen-high flush, then the second-highest card in the flush determines best hand. Should these be identical, the next-highest card counts. A 9 7 5 4 3 flush beats a 9 7 5 4 2 flush. If all five cards in each hand are identical, the pot is split.

Straight: Any five cards in sequence, but not of the same suit, form a straight. For example, ♣9 ♥8 ♦7 ♠6 ♥5 is a straight, as is ♥A ♠K ♦Q ♦J ♠10. A 5-high straight is the lowest (5 4 3 2 A). 4 3 2 A K is not a straight—simply a no-pair hand, ace-high. If two or more players have identical straights, the pot is split.

Three of a Kind: Any three cards of equal rank in a hand is a three-of-a-kind hand. Examples are 6 6 6, A A A, etc. There can be no ties in three-of-a-kind hands since the highest-ranking cards constitute the best hand. Thus, three aces beats three Kings. When holding a three-of-a-kind hand, the other cards are odd cards. (Example: 7 7 7 A 4.) If the two remaining cards formed a pair, the hand would rise in value to that of a full house.

When calling out the value of the hand, simply say "Three 9s," or "Three aces," or whatever.

Two-Pair: When a hand contains two pairs of equally ranked cards, such as K K 5 5, it is a two-pair hand. The combination just mentioned would be called "kings and 5s," or "kings over 5s," or "kings up."

The fifth card with a two-pair hand must be an odd card; otherwise the hand would increase in value to that of a full house.

Should two or more players have two-pair hands, the highest-ranking pair would win. Thus Q Q 2 2 would beat J J 10 10. Should the high pair be identical, the higher of the lower-ranked pairs would win. Thus Q Q 4 4 beats Q Q 3 3. If both pairs are identical, then the odd card determines the winner; Q Q 4 4 9 beats Q Q 4 4 8.

One-Pair: A hand consisting of just one pair and three odds cards is called a one-pair hand. An example would be 5 5 A K Q. When calling out this hand, you simply say "Two 5s," or "A pair of 5s." When two players have a one-pair hand, the highest-ranking pair wins. Should both pairs be identical, the highest of the odd cards determines the winner. Should these be identical, the next highest, and so on. Thus, 2 2 A J 10 beats 2 2 A J 9. Should all the cards have identical values, the pot is split.

No-Pair: This is the lowest-ranking of the hands. It contains five odd cards, all of different ranks and suits, without any sequence. ♦A ♥K ♦Q ♠J ♣5 is an example of a no-pair hand, as is ♦K ♣Q ♣5 ♠4 ♥2. Even if all but one of the cards are of the same suit, it is a no-pair hand. When calling out the hand, the highest-ranking card is mentioned. Should two players have equally ranked high cards, then the next-highest-ranking card determines best hand, and so on. Thus, A K 5 4 3 beats A K 5 4 2. Should all five cards be identical, then the pot is split.

Note: Where two players have equally valued hands, such as three of a kind or a straight, we have assumed that their hands were the highest-valued hands at the showdown. If, for example, one player has a full house, and two others have identical flushes, the flushes would be meaningless because the full house would win the pot.

Draw Poker—Jacks or Better (Jackpots)

Draw poker is the closed version of poker, differentiating it from open poker, which is called stud poker.

Number of players: Two to eight can play; the best game is with six or seven players.

Cards: A fifty-two-card deck is used, without the jokers.

Object of the game: Winning the pot. The player with the best hand at the showdown wins. (The order or rank of winning hands is explained on page 15.)

Rank of the cards: Ace highest, then king, queen, jack, 10, down to 2, which is lowest.

In draw poker there are two betting intervals. After the cards are dealt, anyone holding jacks or better (that is, a pair of jacks, or cards higher in rank) may open the betting when it is his turn to bet. Should any player make a bet, this begins the first betting interval. After all bets have been made, those remaining in the game may stand pat or draw one to three cards from the unused portion of the deck and discard the same number of cards from their hands. This is called the draw.

After the draw is completed, a second betting interval occurs. After this betting interval is over, there is the showdown among the players still remaining in the game.

Usually, this game is played with an ante, which means that prior to the deal each of the players, including the dealer, puts a designated sum into the pot. This is not considered a bet and cannot be withdrawn. Sometimes it is referred to as a "sweetener"; that is, it enhances the pot and encourages players to stay in the game. In a dollar-and-two game, the ante is usually a quarter, sometimes a dime.

It is up to the dealer to make sure that each of the players has anted prior to the deal. The dealer runs the hand he deals, and it is his responsibility to see that correct bets are made and the correct number of cards are drawn. The players deal by turn, the deal moving clockwise.

Once the cards have been shuffled and cut, the dealer distributes them one at a time, face down, beginning with the player on his left, in clockwise fashion. Each player, including the dealer, receives five cards. The undealt cards are placed to one side of the dealer to be used for the draw.

The betting then begins. In jackpots, a player must have at least two jacks in his hand to open the betting. If the first player doesn't have "openers," he checks. The second player is then given the chance to open. If no one can open, the cards are thrown in, all the players ante again, and a new dealer deals out the cards. If the game is "progressive," on the next deal a pair of queens will constitute the "openers"; if the hand is passed around again, kings; then aces.

Any hand higher in rank than a pair of jacks may open the betting. For example, three 4s, 2s and 5s, a pair of queens, etc. are all considered opening hands. But two 10s cannot open; they are lower in rank than jacks. Once a hand is opened, any player, no matter what cards he is holding, can stay in. It is only the opener who must have jacks or better.

The first player to be given a chance to bet is the player on the dealer's left. He is "under the gun." If he doesn't have openers, he checks. Let us assume, however, that he has a pair of jacks. He makes a bet by calling out his bet and placing the money or chips in the pot. If the game is a dollar-and-two game—that is, a dollar or two dollars may be bet and raised—the player calls out "I bet a dollar," or "One dollar."

The player to the opener's left is the next bettor. Now that the betting has been opened, he need not have jacks or better to place a bet. He can call (match the bet), raise (increase the bet by the designated amount of one or two dollars), or fold (drop out).

Suppose the second player has poor cards. He drops out by saying, "I fold," or "I'm out," or some other expression indicating that he is out of the game. He then throws his cards to the dealer face down. The dealer puts them to one side, separate from the remaining deck.

The third player now has the same option of calling, raising, or folding. Let's say he calls. He would simply say, "I call," and put a dollar in the pot.

We'll assume that six players are in the game. The fourth and fifth players fold, but the final bettor, the dealer, raises the bet by a dollar, saying, "I raise a dollar," or "I raise," and puts two dollars into the pot.

Whenever there is a raise, the betting continues to those bettors who made the original bets, giving them the option of seeing (calling) the raise, reraising, or dropping out. Now the betting moves to the original bettor, who calls the raise by putting another dollar in the pot. The third player also sees the raise, and now, prior to the draw, there are three players left to play out the hand. The pot consists of six dollars plus the ante.

We'll lay out their cards and summarize what has happened so far.

First player	J J A 4 9	Bet one dollar, called raise.
Second player	9 5 7 K 2	Folded.
Third player	10 10 6 6 3	Called bet, called raise.
Fourth player	J 4 5 Q 7	Folded.
Fifth player	4 4 8 5 3	Folded.
Dealer	K K Q 6 2	Raised.

Each of the remaining players is now permitted to discard up to three cards from his hand and receive the equivalent number from the unused portion of the deck. The order of drawing is the same as in the original deal.

As each player discards, he calls out the number of cards he wants to draw, which must be the same number as has been discarded. Let us assume that the first player wants to hold the ace as a "kicker"; that is, as a hopeful high card to be matched by the draw. Or perhaps he is holding it to give the impression that he has three of a kind.

(If he did have three of a kind and was a strong player, he would have reraised the dealer, but for the time being we will avoid the fine points of the game and concentrate on the mechanics of the draw.)

Holding the two jacks and the ace, the first player throws in the 4 and the 9, face down, and calls for two cards, saying "two," or "I'll take two." He is dealt two cards face down by the dealer, who collects the two discarded cards and puts them on a separate pile along with those cards given up by players who have dropped out.

The third player holds two pair—10s and 6s. He draws one card, discarding his 3. The dealer discards the queen, 6, and 2, draws three cards, and puts the unused portion of the deck aside. It is not to be used again. The draw is over, and now the second round of betting begins. The cards in the players' hands are as follows:

First player	J J A 5 9
Third player	10 10 6 6 J
Dealer	K K 8 8 A

It is the first player's turn to bet on the second round, since he opened the first round of betting. He has not improved his hand, so he passes. This means that he temporarily foregoes his bet, but has the option to bet later. However, if he had been the second bettor on this round, and some other player had opened the betting, a pass would mean that he was out. It would be the same as folding. But this is not the case here, since the first player is also the first bettor.

If and when the betting came back to the first player, he could not raise. This is a standard rule of betting; unless agreed on by the players before the game, the rule is that you cannot pass and raise, or check and raise. This rule applies only to each round. If a player checks in the first round, but bets in the second round, he can raise in the second round.

The first player now passes, by saying "I pass," or "I check," or by knocking or tapping the cards or his hand on the table. The accepted way and the preferred way of checking is to call it out, so that all the players may hear the actual "check" and not wonder if the tapping meant a pass.

The third player makes a two-dollar bet. He surmises that since the dealer, who has yet to bet, has drawn three cards, he probably had, at best, a pair before the draw. He is hoping that the dealer has not improved his hand. He has also surmised that the first player, who after drawing only two cards has passed, has, at best, only openers. The third player therefore calls out "two dollars," and puts that amount into the pot.

The dealer knows that the third player has drawn only one card, so he has to guess whether the third player has two pair or has drawn to a four flush or four straight. If the third player has made his flush or straight and the dealer now raises, he will be reraised by the third player and probably have to fold.

The dealer doesn't fear the first player, who by checking has foreclosed his chance to raise, so the dealer bets two dollars, calling the bet of the third player. The first player folds.

The third player and the dealer have a showdown. Since the third player made the bet and was called by the dealer, he must show his cards. He shows the two pair, tens and sixes. If the dealer had a weaker hand, he could concede without showing his cards, but he shows the Kings and eights and wins the pot. The dealer collects all the money from the pot, including the ante.

Only one thing remains to be done; the original bettor, who is the first player, must show his openers. Having put his cards to one side after folding, he pulls out the two jacks and displays them. He is not obligated to show the rest of his cards. The deal now moves to the player on the previous dealer's left, who reshuffles the cards and makes sure that all the players have anted. Then he begins to deal.

Strategy at Draw Poker—Jackpots

In jackpots, the first basic rule to remember is that if a player opens and you don't have a better hand than jacks, get out and save your money.

There are exceptions of course, but they are very rare indeed. If you have a four flush or a four straight, and the pot will give you five to one or better on your bet, then stay in. Otherwise get out.

By making it a practice to get out when your cards are weak or when the pot doesn't pay a satisfactory percentage on your drawing possibilities, you will not only save money—over the long run a great deal of money—but you will also find yourself winning at draw poker.

There are also some other considerations in deciding whether to stay or not. If a previous hand opens and you hold a pair of jacks, get out fast; the opener, in all probability, holds a higher pair than jacks. Even if he also holds jacks, you have a pretty dead hand, and a third party staying in will have much better chances to draw and sandbag both of you.

To reiterate: When another player opens, if your cards are not better than his openers, get out. If the pot doesn't pay at least five to one, get out with an open-ended straight or four flush.

What cards should you stay in with after a player opens? Not less than kings. If you have queens it could be that the opener has jacks, but queens do not give you the kind of strength you need to force a win in draw poker. Kings or aces do.

If a player opens in jackpots and you have kings, then raise. If you have aces, raise.

Let us suppose a typical hand. There are six players in the game and you are the fifth, just before the dealer. The first three pass, the fourth player opens. You hold kings and three odd cards. Raise the opening bet. The dealer, if he has only fair cards—let's say 10s—will be reluctant to call a raise, whereas he might have tried to meet an opening bet alone. He should fold, and the first three players, who originally passed, will now have to call your raise or fold. You know they all have weak hands and, at best, hold a four flush or four straight, or a pair lower than jacks. Let us say one of them chooses to call your raise, and the opener, whose turn it is next, does likewise.

The bettor who called your raise draws one card. The opener draws three cards. You can also draw three cards, since, if he had aces, he had every right to reraise you, if he was a sharp player.

You now must count on him for a pair of jacks or queens.

Now it is the opener's turn to bet. The rule is: The opener of the betting before the draw bets first after the draw. He checks. If you bet, and the player who drew one card has not gotten his flush or straight, he will probably go out. But if he raises you, you will be in a dilemma. Has he gotten the straight or flush? Is he bluffing? He is the one to worry about, since, by checking, the opener has told you he has not improved his hand.

The wise course, if you haven't improved your hand, is to check also. Now if the drawer of one card decides to bet, you only have to call his bet, rather than face a raise. He may bet because he has drawn the flush or straight, or he may have drawn a pair and wants to steal the pot, or he may be bluffing. But you can safely see his bet.

If you hadn't raised with your kings, a wholly different game might have ensued. The dealer might have stayed in, and perhaps two of the three original passers. Now, after the draw, if the opener passed and you passed, any of the three players might have bought a third card to a pair or bought another pair, and they might have bet and beat you.

Basically, this is the point: If you hold a pair of kings or aces, you are holding good solid cards, but any fool staying in with 4s might draw a third 4 and beat you. You want them out, especially since they are behind you in the draw and bet. You want to deal only with the original bettor if possible, and that is the main reason for your raise.

At this point, an important factor in draw poker should be emphasized, indeed it may be as important as the cards you hold. I'm talking about the position in betting after the draw. If, in the above example, the first player opened and you were the dealer, then all the other players would be drawing and betting before you, which would give you the opportunity to control the betting.

Let us suppose that in another hand you are the dealer, and you hold aces. The first player opens; the second and fifth players call. You raise with the aces; the opener and the second and fifth players call the raise. The opener draws three cards, the second player draws two cards, and the fifth player draws one card. You can safely draw three cards.

Now, after the draw, the opener checks. In all probability, he has not improved. The second player, who drew two cards, bets, and the fifth player folds.

Since the second player drew only two cards, you have to count on him for a small pair and a kicker, for if he had three of a kind, he should have reraised the opener, or reraised your raise. So now he should have two pair, probably buying his kicker, which could possibly be a king. You now hold aces and 5s after the draw. Raise him, because you are in the perfect spot. The opener now folds, and the second player calls. You show aces and 5s, and he concedes the pot without showing you his cards. You figured correctly. What if he had reraised you? Then you'd call, and hope he was raising on two pair rather than three of a kind.

In jackpots, the position *prior* to the draw is also very important. In a six- or seven-man game, sitting first and holding jacks, I would probably pass. I would pass with queens as well. Who wants these pairs, when you might have to absorb a raise or two to get to the draw, and after the draw, if you don't improve, you are dead? And if you did improve, getting queens up (that is, queens and another pair), all you could do is pass, while in your heart you knew these cards were going nowhere.

If I were first or second man, I would open with nothing less than kings. If I were third man or later, I would open with jacks or queens, and if I were raised, I'd throw them to the wind. Why throw away money on mediocre hands that have to be nursed to defeat?

So much for opening. As to raising, if a hand is opened in jacks or better, and I hold kings or aces, I raise with those cards. If I hold three of a kind in face (picture) cards, I may merely call the bet, since I feel these will be winning cards and I want as many players as possible to contribute to what I feel is *my pot*. But if a player after me raises, I reraise at that point. I figure the raiser is going to stay in and call my raise, and that is more money for *my pot*.

If I hold three of a kind lower than face cards, I raise an opener and all those hands that preceded me in the betting before the draw. I want them out, if possible, because although my three 5s should win, what if some fool with 8s buys a third 8? No, I want him out. And to give him the message, I raise the limit.

If a player opens and I am last or next to last on the draw and bet, I stay in with two small pairs, such as 7s and 6s. But if I am early in the draw and bet—let's say second or third man after the opener—I throw them in. God bless them, but I don't want them. Any raise behind me and those cards are finished. If, after the draw the opener bets, the cards I hold are worthless to call the bet. And the chances of improving two small pairs are eleven to one against me.

Draw Poker—Anything Opens

The rules and methods of play are the same as in jackpots, with one important exception: A hand may be opened without the necessity of having jacks or better. Thus, the first player may open on the cards he holds, regardless of their value. And, of course, after the play is over there is no necessity to show openers.

This game is not as widely played as jackpots because the average poker player isn't expert enough to cope with it. Yet it is a favorite among big-money players and, by taking away the necessity of holding certain valued cards before opening, it lends itself to more exciting play. Rarely are deals passed over completely, as they are in jackpots, because any player can open, and the dealer has an enormous advantage, being the last player to make a bet.

To many players the game seems a "blind" one, and they are reluctant to play for money, especially big money, when they cannot gauge the opposition hands. For example, in Anything Opens, the first player may bet, the second player may raise, the third player may reraise, and the fourth player, if he is a novice, doesn't have any idea of what the first player held to open the pot. So here he sits with 9s and 4s, trembling at the prospect of having to decide whether to bet or fold.

But to the initiated, the student of poker, a game of straight draw poker (Anything Opens) is just as clear as a game of jackpots (jacks or better).

Strategy at Anything Opens

In Anything Opens, the strategy is pretty much the same as in jackpots. I only open with kings or better, and if I am in a strong game, I figure that a player opening has the equivalent of jacks or better. Anything Opens can become quite clear if the above strategy is followed. Thus, recalling the trembling player in Anything Opens who held 9s and 4s and saw the opener raised or reraised, why tremble? Simply throw away those rotters and get out. The opener probably had a pair of face cards, the raiser had a pair of kings or aces or three of a kind (10s or lower), and the reraiser might have held three of a kind in face cards.

Of course, if I see a player raising or absorbing a raise while holding a four flush or four straight, or better yet, if all the players in the game will do the same, then I know my feast that night will be hearty.

Another important tactical move: If you play "dealer's choice"—that is, every player when it is his turn to deal can choose whatever game he desires—choose draw poker, Anything Opens. As dealer, you are in an ideal spot, and if no one opens, a good bet usually wins the ante for you. If the first player opens and you hold strong cards (kings or better), you are in a beautiful position to build a good pot for yourself. Even if you should lose, in the long run this one hand will be for your benefit, since you control the play and the betting.

Other Strategies

If I hold two pair, face cards and a small pair, I usually raise the opener because, again, I want everyone out of the draw.

Suppose I am the dealer, with a pair of kings, and the opener is in along with me. He opened, I raised, he called, and then he drew two cards. I draw two cards also. He then has to figure me for three of a kind, while I figure him for a pair and a kicker. If he passes, I bet the limit. That's usually enough for his faint heart to call it quits.

That is the big advantage in being the dealer. I have held three of a kind against a strong player—he opened, I raised, he called, and then he drew one card. I counted on him for two pair, so I drew one card also, trusting in the odds (eleven to one) against his improving his two pair. When I drew one card, he bet in the blind, and I raised him immediately, also in the blind. He was stuck. He looked at his cards, which I was sure were aces up, and called. I put down my three 4s and he conceded.

Now if I had been in front of him in the betting, I would have drawn two cards, and he might have stood pat, forcing me to check the three 4s. Then a big bet on his part and I'd have no alternative but to fold, or risk what I considered a bad bet.

In draw poker, never go in with a three flush or a three straight. The odds are just too great against your filling in. Never go in with two pair if you must make them into a full house to win. Again, the odds will kill you. Don't buy to an inside straight (8 7 – 5 4). Again, the odds are murder. No pot will hold enough money to compensate you for it.

Watch your opposition. A player raising on four flushes or straights, or a player who goes in on three straights and three flushes, is weak. In draw poker it is fairly easy to spot the strong and the weak. Remember, you cannot bluff a weak player who is about even or winning. You can bluff a strong player, but you must respect his cards. If he draws one card after raising and reraising, he is not looking for a straight or flush; he is looking for your money.

California Club Poker—Jacks or Better

In the California clubs, only draw poker is permitted by statute. A popular game in these clubs, particularly in Gardena (a Los Angeles suburb), is draw poker, high.

The game is played with a joker, which has a special value, *and can be used as an ace, or to form flushes and straights only*. It is not really a complete wild card, but one that is limited.

With a joker in the deck, the odds against making a flush are 3.8 to 1 instead of 4.2 to 1, and the odds against a straight are 4.3 to 1 instead of 4.8 to 1. This is with a four-card holding, of course.

With the joker, aces can more easily be paired, and straights and flushes come more often. When playing in the California clubs, first study our basic strategies and then apply these factors to the game.

In California, there is a special game called "open blind" in draw poker, high. In this game, the player to the dealer's left, the one under the gun, *must open*, no matter what he or she holds. In this game you can play more aggressively according to position. When you're in a late position, you can raise with cards that ordinarily you might just call with, such as jacks or queens, because the opener doesn't necessarily have good opening cards; he or she is forced to open.

Even if you only hold an ace-high hand, you can go in against a blind opener if you're head to head with him and all the other players have folded. You still have a good chance to win the pot.

But like all other poker games, gauge your opposition. Find out who is weak and who is strong, and play accordingly. Respect the strong player and punish the weak one.

Draw Poker—Odds Against Improving

There is no sense in making a bet in draw poker, or any game of poker for that matter, unless the odds being paid to you are greater than the odds against making the hand.

The simplest way to explain this is to examine a two-sided straight, such as 6 5 4 3. There are eight ways to make the straight; either by getting one of the four 2s or one of the four 7s. You know five cards, the 6, 5, 4, 3, and an odd card that you are discarding in order to draw for the two-sided straight. There are forty-seven other cards that you don't know. Of these forty-seven, eight will help you (the four 2s and the four 7s) and thirty-nine will hurt you. The chances, then, of getting the straight are eight in forty-seven, or thirty-nine to eight against, or the approximate odds of 4.87 to 1. We'll call it 4.9 percent, but it probably will be easier to remember that unless the bet you make will pay you back five to one, don't make it when going for a five-card straight.

The following is a valuable chart to keep and study and eventually to memorize. The odds contained in it are approximate, and rounded off if possible, to make them easier to remember.

Holding Before the Draw	Number of Cards to Be Drawn	Odds Against Improving the Hand
One Pair	Three	2.5 to 1
Two Pair	One	10.8 to 1 (11 to 1)
Three of a Kind	Two	8.7 to 1 (9 to 1)
Four Flush	One	4.2 to 1 (4½ to 1)
Two-Sided Straight	One	4.9 to 1 (5 to 1)
Straight	—	—
Inside Straight	One	10.8 to 1 (11 to 1)

The odds against making two pair into a full house are the same as the odds against drawing to an inside straight (10 9 – 7 6). With two pair, however, particularly if the higher pair are queens or better, there is a good chance of winning without being aided by the draw. Without getting your inside straight, it is probably a losing hand even if you pair up one of the cards.

With odds of 10.8 (or to be more exact, 10.75) to 1 against getting that inside straight, you can readily see why anyone going for it is a sucker. How many times could a situation develop where there would be at least eleven times the amount of your bet in the pot? It's really difficult to envision such a situation, except in a twelve-man poker game.

By the same token, if you are sure, from the betting and draw, that a player has three of a kind, and you have two pairs, even aces over kings, you are a sucker to go for the full house because, again, the odds against buying that ace or king are prohibitive at 10.8 to 1.

Any bet made against the odds in poker is a potentially losing bet, and if these add up in the course of an evening or, worse still, in the course of a year or a lifetime, you're going to be a very heavy loser at poker. Knowing these odds will definitely give you the edge on those players who don't know them, and will save you a lot of money in bets not made.

More Odds Against Improving a Hand in Draw Poker

Cards Held Before Draw	Number of Cards Drawn	Improving To:	Odds Against Drawing
One Pair	3	Two Pair	5 to 1
		Three of a Kind	8 to 1
		Full House	97 to 1
One Pair with the Ace Kicker	2	Aces up	7.5 to 1

More Odds Against Improving a Hand in Draw Poker

Cards Held Before Draw	Number of Cards Drawn	Improving To:	Odds Against Drawing
		Any other pair	17 to 1
		Three of a Kind	12 to 1
		Full House	119 to 1
Two Pair	1	Full House	11 to 1
Three of a Kind	2	Full House	15.5 to 1
		Four of a Kind	22.5 to 1
Open-End Four Straight	1	Straight	5 to 1
One-Sided Straight or Inside Straight	1	Straight	11 to 1
Four Flush	1	Flush	4.2 to 1
Four-Card Straight Flush, Open-Ended		Straight Flush	22.5 to 1
		Any Improvement	2 to 1

Irregularities in Draw Poker

Irregularities in draw poker may occur at various times because of the additional factor of the draw, but we will deal with irregularities in chronological order of play, beginning with an incorrect deck.

Incorrect Deck of Cards: If, at any point during the hand being played, it is ascertained that the deck does not consist of fifty-two cards, all different, forming the four suits of thirteen cards each, any player may, upon bringing this fact to the attention of the players, declare the deal void. All moneys and chips bet on that hand are returned to the players, but this does not affect any previous hands played with the incorrect deck.

No shuffle: If the deck has not been shuffled, then at any time prior to the betting on the second round of play *after* the draw the hand can be called dead by any player, and all money and chips returned to the players.

The reason this rule goes into effect after the draw is that prior to that point it may not be ascertained that the cards had not been shuffled. After the draw, players seeing duplications of the previous hands may first become aware of the situation.

Exposed Card During Shuffle: If a card is exposed during the shuffle, it must be replaced and the cards reshuffled.

No Cut: If the cards have not been cut, then at any time *prior to the first bet* any player may point out this fact and declare a misdeal.

If the cards have not been cut, but a bet has already been made, there is no misdeal, and play goes on.

Exposed Cards During the Cut: If one or more cards are exposed during the cut, it is a misdeal, and the deck must be reshuffled.

Exposing a Card During the Deal: If, during the deal, the dealer exposes a card of any player, there is an automatic misdeal, and the cards must be reshuffled.

The one exception is when the dealer exposes one of his own cards. Since he is responsible for the deal, he cannot call a misdeal and must play the hand.

Too Few or Too Many Cards Dealt to Any Player: If, after the deal is completed, any player has too many or too few cards, it is a misdeal.

There is one exception and it hinges on the order of the deal. Suppose, for example, there are seven players in the game, and each of the first five players has received five cards, but the sixth and seventh players, in turn, have not received five cards. If this fact is brought out before any of the players opens the betting, the dealer is permitted to give those two players their cards then and there, *prior* to the betting. But if the betting has been opened by any player, it is a misdeal.

Dealing More Than One Card at a Time to a Player: If any player receives two cards at one time, it is a misdeal if this fact is pointed out *prior* to the betting.

Skipping a Player in the Deal: If a player has been skipped, it is a misdeal, since it would be necessary to deal him five cards at one time to put him in the game. This fact must be brought out *before the betting,* however; otherwise, the skipped player merely stays out of the hand.

Wrong Dealer: If, prior to the betting, it is ascertained that the wrong player is dealing, it is a misdeal.

Exposing One's Own Card or Cards in the Play Before the Draw: If any player exposes any of his cards, the deal stands. If any player has one of his cards exposed unintentionally by any other player, the deal also stands, since it is the obligation of each player to be responsible for his own cards. If the exposure is intentional, however, it is a misdeal, if it occurred prior to the betting. If it occurs after the player whose card has been exposed has bet, he may take back his bet and withdraw from the game for that hand, or may play out the hand, at his option.

Betting: Once a bet is made it must remain in the pot, whether or not it was made in the proper turn or in the proper amount.

More About Betting in Improper Turn: If a player bets out of turn, either prior to or after the draw, his bet stands. When it is his regular turn to bet he must leave that bet in and cannot alter it, unless there has been a prior raise. In this case, he must either meet the raise, or reraise if he wishes. If he doesn't care to meet or call the raise, he simply forfeits the bet made out of turn, and cannot retrieve it.

If a bet is made prior to the improper bet and is less than the improper bet, the improper bet is considered a raise and cannot be altered. If a bet is made equal to that improper bet, the improper bet cannot be raised.

An Oral Bet: If a player makes an oral bet, such as "I call," or "I raise," he is bound by his call and must make that bet, since it is the custom in poker to call aloud the bet just prior to or at the same time as making the bet. If a player makes an oral call of "I fold," or "I'm out," or any call signifying that he is out of the play, he cannot then make a bet, but must drop from the play by closing up his cards.

If an oral bet is made out of turn, a player is bound by the bet in the same way as if he'd made a bet out of turn, and the same rules prevail.

If it is obvious that the player is actually joking, it is up to the discretion of the players whether or not to penalize him by holding him to his bet. It may be permitted once, but after that the player having fun with oral bets should be penalized by being forced to make the bet he called out, or to fold his cards if that's what he called out.

Passing or Checking Out of Turn: If a player checks after a bet is made, and does so out of turn, he is considered to have folded his cards. The same holds true if he says "I pass." If he checks out of turn but there has been no bet made, his check or pass does not necessarily mean a desire to fold the cards and he, therefore, does not have to.

Folding or Dropping One's Cards: Once a player folds his cards, by so announcing, after a bet on that particular round has been made, he cannot reconsider, even if he did it out of turn. His hand is dead. Any statement of folding, or the actual throwing or discarding of the cards toward the center of the table or to the dealer, or any other method of indicating a folded hand, means that his hand is dead as of that moment.

Dealing an Exposed Card on the Draw: If any card is exposed by the dealer during the draw, that card is dead and is put to one side, face down, with the discards, even if the player drawing decides that he wants it. He has no such option.

If the dealer deals himself an exposed card after the draw, that card is good because the dealer is responsible for the deal.

Dealing Too Few Cards: If, prior to the betting, any player discovers that he has not been dealt enough cards on the draw, he may demand and must receive the number of cards he is short. If a player discovers that he is short and the deal is not over, the next cards from the top must be dealt to the player who is short. Once the betting has begun, a player with a short hand is stuck with that hand.

Dealing Too Many Cards After the Draw: If any player is dealt too many cards, thus giving him more than five cards after the draw, *and he has not looked at his cards, or placed them into his hand,* the excess card or cards can be placed with the discards.

If he has placed them into his hand but has not looked at them, the dealer may take away *one* of the excess cards and place it face down on the discard pile.

If he has looked at the cards, his hand is foul and dead, and he cannot share in the pot. If, however, the fact that he saw the cards is not discovered until after the pot is taken by this player, the hand is considered legitimate. If the fact of too many cards in his hand is discovered at the showdown, the hand is foul, and he is not a participant in the pot.

Drawing Out of Turn: If a player misses his draw through the fault of the dealer, he may draw cards immediately after the error is discovered, unless it is discovered after the betting has begun, in which case he is stuck with his hand.

If the player misses the draw through his own negligence, he is stuck with his hand. If he has discarded any cards, he plays with the cards in his hand. The reason for this strict rule is that, otherwise, it would be to the advantage of a player to wait and see what the others have drawn before making his decision.

Misstating a Hand at the Showdown: If a player misstates a hand, giving it a lower rank than its true value (for example, calling kings when he has kings up), he is bound by the call if the pot is collected and mingled with the funds of the other player. However, if the pot has not been mingled, and the error is discovered by the erring player or any other player, the hand is reevaluated. In other words, "the cards speak for themselves."

If the player miscalls the cards by giving them a higher value, the same rule applies. The cards speak for themselves unless the money or chips have been mingled.

Conceding the Pot or Hand: Once a player concedes, and has discarded the hand he loses the pot. If he concedes, but still retaining the cards, puts them down, face up, and has been mistaken in conceding, and this fact is pointed out by any player, the cards again speak for themselves, and he wins the pot.

False Openers: It is necessary for the opener in jackpots to show his openers at the showdown, whether or not he has won the pot. The proper procedure when folding is to put the openers to one side and not to throw them into the common discard pile. If the openers have been split—for example, a player holding J J 10 9 8 may split the jacks and go for a straight—the discarded jack should have been put to one side so that it could later be shown.

If there is a showdown and the opener is involved, his false openers automatically cause his hand to be dead and he cannot participate in the pot. If there is only one other player in the showdown, the other player wins. If more than one, then the best of the remaining hands win.

If the opener had false openers and he bet and was not called, his bet is forfeit and remains in the pot for the next deal.

If the opener bet, and others called and then folded after the draw so that just the opener remained, all the money in the pot should be redistributed to the players who made bets.

Insufficient Cards for the Draw: In the event that there are not sufficient cards remaining for the complete draw, the dealer shall gather all previous discards (but not those of players yet to draw) and shuffle them and cause them to be cut by any player still active in the game, and then deal them out to the players yet to draw.

If the opener has put his discards aside to show an opening (if he split the openers), then those cards are not to be used in the new shuffle. But all other discards (again, not those of players yet to draw) are used in the shuffle.

Five-Card Stud

This game, together with seven-card stud, constitutes the game of open poker as most commonly played. In five-card stud, each player is dealt five cards; the first card is dealt down and the other four are dealt up.

Number of players: Five-card stud can be played with two to nine players; the best game is with between six and eight players.

Cards: A fifty-two-card deck is used without the jokers.

Object of the game: As with all poker games, the object is to win the pot. The player with the strongest hand wins at the showdown. For the order or rank of the hands, see page 15.

Rank of the cards: Ace highest, then king, queen, jack, ten, down to 2, which is lowest.

Unlike draw poker, the game is not played with an ante, although, if the players, agree, there may be one. Usually, if there are only four to five players an ante is used; this might be necessary to increase the pot and thus entice the players to stay in the game when they have poor hands.

Each player takes his turn dealing. The turns pass clockwise around the table. After the dealer shuffles the cards, he puts the deck down in front of the player to his right to be cut. If that player decides not to cut the deck, any other player at the table has the privilege of cutting the deck. After the cut, the dealer deals each player, including himself, one card face down, starting with the player at his left and going clockwise.

Only the player receiving the "down" card may see it. After each player has one downcard, or "closed" card, the dealer deals another round in the same sequence, this time face up.

After each player has been dealt two cards, one down and one up, the player with the highest open card begins the betting. If the dealer has the highest card, he begins. Unlike draw poker, the order of betting is determined by the high hand showing among the open cards, rather than by the sequence in which the cards were dealt. If two players have identically high cards, then the one of them closest to the dealer's left begins the betting.

The usual rule is that the holder of the high card cannot pass or check on the first bet. This applies only to the initial bet. After another card is dealt face up, the high hand can check or pass.

Let us suppose there are six players in the game and the dealer has dealt himself the high card, an ace. He opens by betting the amount that has been previously agreed upon. If it is a one-and-two-dollar game, he may bet either one or two dollars, unless the players have agreed that two dollars can only be bet on open pairs on the last card. Let us assume that this is not the case and the dealer or any other bettor can bet either one or two dollars, or raise one or two dollars.

The dealer bets by throwing the money (or the chips) into the pot. Now the betting proceeds clockwise, starting with the player to the opener's left. If that player had had the ace, he would have opened the betting and the player to his left would then have been the second one to bet.

The player to the dealer's left has an 8 showing and folds his hand. In other words, he drops out of the hand and is not eligible to collect the pot, or to participate any further in the betting on this particular hand. He can announce, "I fold," or "I drop," or merely turn over his open card and place it on top of the card which was dealt face down.

Many players are sloppy and turn over the face-down card and show it to a few or all of the players. This is bad poker etiquette and should immediately be pointed out as such by the dealer; or if he does not speak up, by any other player, so that it doesn't happen again. I have never seen it done by an expert or strong player; only weak players and consistent losers seem to do it. Anyway, after both cards are turned down they should be held there in front of the player until the round is over and then given to the dealer, who should place them in a separate pile, face down.

After the player with the exposed 8 folds, the player to his left has the option of betting. He holds a king and bets one dollar. He could have raised the bet also, but he elects to call. All other players fold, with the exception of the player to the dealer's right, who has an exposed 9 and calls the bet.

Now, of the original players we have only three left after the first card has been dealt. The cards look this way:

Dealer	? A
First player	? K
Second player	? 9

The question marks stand for the unseen "hole" cards.

At this point, a word about strategy. It is bad poker to chase an ace with lower cards. If the player holding the king does not have a king or an ace in the hole, he is a poor player. If the holder of the 9 doesn't have a 9 or an ace in the hole, the same thing can be said for him.

The dealer now deals another round of cards face up. The first player is dealt the first card, the second player the second, and the dealer the last. The dealing doesn't follow the order of betting, but the sequence of players in clockwise fashion, starting with the player at the dealer's left. After the third card is dealt, the hands are as follows:

Dealer	? A 6
First player	? K J
Second player	? 9 10

The dealer, holding the top card, the ace, bets two dollars. Since the others have weaker cards, as far as he can see, he will bet the limit and make them pay to stay in the game. He is also testing to see if either of them will raise him, at which point he might then disclose the relative strength or weakness of his hand by calling the raise or reraising.

Both players call the two-dollar bet, and another card is dealt face up to each of the players. Now the hands look this way, with the hole cards exposed only to our view:

Dealer	A A 6 5
First player	Q K J 10
Second player	Q 9 10 10

Although we can see that the dealer is holding the high hand, the open high hand is the two 10s held by the second player. He looks over the other hands. The holder of the ace, the dealer, has bet boldly, and the first player may have a pair of jacks or kings, or may have nothing. If he, the second player, checks, and the dealer bets two dollars, then he must assume the dealer has a pair of aces. If the second player checks and the dealer checks and the first player bets, the first player would have a high pair, certainly higher than the pair of 10s showing. Perhaps, if the second player bets, he will bluff the other players into believing that he has 9s and 10s. Perhaps he might even steal the pot with a bold bet.

So the holder of the pair of 10s bets two dollars. The holder of the aces must make a calculation, and it must be based on the second player's strength as a poker player. If the second player has a reputation as a strong player, the bet must be respected; if his reputation is weak, then the bet must be met and surpassed. Now, having sat through half an evening of poker with the players around the table, and having seen the second player go into most hands with wild hopes of buying better cards, the dealer, a strong player, knows that the second player is weak.

The dealer raises the bet and makes it four dollars, and now the first player—who went in with cards he should have stayed out with, perhaps on a hunch, or for whatever reason poor players persuade themselves to bet and lose money—finds himself sucked in. His chances of getting a straight are as follows: He sees one 9 and one ace, either of which are necessary for him to get that straight; he knows his own four cards and three cards of each of his opponents; he has seen the three cards of the players who went out. Thus, there are thirteen cards he knows and thirty-nine that are unknown. Of these thirty-nine, there are six cards (three 9s and three aces) that will give him the straight. The odds against his making it are 33 to 6, or 5½ to 1. He must bet four dollars, and so far the pot contains fifteen dollars. (Three dollars were bet on the first open card, six more on the second card, and six so far on the third open card.) He is getting 15-to-4 odds on his money, a little less than 4 to 1, and the odds against making the straight are 5½ to 1.

It is a sure losing bet. But his cards look so good, and what if he buys a pair? That will help him also, he thinks, as he throws his four dollars into the pot. The second player, now having gotten the message, decides not to bluff the dealer by reraising, for he figures him for aces now and any improvement of the dealer's hand will put the second player in a really bad spot. He calls the reraise, but it would have been wiser to fold and not throw good money after bad.

All bets are now in, and the final card is dealt. The final hands are now:

Dealer	A A 6 5 7
First player	Q K J 10 J
Second player	Q 9 10 10 4

The second player is the first bettor and, cursing the 4, he passes. The dealer is next to bet, and now his only worry is the first player. Perhaps the jack gave him two pair. But if that were so, why didn't he raise the first two-dollar bet and find out the intentions of the dealer and the value of the dealer's hand, or force him out? Perhaps he was being cagey, but there is now one way to find out—bet, and then see if the first player raises. So the dealer bets, and the first player, looking at his cards, is not contemplating a raise. He is wondering whether to call or fold. He calls, the second player folds, and the dealer shows the aces and wins the pot.

The deal now goes to the player on the dealer's left, who shuffles the deck, gives it to the former dealer to cut, then begins dealing out the cards.

Strategy at Five-Card Stud

To a skillful player, five-card stud has its handicaps. The game, for the most part, is an open one. A good player will find himself going out hand after hand, until he finally has cards that can win, and then, to his dismay, the other players fold up *their* cards.

If you are a good poker player, you don't go in with losing cards; that is, cards of lower value than those held by the first bettor. Thus, if an ace is showing and you have a king in the hole, you don't spend the whole hand chasing that ace, hoping that the original bettor doesn't have aces back to back. If, on the other hand, you stay in the pot only with the best cards, you will soon get a reputation as a "tight" player. You will thus find yourself an object of contempt by the weaker players, who will complain that you go in "only with good cards," as if that were an insult.

So, once you have strengthened your game, try to avoid five-card stud. If you must play the game, play for as high a limit as you can find. If you stay in only with strong cards, cards that beat the others on board, you are going to be a winner at the end of the evening and have a lot of enemies, particularly if you are playing with poor players. So the strategy for five-card stud will be divided into two parts. First, the cards to stay in with.

It is not always possible to tell if you have the best cards in five-card stud. For one thing, in a seven-man game, you may hold queen, 8, the queen in the hole. The highest card showing is a jack. The holder of the jack is the initial bettor, and after two players see the bet and two others fold, another player raises, and it is your bet.

You look at the raiser's open card and see a 7. You now calculate that he has either a pair of 7s, an ace in the hole, or perhaps a king in the hole, or he is bluffing. If it is a bluff, the timing and the low open card are both bad. So you call the raise, the jack sees the raise, as do the other two players who have stayed in, one with a 6 and the other with a 3.

Another calculation is made. Either those other two players have pairs or they have high hole-cards. If they have high hole-cards, there are a lot of kings and aces in the hole, and your queen might just stand up.

On the next round, the hands look as follows:

First bettor	? J K
Second bettor	? 6 4
Third bettor	? 3 8
Fourth bettor (raiser)	? 7 10
You	Q 8 2

If the first bettor bets again, holding ? J K, right into the raiser, it is time for you to depart rapidly from the game. If he checks, and all the players check to the raiser, who bets, a raise by you might knock out all the others. However, the first, or opening bettor bets his ? J K. The second bettor calls, the third calls, the fourth raises, and you turn over your cards. You do it for several good reasons. For one thing, you will be chasing after a pair of 7s or an ace in the hole. To improve against the 7s, you must start with your queen and an 8. Another 8 has already been shown, and either of the first three bettors might be holding a queen in the hole. Even if they're not, you still have to buy it, and at this point, knowing thirteen cards (your three, the other eight, and two that folded), you know there are now three chances of buying the queen out of thirty-nine remaining cards—odds of twelve to one against you. If you can buy the queen, the first player can buy his king, and the raiser can buy his ace in the hole; or if he has a pair of 7s, he can buy the 10 at the same odds.

After you fold you watch the play, which is important because you want to see how the others play, want to know their relative strength so that when you stay in you can gauge their next move. The first bettor calls the raise, the second bettor calls the raise, and the third bettor calls the raise. What mysterious cards are they holding? Well, the first bettor might have a pair already, or three big cards, or perhaps a small card in the hole, but, holding the high card on the table, he is reluctant to get out.

The second player holds either a small pair or an ace in the hole, or perhaps he is getting ready to work on a small straight. The third player holds either a pair of 3s or an ace in the hole, or he has a hole in his head. Another round of cards is dealt:

First bettor	? J K 4
Second bettor	? 6 4 2
Third bettor	? 3 8 Q
Fourth bettor	? 7 10 9

The first bettor bets again. The second bettor turns over his cards and folds them away; he probably was going for that straight, but didn't want to go for an inside straight, needing the 3 with one already showing. The third bettor seems encouraged by his last card and calls the bet. The fourth bettor raises, and the first bettor reraises. Aha. Either the first bettor was praying for a 4, or, more likely, he did have jacks back to back, or when he bought the king it gave him kings.

The third bettor is baffled by the reraise; after all, he just bought a queen. Now he folds, keeping his record (of continually building up pots) clean. His little pair of 3s has not carried him far enough. The fourth bettor now gets some kind of message, but calls the reraise.

The last round:

| First bettor | ? J K 4 J |
| Fourth bettor | ? 7 10 9 10 |

Two buys of open pairs. The first bettor bets the limit. The fourth bettor waits a minute, looks at his bottom card as if to change it, and folds. The first player takes the pot.

We now come back to our basic premise. We can stay in with cards that seem to be the best on the table, like our queen in the hole, but once it becomes apparent that we are second best, we should be out. If you hold a face card in the hole and no face card shows, you can stay in. If there is a face card showing and you have a higher one in the hole, stay in. If the face card held by the opener equals your hole card, get out.

These are very simple, basic rules. Always stay in with an ace in the hole, either until you see an open pair, or until it becomes apparent that one of the players has a pair. If no other ace has shown, stay in until the fourth card is dealt. Then, if you don't improve, get out.

Try to stay in with the best cards, or with high cards that might be best, and you will become a winner, all other factors being equal. If you hold a high pair back to back, let the others stay in, especially if they are not buying a card as high as yours. For example, if you hold kings back to back and the highest card on the board is a queen, don't raise until the fourth card. Let them all stay in.

If a player holds a three flush or three straight (including the hole card), or is betting as though he holds those cards (for instance, raising on ? ♦5 ♦9) and you hold Q Q 4, have no hesitation in reraising him; the odds are so heavily against his buying the remaining two diamonds that you are almost a sure winner.

Of course, don't raise on three flushes or three straights; don't even stay in with those cards unless they are also high cards. For example, get out with ♥2 ♥6 ♥7, but stay in with ♥ J ♥K ♥8. The same principle holds true with straights. And never, never raise with those three flushes and straights. Even if you hold a four flush, don't raise, because most calculations will reveal the odds at 9 to 2 against your buying the necessary fifth card.

In other words, don't raise on expectations; raise when you've got the goods. Stay in when you have the good cards.

One more thing. As I said at the beginning, if you only stay in with top cards you will get a reputation as a tight player, so that when you do stay in you'll be cursed. That's all right, as long as the other players stay in also. But along with the muttering, they may go out. So alter your strategy; play some weak cards out, so long as there is no raising. And once in a while raise on absolute garbage. Keep them guessing. Don't let them know how strong a player you are.

Seven-Card Stud

Seven-card stud has, in recent years, become a popular variation of poker and may be *the* most popular form of poker. The extra two cards, both of which are seen only by the player, account for its popularity. It makes the game a wilder one, with larger pots and more players staying in. Instead of having only the five cards dealt them to choose from, the players at seven-card stud have the option of picking the best five of the seven cards dealt them.

Number of players: Since there are seven cards dealt instead of five, the best game is played by six to eight players. Eight should be the maximum, though in draw poker and five-card stud, nine or ten players could play if necessary.

Cards: The game is played with a fifty-two-card deck, without the jokers.

Object of the game: To win the pot.

Rank of the cards: Ace highest, then king, queen, jack, 10, down to 2, the lowest.

There is usually no ante required because, with three cards in every seven unseen by the other players, the game can be exciting even played by only four or five players.

As in draw and five-card stud, each player takes a turn dealing. The deal is passed clockwise around the table as in the other game. Where only one deck is used, the dealer shuffles the deck. Where two decks are used (one as a spare), the deck just used is shuffled by the player to the dealer's left and then placed at that player's right, to be cut when it is his turn to deal. Prior to the deal the cards are cut by the player to the dealer's right, and if he should refuse to cut them, then any other player has the right to do so.

The dealer deals each player the first card face down, commencing with the player at his left and going clockwise around the table. After each player, including himself, has received one card face down, he deals another card face down to every player, and then an upcard (open card). Thus, the third card is the one seen by all the players in the game.

As in draw and five-card stud, it is the dealer's job to run the game. In stud poker he announces who has the high hand and who is, therefore, the one to bet. Even if the dealer folds his cards, he continues to deal and call the game and to make certain that the right bets are placed and the order of betting is correct. To a serious poker player, there are few things more aggravating than a player betting out of turn. It disrupts the game; it complicates the betting, and usually it causes discrepancies in the pot amount. A serious player bets in turn, and expects others to do the same, and should point out the first time someone disregards the rule. If the offender persists, the serious player has two choices; ask him to leave the game, or leave the game himself, because to be irritated and annoyed is to plant in oneself the seeds of defeat.

The holder of the open high card is the first to bet, and on the first round he usually must make a bet. After he bets, the player to his left makes the next bet, and so on clockwise around the table. In the next round, if another player has the high open hand, he bets first, and the player to his left is then the next bettor.

In five-card stud, the first card shown "up" may very well determine the play of the hand. In seven-card-stud, since there are two cards in the hole, an ace showing doesn't have as much strength, for the holder of the deuce may have two more in the hole, and the second card dealt face up may give him four of a kind. It is this blind aspect of the game that makes it appealing, plus the fact that there are so many cards dealt.

A strong player prefers seven-card stud because, if he plays well, he can entice the weaker players to stay in the game with inferior hands, thus enabling him to win much bigger pots. In five-card stud, if the strong player shows a pair of aces on the third card (? A A), he is sure to drive out all the other players, except those who dream of buying the moon, stars, and sky. But in seven-card stud, a pair of aces showing doesn't have that impact. By the time they show, each player has been given four cards, and all the weak players, with their three-card flushes and straights, their low pairs and their cards reading J 9 8 7, are dreaming of the buys they need. They will stay in to the last card, still hoping. After all, they have only been dealt four cards, and there are three more still to come, and among those three—ah, among those three . . . And so they see the raise and reraise, happily throwing in the chips, because their motto is "Where there's faith, there's hope." But this is not quite the kind of faith meant by that pious motto.

After the first bet has been made in the game of seven-card stud, each player in turn, starting with the player to the first bettor's left, has the option of calling the bet, raising, or dropping out. Let us assume this is a six-player game and four of the five remaining players call the bet, with only the dealer dropping out.

After the bets are made, the dealer deals out another card, face up, to each of the remaining five players. At this point, the cards are seen as follows:

First bettor	? ? A 10
Second bettor	? ? 3 5
Third bettor	? ? 8 K
Fourth bettor	? ? 6 6
Fifth bettor	? ? Q J

It is now the fourth bettor who has the high hand, and the betting will proceed from his left after he has made a bet or checked. This being the second round of betting, he has that option. We'll assume this is a one-dollar-to-five-dollar game, with any amount between those two figures allowable as a bet or raise.

The fourth bettor bets two dollars; the fifth bettor calls. The first bettor raises it to five dollars; the second bettor calls. The third bettor folds, and the fourth and fifth bettors see the raise by putting in three more dollars each.

The next card is dealt face up, and the cards are seen as follows:

First bettor	? ? A 10 7
Second bettor	? ? 3 5 J
Fourth bettor	? ? 6 6 2
Fifth bettor	? ? Q J K

The pair of 6s are still high and, therefore, the fourth bettor has the option of betting or checking. Unless the players have made up a special rule beforehand, a checked hand cannot be raised.

The fourth bettor bets two dollars again, betting into the raiser, who is the first bettor. The fifth bettor calls. The first bettor is now a little wary of the fact that the fourth bettor bet into him, so he calls, and the second bettor calls.

The sixth card is dealt face up by the dealer. The hands, now seen in their entirety only by us, are as follows:

First bettor	8 A-A 10 7 7
Second bettor	2 2-3 5 J 5
Fourth bettor	6 10-6 6 2 9
Fifth bettor	9 8-Q J K 4

The 6s are no longer the open high hand; the 7s in the first bettor's hand are high. He is worried about the 6s but figures a bold bet will prevent the fourth bettor from raising him. He is afraid of checking, for that would show the fourth bettor that he is conceding control of the betting to him. So, having once raised, he now bets five dollars. The second bettor, in with junk, has improved his hand to a point where he feels he cannot afford to drop out. After all, he might be bluffed out with his two pair. So, after hesitating, he throws in five dollars, which he might just as well have saved, for the odds against filling in two pair and making a full house are roughly eleven to one.

The fourth bettor, remembering that the first bettor did not raise him in the previous round and that the first bettor raised without a 7 showing, can only figure the first bettor for aces over 7s. If he is wrong, he will be reraised, and he may be reraised even if his calculations are correct, to try and bluff him out. So he raises the bet by five dollars and throws ten dollars into the pot.

The fifth bettor, having gotten face cards that looked better and better, made the mistake of being ashamed to drop out with such good-looking cards, for fear that the other players would think he plays too close to the vest, or is stingy. But the 4 has dampened his enthusiasm for the hand considerably, and he turns his cards over.

Now, the aces over 7s in the first bettor's hand are obviously weaker than the fourth bettor's 6s, backed up most probably, the first bettor thinks, by another 6. Or perhaps the fourth player already has a full house. But since he is not the strongest of players, and the basic rule that one does not throw good money after bad in poker has never gotten through to him, he throws in five more dollars.

It is surprising how much ego is tied up with poker hands. The first bettor, like so many others, is afraid of being bluffed out of the hand and, worse, having everyone else know it.

The second bettor, now faced with still another raise and another five dollars to throw into the pot, has had enough. He folds his cards.

Now only the first and fourth bettors remain. The last card is dealt face down. "Down and dirty," is the way dealers like to call it.

The final hands, preparatory to the last bet, stand as follows:

First bettor	8 A	A 10 7 7 8
Fourth bettor	6 10	6 6 2 9 Q

Now the first bettor has three pair. But since he can only use the best five cards of the seven dealt to him, his best hand is aces over 8s. He is still high bettor, with his 7s showing, and he checks. But when the fourth bettor bets five dollars, the first resists the impulse to call and folds his cards.

The fourth bettor wins the pot. Since he was not called, he turns over his cards, so that they are all face down, and throws them to the player whose turn it is to shuffle them. A new deal begins.

Strategy at Seven-Card Stud

The game of seven-card stud is, in many ways, an ideal game for a superior poker player. Because of the three concealed cards and the fact that seven cards are dealt, of which only the best five may be used, many poor players stay in on wishful thinking, contributing to pot after losing pot.

The single most important skill in seven-card stud is in knowing whether to stay in or fold after the first three cards are dealt. At that point the good player has a clear view of his objectives. He knows what he needs to buy and, viewing the open cards, calculates the odds. This gives him an enormous advantage over that great body of players who hope to buy cards to form *something,* although at the outset of the deal they cannot say with certainty just what that something is.

I will list the only cards to stay in with after the first three cards are dealt. There are exceptions, but it's best not to go into them now. The basic thing to remember is that if any of the following groups of cards are dealt to you, stay in; if not, go out. Knowing just this will save you a lot of money and make you a potential winner. Stay in on:

Three of a kind, such as 6 6 6. This seems, and is, elementary. Don't raise with these cards however. The important thing about seven-card stud is that cards are concealed. Here, the meat of your hand is concealed. You will be going for four of a kind or a full house. If, on the next round, another player raises, then reraise him. But you can wait till the fifth card to raise. You want as many players in as possible with these cards; they should be winners.

A high pair and an odd card. Any face-card pair will do, such as jack jack 4. Again, an elementary hand to stay in with. You are looking for two pair or three jacks, then a full house.

A middle pair and an odd card. I consider a middle pair to be 8 8, 9 9, or 10 10. If a higher pair doesn't show on the table by the next round, or a player isn't betting as though he had a higher pair, stay in till the fifth card is dealt. If you don't improve by then and there are three or more players in besides you, you will probably not win with these cards combined with a smaller pair, so that's the time to fold them.

A small pair and a high card. For example, 3 3 king. Here I stay in through the fourth card. If the fifth card doesn't aid me and another king has been shown, I'm out. I have four chances out of thirty-eight of buying, or odds of about 8 to 1 against improving my hand. I don't want to stay in the last two rounds of betting hoping to buy against those odds—too much punishment. If I had kings and 3s by the fourth card, then I would be raising, making the others pay or forcing them out.

Three to a straight. For example, 7 8 9 of different suits. The higher the straight, the happier I feel. Now I stay in and get a fourth card. If it is an odd card, say a queen or 2, I stay in one more round. If on the fifth card I show no improvement, I throw the cards in. No ifs, ands, or buts. Hoping to buy two to a straight on the sixth and seventh cards is as bad as drawing two to a straight in draw poker. The odds against this in draw poker are astronomical. They are as bad in seven-card stud. Why be a sucker? Out!

Three to a suit, such as ♠K ♠8 ♠6. The same rule holds true; if I don't improve on the fourth card, I wait one more time. If no improvement on the fifth card, I am out of the game.

The only other cards I would stay in with are ace king and an odd card. But if there is no improvement on the fourth card, that's it, folks. Goodbye. Now, I might hold ace, queen, and an odd card and stay in also, depending on financial position (if I am a moderate or big winner); again, for only one round. No improvement and it's all over. What if I pair the low card? Then I would be in the same position as holding a low pair and an ace, as discussed above—I stay in to see the fifth card. If no improvement and another ace is showing, I'm out. If another ace has not shown and the cards on the table look as though there are straights, flushes, and full houses showing, I will probably pull out. I have no strength because I have yet to buy the card I need. If I raise on cards I don't have yet, I'm a sucker.

There you have it, for seven-card stud staying-in cards. Nothing will induce me to play other cards. I don't want to start with a losing hand right off and absorb punishment trying to get to the sixth and seventh cards, only to find that I still have nothing, or have bought a weak pair.

If I am a big winner, or if I want to convince the other players that I am not really that tight a player, I may stay in with weaker cards very, very occasionally, but at the first sign of a raise, I am gone.

If you learn nothing else but the basic strategy of poker and the cards to stay in with, as enumerated here, I don't see how you can be a loser.

Now, if the cards you hold are good, what about the betting? My rule of thumb: If I believe my cards are very strong, strong enough to win by themselves without buying another card (example: three of a kind), I want everyone in the game and I don't raise until the fifth card. If another player raises, I may reraise him on the fourth card, but not before.

If I hold aces up, or kings up, and I have the opportunity to raise, I raise. I don't want three of a kind or a flush or straight beating me. By the fourth round, if I have aces up and someone is working on a straight or flush, that person has to buy to beat me. And he must pay heavily for each card he buys. I raise.

If I have a four flush or four straight, I don't want to raise; no matter what the situation, the odds are against me. But if I hold ♣K ♦K ♦9 ♦5 ♦4 I raise, feeling those kings are a good umbrella, and there are a lot of cards I can buy, in addition to the remaining diamonds, to win the hand. Of course, this strategy is dependent on the other hands. If another player has aces showing or three of a kind showing, there's no sense in raising. And there's a good chance, if the other player had been raising before that third 8 came out, I would be out, dumping those lovely cards. Why? Because I want to win, and coming in second has no value. This is basic and should be impressed deeply into your consciousness; what good are beautiful cards if they can't win?

So remember, if you have the best cards and want everyone in, hold off raising. If others can stay in and possibly beat your cards, make them pay to stay in, providing you have the best hand (or think you have) on the table. If you are second best, but with very good chances of buying to be best, stay in. But if you are second best and have very little chance of buying, get out.

Irregularities in Stud Poker

An Incorrect Deck of Cards: See *Irregularities in Draw Poker,* p. 27.

No Shuffle: If the deck of cards has not been shuffled, then at any time prior to the first bet, the hand can be called dead by any player.

Exposed Card During Shuffle: See *Irregularities in Draw Poker,* p. 27.

No Cut: See *Irregularities in Draw Poker*, p. 27.

Cards Exposed During the Cut: See *Irregularities in Draw Poker,* p. 27.

Exposed Cards During the Deal: If, during the deal, cards are seen exposed in the deck, it is a misdeal if there has been no betting. If there has already been a bet, those exposed cards are placed face down at the bottom of the deck. Since some players have seen them, all players in the game are entitled to know these cards before they are placed on the bottom.

If a card is dealt face up or is otherwise exposed on the first round in five-card stud, or on the first or second round in seven-card stud, the player keeps that card, turns it face up, and receives the next card face down.

Dealing Too Many Cards to Any One Player: If the dealer has dealt too many hole cards to any one player and that fact is discovered before any betting has occurred and before the player has looked at his hole cards, then the dealer shall select either of the extra hole cards and place it unseen at the bottom of the deck. However, if betting has begun, or if the player has seen his hole cards, then his hand is foul and dead and is collected by the dealer, though the player may remove any money he has placed in the pot.

If, at any point after the first round, a player discovers that he has too many cards, his hand is dead as of that moment. However, should this be discovered after the pot has been collected and mingled by that player, then the hand stays as a good hand.

Dealing Too Few Cards to Any One Player: When too few cards are dealt to any one player and that fact is discovered before the betting commences, the dealer may deal one, and only one, additional card to that player. Thus, if the player is shy two cards, his hand is dead and he is out of the game.

If the fact that a player has too few cards is discovered after the first bet has been made, or after the first round, his hand is dead. Should he win with this hand and the error is not discovered until after the pot has been collected and mingled, then, and only then, is the hand not foul.

Since it is the duty of a player to count his cards, in the event he has been dealt too many or too few cards and this fact is noticed after he has made any bets (ante does not count), he forfeits those bets and his hand is dead.

Dealing Too Many Hands: Should the dealer deal out one or more extra hands, and this fact is discovered while only hole cards have been dealt, then the excess cards shall be taken up and put, sight unseen, at the bottom of the deck.

Should the extra hand also contain an exposed card, the exposed card shall be shown to all players, then, with the hole card, which is not to be shown, placed at the bottom of the deck.

If any player shall have looked at any hole card of an extra hand, that player then plays that hand, and another hand is designated as the extra hand. If all the players have looked at their hands, and the hole card of the extra hand has been seen by one player, he shows it to all the other players, and the extra hand is then placed at the bottom of the deck.

Dealing Too Few Hands: If the dealer has dealt out one fewer hand than players, and this is discovered before any players have looked at their hole cards and before any players have received an up card, then the dealer may take the top card and deal it to the left-out player. Or, if there are two hole cards, he may ask each player to move one card to the player on his left, and then deal out two cards by dealing one to each player who does not have two hole cards.

In no event can the dealer be permitted to deal two consecutive cards to any one player.

Should it be discovered that the dealer has skipped one or more players after either the hole card has been seen or an exposed card been dealt, then the game is played with only those players who have been dealt cards.

Skipping a Player During the Deal: If, after the hands have been established, the dealer skips one of the players during the dealing of an upcard, then that card is moved over to its rightful place and the deal continues. It is not a misdeal, and the player who wrongly received the card cannot keep it.

In seven-card stud and in some other forms of stud poker, the final card is dealt face down. Should a player be skipped and the card is not seen by the player who gets it, it also is moved over. If it has been seen, then at the moment the mistake is discovered the top card of the undealt deck is dealt to the skipped player and the deal continues.

Exposing a Card for the Next Round: If a card for the next round of betting is accidentally shown by the dealer, so that it is known before the previous round is over, this card is discarded and put on the bottom of the deck and the deal continues in proper order.

Exposing a Final Card in Seven-Card Stud During the Deal: If the dealer deals the final card in seven-card stud as an exposed card to any player, then, since the player is at a disadvantage, there can be no raises on the final round by any player, including the player with the exposed card.

Exposing One's Own Hole Card: Any player exposing his own hole card must bear the brunt of his mistake. There can be no misdeal for exposing one's own card.

A player should not expose his hole card, or cards, when folding his hand. If any player sees this hole card, then all the players are permitted to see that card.

Betting Out of Turn: If a player makes a bet out of turn, that bet stands and he cannot withdraw it. When it is his proper turn to bet, and the bet is equal to another player's previous bet, his bet stands and cannot be raised. If his bet is insufficient, it must be added to equal another player's bet made previously (not a raise). If the player refuses to do so, he automatically drops out of the particular game; his cards are dead, and the bet is forfeited. If the bet previous to his was a raise, he may call, or reraise, or drop out. If he drops out, his bet is forfeit. If the bet previous to his was less than his bet out of turn, his bet is considered a raise and must stand as such.

Oral Bets: If any player announces his bet orally, then he is bound by his statement and must make that bet. An oral bet made out of turn is treated the same as a bet made out of turn.

Dropping Out or Folding Out of Turn: A player must wait his turn before dropping out of play. Should he do this out of turn, it should be brought to his attention by the dealer and he should be warned not to repeat it. Should a player drop out, out of turn, he is bound by this decision and cannot reinstate his hand. His hand is dead as of the moment of his announcement.

Dealer's Mistake in Calling: Should the dealer designate the incorrect hand as the high hand and a bet is made, it may be called to the attention of the other players by any player. The bet shall then be returned, and the correct hand shall then open the betting.

If either the dealer or any player calls the wrong hand as the winning hand, "the cards speak for themselves." Winning cards, based on rank of hands, win the pot, not the call of the cards.

However, should an incorrect call be made and the wrong hand takes the pot and the funds are mingled, that win stands.

Wrong Concession: If a player on the showdown concedes his hand *before the pot is taken in,* and if, when his cards are exposed, it is shown that his cards win the pot, the cards-speak-for-themselves rule applies and he wins. However, should he concede and discard his cards, his hand is dead and out of the game.

Lowball

Lowball, or as it is commonly called out West, Lo Ball, is poker with the lowest hand winning. So the ranking of the hands is reversed, with a few exceptions. Obviously, it would appear that the worst possible hand to get in lowball would be a royal flush, but in lowball we eliminate flushes and straights from consideration, and the ace is always considered the low card in the deck.

To illustrate: A holding of A K Q J 10 should read, in lowball, K Q J 10 A, and the player holding the hand would announce he has "King queen high."

Since, in lowball, any hand with no pairs is superior to a hand having a pair, the method of calling such a hand (without a pair) is to announce the two highest cards. Thus, holding J 9 6 5 2, you announce, "Jack 9 high." If your opponent holds Q 5 4 3 2, you would win, despite the fact that the remaining four cards, other than the queen, are lower than yours. In lowball, the high card counts in determining the rank of the hands. The lower the first card, where there is no pair in the hand, the better the hand.

At this time, it would be best to give the relative rankings of the hands.

The best possible hand to hold is 5 4 3 2 A. It doesn't matter if all the cards are of the same suit. Remember, straights and flushes do not count at all in determining the best hand.

5 4 3 2 A is called a "bicycle," or a "wheel." When a player announces he holds a wheel, only another "wheel" is going to tie that hand.

6 4 3 2 A is next in rank.

6 5 4 3 A is next.

6 5 4 3 2 follows.

Obviously, 6 4 beats 6 5, but 6 5 3 beats 6 5 4. If necessary, the hand may be determined by the lowest card held. For example, 8 6 5 4 2 beats 8 6 5 4 3.

The rank of unmatched hands goes up to K Q J 10 9, which is the highest of the unmatched hands, but this beats 2 2 3 4 5. In rankings of hands, any unmatched hand beats any hand holding a pair.

If two hands each have a pair, the lower of the pairs wins. Thus, 8 8 J K 5 beats 9 9 4 3 2.

If two hands each have identical pairs, the highest remaining card in each hand is examined, and the lowest high card wins. That may sound a little complicated, but in practice it means that 4 4 9 3 2 beats 4 4 10 3 2. And 6 6 Q 9 A beats 6 6 K 4 3. In the winning hand of 6s, remember that the ace counts as low card.

To continue the ranking of the hands, consult the ranking of poker hands (p. 15). Leave out the hands that reflect straights and flushes, and reverse them for lowball. Two pair in lowball is better than three of a kind, etc.

Draw Poker, Lowball

The game is played exactly as draw poker, but you cannot play jackpots. The best way to play is Anything Opens. The same rules apply as to the draw and showdown.

The strategy in lowball draw poker is to go in with an unmatched hand if possible. If you don't have one, then go in with no better (or, in this case, worse) than a pair, throwing away one of the matching cards and drawing one card, but only if your highest remaining card is a 9. It doesn't pay to draw more than one card—a sure sign of a weak player.

Let us study a game of lowball draw poker. Six hands are in the game.

First hand	10 10 7 6 5
Second hand	Q 9 5 5 2
Third hand	8 8 J 3 A
Fourth hand	7 6 5 4 4
Fifth hand	Q Q 9 9 3
Sixth hand	K J 7 7 3

The first hand checks, as do the second and third. The fourth hand bets, the fifth hand folds, as does the sixth hand. The fifth hand, to have any chance at all, would have to discard both queens and a 9. It is not recommended to draw two cards in lowball draw poker; to draw three cards is suicide. The sixth hand, even if he breaks up the 7s, still has two big cards, the king and jack, that are poison, and he also would have to draw three cards, and so he's out.

The first hand is a fair one. If he discards the 10 he might draw a higher card or match one of the lower cards for a pair. I wouldn't stay in with those cards. The second hand is a sucker; he calls, getting ready to discard the queen and 9 and some more of his cash. The third hand thinks long over this disarray of cards (we are in our usual mediocre game), thinking that he is going to win if he throws away an 8 and the jack, and buys two low cards not matching the others. If he buys those two cards he dreams about, he deserves to win, because he is sliding rapidly down the greased pole of failure.

The draw begins. The first hand draws one card, throwing away the 10. The second hand throws away the 5 and queen and draws two. The third hand throws out the 8 and jack (he should have thrown out the hand) and draws two. The fourth hand draws one card, discarding his 4.

Now the hands appear as follows:

First hand	K 10 7 6 5
Second hand	J 9 5 2 2
Third hand	8 6 6 3 A
Fourth hand	J 7 6 5 4

The fourth hand has weakened a little. He bets. The first hand decides to raise and perhaps bluff the pot. The second hand, after the raise, decides his 2s are losers and he folds, as does the third hand. Now it is the fourth's turn; he calls the raise. If the first hand had raised at the outset (and tried to bluff) and then stood pat, not drawing any cards, the fourth hand would be in trouble, having to worry about his bet. But the first hand has drawn a card, and his bluff is called. He announces "King 10 high," and the fourth hand shows jack 7 high and wins the pot with what is a weak hand for lowball draw poker.

Strategy at Draw Poker, Lowball

The two major considerations in this game are the ante and our position during the game. If the ante is low (less than 10 percent of the minimum bet) our play should be conservative, because "stealing the ante" is unimportant. The same may be said for a normal-ante game, when the ante is 10 percent of the minimum bet (50¢ for $5). When the game gets into high-ante ground, we have to alter our game. For example, if there are eight players at the table, and the ante is 20 percent of the minimum bet, or $1 in a $5-$10 game, then we have $8 out there on the table to grab. In this case we shift gears and play as aggressively as good play allows.

Now, let's turn to position. In draw poker, position changes on every deal, with the dealer (or in casino games when there is a constant dealer, the "designated" dealer) having the best possible position, for he or she bets and acts on his or her cards last on at least one round of play.

The later the position, the better the situation for the player. In late position, if someone previously has bet, we can raise with impunity, without worry about being reraised by someone behind us. Or, if no one has opened, we can open with weaker hands.

Let's divide the position at the table into three parts. Early position is the first four places in an eight-man game. Middle position would be the fifth and sixth spots, and late position would be the last two places, seventh and dealer. Some may consider fourth spot middle position as well, but for purposes of our discussion, we'll relegate it to early position.

As in most other games of poker, what to open with is of prime importance. We never open with a hand, even a pat hand, headed by a jack, queen, or king. In late position, we can open with a 10-high pat hand, in fourth, fifth, or sixth position with a 9-high pat hand, and in early position, in this case the first three spots, we'd need an 8-high pat hand to open.

When drawing one card—never do we play a hand that needs more than one card to improve it—we need a 7-high hand in the first four positions, an 8-high hand in the middle positions, and a 9-high hand in the seventh position, and only as dealer can we open with a 10-high drawing hand.

With a 7-high pat hand, we must raise, no matter what position we're in. It is a favorite to win, as are any hands lower than 7-high and pat, of course. With an 8-high pat hand, we raise if we're in the last three positions; otherwise we call.

When we have drawing hands, it's tough to raise because one drawn card can destroy our hand, by pairing one of our cards or giving us a face card. But should our drawing hand be extremely smooth, such as 4 3 2 A or at the worst, 5 4 3 2, and we're in late position with a large ante, we can raise and take a chance at winning a big pot. However, we must emphasize the importance of position here, because in early position we can't afford to raise with these cards. If someone behind us reraises, we have to go down to the river with our cards, and a bad draw can destroy the hand.

After the draw, if you've bought a 7-high hand, no matter how rough or smooth, you can raise, if you're in late position and the players before you haven't raised. Play aggressively, and punish the weak players who are drawing two cards or who think a pat hand headed by a face card is playable.

We should now fully explain what a "smooth" or "rough" hand is again. The lower the remaining cards other than the high card, the smoother the hand. The higher the remaining cards, the rougher the hand is. Let's take an 8-high hand to illustrate this concept. An 8 7 6 4 3 is a rough hand. An 8 4 3 2 A is the smoothest possible 8-high hand.

In draw poker, lowball, there will often be a "blind," a player, usually the one under the gun, or first to make a decision, who must open no matter what cards he holds. This is the player to the left of the dealer. Suppose that in a $5-$10 game, there's a blind. He must open on the first round with $5, no matter what he holds. When you're the blind and it's a "live blind," when it's your turn to bet again, you can raise, if no one else has raised. And, of course, you can reraise, if there's been a previous raise of your bet.

When holding cards as a blind, if there's been no other action but calls of your blind bet, then draw as many cards as you need. You've been forced into the game; you can draw three cards to improve your hand if you have to. But unless you're in this position, never draw more than a single card.

California Club Poker, Lowball

In many communities in California, and in particular Gardena, the "poker capital" of California, draw poker is permitted as a legal game. In lowball a joker or "bug" is added to the deck, and can be turned into any card the player desires.

There's also a blind bettor in these games, the player to the left of the dealer. This factor, plus the addition of a joker, makes it different from the normal private game.

When you hold a joker in your hand, the likelihood of pairing becomes dramatically less, since you can't pair a joker. You can thus play much more aggressively, and your hand, headed by a 7 as a four-card holding, becomes stronger in early position, and headed by an 8, becomes stronger in middle positions. The seventh position can be played with a rough 9, and the dealer can play a rough 10 with a joker in the hand.

Stud Poker, Lowball

Lowball can be played in either five-card stud or seven-card stud. It can be rather a dull game in seven-card stud (a better game is high-low).

When stud poker is played as lowball, the lowest *card* showing opens the betting, and the lowest *hand* showing opens the betting in each round, with the same rules applying as in ordinary stud poker.

The strategy in lowball five-card stud is similar to that of regular five-card stud, but in reverse order: If you have a pair, get out; if you hold high cards (face cards), get out. The interesting aspect of lowball stud poker is that one card, at any time, can ruin a hand. We'll play one out to show the hazards.

There are six players and we'll look at all their cards, explaining the strategy.

First player	9 10
Second player	K 4
Third player	8 3
Fourth player	Q A
Fifth player	2 7
Sixth player	K 2

The fourth player opens with the ace, always a low card in lowball; the fifth player sees the bet, and the sixth player calls also, because his bad king is hidden away. The first player, holding mediocre cards, decides to try one more round and calls. The second player, a strong player, has bad cards; he is not interested in seeing anything but his money intact and folds. The third player has a good hand and calls. The next round of cards is dealt.

First player	9 10 6
Third player	8 3 9
Fourth player	Q A A
Fifth player	2 7 3
Sixth player	K 2 10

The low hand is now the fifth player, holding 7 3, and he bets. The sixth player, still not matched, decides to try another round and calls. The first player calls. The third player, in the favorable position of betting last, raises. The fourth player, with the only pair showing, goes out. The fifth player reraises. Now the sixth player folds, but the first player hangs in. And the third player, seeing a 7 3 against his 9 8, stays in and doesn't reraise. Another round is dealt.

First player	9 10 6 3
Third player	8 3 9 10
Fifth player	2 7 3 Q

Now the first player has the best cards. Seeing that the queen has hurt the fifth player, and seeing that the third player has 10 9 showing and would need a lower card than the 6 to beat him, he bets the limit. Both the third and fifth players call. Now, in lowball, the next card could be ruinous, whereas, in the regular game of stud, a good player would not be chasing better hands to the last card. The final round is dealt.

First player	9 10 6 3 9
Third player	8 3 9 10 7
Fifth player	2 7 3 Q 7

The first player is still low. His 10 9 6 3 is a little better than the third player's 10 9 4 3, but in his heart he knows he has been doomed by the last card, which matched a 9 into a pair. The fifth player is already preparing to fold his cards, but he waits to see the betting. The first player checks, and the third player now bets. He calculated rapidly that if the first player holds a 7 5 4 or 2 in the hole, he would have a lock on the game, and it would certainly be worth a bet. The fifth player folds, and the first player, even though he is beaten on board, calls, afraid (as are most weak players) that he will be bluffed out. He gets the bad news as the third player turns up the hole 8, and he curses his luck.

Seven-Card Stud, Lowball

This game is widely played in the Nevada casinos, where it is also known as "razz." Of all the casino poker games, this entails the most luck because all hands become drawing hands to the end. This is true of all lowball stud games, where a couple of bad cards can destroy the hand that starts the best, whereas in stud poker, if you hold three aces at the outset of play, you'll probably win the pot no matter what you draw down the line.

Here's a perfect example of how bad buys destroy a tremendous opening hand in seven-card stud, lowball. The player starts with 4 2 A, then gets 6 on Fourth Street. At this point he has cards that are beautiful, a smooth low headed by the 6. Now he buys 6 K J and ends up with garbage, for his best hand is J 6 4 2 A. And so it goes.

The game is played exactly like the high version of seven-card stud, except in private games the low hand acts first, or brings it in throughout all the rounds of play, whereas in the casino game, high hand brings it in on Third Street, and thereafter the low hand acts and bets first. There is usually an ante in casino games.

Strategy at Seven-Card Stud, Lowball

You've got to start with solid low cards, the lower the better. You don't want to be playing hands with two low cards and any high card, even a 9. At worst, you'll start with an 8 high hand, when you see that the board is either high or has your possible pairing cards. For example, if you open with 8 6 5, which is a pretty rough low hand, you might stay in if the board shows J, Q, 6, 5, 10, 8, 4. Of all the cards, only the 4 is going to hurt you. The other high cards mean one less of these dealt to your hand, and the 6 and 5 on board mean that there is one less of each to pair your hand.

In this case the 8 6 5, with any card exposed, could call for an immediate raise on your part. You'll be putting it right to the hands holding the 6, the 5, and the 4, and the strong possibility is that they don't stand perfect, and a couple of them may have to fold.

Therefore, in razz (the name of lowball seven-card stud in casinos), it's important at the outset to not only study your own cards, but to reflect on what is out there against you. At this time, all you can see is the board, and that must guide you.

Another concept that's important is the smoothness of your hand. A hand of 9 2 A is very smooth, except for the 9, of course, but it might be worth a round of play if the 9 is exposed as your door card. Then again, if the board is full of lower cards and there are a couple of raises, you might as well throw them away.

You've got to play carefully in razz, going in with very low cards, headed by a 7 if possible, because in the course of the next four rounds of drawing cards, you have to figure that many of your hands will eventually be destroyed by poor draws. If you start with a mediocre hand, it will become worthless in short order.

Once you get to Fifth Street, and hold a very smooth four-card drawing hand, while your adversary holds a rough 9, such as 9 8, you can bet into him and even absorb a raise, but should his 9 be smooth, then you're an underdog with your drawing hand at this point.

On the other hand, if you hold a made hand, headed by an 8 on Fifth Street, you're a definite favorite over any drawing hand. You must play aggressively here, getting full value for your hand. Your opponent must pay for his attempt to beat you.

Razz attracts weak players, who will stay in with all kinds of strange hands that you wouldn't touch with a ten-foot pole. When you're in against them, raise and reraise and make them pay for their mediocrity. But don't fall into the trap of praying for good drawing cards to help a mediocre hand—get rid of it and patiently await your moments.

High-Low Poker

This game is a combination of regular poker, in which the high-ranked hands win, and lowball, in which the lowest hands win. It can be played as either draw or stud poker and, if played as stud poker, as either five-card or seven-card.

Each player in high-low has the option of playing for low hand, high hand, or high-low hand. In draw poker and five-card stud, there is usually a separate high hand and low hand. But in seven-card stud there are many occasions in which one player may hold both the high and low hand.

Whereas the rule in seven-card stud is that only the best five cards can be used for the high hand, in high-low all the cards can be used for a high-low hand. In other words, any five cards can be used for the low hand and any other five cards can be used for the high hand when calling high-low. If a player prefers to call low, he can only use five cards; and only five cards if he calls high.

There are three options open to the player in high-low poker: He can call high—that is, he claims that he has the best high hand; or he can call low, claiming that he has the best (lowest) lowball hand; or he can call high-low, claiming that he has both the best high hand and the best low hand.

Since every player in the game has three options in calling, there may be a couple of players calling high, a couple calling low, and one calling high-low. If a player calls high, he has to beat the other high callers. If a player calls low, he has to beat the other low callers. If a player calls high-low, he not only has to beat the high players, but the low players as well. An example:

Player *A* calls high—he holds A A 8 8 2.
Player *B* calls high—he holds 5 5 5 6 9.
Player *C* calls low—he holds 8 7 6 3 2.
Player *D* calls low—he holds 10 7 4 3 2.

If only these four players call, the pot will be split two ways. Half the pot will go to player *B* holding the best high cards, and the other half of the pot to player *C* holding the best low cards.

But let us suppose that, in addition to these four players, Player *E*, at the showdown, calls high-low. For his high hand he shows ♥K ♥Q ♥9 ♥8 ♥6, a flush, which is the best high hand; and for his low hand ♥9 ♥8 ♥6 ♠4 ♦3. It is not the lowest hand, since Player *C* holds an 8 7 high. Since Player *E* called high-low, but could only win the high hand, he forfeits any winnings and doesn't participate in the pot. *B* and *C* divide the pot, even though *B*'s high hand is lower than *E*'s. In order to win the high pot, *E* would have to have called high only. Not having done this, and losing the low pot, he loses all.

Draw Poker, High-Low

This is played the same as regular draw poker, except that after all the betting is over each player must announce whether he is going after high, low, or high-low. The most equitable way of declaring is for each of the players at the showdown to place his hands (real hands, with fingers) under the table, select one of three chips (white for low, blue for high, and red for high-low), hide the selected chip in his hand, and have everyone open their hands at the same time.

If there are three players at the showdown and two have declared high and one low, the low declarer can immediately take half the pot, while the other two determine the high winner by showing the cards.

An interesting variation: If there are more than two players at the showdown, or if there are two and they both declare the same way, an additional bet can be made. The original bettor after the draw makes the first bet. If there are three players, one calling low and the other two high, the low declarer removes half the pot while the other two make their bets, enhancing the pot, which is won by the best hand of the high declarers.

If there are four players at the showdown, two declaring high and two low, then the betting on the last hand, after the declaration, involves all four.

Thus, if the high players are raising each other, while the low players are content to call, the low players must go along with the betting.

If there are four players in the showdown and two call low, one calls high, and one high-low, then again the next round of betting after the declaration involves all four.

If there is no additional betting after the showdown and one player calls high, two low, and one high-low, the cards are displayed. If the high-low caller has both the high and low hand, he wins the entire pot; if he loses to either a high or low hand, he forfeits his hand, and the pot is shared by the high player with the highest hand and the low player with the lowest.

If the players don't have chips, they can use coins for the final declaration. A nickel can mean low, a quarter high, and a dime high-low.

What kind of hand would win high-low at draw poker? A holding of a low straight—for example, 6 5 4 3 2—could win low and high, since straights don't count in valuing a low hand. Or a low flush, such as ♠7 ♠6 ♠4 ♠2 ♠A could win low, and the same hand, valued as an ace-high flush, wins high. It would beat a holding of ♥K ♥Q ♥9 ♥5 ♥4, since we know that the highest card of a flush determines its ranking in relation to other flushes, and as a high hand, an ace-high flush beats a king-high flush.

Five-Card Stud, High-Low

Since the hands are fairly obvious, some games are played with the declaration made before the cards are dealt. However, I think there is still enough mystery in five-card high-low not to need this artificial incentive. For example, the following hands:

First player	? 8 10 9 6
Second player	? 2 4 K J
Third player	? A 8 8 10
Fourth player	? 9 4 A 3

The question marks represent the unknown hole cards. Now, if we are the first player and our hole card is the 2, can we safely call the low against the fourth player? What if our hole card is the 10? Can we call high safely against the third player? Let us assume that we don't know any of the hole cards; that we are not the first player. Each player puts out his fist, holding a chip, ready to call.

The first player calls high, the second player calls low, the third player calls high, and the fourth player calls high. The hands are revealed. Now, as in draw poker, an interesting variation might be to have another bet.

But before another bet may be made, the second player, somewhat to his surprise, being the only low declarer, takes in half the pot. His hole card was a 4. The final hands are:

First player	10 8 10 9 6	
Second player	4 2 4 K J	Low declarer
Third player	7 A 8 8 10	
Fourth player	A 9 4 A 3	

The fourth player is the high-card winner. By this time, you are wondering about the calls, but it is an example of poor players staying in with cards that weren't meant to be played out, and thus the variations. The only legitimate high player was the fourth player. All the others had bad low hands and bad high hands. They were neither here nor there.

When playing five-card stud high-low, gauge your hand at the outset. Go for either high or low and play the hands according to the respective strategies for each kind of hand. If playing a high hand, remember the rules outlined in the section on strategy for five-card stud; if playing low, remember the rules of strategy for lowball in five-card stud. Don't mix them up, and don't just hope something will develop. Nothing ever develops but a losing night.

Seven-Card Stud, High-Low

I consider this one of the most exciting poker games. There is usually a lot of betting, a lot of action, and a good chance for a strong player to win a lot of money. Remember that seven-card stud is a favorite of a lot of bad players because they have a lot of cards to buy, and hope springs eternal, etc. Imagine their delight with seven-card stud high-low. Now they can always be in there buying, not knowing what can develop.

But you must remember that if you play that way—hoping and praying for something to develop, but not knowing which way you want them to develop—you are a loser; you are a poor player, a sucker. You must know where your hand is headed. You must determine, right at the outset, the kind of hand you want, high or low, and then abide by the strategic rules as outlined in lowball seven-card stud, as well as those in the section on seven-card stud.

Never play for high-low. I cannot state this emphatically enough. That doesn't mean you may not call high-low and win, but don't play for it at the outset; play either high or low. If high-low develops, all well and good, but keep it in abeyance unless you can be sure you win both high and low. Because if you lose either way after calling high-low, you lose everything.

The following is a good example of a hand that develops into a high-low hand *after* being played for high:

At the first deal, you are dealt ♣K ♣4 ♣6. All well and good. Since it is a three flush you stay in.

Then you are dealt ♣K ♣4 ♣6 ♦A. Even though you haven't improved your hand, you have an ace and can wait one more turn to improve.

♣K ♣4 ♣6 ♦A ♣A

Now, you not only have a four flush, with three more opportunities to buy a club, but have aces, with three more opportunities to buy another pair or, better yet, another ace. Aces up usually is a winning hand.

♣K ♣4 ♣6 ♦A ♣A ♠3

The three of spades doesn't look too good for a high hand, but you can still buy a lot of cards for high. But now, in high-low, you suddenly realize that your low hand is 6 4 3 A. If you buy a 5 or 2 you should have a lock on low. Even a 7 would probably win. As for high, a buy of a club—any club—or a 4, 6, 3, or an ace and you will probably win at high. Should you raise with these cards? Well, it would depend on how many of the cards you need can still be bought, but a good rule is: Don't raise when you still need to buy to win; raise when you know your opponent needs to buy to beat you.

The final hand:

♣K ♣4 ♣6 ♦A ♣A ♠3 ♣5

By playing for a high hand, there was a possibility of a low hand forming. And the final hand? A perfect high-low call—an ace-high flush and a 6 5 4 3 A low. It should be enough to take in the pot.

High-Low Split—Nevada Casino Game

Seven-card high-low as played in the Nevada casinos is known as high-low split. The main difference between this game and the private game of high-low is that "the cards speak for themselves"—in other words, there are no declarations at the showdown. The players put out their hands, all cards face up, and the best high hand wins half the pot, the best low hand the other half, or, if one player has the best high and the best low, he wins or "scoops" the entire pot.

This feature of "cards speak for themselves" cuts out a bit of psychological play at the showdown, and the only reason now to disguise your hand is to get more value for your cards in the betting.

Unlike the private game, in the casino game of high-low split what we attempt to do is "scoop" the pot, that is, win both sides. This means that we must concentrate on low hands, hoping they turn into high hands as well.

Since low hands are basically drawing hands because a series of poor cards can destroy them, you must play them tighter with the thought of coming into Fourth Street, where you see your fourth card, with a solid low hand. For example, if you hold 7 6 4 on the first three cards and then get a face card (J, Q, K), you've got to throw the hand away. Otherwise you'll fall into a trap of feeding pot after pot while you try to get perfect draws with the last three cards available on the draw. No, you must be solid going into Fifth Street and beyond, all the way down the river.

There'll be times when you will start with the high hand, of course, but it will only win you half the pot. What you want is to develop hands that can scoop the pot, and if things don't develop that way, at least you may be able to escape with half the pot.

In the casino game there's always an ante, and on the opening round the high card brings it in. Thereafter, the low hand bets and acts first, which is different from procedure in the private game.

High-low split can be an exciting game, but it's also a big action game, so our suggestion is that you start in a smaller game in the casino and see if you can make money at it before moving to bigger-stakes games, where you're coming up against better players, some of them pros.

Texas Hold 'Em

This is becoming one of the most popular of the Nevada casino games, and each year during May, the Horseshoe Club of Las Vegas holds a world championship tournament in which Texas Hold 'Em, or just Hold 'Em, as it is often called, is the featured game. The winners of this tournament have been such legendary players as Johnny Moss, Amarillo Slim Preston, Doyle "Texas Dolly" Brunson, "Texas Jack" Strauss, and Stu Ungar.

How the Game Is Played

There is usually an ante, and then each player gets two cards face down, known as "pocket cards." There can be as many as fifteen players in the game, but the best games are played with from eight to eleven participants because, in addition to these two cards dealt each player, another five cards are placed out on board as community cards, and so, even with eleven players, only twenty-seven cards from the deck will be used.

After each player gets two cards, there will be three cards dealt face up at one time, known as the "flop." Then another card is dealt face up, known as "Fourth Street," and finally a fifth card, known as "Fifth Street," is dealt. Altogether there are four betting rounds.

A normal fifty-two-card pack of cards is used, without the jokers, and the rank of the hands and cards is the same as in high poker.

The Deal

In casino games there is a house dealer, but since position is important in Hold 'Em, a button is moved around the table to each player, moving in a clockwise manner. This button signifies an imaginary dealer.

After the dealer shuffles the cards, he burns one, that is, pulls the first card off the top of the deck and removes it from play, without showing its face to anyone. Then a card is burned on each additional round of play.

First Betting Round and Ante

There is usually an ante in casino play. After all the players have anted up, the dealer will shuffle and burn the top card, then deal one card in turn to the players, starting with the player to the button's left. Each player gets two cards face down before the first betting round. Then, if there is a blind, the first player to the button's left makes a minimum bet, which is mandatory, no matter what cards he holds, then each player in turn, commencing with the player to his left and going around the table, must call the bet, call a raise if there is one, or fold. After all bets are in, the dealer burns another card.

Second Betting Round and Flop

Three cards are now dealt face up on the table. These are community cards and can be used by all the players to form their best hands. Eventually five cards will be dealt out on the table, and the player combines any three of these cards with his own two cards to form his best five-card poker hand.

For example, suppose a player has been dealt ♦K ♠A, a rather strong opening hand for Hold 'Em. The five cards on board are ♦4 ♥9 ♣A ♠4 ♣8.

The best hand this player will have will be aces over 4s, making use of his own ace and combining it with the pair of 4s and other ace on board.

But on the flop, the players see only three of the cards they can use, and must make decisions based on these cards and the possibility of improving their hands with the two cards still to be dealt face up.

After the flop the betting starts once more with the player to the button's left. If he has already folded on the first round by not seeing a subsequent raise, then the player closest to the button's left still in the game makes the first bet. If this were a $10-$20 game, the bets would still be in the $10 range, with raises also increments of $10.

Fourth Street—Third Betting Round

Now another card is burned and then the top card is placed alongside the three cards of the flop. The bets are now in the higher range; $20 in a $10-$20 game with increments only of $20 for raises.

Once again, the betting starts with the player closest to the button's left, and goes around the table in order.

Fifth Street—Fourth Betting Round

The fifth card is now dealt face up, and at this point there are five cards face up on board. The betting once more starts with the player closest to the button's left, and again goes around the table. If more than one player remains in the game after all bets and raises are in, then there's a showdown.

The Showdown

The player called first shows his cards. Then if any player in turn feels he can better that hand, he shows his cards. The best hand, that is, the highest hand at the showdown, wins. Any player can concede the pot by not showing his or her cards at the showdown.

Strategy at Texas Hold'Em

As with most poker games, the most important consideration and chief strategy is what cards to stay in with. There is a round of betting before the flop, when the player is seeing very little of the future possibilities, only his or her two pocket cards. And remember, you'll be sharing the board with all the other players. If you hold a pair of 6s in the pocket, and the eventual board is ♦2 ♣4 ♠10 ♥10 ♥9, then your best possible hand is 10s over 6s, using the 10s on board as your higher pair. But if any other players hold higher pairs in the pocket, they'll beat your hand. For example, if a player holds a pair of 8s, he'll have 10s over 8s. Or if a player holds J 9, he would have 10s over 9s, combining the lone 9 with his pocket 9 for the pair.

That's why, as we shall see, small pairs in the pocket have little value in Hold 'Em.

The following are the best possible hands to hold at the outset of play:

Best: A A, K K, A K suited (same suit), A Q suited, Q Q, A K off-suited, K Q suited.

Next best: J J, 10 10, 9 9, 8 8, A J suited, K J suited, Q J suited, J 10 suited.

Marginal: A Q offsuited, K Q offsuited, lower pairs than the 8s.

When discussing these hands, we must also talk about position. Let's divide position as follows: the blind through fourth seat, early position; fifth through seventh, middle position; eighth through eleventh, late position. Unlike other stud games, where position will change according to what the players show on board, in Hold 'Em the position never varies from the first betting round through the showdown.

The worst—i.e., the earlier—the position, the stronger your cards should be. Don't stay in with marginal hands in early position, and if there are raises already and you have marginal cards, throw them away.

With stronger cards, be the raiser, take control of the game. If you hold aces, you must raise before the flop, and establish your strength. You're top dog and can hold those aces as winning cards to the end; you can't afford to call and let some marginal hand sneak in, such as a pair of deuces that might find another deuce on the flop and whip you.

Any of the three best pairs calls for an immediate raise, as does A K suited or offsuit. The A K either suited or otherwise calls for a raise even though it's a drawing hand, which means you have to improve that hand to win the pot, because if you catch the ace on the flop or board, the king with it makes it the best possible second pair.

The later the position, the looser you can play your cards. If there has been no raise and you hold marginal pairs, such as 7s, you can stay in and get to see the flop for just one bet. You can even stay in with cards such as connected 7 8, or 8 9 suited, for there are drawing chances with a straight and flush, but you can't absorb raises with marginal cards before the flop. Stay in with strength, and make the others pay to see and beat your strength.

After you see the cards on board, you'll be in a better situation to gauge what you're up against. If you hold kings, but an ace flops and the raiser at the first betting round before the flop is in there raising again, you have to feel you're up against aces and your kings have lost much of their value.

Don't fight the cards you see, and in Hold 'Em, as in all other poker games, keep alert and get a feeling for the strength of your opposition.

When playing this game in a casino, start with a small game, and work your way up. If you can't beat the players in the $1-$4 games, don't go to the $5-$10 games or higher. Improve your game before increasing your risk, and you'll do all right.

Special Features in Poker

Wild Cards

Some poker games, whether draw or stud, are played with wild cards. The most popular wild cards are deuces, because of their original low value, and jokers. In games in which a wild card is incorporated, the highest-ranked hand is five of a kind. Thus 8 8 8 8 Jkr (the joker being wild) constitutes five of a kind and is of higher value than a royal flush.

The wild card can be used to indicate any card of any suit. For example, if deuces are wild, a hand such as ♥K ♥8 ♥7 ♥4 ♠2 is considered a flush, J J J 2 becomes four jacks, and ♣A ♣K ♦2 ♣J ♣10 is a royal flush.

There are other cards that are sometimes used as wild cards; one-eyed jacks, 3s, or black 4s. The variations are endless. In some games, the card after the first deuce dealt becomes the wild card.

You may find yourself in games with wild cards and, especially, games where it is "dealer's choice"—that is, each dealer selects the game of poker he wants to play and announces the wild cards as well. A strong player can easily cope with these games.

When playing with wild cards, simply upgrade, by one level, the cards you need to stay in with and the cards you need to win with. If Queens up can usually win in seven-card stud, then, with a wild card, count on three of a kind to take the pot. If the wild card is in someone else's hand, and you need to buy your card, and it is the fourth round or later, get out. Be wary of the wild cards because each wild card introduced makes the game a little more dependent on luck and a little less on skill. Not enough to upset a good player, but the premium on skill is reduced a bit.

If the game turns into a wild-card mania (suppose all deuces, 7s, and black jacks are called wild), get out of the game. This is not for you—there are too many unknowns to handle the game. Likewise, avoid games where the card after a certain card becomes wild. If the dealer announces he is playing seven-card stud and that the first card after an open deuce is the wild card, take your business elsewhere.

Sometimes in an otherwise normal game there is one wild man who, when it is his turn to deal (if it is dealer's choice), announces this barrage of wild cards. Just fold your cards during that deal, unless at the outset you are dealt a slew of wild cards. Then, in the regular games, punish that wild man, because you know 1) he is a poor poker player and 2) he goes after big hands in a desperate way. If this isn't so, why the hell is he playing these games?

In this chapter on poker we have stayed mainly with the basic games of draw and stud, both five-card and seven-card. These are certainly not the only variations of poker there are, but if you know these strategies, you can handle most any other. Remember, the heart of the strategy is to win the showdown, and, to do this, start with good cards, play with good cards, go out with bad cards. If your cards are the best, make everyone pay heavily to stay in with you, or, if you prefer not to scare everyone out because your cards are overwhelmingly best and hidden, sucker them in by not raising.

Other games that are played are older games with new names. Cincinnati, with its variant, criss cross, is today played as the iron cross.

In this game, each player is dealt five cards face down, as in draw poker, and five cards are placed in the middle of the table face down, to form a cross, like this:

X
XXX
X

One card at a time is turned over by the dealer, and after each card is turned over that card may be used by any of the players in the game to match with his cards. A player holding A Q Q J 8 can then use a queen turned over in this way to give him three queens. Any player in the game can make use of the upturned cards which remain in the center of the table. After each upturn there is a betting interval.

It can be readily seen that each player has ten cards to pick from and can use the best five out of ten. It's not different from a ten-card-stud game, with five cards down and five cards showing. Why not ten-card stud then? Because there aren't enough cards to play it. You'd be limited to five-man games. In the Iron Cross you can have nine players and still have two cards left over.

What to do in this game? Well, queens up are not going to win here, and a flush is a mediocre hand. There are going to be plenty of full houses. You must play at the outset with matched cards, as in seven-card stud, but if the cards right from the first upturn are not benefiting your hand, throw them away.

There is also a very potent variation of stud poker, called six-card stud, high-low. I once sat in some wealthy man's living room, watching a game of six-card stud, high-low. When I asked one of the players what exactly the game was called, he said simply, "guts." It was true, because in this game there was not only skill involved, but that other quality, courage. To put it colloquially, you needed a big pair of balls.

It was played as follows: There were seven players, and two cards were dealt to each, face down. I should add that the game was pot limit, no table stakes, and the man who ran the game knew all the players, and their financial reputations. He also knew their card reputations, because he was an extraordinary player.

After the two cards were dealt face down to each player, each player anted five dollars, just to "sweeten" the pot, so there was thirty dollars in it. Then each player looked at his two cards and selected one to show. The other was his hole card. Since the game was high-low, I assumed that some players tried to disguise low hands, and others high hands. High hand bet first. After the betting round was over, another card was dealt, face up. Then another betting round. Then another face-up card, and another betting round, until each player had five cards, four up and one hole card.

After this betting round, another card was dealt face down to each player. Now there were six cards in each hand, four up and two down. Another betting interval. By this time, with more than two players in the game, the pot was large, very large. After what should have been a final betting interval leading to a showdown, came the tingler; each player had the right to return one of his cards and receive another card from the unused portion of the deck. If a player gave up a closed card, he got another closed card; if he gave up an open card, he got an open card.

Now, with each player having a new card, another betting round ensued, and now came the calls of high, low, or high-low.

Allow me a brief aside at this point. I was at this game because of a friend of mine who was starting to play poker for enormous stakes. He invited me along. He was collecting art at the time, buying paintings with his winnings. He had played in some big games against dilettantes who imagined themselves good poker players. They were just fair, and since my friend was very good, he was beating them left and right—and filling his walls with art. I'll continue the story after this hand.

My friend was number three player. Against him was the host, number one; a millionaire, number two; and one of the shrewdest players I have ever seen, a dark-haired, slit-eyed player to be known henceforth as number four. Compared to him, the other three players were out of their element.

My friend was having a moderately good evening, winning something like five or six hundred dollars. The game was played with chips, and a hostess served very fine steaks and good wine and drinks.

The host dealt, and the first cards showing were as follows:

Number one	? J
Number two	? 4
Number three	? 3
Number four	? 10
Numbers five, six, seven	Inconsequential. They folded fast.

High hand had to open. The minimum bet was five dollars. Number one opened with that bet; numbers two and three saw the bet; number four raised it to twenty dollars; numbers one, two, and three saw the raise. Now in the pot—$110.

Another card dealt. I looked at the cards, then at the players. The host was tall, slim, smoking a long cigar, also thin. He looked unruffled by it all. It was his handsomely furnished apartment, his hostess, his cards, his table. I surmised that most of the furnishings has been bought with his winnings at poker, or at rubber bridge, where I had heard he had a fearsome reputation. I half expected the inlay on his coffee table to consist of bits of clubs and spades, or perhaps the hapless bones of losers, ground down finely.

Player number 2 was a millionaire but looked like a dishevelled bum, or perhaps an aging pinochle player, playing with his cronies in the park on an abandoned checkerboard table. He smoked incessantly; his fingers were brown with tobacco stains. But he had the money, he had the skill, and he had the courage for the game. True, much of his backbone was financial, a garment-industry business inherited from his family. Unlike the host, who was wearing an English-cut suit, number two was in shirtsleeves, and his stomach and part of his undershirt protruded over his belt. He sweated a lot, he grumbled a bit more, but he knew how to play poker.

Player number three was my friend. He wore a Hathaway shirt, candy-striped in the latest fashion. He had the build of a middleweight, and he had fought as one in college. He smoked Camels and really looked like that guy on television who doesn't want the cigarettes dipped in mint, but wants the real straight smoke without gimmicks. That's what my friend wanted; no gimmicks, just good cards and bourbon and brandy. He was a strong player, and his eyes tightened into crinkly edges as he examined the cards, examined the other players. At that time he was about thirty-two or three and had an apartment in Greenwich Village, a business of his own, a sports car, and friends in the theatre. He had a lot.

Player number four looked like a criminal lawyer. He was about fifty, with graying kinky hair that looked as though it was fashioned by one of those Japanese gardeners who plant on the sides of mountains. He had deep blue eyes, slit eyes, but now and then, when he relaxed and rubbed them, or got up to stretch, or when he contemplated the hostess' thighs, his eyes opened wide. Aha, I thought, make a note; when a card player likes something, his eyes open wide. Yes, but this card player never opened them when looking at the cards, only at the thighs. He wore a marriage band, and I wondered what his wife was like.

The host was the youngest of the bunch. He was just about thirty, certainly no older, one of those sharp young men so prevalent in New York, already making it and going to make it even bigger. I wondered if the smoke and the cards wouldn't wear him out early, but that was only a surmise on my part—he's still going strong, now about thirty-five or six. The millionaire, player number two, I'd say was the oldest, close to sixty, and had seen a lot of cards in his day, and a lot of money.

In the next round the following cards were dealt:

Number one	? J 8
Number two	? 4 A
Number three	? 3 2
Number four	? 10 7

Ace 4, held by number two, was high. The ace was high for purposes of betting or being used in a high hand, but it could be counted as the low card in a low hand.

Number two bet ten dollars. Number three, my friend, studied the cards, then called. Number four again raised, to fifty dollars. Number one, who wouldn't contribute an ash from his cigar to a losing cause, folded the cards, went into the kitchen, and poured himself a glass of water.

Number two sat back, puffed on his dying cigarette, and looked over at number four's cards. He called the raise, as did my friend. Total in the pot, $260.

Another round of cards.

Number two	? 4 A Q
Number three	? 3 2 3
Number four	? 10 7 2

My friend's hand was high. He looked carefully at the cards on the table. Number two could be high or low. Number four looked low at this point. He checked.

Number four bet a hundred dollars. Number two, after some hesitation, called, as did my friend. Total in the pot, $560.

Another round of cards dealt.

Number two	? 4 A Q 7
Number three	? 3 2 3 5
Number four	? 10 7 2 4

My friend was high again. He bet fifty dollars. Number four raised it to three hundred. Now number two looked at the cards as though he were examining his death warrant. He got up, asked for a new pack of cigarettes, which was hurried to him by the hostess. The four players out of the game watched, the host lounging around, a slight smile on his face. Why was he smiling I wondered?

After number two unraveled the cellophane on the pack of cigarettes, he asked for a drink, and got a scotch and water. He drank slowly, apparently washing out his mouth with the liquor, then bent down and turned over his cards.

That left my friend and number four. It was my friend's turn to bet. The raise had been to $300. My friend now took his time. Then he called the bet. The pot now held $1,160.

Another card dealt, this one down.

| Number three | ? 3 2 3 5 ? |
| Number four | ? 10 7 2 4 ? |

My friend, still cursed with being high, checked. Number four bet $500. My friend called. Total in the pot $2,160.

Now each player could exchange a card. My friend, who was first, did nothing for about five minutes. He didn't even look at his hole cards, but just stared at the cards. (He told me later that if he had looked he might have given away a clue as to their value.) I guessed he was trying to determine how number four was going to call, and whether number four would go for high or low. Who could tell?

My friend threw away the last down card dealt to him. Number four threw away the 7. There was a murmur at the table. The 7? What the hell did he have? We had all expected the 10 would go; then number four would call low; and my friend, who, after all, could have two pair or three 3s, would call high and split the pot. Two cards were exchanged. It looked like this before the final bet and call.

| Number three | ? 3 2 3 5 ? |
| Number four | ? 10 9 2 4 ? |

My friend, being high, checked. I could see he wanted to ask to split the pot, expecting now that number four would also check and offer to split. But number four bet $1,800.

A shocked silence. For the first time my friend, who had withstood all the betting up to now, was visibly unnerved. Why eighteen hundred? What for? He sat down in a corner, asked for a drink of water, wiped his forehead, returned to the table, looked at the cards of number four. Eighteen hundred on what? For what?

He could have folded, rather than go through this agony, but I figured that he was purposely put to the test. To perhaps make a wrong decision? Misread the hands? Who knows. Anyway, he called the bet.

Each man took three chips and they turned away from each other. White was low, blue high, and red high-low. It was foolish to call high low with two players, I thought. Or was it? Could either player call high-low? I still doubted it.

Their respective fists were on the table and then opened. Both called low. Another stunned silence. My friend was clearly upset. He had called the bet, and so number four opened up first. But under the rules of the game, no man could concede. The whole table had the right to look at conceded cards, since each player had the right to know the style of the other players because of the high stakes.

Number four's cards looked like this:

3 10 9 2 4 A, or in low terms, 9 4 3 2 A.

My friend had:

A 3 2 3 5 9, or in low terms, 9 5 3 2 A.

Number four won. My friend cashed in, paid by check, and we left together a short while later.

What had happened? Well, number four had made an awfully bold move throwing away that seven, because he seduced my friend into believing he was going to call high after that. But number four had figured that if he got a high card, or matched a pair, he could call high anyway, and he would take his chances on calling low if he bought, as he did, a nine or lower card.

If he had thrown away his 10, he would have telegraphed a low hand. He had four beautiful low cards and could have bought a 5, possibly giving him a lock on high and low.

Anyway, my friend had taken an awful beating. It was the beginning of a lot of beatings. He was a mackerel who, having eaten a lot of minnows, thought he could nibble at the sharks. A bitter lesson. The artwork he had invested in was bad, too, and today it still hangs on his walls—he can't get rid of it for anything near what he paid.

I came out of that apartment learning a lot; learning not to play above my head and learning, also, not to play above my finances. As the host so aptly put it, in an idle conversation, "When you play for those stakes, the game moves out of the realm of odds into the realm of psychology. And then courage counts. And there's nothing so helpful to courage as good cards and a lot of money."

He's too cynical for me. I don't accept that definition of courage at all. But my friend did, and tried to play by it, and was wiped out.

A Poker Story

Here is another story, the narrator of which shall be nameless.

It was a low point in my life. I had just been divorced and in the final settlement I gave my wife the house, the car, the money in the bank. I carried out my belongings in a duffel bag left over from my army days. My two kids cried, and I felt lousy, but there was nothing else I could do. There was no sense in hanging on; I had hung on for two extra years, and it was hell.

I took a room in the St. George Hotel in Brooklyn. I was still working in Brooklyn with a management company, going around to various apartment houses in Brooklyn and the Bronx, checking out complaints, etc. I was sick of the work, but it gave me time for myself. I was working on a book and I felt that the book would be my entry into a new life.

Since I lived on an all-men's floor in the hotel, my social life was nil. I spent my days working, my nights writing my book on the one thing I had salvaged from my marriage, my typewriter. I had a few hundred in my checking account and no savings whatever. And without a car I had no mobility.

One of my friends worked for network television in Manhattan. He was a writer, had written a couple of screenplays and was making good money. On a couple of occasions he invited me for dinner, and there I met a character I'll call Ben. Ben looked familiar, and then I realized I had seen him often on television, either smoking a cigar or playing a rugged cowboy smoking cigarettes. He had the kind of face that denotes masculinity to a television audience—a square heavy face with crinkled eyes, a shock of brown hair worn long, a firm jaw, and good teeth.

He was at dinner with a striking, sexy girl who wore a knit suit and spent half the evening stretching her arms above her head. I kept my eyes on her, rather than on the roast beef on my plate, which was a little too well done for my taste. Of course, at that time my favorite meals were served at Nedicks and Chock Full o' Nuts, but still, I did have some taste left.

The talk turned to cards and poker. My host, the writer, never gambled. His father had been a heavy gambler who had lost his business to bookies, and as a result his son wouldn't go near anything that resembled a betting situation.

Ben spoke of the card games he had been involved in and discussed a couple of winning hands and some shrewd playing (he said) on his part. He asked me if I played poker.

Actually, I considered myself a pretty good player. I said I played, and he asked me if I was interested in coming over to his place that Friday night for a game. I was hesitant. I didn't know what stakes he played for, but, from his description of his winning hands, I had the idea that he played a pot-limit game. And I had about three hundred in the bank.

I really don't know why I finally agreed. Maybe it was the girl he was with. I have an idea it was her knees rubbing against my knees that did it. I would probably see her again at his place; maybe something would develop. I didn't have his rugged looks, it was true, but I had my own charm and style of life. A suite at the St. George, I could tell her, extensive real-estate experience, a budding writer. . . . Anyway, I didn't like Ben. He seemed like a vain boor.

In any event, that Friday night I found myself in a slum block on East Tenth Street near First Avenue, going into a stinking hallway and up three flights of moldy stairs to this decrepit apartment. A woman answered my knock. It wasn't the same one I had met before. This woman, it turned out, was Ben's wife, and though she was no older than thirty, she looked tight and haggard. I was wearing a suit and shirt and tie, of all things, and I asked her where I could wash up. She pointed to a room down a dark hall.

I passed a couple of little kids sleeping on bare mattresses on the floor in an open bedroom, and found the bathroom, which contained a large sink that was grimy and smelled of yellow soap. There was only cold water. I rinsed my face and hands, found no towel and wiped myself off with a handkerchief. I then went back into the kitchen where the poker game was going on. Ben's wife was sitting in the bedroom as I passed, staring out of a cracked window and smoking a cigarette.

There were seven men at the table. I was the eighth. I took off my jacket, opened my collar, and rolled up my sleeves. Ben gave me a nod of recognition. He took out a box filled with money, chips, and checks.

"How much do you want?" he asked.

I hesitated.

"We play table stakes, pot limit," he said. "Want five hundred?"

I shook my head. "Three hundred," I said.

He gave me stacks of red, white, and blue chips. "The whites are one, the reds five, and the blues twenty-five."

I counted them out. They added up to three hundred, all right, and I was in business. The game was on. They played dealer's choice, and the games played were draw with anything opening, jackpots, five- and seven-card stud. They didn't play lowball or high-low, in any variation. No cards were wild. It was normal, popular poker without any frills.

I had given him a personal check for three hundred, made out to Cash. He looked at it, then looked me over carefully. "It's good, isn't it?" he asked, and the way he asked indicated a streak of nastiness I had not encountered before. Of course, I didn't know him from Adam, having met him once at my friend's house. But he had invited me, and I now surmised that he took me for a sucker. I just had that feeling. I felt, however, that I was anything but, for I could spot a crooked game, I knew card tricks myself, and I knew poker.

I could see that Ben was losing. He cashed a residual check and got more chips from the box.

I looked around the table. The men were all in their twenties or early thirties. The dealer was a young man with a scanty beard. He was dealing a game of five-card stud. I anted a quarter, then folded my 6 and deuce.

It took about five deals before I called a bet. After all, if I lost that three hundred I would start about even with the world, with no money to my name, the hotel rent coming up the next Monday, and also a check to be sent for child support and alimony.

I won a couple of small pots and was ahead right from the start. I dropped out of a seven-card-stud game where Ben lost to aces up. He had queens up. After losing, he demanded to count the cards. He counted them and claimed there were only fifty-one. He had a vicious temper and was practically snarling as he counted, shining white teeth gripping that cigar and breaking it in two.

"Fifty-one cards," he shouted. "You cheating bastard!"

The winner of the hand, a man who had the movements of a dancer, counted them again, dropping each card on the table. "There's fifty-two there, Ben," he said.

"Screw you," said Ben. "You counted wrong."

He looked around the table, then fastened his eyes on me. "You count them," he demanded.

I shook my head.

"Why not?"

"It's between you two," I said. "I don't want to get involved."

Ben recounted them, then cursed and started tearing the cards, a few at a time. After tearing about ten of them, he threw them all on the floor.

"Shit," he said, standing up menacingly. The dancer stood up also; he later was the star of a television series, and his body was lithe and muscular. I guess Ben thought better of starting a fight and hurting that profile, which was getting him all those royalty checks. Instead, he went and washed his face in a sink in the corner, then came back to the game, his face and hair wet.

I continued to play very carefully. A couple of new decks were put into the game. I won two draw-poker pots in succession, one of which I dealt. In dealer's choice, I knew the odds favored draw poker for the dealer, and I wanted all the odds in my favor.

In each game there was a quarter ante, and with seven players the first bet was considered a two-dollar bet. After that, the total of the pot could be bet, subject to the stakes you had on the table. Anybody could add to their stakes, but not during the play of the hand. A limit of a thousand dollars was set as the stakes for each player. If he didn't have much of a stake, his bets were put aside during a hand and calculated separately.

The game droned on. Time went on. It was almost two in the morning when I counted my chips. I had doubled them exactly. I had six hundred. Two of the players had left at midnight, then another left at 1:30. There were five of us playing now.

It was the dancer's deal. He dealt seven-card stud, and I dropped out early, but the other four stayed. The betting became frantic. Ben won the pot on a straight, then won three more pots in succession. Suddenly he had become a very big winner. He fondled the chips, he lit a new cigar, and his deep dimples showed when he smiled. He was all smiles now.

Ben dealt, and lost a small pot. Then the deal went around the table again, with Ben picking up two more pots, one a very big one in seven-card stud. I won a nice draw-poker pot, and my chips totaled $750. Then Ben dealt again. It was a game of seven-card stud.

I looked at my hole cards. I had a ♣7, ♣8, and ♦8 showing. The bet went around the table, with an ace betting two dollars, me calling, the dancer calling, another player with a jack calling, and Ben with a ♠K raising to ten dollars.

The ace called, I called, the dancer folded, and the jack called. Another card was dealt. I got the ♥8. The ace got a deuce of a different color, and the jack got a 3 of a different suit. The ace checked. I bet ten dollars. Ben made it fifty. The ace hesitated, then called. I called. The jack called. Ben had bought a ♥5.

Another card dealt. Now I had ♣7 ♣8 ♦8 ♥8 ♣9. My hole cards were the 7 and 8 of clubs. The ace-high hand had a pair of deuces with it. Ben's top cards showed ♠K ♥5 ♦K.

Ben was high. He counted out chips and put $150 in the pot. The ace-high hand hesitated, looked at his hole cards. I knew that was bad for him. If he had the goods, he wouldn't have to look. He lit a cigarette, and while he made up his mind, I took a good look at him. He was about twenty-five, with dark curly hair. He had aspirations toward directing and was an assistant director, I found out later, on a daytime TV show—which meant that he went out for the coffee.

He had a good-looking face, but there was something weak about it. It wasn't his features, which were all smooth and straight and noble, but something around his eyes that betrayed him. He looked at Ben's kings, looked at my 8s, then bet the chips. He was a big loser, and this was about the fourth time he had replenished his chips.

I thought about raising, but it was now fairly certain that Ben might have three kings. He was riding a good winning streak with all the good cards coming to him and, on top of all that, he was dealing. I had watched his deal and the shuffle. It all looked good to me. I called the bet. The jack-high hand folded.

Ben picked up the cards and dealt out another top card. Man, how I hungered for that other 8. I just *felt* that it was there. I had confidence in the cards. I waited for it. The assistant director got the first card, a ♠10. I got a ♣10, and Ben got a ♦5.

Ben now had kings over 5s showing. And he had two goodies in the hole. I now had a possible straight flush and three 8s. Ben was still high. He looked at my stack of chips, then bet $250. The ace folded, and I guess Ben was waiting for me to fold, but I called his bet.

He was surprised. He dealt the next cards quickly, face down. Only Ben and I were left in the game. Ben had plenty of chips to bet, and I had $350 left. I took the last card, shuffled it with the other two hole cards. Ben looked at his card, then threw in $350 in chips, just about what I had left.

I looked at his face. He was smiling. He had over $700 in the pot and he was sure it was his. I still hadn't looked at my hole card, but it suddenly dawned on me that Ben had a full house, kings full, and I needed to buy to beat him. I had to buy or fold. A club flush wasn't good enough, and 8s full weren't good enough either. Suddenly I was sweating.

I looked at my hole cards. First, the ♣7; well, I knew that card. Then the ♣8; well, I knew that one also. Slowly, I squeezed that last one. I was praying for an 8. Come on, eight.

It wasn't an 8, it was the ♣J. I had a straight flush, a lock on the game. And there was Ben, with that smiling face, his left hand on his pile of chips, the right hand also poised, ready to pull in the pot.

I tried to keep a straight face. I bent my head down and shoved the $350 in chips forward. His smile broadened.

"I bet the $350 and raise a thousand," I said.

Ben turned white as a sheet. In a moment, perspiration drenched his face.

Someone said, "You can't raise; you're limited to your stake. All you can do is call."

So I called.

"What you got?" Ben demanded.

"I called *you*," I reminded him.

"Cowboys full," he said, gaining heart as he moved to take in the chips. He had three kings and three 5s.

I showed my straight flush.

"Son of a bitch!" he screamed. "Son of a bitch!" He stood up, full of fury. He showed the seventh card to the players. "Look what I pulled in, the fucking 8." Sure enough, he had bought the ♠8 on the last card.

He flung the cards at me, splattering my face with them. I said nothing. I gathered in the chips.

"I'm cashing in," I said.

"Come on," he said, "the night's young."

"Just cash me in."

I collected my money. I now had almost $2,000. I pocketed my check, his residual check, some traveler's checks, and some cash. I adjusted my tie and put on my jacket.

"The next time you throw a card in my face . . ." I said to Ben, buttoning my jacket, but I didn't finish the sentence.

He said nothing and looked away.

The next day I checked out of the St. George Hotel, bought a small second-hand car, put my duffel bag into the trunk, and headed west, to other stories and other adventures. Ah, poker. It had been a lovely night of cards.

III

Rummy

♠ ♥ ♦ ♣

Introduction

This is the basic game from which all other rummy games are derived. It is very widely played and can be enjoyed at all levels; as a social game for children, adolescents, and adults; and as a gambling game. However, its basic popularity, if it is played for money, is at a low-stakes level, whereas the games that developed from it, notably gin rummy, are considered the big gambling games.

If a player learns this game—the basic game of rummy, sometimes called rum—he can then progress to the other variations of rummy, because it is the principal foundation of gin rummy and the others.

Rules of Play

Number of Players: It is a game for two to six players and is not a partnership game; every man plays for himself.

Cards: A standard deck of fifty-two cards is used, without the joker.

Rank of the Cards: The king has the highest rank for scoring, followed by the queen, jack, 10, down to the ace, which is the lowest-ranking card, or low card.

Object of Game: The first object of the game of rummy is to "go rummy," which means to have a hand without any odd cards. In order not to have odd cards, the player's hand must contain either matched sets of cards, or sequences in the same suit. A matched set consists of three or four cards of the same rank, such as three 8s, four 7s, three kings, etc. A sequence

85

is three or more cards of the same suit in order, such as ♠8 ♠7 ♠6 ♠5, or ♦K ♦Q ♦J. These matched sets and sequences are called melds.

In a sequence the ace can only be used as a low card, since its rank is lowest. It cannot be matched with a king and queen to form a sequence, but may be used with a 3 and 2, or 4, 3, and 2.

In the event that a player does not go rummy, his object is to have the lowest-valued total of odd cards in his hand at the end of the game.

The Deal: Once a player is selected to deal first, by drawing either the low or high card, the deal passes clockwise around the table. If two play, the deal alternates. The dealer shuffles the cards and passes them to the player on his right to cut. If that player refuses to cut the cards, any player may exercise the option of cutting. After the cards are cut and re-placed, they are then dealt, face down, one at a time to each player, includ-ing the dealer, in clockwise fashion around the table, until seven cards are dealt to each player.

Some rule books may recommend as many as ten cards being dealt to each player, but the standard deal is seven, and this is used when two to five players participate in the game. Obviously, the number of cards dealt reduces the stock (those cards not dealt but placed in a pile in the center of the table, to be drawn by the players). Therefore, in five-handed games sometimes only six cards are dealt. The same is true of six-handed games. Even so, in a six-handed game with each player getting six cards, only sixteen remain in the stock. So the best game is four-handed, with each player getting seven cards, as described above.

After the deal is complete, with each player receiving six or seven cards, the remainder of the deck is placed in the center of the table so that it is accessible to all the players.

After all the cards are dealt, it is the custom in some games to place the next card face up, to form the upcard, and place this next to the stock. This card then becomes the bottom of the discard pile, upon which the other players will discard cards, face up.

In games like gin rummy, where the upcard forms the basis of the score and has a definite value in that way (see *Oklahoma*), the use of an upcard has a practical meaning. But the better practice in rummy is not to have an upcard, since its value is basically to the first player after the dealer. He can reject or take the card, or pick next from the pile. Also, in most rummy games, the stock is rather depleted by the deal, the upcard eliminates a card from play unnecessarily. Therefore, I suggest that the up-card not be used for rummy, or straight rummy, as it is sometimes called.

Another rule to be commented on: In some books, it is stated that in two-handed straight rummy the winner of the deal gets the next deal. I am firmly against this rule in any game, except certain ones like knock rummy where the deal is a disadvantage. But where the deal is an advantage, or neutral, as in rummy, it should be alternated so that the dealer doesn't take advantage of the neutrality of the deal and put it in his favor. (See chapter on Cheating.) So, in two-handed games of rummy, the deal should alternate. It will be noted, however, that in gin rummy the loser of the previous deal should be the dealer.

Scoring: In determining the total number of points in a player's hand, the king, queen, jack, and 10 each count as ten points. All other cards have the same total as their spots, or rank; the 5 equals five points and the ace, one point. Once cards are in matched sets, or sequences of three or more, these melds have no point value. Thus, a hand with ♣5 ♠5 ♦5, ♥10 ♥9 ♥8, and ♠J would have a point of ten, with only the jack counting toward the point total.

Play of the Hand

The player to the left of the dealer (called the eldest hand) makes the first play of the game, and thereafter the play continues clockwise around the table. If only two players are in a game, the play alternates between them.

The first player picks up the top card of the stock and if he can use it, retains it, discarding any other card; if not, he may discard it by putting it face up on the discard pile. Note: As I have not recommended an upcard, the first player's discard, face up, starts the discard pile, which is used by all the other players in the game.

After a card is discarded, the next player may pick up that card if he can use it, discarding any other. If not, he may take one from the stock, discarding it if he so desires, or, if he can use it, discarding any other card from his hand. However, if a player picks up a card from the discard pile, he cannot immediately return it to the discard pile, but must wait one round until he discards it. Also, in rummy it is important to remember that when there are more than two players in the game, the only one who has a right to use the card on top of the discard pile is the player whose turn it is. Another player, even if he could use that top discard card, cannot take it. Nor can he take it when his turn comes, since another card or cards will have been placed on it by then.

The play continues until a player goes rummy—that is, he has all matched cards, or sequences, or both in his hand—or until the stock is exhausted.

At that point, there are several possible variations to the game. My recommendation is the one called block rummy.

Block Rummy

When the stock is exhausted and the final discard has been refused, all the hands are then shown, and the player with the lowest score wins. If two or more players tie for low score, then they share the winnings.

After the stock is exhausted, all the players put down their melds first, which of course, consist of matched sets and sequences. When these are down on the table any player may *lay off* cards.

Laying Off

Laying off is applicable to any variant of straight rummy. It is the process by which any player may, if possible, add his odd cards to any matched set or sequence shown by any other player at the conclusion of the game, after the stock has been exhausted. The object of the layoff is to reduce the number of points you are left with in your hand.

Suppose, for example, that after a player puts down his meld, he has three odd cards, the ♣9, the ♥4, and the ♦2. He looks around the table and finds that one player has three 9s in a matched set. He may lay off his ♣9 on that matched set, thus reducing his hand by nine points. If the other player had only two 9s, however, they would only be odd cards, and our player could not lay off his 9 to form a matched set.

Thus, it must be remembered that cards can be laid off only on melds, not on odd cards. If the same player who had the ♣9 saw another player's sequence of ♥7 ♥6 ♥5, he could also lay off his ♥4. In doing all this, instead of an original point count of fifteen (9 + 4 + 2), he has reduced his point-count total to two.

In some books on the game, it is recommended that as each player gets a meld during the play of the game, he must immediately put his meld on the table, and any player may lay off cards on that meld. Once a player has laid off all his odd cards, if he gets a meld, he may lay it down and go rummy, without making a discard.

Now, from this game we can see the derivation of 500 rummy (see Chapter VI), where all melds are in the open. In the other method, where no melds are shown till the end of the hand, we see the derivation of knock rummy and gin rummy.

My recommendation: For a social game, or if the game of straight rummy is to be played by children, the melds can be put down as they are formed and laying off should be allowed during the course of the game.

As a money game, the melds should be retained until the player goes rummy, or until the stock is exhausted, and then the cards may be laid off—only at the end of the game.

Other Variations of Play

Where melds and layoffs are retained till the end of the game, then sometimes, when the remaining number of stock cards equals the number of players, the melds are placed on the table by all players. Each player retains his odd cards, but may lay them off prior to the last play of the game. After the last card from the stock is used, the odd cards not laid off are counted by each player, and the one with the lowest total wins the game. If two are tied for low, they both share in the winnings.

Another Variation: This one is good only in social or children's games, since strategy is mostly eliminated. In this variation, the players must go for rummy. To do this, *the discard pile is turned over* after the stock is exhausted, forming a new stock, and play goes on until one of the players goes rummy.

Winnings

The payoffs in rummy may be in units: One unit for having the lowest score; two for having rummy; four for getting rummy on the first pick, or having a complete sequence in a suit to form the rummy, such as a six- or seven-card sequence in diamonds, clubs, etc.

In another method of paying off or scoring, the point total forms the basis of the winnings, and the difference between the winner's total (which will be zero if he has rummy) and the loser's (or losers') is the amount paid off to the winner.

Strategy

Remembering which cards have been discarded and which cards have been picked up by your opponent, or opponents, is the basic strategy of rummy. With this knowledge you can do two things: a) avoid discarding cards that will help your opponent and b) avoid holding cards that cannot be made into sequences and matched sets because the cards necessary to fill them in have already been discarded.

Again, as in so many other card games, it is important for the player to develop his memory so that his skill at the game will improve. In certain variants of rummy, such as gin rummy, it is all-important, and it is valuable in the basic game of rummy as well. Without a knowledge of the cards played, the player at rummy is literally groping in the dark.

Once card memory is developed, it can help in many other ways. Knowing the cards already discarded, and knowing the cards in your own hand, you can then get a picture of your opponent's hand, even though he has not taken any cards from the discard pile. This will help you in the overall strategy of the game, which is to go rummy before your opponent does. If you can avoid feeding him cards he needs, and avoid taking in and holding cards that cannot be improved, then half the battle is already won.

Having mastered that aspect of the game, the rummy player should now turn to the possibilities and probabilities in his hand. If a player is holding two 9s, and one has already been discarded, then there is only one chance of getting the other 9. So, if he holds ♥9 ♣9 ♦4 ♦5 ♠10 ♠J ♠Q ♠K, and the ♦9 has already been discarded, it would be wise now to discard one of the 9s rather than split up the possible sequence in diamonds. This sounds elementary, and probably is in this simple hand, but so often a player will go against probability because of a hunch, or otherwise. Play with the odds. The odds favor a ♦3 or ♦6, two chances, rather than the ♠9, one chance. You can't buck two-to-one odds and expect to win.

A question that often comes up is whether to save a matched set of one rank, such as a pair of 5s, or to save two of a sequence, such as ♠9 ♠10. The answer to the query involves the consideration of several factors. If your opponent has picked up a 4, he may be using it in a sequence that involves the 5, thus eliminating one of your chances to buy the 5. Whereas he might have already thrown a couple of jacks and the jack of spades might be dumped next.

Thus, we come back to the basic strategy of the game, remembering the cards. To play well, as was said before, you must memorize what is out, what has been played. Then, with this knowledge you must calculate. What is the opponent holding? When he picked up a certain card, did he use it for a matched set or for a sequence? What is he likely to throw you? If he has thrown a new card after half the stock has been used up, does he hold another of the same rank and is he preparing to throw it also? Or has he matched the other one, and therefore, a certain suit will be dangerous?

As you analyze the play of the hand in rummy and in all its variants, you'll find it's not the simple game of luck it might appear. Skill plays an important role, and the player must be alert to all the innuendos of play.

Once you are skilled at memorizing and calculating your opponent's hand and play, you may be able to "block" your opponent from rummy. Suppose, by calculating the hand from the cards discarded and picked up by your opponent, you find that he has three 6s and a matched sequence of ♣A ♣2 ♣3. If you know that the ♣4 was discarded early in the game, and you hold onto a ♥6, there is no way your opponent is going to get rummy. But if you hadn't bothered calculating and remembering, you might inadvertently throw the 6 and quickly lose the game.

As stated earlier, play the odds. Don't save possible sequences with an ace or king involved, because they are one-sided. It is preferable to save two-sided sequences because you have twice the number of possibilities of improving the hand. Don't save pairs of matched cards that are dead through discarding, or dead because the others are used by your opponents. In this way, you will use the probabilities to your benefit and definitely improve your chances of winning.

Irregularities

These rules are generally applied to rummy or straight rummy, knock rummy and 500 rummy. (For gin rummy irregularities, see Chapter IV.)

An Irregular Deck of Cards: If, at any time during the game, it is discovered by any player that the deck is irregular—that is, that there are less than the number of cards required for the game, or too many cards, or cards that duplicate each other, or any other irregularity in the number or makeup of the cards—that game is void. And if the scoring is on a cumulative basis, then all previous scores involving that deck of cards are also void.

However, if a complete game has been finished, where the score had reached the necessary cumulative total to end the game prior to the discovery of the irregular deck, then that score or game stands. This is also the case where each game was played on an individual scoring basis and previous games had been completed in this manner.

An Irregular Hand: If a player discovers that he has an irregular hand, having either too many or too few cards in it, and play has already begun by one player playing a card from his hand or picking up a card from the stock or from the discard pile or the upcard, then only that player's hand is dead, and he must place his hand face down before him and not participate in the game. But he must, nevertheless, pay off any player who wins the hand. If only two players are in the game (a two-handed game), then it is a misdeal, and the entire deal is void.

If more than one player has an irregular hand, it is also a misdeal.

If a player discovers his irregular hand before any play has been made, it is a misdeal. The game is void, and there must be a new deal.

Exposed Cards: If a player accidentally picks up another player's card during the deal and exposes it, or sees it, then there is a misdeal.

However, if a player turns up or exposes a card belonging to himself, the deal stands. Each player is responsible for his own cards.

If, during the deal, a card is discovered to be face up, or exposed, in the deck, there is a misdeal.

During the play of the game, if a card in the stock is discovered to be face up or exposed, the card is put face down, the stock is shuffled, cut, and the game continues.

Irregularities in Discarding: If a player discards more than one card, he may retract one of the cards unless the next player has already taken one of them, in which case, he must retract the card not taken. If another player has already played, but not picked up either of the discards, the player with two discards has an incorrect hand. On the next turn he cannot meld, but must pick a card and discard one of the two cards already on the table. He must continue to do this at his turn, without melding, until his hand is correct.

If a player discards without drawing a card, he may pick a card from the stock before the next player has his turn. If the next player has made his play, then the offender has an incorrect hand and must draw a card without discarding until his hand is correct. While in this condition, he cannot meld.

Invalid Meld: If a player puts down a meld which in fact is not a legal grouping of cards, they must be replaced in his hand at any time before the cards have been mixed together. However, any card which has been laid off on it may be left on the table, but no card may be added to the layoff unless three cards or more, which in themselves form a proper meld, were laid off in this fashion.

Improperly Going Out: If a player improperly announces that he is going out, when in fact he cannot, he must at that time place all melds on the table and lay off all cards that he can from his hand, and then play with those cards remaining. Play goes on, and the player making this improper call remains in the game.

Incorrect Scores: If a player has incorrectly stated his score, it may be corrected before the cards are put together, or mixed together. Thereafter, his score, incorrect though it be, stands. However, if the *recording* of the score is incorrect, this may be corrected at any time prior to the time the final total is reached, or before a settlement is made.

Playing Out of Turn: If a player takes either the upcard or a card from the discard pile and discovers that he has played out of turn, or it is brought to his attention before he has mingled the card with his cards, he must replace that card. Then the player whose proper turn it is may play.

Should this fact not be discovered until after this player has made a complete play out of turn by placing another card on the discard pile, then the player whose turn it was misses his turn. The reason for this rule is that each player must not only protect his cards, but his turns at play. If more than one player missed his turn, all those players simply lose a turn.

If a player has taken a card from the stock out of turn, but has not looked at it, he must replace it, and the player whose correct turn it was may play.

If the player playing out of turn has looked at the card from the stock, and then made a play, the intervening players lose their turn.

If, however, this offending player has looked at the card but not made his play, play reverts to the correct player, and when it is the offender's turn, he must make a discard from his hand but may not meld for that round.

Drawing More Than One Card from the Stock: If a player draws more than one card from the stock, that second or extra card must be shown to all the players by turning it face up on top of the stock. The next player has the option of taking it or not. If he doesn't want it, it is put face down on the stock, the stock is shuffled and cut, then play continues.

IV

Gin Rummy

♠ ♥ ♦ ♣

Rules of Play

Number of Players: Gin rummy is one of the best card games for two players. It can also be played as a partnership game, in which each player of the partnership plays against an opponent from the other partnership. It can also be played by three players (see *Captain*). In captain, one player plays against the other two, but only two players are involved at any one time.

Deck: The standard deck of fifty-two cards is used, without jokers.

Rank of Cards: The king is highest, followed by queen, jack, 10, down to the ace, which is lowest.

Value of Cards: To determine points, the king, queen, jack, and 10 each have a value of ten points. Every other card has its spot value (a 5, five points), and the ace has a value of one point.

Object of the Game: The object is to form sequences or matched sets, so that the total number of points remaining is ten or below. The ultimate object, if possible, is to have a hand consisting only of matched sets or sequences, or both, so that there are no points in the hand, and the player goes gin.

Cut and Deal: At the beginning of the game, the cards are cut to determine the dealer. Usually high card deals, although the players may determine that low card deals. After the dealer is determined, he shuffles the cards and then allows his opponent to cut. The opponent should always have the option of cutting, or of giving the cards another shuffle if he feels that they have not been shuffled sufficiently. But in that event, the dealer then has the

97

option of a final shuffle. He then hands the cards back to his opponent to be cut, after which the deal begins.

The dealer deals his opponent and himself ten cards each, all dealt face down in alternate sequence. The twenty-first card is turned up by the dealer. This is the *upcard.* The balance of the deck, called the *stock,* is placed beside the upcard. The game is played down to the last two cards of the stock.

The opponent (as we shall call the nondealer) has the option of taking the upcard or refusing it; if he picks it up, he must throw out another card, keeping his hand at ten cards at all times. The card he throws out is called a *discard.*

All discards are placed face up, one on top of the other. In some games the pile of discards may be sloppy, enabling each player to see previous discards, and at times to push aside some discards and look at previous ones. This is incorrect procedure. The pile of discards should be kept as square as possible so that only the last discard is visible to each player. Part of the skill of gin rummy is in remembering the discards.

Should the opponent not want the upcard, he says "I don't want it," or "It's yours," or a similar phrase. Now the dealer has the right to pick it up, or, at his option, to refuse it also. If he picks it up, he must discard another card from his hand and place it face up next to the stock. If he refuses it, he says "I don't want it," and now the opponent picks up the top card of the stock, puts it into his hand, and prepares to discard one card. He may discard the one he has just taken from the stock.

Sequences: Sequences are formed in one suit by consecutive cards, such as ♣J 10 9 8, or ♦ 3 2 A. For purposes of sequences, the ace is a low card and *cannot* be matched with the queen and king, as A K Q, to form a sequence. The ace, being the low card, can only be matched with the 3 2 A to form a proper sequence.

In gin rummy a sequence can be as long as ten cards, for example ♠Q J 10 9 8 7 6 5 4 3, or it may be as short as three cards, this being the shortest possible sequence. When a sequence is formed, those cards in the sequence have no further point value. Thus a player can get down to ten points or go gin only when he has eliminated points by sequences or matched sets.

For example, ♦ Q J equals twenty points, but ♦ Q J 10, being a sequence, equals zero points.

Matched Sets: Matched sets are cards of the same rank, such as three queens, or three 5s, or three aces. When at least three of the same rank are held, it is a matched set. Four of the same rank is also a matched set, but two of the same rank is not.

For example, ♣K ♥K equals twenty points, but ♣K ♥K ♠K equals zero points.

A hand can consist of matched sets and sequences in any combination, but the same card or cards *cannot* be used in both.

For example ♥ 4 5 6 cannot be used together with ♦ 6 and ♠ 6 to form both a sequence and a matched set. The player must choose one or the other, since it is necessary to have a minimum of three cards in either a matched set or sequence. Thus, if the sequence is counted, the two 6s equal twelve points; if the matched set is used, the ♥4 and ♥5 equal nine points.

If, however, we have ♥3 4 5 6 and ♦6 and ♠6, then we have a sequence of ♥3 4 5 and a matched set of three 6s, both equaling zero points. So the rule to remember is that either a matched set or sequence must consist of three cards to be equal to zero points.

Examples of points in hands:

Hand one	♥K Q J - ♠9 8 7 - 3 3 3 - 9	=	9 points
Hand two	♦6 5 4 3 - J J J - A 2 4	=	7 points
Hand three	♣10 9 8 7 - 5 5 5 5 - 8 2	=	10 points

A player with any of the above hands could "knock," since he had ten points or less. (See *Knocking* below.)

Examples of gin hands:

Hand four	♠8 7 6 5 - ♥ 8 7 6 - ♥ 3 2 A
Hand five	♣9 8 7 - 4 4 4 4 - A A A
Hand six	♣K Q J 10 9 - ♦ 7 6 5 4 3

Knocking: When a player has ten points or less in his hand, he has the option of knocking. To knock, he puts his discard face down on the discard pile and announces he is "knocking." He then lays out his hand on the table, putting his sequences, together with his matched sets, to one side and his odd cards away from these, so that his opponent can easily see the cards and count the points.

If the players are playing the modern version of gin, the upcard determines the knock. If the upcard is anything lower than a 10, the knock must be the value of the upcard or lower.

If the player holding hand number one above were to knock, he would put his discard face down first, announce he is knocking, and lay out the cards as shown below.

♥K Q J   ♠9 8 7   3 3 3   9

He would then announce, "Nine points."

His opponent now lays out his cards as well and, before taking his own count, has the privilege of *laying off* unmatched cards in his hand on the knocker's hand. If he had an unmatched ♥10, or ♥10 and ♥9, he could lay those cards off. If he had a ♠10 and ♠6, or ♠10 J and ♠6 5, he could lay those off as well. If he had the fourth 3, that also could be laid off. When cards are laid off they are considered to have zero point value and do not count in the total point-count in the hand of the player laying them off. They also add no value to the knocker's hand.

For example, after the knock with the number one hand, the opponent is holding the following cards:

888 - ♠ 5 4 3 2 - ♥ 10 - 7 7

The total point-count is twenty-four, but after the ♥10 is laid off on the sequence of hearts, the count is fourteen. Since the knock card was a 9, if we subtract nine from fourteen, the point total of five is credited to the knocker.

If the opponent of the knocker has a total point-count *tying or below* the knocker's, then the opponent wins. This is called underknocking, or undercutting.

If the opponent of the knocker can lay off his unmatched cards, and the remaining cards in his hand are sequences and/or matched sets with a total point value of zero, then he is said to have *ginned off* on the knocker and he wins bonus points. Bonus points are also awarded in the event of tying or *underknocking* the knocker, or going gin.

Let's look at this hand. The player knocking held:

♥ 9 8 7 6 5 - 4 4 4 - A A

He knocked with two. Because of the five-card run in the heart sequence, and the unlikely prospect of having his opponent throw him an ace for gin, he thought it better to knock.

His opponent held:

Q Q Q Q - ♠ 8 7 6 5 - ♥ 10 4

He also had a bad hand for gin, with two four-card sequences, but he held the odd hearts, knowing the knocker was holding hearts and also 4s. He now lays off the ♥10 and ♥4, thereby eliminating all odd cards in his hand and giving his hand a point total of zero, and gins off. He gets thirty points plus the two points the knocker knocked with, and three bonus boxes.

If the knocker has gin, the opponent cannot lay off any of his cards.

Gin: This is what gave the game its name and it occurs when either of the players has no odd cards in his hand, all the cards falling into groups of matched sets or sequences. Here are a couple of examples of gin hands:

♠ Q J 10 9 - 5 5 5 - A A A
♦ 8 7 6 - J J J J - ♠ 4 3 2

When a player goes gin, he gets a bonus of twenty-five points, two bonus boxes, and the total amount of points remaining in odd cards in his opponent's hand. The opponent cannot lay off or gin off; his points are frozen as of that moment. If he holds thirty-nine points in odd cards, that is added to the twenty-five points for gin, giving the player going gin a total of sixty-four points, two bonus boxes.

If one player had gin in his hand but overlooked it, and his opponent went gin, the opponent gets the credit and wins twenty-five points and the two bonus boxes.

Other Rules of Play

Play of the Cards: A card is considered drawn when it has been taken off the discard pile or when it has been moved from the stock by a player. If a player is merely adjusting the stock, he must so announce before touching it.

A card is considered discarded when it is on the table, having left the player's hands. If the player is still holding it, even though it is on the table it is not yet a discard.

A player cannot discard the same card he has picked from the discard pile on the same turn. If he does this, he can be forced to put it back in his hand, and to discard another card.

If a player removes a card from the stock before the opponent has discarded his card, the player must draw the stock card and cannot use the discard.

If the nondealer, at the beginning of play, should pick up the top card from the stock without asking the dealer if he wants the upcard (twenty-first card), the dealer may still take the first upcard, and discard a card, which the nondealer cannot pick up. His own discard must now be placed upon the dealer's discard.

If the score has been incorrectly counted—that is, the total amount of points from the cards held—this may be corrected as long as the cards are on the table. But once they have been mingled, the score stands, since it would be impossible to refute or affirm the count.

If the scorer incorrectly adds the points, this may be corrected at any time; or if the scorer writes down the wrong number of points, this also can be corrected at any time.

After one player has put down his melds and knocked, and the other player has laid off cards on those melds, the melds stand and cannot be changed or rearranged. But prior to the laying off of cards, the melds can be changed or rearranged by the player knocking, providing that they give him a legal knock.

If a player calls a knock and has fewer points than his call, the cards speak for themselves. If a player knocks and has gin, the gin counts.

However, should these errors be discovered after the cards have been mingled, then the original call stands.

If a player calls "knock" or "gin" and has made a mistake, but his cards have not been exposed, nor have his opponent's, then there is no penalty and the game goes on. But should his cards be put down, he must then retrieve them and play out the game, his penalty being the inadvertent showing of his cards.

If, however, his opponent has shown his cards, then the player mistakenly calling "knock" or "gin" must play out his cards from the table in an exposed position, while his opponent may retrieve his own cards and play them out from his hand.

Scoring

If a player knocks, his opponent's points above the knocking points are credited to the knocker. As an example, if the knocker had six points, and his opponent eighteen after his layoffs, then the knocker is credited with twelve points.

If a player has gin, he gets credit for all the points in his opponent's hand, plus a bonus of twenty-five points.

If the opponent ties or underknocks the knocker, he gets credit for the knocker's points, plus a bonus of twenty points. (Some players may agree on ten points.) If the opponent gins off, he gets credit for the knocker's points, plus thirty points. (Some players agree on twenty points.)

At the end of the game, which occurs when either player reaches a hundred points, the winner gets a bonus of an additional hundred points, plus twenty points for each individual score he had. Then, after his score is totaled, he subtracts his opponent's score and gives the opponent twenty points for each individual score he had. The net total is his winnings.

A score sheet would look something like this:

A	B
12	7
39	34
78	
109	

Each time a hand is won the score is added to the points already totaled. Thus *A* won 12 points; then 27 more; then 39 more; then 31 more, for a total of 109. He gets an additional 100 points for winning the game, and since he won four individual hands he gets 80 more points for a grand total of 289.

His opponent had 34 points, plus 40 for the two scores he made (7 + 27), for a grand total of 74 points. Subtracting this from 289 shows a net total of 215 for the winner.

In the event that the loser scores no points at all, he is said to be *shut out*. Other terms frequently used are *schneidered* or *skunked*. A player who has not yet scored any points while the game is in progress is said to be *on a schneider*.

In the event of a schneider, the total points the winner receives are doubled.

Variations

The game of gin rummy has undergone changes since it was first introduced. It is probably the most popular of the two-handed games, since it can be played socially as well as for stakes, and some games are played for very big stakes at that. Its popularity has extended beyond the United States, and I recall a James Bond movie that opened with a gin rummy game played in the Bahamas, in which one of the players was cheating via an earpiece tuned in to a confederate's walkie-talkie. The confederate, a good-looking woman of course, was sitting in a hotel room overlooking the game at poolside with a pair of binoculars, calling out the opponent's hand to the cheater. *Moral*: Never play in sunny climes with your back to the hotel; never play anyone wearing an earpiece; and, if you're in the Bahamas, never play gin rummy.

Naturally, James Bond saw through the whole thing, called a spade a spade, and eventually was fighting sharks—real ones, not the card mechanics you're going to read about later in this chapter.

Two changes occurred in gin rummy that made it a faster-scoring game with bigger scores and bigger payoffs. The game of Oklahoma gin was introduced, and was a fad for a while, but the one important thing modern gin rummy has taken from this game is the use of the upcard, the twenty-first card dealt, to determine the knock card.

Oklahoma

Before Oklahoma, the upcard was just there, without any particular importance attached to it. Oklahoma gin changed all that. Now, whatever the upcard, that became the knocking card. Whereas before you could always knock with ten or less, now, if the knock card is a king, queen, jack, or 10, you can knock with ten or less, but if it is a 9, nine points or less is the knock; if it is an 8, the knock is eight points, and so forth. And if there is an ace showing, both players must go for gin. No matter what the knock card (upcard), each player can still go for gin.

For example, the upcard is a 2. Neither player can knock unless their odd-card count is two or less; and at their option, either player or both can go for gin. One doesn't have to announce that he is going for gin, one merely announces it when he has it.

Another innovation: Not only did the upcard become the knock card, but if it was a *spade,* that particular hand was played for *double the point count.*

If the upcard was the ♠6, and one player went gin, he would collect double the total points in his opponent's hand, plus double the normal bonus points for going gin. After a while, the standard bonus total for gin became twenty-five points. With a spade as the upcard, and the opponent holding twenty-three points in odd cards, a player going gin would collect twenty-three times two, or forty-six, plus twenty-five times two, or fifty, for a total of ninety-six points. With these innovations, point totals began to mount.

Whenever there was an ace of spades as the upcard, if either player went gin before the stock was exhausted, he would have at least fifty points to his credit.

With this innovation, another factor entered into gin. The point count was still important, but gradually it was the *boxes* that determined the stakes. Boxes are individual scores. In the following scoresheet, *A* has three boxes, and *B* has one.

A	*B*
12	7
26	
49	

If a scoresheet looked like this . . .

A	B
21	6
34	8
59	19
	32

. . . then *A* has three boxes, but *B* has four, despite the fact that *A* has more points than *B*.

As Oklahoma gin caught on, and its upcard and spade aspects were added to regular gin rummy, the scores of individual games began to increase. Instead of the 100 points necessary to win a game, the scoring was increased to 150 or 200 points. And then a new factor entered into the scoring. It was called Hollywood.

Hollywood

In Hollywood, instead of the normal columns *A* and *B,* or *Me* and *Him,* or *We* and *They,* there were six columns, looking like this . . .

A   A   A   B   B   B

. . . with a line down the middle separating the three *A*s from three *B*s.

Now, if player *A* scored fifteen points on the first hand, it looked like this:

A   A   A   B   B   B
15

If *B* won the next hand and scored nineteen points, the score looked like this:

A   A   A   B   B   B
15   19

Now, for the innovation. If *A* scored another sixteen points on the next deal, the score looked like this:

A   A   A   B   B   B
15 16   19
31

Note: *A* now has three boxes to his credit, and *B* has only one, despite the fact that *A* won only one more hand than *B*.

What Hollywood gin did was to make the scores cumulative and increase the importance of boxes in a count. The scoring is now as follows: If *A* wins one hand, he gets the score in the first column; if he wins again, he gets the single score in the second column, and the first and second scores are added together in the first column. If *A* wins another hand, he gets a single score in the third column, two scores in the second, and three in the first. Let us say that *A* scored ten points each time, to make it easy to understand:

```
A   A   A
10  10  10
20  20
30
```

If *A* scores again and gets eleven points, the columns now will look like this:

```
A   A   A
10  10  10
20  20  21
30  31
41
```

That's Hollywood gin. To the scoring of points was added the bonus in boxes. Here's how it works: For every gin hand, two bonus boxes; for every underknock, one bonus box; for every gin off, three bonus boxes. These are shown in the following manner. Let's say it is the first deal and *A* gins. *B* has twenty-nine points in odd cards in his hand. Thus *A* gets twenty-five for gin, plus twenty-nine, for a total of fifty-four. (It's not a spade hand.)

```
A   A   A
54
(2)
```

That (2) indicates the bonus boxes for gin that *A* gets. These, as well as points, are cumulative. Suppose that *A* ginned on the second hand as well, and caught his opponent with sixteen odd-card points. 25 + 16 = 41. Then also there are two bonus boxes.

A   A   A
54 41
(2) (2)
95
(2)

At this point *A* has six boxes in the first column and three in the second. As boxes were used, the point total was then used merely as a reflection of boxes. When either player reached 200 points in his hand, he got credit for game and got five extra boxes. The use of boxes spread among the gamblers for stakes because it was easy to calculate. Instead of much adding and subtracting of points, as in the old form of gin, the boxes could be counted and then a value put on the net total of boxes. Suppose two players, *X* and *Y,* are playing gin rummy. They are playing the modern form, using the upcard to determine the knock, using the Hollywood style of cumulative scoring in three columns, doubling spades, and counting only boxes. They play for 200 points per game. A finished complete game, with *A* winning, would look like this: [Remember, all (   )s are bonus boxes. The stakes are one dollar a box. If there is a schneider—that is, the loser not scoring at all—in one column, the scoring is doubled. For the first illustration there are no schneiders.]

X	*X*	*X*		*Y*	*Y*	*Y*
14	19	38		11	29	72
33	57	(2)		40	(2)	(4)
71	(2)	98		(2)	101	85
(2)	117	(4)		112	(4)	90
131	(4)	119		(4)	*114*	—
(4)	138	173				
152	182	(4)				
206	(4)	188				
(4)	197	212				
	221	*(1)*				
	(1)					

Before we take the box count, you can see that *X* had one gin hand where spades was not the upcard, the (2); two where spades was the upcard, the two (4)s; and one underknock, where the upcard was not spades, (1). *Y* had one gin with spades and one without. Once *X* reached 200 in his first column, that column was finished and received no more points. At that point, the first column of *Y* also received no more points. (There was one more deal that *Y* won in the second column, and two more he won in the third column after the first column was finished.)

Also, when playing boxes you could merely put down 200 as the final total, since points don't count per se, but I gave the true addition so that the columns could be understood. Now, for the total of boxes.

In the first column, *X* had sixteen boxes. He gets five extra as a bonus for game, giving him twenty-one. In the second column, he has eighteen plus five for a total of twenty-three. In the third he has seventeen plus five for a total of twenty-two. Gross total of boxes: Sixty-six.

Y has nine boxes in the first column (no bonuses; he didn't win any games by reaching 200 points). In the second column he has nine also, and in the third he has seven, for a grand total of twenty-three.

Subtract twenty-three from sixty-six, and that equals forty-three boxes, or forty-three dollars won in this game for *X*. Let us assume that *Y* won no games whatsoever; that he had a clean slate in all three columns. He would have lost 66 × 2, or 132 boxes, or dollars.

It is possible for a player to be schneidered in one or two columns as well as all three. In those schneidered columns the boxes are doubled for the winner, and the bonus-game box total of five is doubled to ten.

It is also possible for one player to win two games, reaching 200 points in both, and the other player to reach 200 points in the third game.

In the illustration of *X* and *Y*'s game, you could see how difficult it would be to add all the numbers and subtract the other scores. Boxes simplify it. It's the way the big-stakes games are played today.

A brief summary of the modern gin rummy game:

1. The upcard is the knock card. An ace as an upcard means both players have to go for gin.

2. Spades as an upcard suit means that the scoring is doubled. Bonus boxes are also doubled.

3. Each individual score is a box.

4. Each gin score is a box plus two bonus boxes.

5. Each underknock is a box plus one bonus box.

6. Each gin off is a box plus three bonus boxes.

7. The first player to reach 150 or 200 points in a game (it is up to the players before the game to determine the winning total; the lower the total, the more chances for schneiders) wins five additional bonus boxes.

8. The scoring is cumulative, including the boxes.

9. The final result is tabulated by the net total of boxes, and the payoff is a fixed sum per box.

10. If a player scores the total points necessary for game (150 or 200) and the loser has no points in that column, the box total is doubled, and the bonus-box total for game is doubled also, from five to ten.

11. A game is deemed complete when the three columns of either player, or a combination of the two players, has reached the total necessary for game (150 or 200 points).

12. Bonus points: twenty-five for gin; twenty for underknock; thirty for ginning off. If a spade, double the amount.

Partnership Gin

Gin can be a very exciting game when two sets of partners play each other. Partners can be selected by high or low cards drawn, or they can be prearranged, as they often are in big money games. Where four players are of unequal strength, the partners are switched; if there is one weak player, each of the other three players has that weak player as his partner during one of the complete games.

The ideal way to play partnership gin is by the modern game, where the upcard is the knock card, spades are double, and boxes as well as total points count. Usually, a score of 200 to 250 points is required to win at partnership gin, since the scores can be quite enormous if both partners win at the same time in a spade or gin hand. The scores in partnership gin are always combined, with both partners' scores counting. Here's how it works.

If *A* and *B* are playing *C* and *D*, high card determines the dealers at the outset. If *A* and *B* are selected as the dealers, *A* deals to *C*, and *B* to *D*, and thereafter, on each deal the sides are alternated. On the next deal *A* will play *D*, and *B* will play *C*, and so on. Each plays with a separate deck.

Since there will be two separate games going on, two decks are absolutely necessary, and I prefer three. I place the third deck to one side, and on each deal the top card is turned over, which is used to determine the knock. In this way, the same knock card is used for all players.

With an outside card used as the knock card, the dealer deals out eleven cards to the nondealer and takes ten for himself. The eleventh card is used by the nondealer in his hand, but he must discard any one of his 11 cards. Then it is the dealer's turn to play, and the game goes on as in regular gin rummy.

Suppose the knock card is a 9. Each game goes on separately, with no player permitted to help his partner. Let's assume that *A* has a very good hand, knocks almost immediately, and gets thirty-four points. His partner, *B*, who is playing *D*, now is quite cognizant of that point total. Since going gin is worth twenty-five points, he must keep his score below nine for his partnership to win. Let us assume that *D* knocks and wins eighteen points. Since *A* and *B* won thirty-four, their net total is sixteen points, and the score sheet would look like this:

AB   CD   AB   CD   AB   CD
16

Only the partnership with the best score for the particular hand wins that hand. Thus, if, on the next hand, *A* beats *D* and wins nine points, and *C* beats *B* and wins fourteen points, the score sheet would now look like this:

AB   CD   AB   CD   AB   CD
16   5

Suppose, on the next hand dealt, an ace shows as the knock card and everyone must go for gin. *A* gets gin and thirteen extra points, and *D* gets gin and ten extra points. The *AB* team gets credit for three points and two bonus boxes, since they won the most points, but no boxes, because both sides ginned.

And, if *A* went gin and got nineteen bonus points on the very next hand, for a total of fourty-four points (25 + 19), and *C* won forty-eight points just by knocking, then the *CD* team would win four points, but no boxes.

Should *A* play *C* to a standoff on the next hand, then the only score that would count is the *BD* score, which determines the winning partnership of that hand.

If both members of a partnership get gin, they get all the bonus points, plus four bonus boxes; and if it is spades, the scores are doubled, as are the boxes. Thus, in a spade hand if both partners go gin, they get a minimum of 100 points (25 × 2 each for gin), plus eight boxes (4 + 4), plus double all the points that were in the opponents' hands.

With these large scores possible, the games are usually played for 200 or 250 points, and schneiders count double.

The playing strategy is similar in all respects to regular two-handed gin, but the scoring is a vital factor. Since only the team with the best score wins the hand, a player may point out the score to his partner and inform him that he has to be under a certain total for them to win. For example, if an ace is shown as the knock card, and *A* has already won with gin and scored twenty additional points, he will inform his partner, *B,* to stay under twenty so that if the opponent gins, the *AB* team will still be ahead.

It is truly a partnership game in scoring, and a player must always take this into consideration, and not play selfishly, disregarding the score.

After one partner knocks or gins, he may not help the other in the play of the hand. The best rule is that a player should always be allowed to an-

nounce the score and inform his partner of the scoring situation, but thereafter he should not interfere in the play of the partner's hand.

Captain

If three players desire to play gin rummy at the same time, the ideal
game is captain. In captain, all the players participate, two of them as partners against the captain.

All the rules of gin rummy are in effect. The scoring is the same. The
only difference is that one player (the captain) plays against the other two
players, who are partners.

The three players draw for high card. High card becomes the captain,
next-highest card is the next captain, and the lowest card drawn is the final
captain.

A captain plays every hand of the game against one of the two partners, who alternate as follows: A partner plays the captain until the partner
loses a hand; then the other partner plays the captain until he also loses a
hand. If one of the partners does not lose a hand, he continues to play
against the captain until the end.

Let's suppose that *A* is captain, and he is playing *B* and *C*. The game
is the modern one, with an upcard and Hollywood scoring. *A* plays *B* in the
first game. *C* stays out. He can only play *A*, the captain, should his partner
lose a hand. *A* wins the first hand from *B*. The scoresheet looks like this:

A   BC   A   BC   A   BC
21

Since *B* and *C* are partners, any hand either of them may play affects
the other as well. Their scores are not separate, but count as one partnership score.

In order to have a fair score, each of the three players involved should
play out a full game as captain. Thus, if one of the players is not of the same
caliber as the other two (either weaker or stronger), each player will have
had the opportunity to be partners twice and captain once.

Now that *B* has lost a hand, *C* plays *A*. On this hand *C* gins and gets
A with twelve points in his hand. The scoresheet would look like this now:

A   BC   A   BC   A   BC
21 37
    (2)

C and *B* have gotten credit for the gin, plus twelve points or a total of thirty-seven points, plus the two boxes (2).

Since *C* won the previous hand, he plays *A* again. Remember, the captain plays all the hands during the game in which he is captain, whether or not he wins.

Should *C* win again, he would continue to play *A* until he (*C*) loses a hand. Then *B* would play *A*.

After the complete game is over, *B* would become captain and play against *C* and *A*, who would be partners.

In the settlement, if the captain has won he collects equally from the other two players, as though each had played him individually. Should the captain lose, he pays off each of the partners individually.

Captain is a good game, but I believe it is slightly inferior to two-handed or partnership gin. I personally would rather sit out a complete game and play just one player at a time. But for three players who want to participate in the scoring and playing without waiting out a game, captain is the solution.

Strategy

The game of gin rummy has an element of luck in it, but there is a great deal of skill involved, and in the long run, the skillful player is going to win a lot of money playing unskilled players. There are a few basic rules to be learned before discussing the finer points of gin rummy strategy.

First: Reduce your hand; get your point total down. If you have a choice of getting rid of a higher-valued card or a lower-valued one, get rid of the higher one. The hand should be played with two objects in mind: Getting the points out, and organizing the hand to play for knocking or gin.

Let's look at a typical hand. The cards have already been sorted.

♥ K Q   ♦ 10   ♠ 10   ♣ 8 7   ♥ 6 4 3   ♦ A

The upcard is the ♠ 8, and we are playing the modern version of gin—with Hollywood scoring, the upcard as the knock card, and spades counting double. This is the first deal of the game.

The first thing to do is look at the cards and see what your plans are for the hand. So few players bother to do this. They just play willy-nilly and hope for the best. We hope for nothing. We make our luck by knowing what we want.

The first thing we notice is that we have no sequences and no matched sets. Our point total is sixty-nine, and on a spade hand, too. If our opponent ginned immediately, he would get 188 points (69 × 2 = 138, + 50 for gin) and four bonus boxes. A catastrophe for us, putting us deep in the hole immediately, for we would lose the first game (150-point game) on a schneider.

The knock card is an 8, a medium card giving us little breathing room. Our opponent might knock, and we'd have to give him at least 120 points immediately. Our first goal is therefore to reduce our hand.

What's expendable? Get rid of ♥ K Q immediately. Only one chance of buying a ♥ J. That takes care of our first two plays.

All right. Neither of us want the ♠ 8. Our opponent picks the first card and discards a ♣ Q. We pick up a card from the stock—♦ 7. We put it next to the ♣ 7 and get ready for the discard. Do we throw the ♥ Q? No sir, because if our opponent picks it up to match a sequence of ♥ J 10, we're stuck with that damned king. Get rid of the king first. If our opponent picks it up, he has kings, and we can then throw out the ♥ Q.

We throw out the ♥ K. Our opponent picks up a card from the stock and throws out ♦ J. We pick up the ♠ 2 from the stock and discard the ♥ Q. Our opponent disregards this card, picks a card from the stock, and discards the ♦ 9. We pick up a card from the stock and buy the ♣ 5. We now hold eleven cards, as follows, and have to get rid of one of them.

♦ 10   ♠ 10   ♣ 8 7   ♦ 7   ♥ 6 4 3   ♠ 2   ♦ A   ♣ 5

We mentally put the ♣ 5 with the ♣ 8 7. We don't want to get rid of the odd 2 and ace in a spade hand, so we throw the ♦ 10. The ♦ 9 and ♦ J have already been dumped by our opponent, whom we hope has as great a load of garbage as we have. We now have fifty-three points, a drop of sixteen points but still a dangerous carding after all these draws. Our opponent disregards the ♦ 10 and picks a card from the stock, discarding the ♠ K. A king now? He probably just picked it up. We pick, get a ♠ 3, and dump the ♠ 10. We know it's fairly safe because the ♠ 8 is the knock card and our opponent is discarding big cards, not holding ♠ J Q hoping that we have the 10. He might, but he picks a card from the stock, hesitates, and throws the ♠ 7, which we snap up. Our hand looks like this:

♦ 7   ♣ 7   ♠ 7   ♥ 6 4 3   ♠ 3 2   ♦ A   ♣ 8 5

We have eleven cards and have to discard one. The logical choice is the ♣ 8. We know our opponent isn't saving 8s (the knock card was an 8), and he'd have to be holding ♣ 10 9 to pick it up. He threw out the ♣ Q so it's unlikely that he's holding the ♣ J. We dump the ♣ 8.

Our opponent disregards it and picks from the stock. He throws the

♣10. We can be sure he just picked that beauty up from the stock. We pick from the stock and get the ♥2. Now we hold:

♦7 ♣7 ♠7 ♥6 4 3 2 ♠3 2 ♦A ♣5

What to discard? We haven't seen a 9, 8, or 7 of hearts yet. Neither have we seen a ♥5. If we throw the ♣5 and our opponent doesn't need it, he might come back with the ♥5. Or he may be holding a run in clubs with two 5s and give it to us. So we throw the ♣5, a card just a little lower than our high card, as bait. Our opponent grabs it up, whistles and shows signs of life for the first time and, after a moment's hesitation, throws the ♣6. He's telling us something. What? He has 5s. He held two 5s and now the ♣6 5. So he has three 5s. Okay. We pick the ♦2 from the stock, and what do we do? We knock. It's the first deal; our opponent also would like to knock but he's had trouble with his hand—we can tell that from the play of the cards.

In gin, get on as soon as you can. It puts you on the scoresheet, saves a schneider, gives you the psychological advantage. What are the disadvantages? Well, our opponent might underknock or, worse, gin off. But we know he has only a three-card match in 5s. He might have another run or lay somewhere, but that looks like it. We knock with eight points, discarding the ♥6, turning it over and announcing, "Knock with eight points." Our opponent looks over our hand, which looks like this:

♣7 ♦7 ♠7 ♥4 3 2 ♠3 2 ♦2 A

He puts down his cards,

♥5 ♦5 ♣5 ♥A ♣A ♠A ♣3 2 ♦4 ♠4

He can't lay off anything, and has thirteen points. So we win ten points (5 × 2) and we're on the first column.

Our strategy paid off. First, with a load of high cards and no matched ones, we started reducing our point total. Then we knocked as fast as we could.

We can see how important our 7s were. Being in the middle they blocked up all sorts of sequences and stopped our opponent from getting any effective sequences. That's something to remember. Sevens are key cards. They can make the most combinations, and control of them controls the game in many instances. It just so happened that we had them, and they gave us that advantage.

More Strategy

After that illustrative hand (I was going to say illustrious hand), certain elements of sound play present themselves. Let's examine them, one at a time.

1. At the outset, study your hand to see what your goals will be. It may be a poor hand for gin, or a good hand for gin. It may be a dangerous hand, full of high cards, where your immediate goal is just to reduce and get rid of the high cards. In any event, have some plan in mind. All factors should be taken into consideration, such as:

The score. If you are on the scoreboard and your opponent is not, and this is the second hand played, and you have really good gin possibilities, go for gin. Generally, with this kind of hand, you will have a low point total, perhaps lower than the knock card. In such instances, you can assume that your opponent is trying to knock and get on, and there are many good scores to be made, underknocking him or ginning off, or finally getting gin.

If, in the above situation, you have good gin possibilities, but the knock card is an 8, 9, or 10, and in order to go for gin you'll have to save some high points, don't do it. Again, your opponent is anxious to knock and at the first opportunity he will. Hold off that gin and go for a knock, and get on the second score.

Your opponent. If you are playing a very strong player, you must play a more careful game and remember practically every discard and play. After your opponent picks up a card, whether he is weak or strong, you should study the situation and know (or have an educated guess based on percentages) what he is holding. After more than half the stock has been used up, you should have a very good idea of what he is holding.

If the player against you is weak, he will probably go for gin more often than the strong player, disregarding such factors as knocking to get on the score. Punish him by knocking as soon as you can; don't play his game by going for gin yourself. Keep knocking and adding up the points. However, if it is late in the game and he has not knocked, be careful. He may be holding just one odd card, and it may be impossible for you to knock without being ginned off or underknocked. In that case, you must use your superior skill. You should already know what he has in his hand by the play of the cards and refuse to give him a card he needs.

The knock card. If the knock card is high, 8 or above, all factors being equal, a knock is more imminent than if the knock card is a middle one—5, 6, or 7—or a low one—4, 3, or 2. The higher the knock card, the quicker you must get rid of your big cards. If the knock card is a low one, it might pay to hold a sequence of 9 10 rather than get rid of them and be left with a hand full of odd cards. If the knock card is a spade, whether high or low, dump these big babies out fast.

However, if I am winning and on all three scores, and my opponent is on a schneider in one or more games, and the knock card is a spade, 7 or below, I play aggressively, going for higher sequences rather than discarding 9s and 10s to reduce the hand. The moment my opponent picks up a discard, however, I get rid of the big cards.

Conversely, if I am losing and on a schneider myself, then in a spade hand I play completely defensively, reducing at all costs unless a discard will match a card I know is in the opponent's hand. By playing this defensively, you are not completely crushed by one bad hand.

2. In the play of the hand, I like to keep 7s in my hand if possible, either in sequences or as a matched set, since they are important in stopping an opponent from getting really long sequences. I think they are the key cards of gin rummy, and I hoard them. If I throw a 7 and it is picked up, I may find myself in a bad defensive position.

Conversely, those cards in which there is very little possibility of sequences, such as a king or an ace, I may discard. I say may for the ace; I will always dump a king right at the outset if possible, because it is the highest card, ten points, and the possibility of using it is limited. Also, if it is picked up I usually can easily tell whether it is for a sequence or a matched set. Thus, with holdings of K Q, I always dump the king before the queen in the same suit. There also, I will not hold those cards waiting for the one chance of a matching jack. I'd rather get rid of those twenty points and get two odd cards.

3. If there is a choice, try to form sequences rather than matched sets. Thus, if you hold ♣5 6 7 ♥7 ♦7 and must discard one of these cards, get rid of one of the two red sevens. You have only one chance of buying another seven, but two chances of getting a ♣4 or ♣8. That's two to one, which are good odds any day.

Cheating at Gin Rummy

Of all the popular card games played for money, gin rummy is perhaps the easiest to cheat at. It is a cheater's ideal game. He plays against only one opponent and he can control the cards every time he deals. He can also cheat his opponent without detection just by knowing certain fundamental things about shuffling. And he can cheat without even touching the cards if his opponent is a sloppy player.

There is one rule in gin rummy which is to the cheater's benefit and which I consider to be completely irrational; the winner of the previous hand deals the next hand. It is a terrible rule, for what it does is allow a cheat to have control of the cards from the beginning of a game to its end, without the loser, or sucker, being able to even deal a hand. This rule can only benefit a cheat; it has no other value.

The correct rule should be: *The loser of the previous hand deals.* I cannot emphasize this enough. To allow a winner in a game like gin rummy to deal the next hand is just encouraging cheats to play gin rummy, which is often the case.

The crooked dealer who can manipulate cards has an enormous advantage. By shuffling the cards he can control them so that he knows one or more cards in the deck. This is usually enough, all other factors being equal, to allow him to win most of the time.

The Mechanic's Grip in Gin Rummy

Before you sit down to play gin rummy, or any card game for that matter, you should know what the Mechanic's Grip looks like. (See *Cheating,* Chapter XIV.) Study the grip, and if you ever see anyone using it, run away from the game as fast as you can.

What the dealer can do, using the mechanic's grip, would take many pages to explain here (again, see Chapter XIV), but basically he can control the top card or cards, bottom card or cards, shuffle the deck so that the cards remain in the same order, retain tops and bottoms, and so on. You can cut the cards to your heart's content after he finishes shuffling them with the mechanic's grip, and you'll still be in trouble. A mere cut or cuts is not going to help you. You must thoroughly reshuffle the cards. Better yet, get out. Only a sucker lingers in a game that he knows is not on the level.

There are card mechanics who modify the grip so that it is not too obvious. But once you know what the mechanic's grip looks like, you should be alert to any grip where the bottom or top cards can be withheld. Also, look for the "injog" (Chapter XIV) because the whole deck can be shuffled and put back together again in the same order with this method. All your cards will be matched by the cheat; he'll just be waiting for you to discard the ones he needs.

The Correct Way to Shuffle

You can be cheated by badly shuffling the cards yourself. An alert opponent, even if he's not a card mechanic, can follow the progress of your shuffle and take advantage of it. I've seen too many players who take the deck, split it in half, riffle the cards once or twice, and present them for cutting. If an alert opponent knew that there were three 9s and three kings on the top, he'd know they were still together. He'd refuse to cut, and then, when he'd been dealt two 9s or two kings, he'd patiently wait for the third, which in time you'd have to feed him.

Why cheat yourself with an inadequate shuffle? Learn to shuffle the cards so that they are thoroughly mixed. (See *Shuffling,* Chapter I.) Practice your shuffle, both the riffle and the overhand shuffle, and alternate both of them.

Exposing Cards

You can consider yourself the most skillful player in the world but if during the shuffling process you expose one or more cards, you can take all that skill and shove it, because you're going to end up losing in the long run.

The worst thing you can do while shuffling is to square up the pack so that the bottom card is exposed to the opponent. I've seen a lot of games of gin rummy in my time, and I've played a lot of games as well, and I'm always amazed at the shuffles of some players. They blithely expose the bottom card, reshuffle, expose another bottom card, deliver the cards to be cut, and in the process expose still another card. Three cards that the opponent knows and can take advantage of. How can such a dealer ever win?

It is never necessary to lift the cards during the shuffle so as to expose them. You should practice shuffling until you master the method of not exposing cards.

At the same time, beware of the player who, during his shuffle, turns the deck towards him, so that all the exposed cards are facing him and all you see are their backs. Tell such a player that you wish to shuffle the cards after he is done, and then, if he protests, tell him that you won't stand for that kind of shuffle. If he refuses to alter his shuffle, then get out of the game. You'll only become aggravated, and that can ruin you.

Also, the sloppy shuffler has to be watched, the one who is continually dropping cards all over the table and the floor, probably making mental notes of them. There are a lot of petty cheats in this world who don't really have the skill to cheat, so they hide behind sloppiness.

Although I cautioned you about shuffling the cards poorly by riffling them only once or twice, you're going to encounter a dealer (I have—many, many times) who gives them a fast shuffle once, maybe twice, then lays them down to be cut. Pick those cards up and give them a careful shuffle, or demand that he do it. This is another method used by clumsy cheats, because they figure that all the melds and lays will be equally divided and they will simply wait for discards. Even though you have the same knowledge, there is no sense in playing this kind of half-assed game of gin. Make sure those cards are shuffled properly.

Another method of being cheated is based on a principle that not too many players know, but which, if used against them, can be deadly.

In the ordinary riffle shuffle, the cards alter their position; otherwise there would be no sense in shuffling in the first place. What happens is fairly obvious, but not many players have thought about it. If a card is second in the deck, after a riffle it moves down in position twice minus one, or to third position. After another riffle, it again moves twice minus one ($3 \times 2 - 1$), or to fifth position. On the next riffle it is ninth.

Try it. It will be difficult at the beginning to exactly place the card, but with a careful riffle you will find that the card will be within two or three cards of the correct place. Now, a cheat can just keep riffling one or two or more cards and place them near the bottom of the deck. Then you cut the cards, and these same cards will be in your hand or his. He'll be cheating you honestly. In other words, you'll be cheated by a legitimate riffle, just because he knows more than you. Well, now you should know as much or more than he does.

Cheating After the Deal

You're the nondealer, and the cards have been shuffled and cut to your satisfaction. You are now dealt the ten cards face down. Right here you can be cheated blind and not know it unless you are alert. As I said before, gin rummy is a cheater's ideal game. Here's how you can be cheated.

While you're busy picking up your cards and placing them in proper order or sequence, the dealer palms three extra cards (or as few as one or as many as ten) and picks up his cards with the extra cards. While you're still placing your cards, he quickly examines his, decides what he'll keep, and then fans the stock to make it easier to pick up cards. (This is legitimate.) But at the same time, with a palm, he places cards back on the fanned stock. Now, not only has he improved his hand, but he knows the next one to ten cards in the stock.

How to prevent this? Simple. Don't pick up your cards right away. Watch the dealer all the time. When he is finished dealing, has decided to fan the deck, and then has picked up his own cards, you can pick up yours. Don't get your nose buried in them either. Keep alert.

Some players like to fan the stock (it's been recommended in card books as an antidote to cheating), and others like to keep the stock squared. I personally think the two methods about equal. Some cheats can pick up more than one card at a time from a squared stock, and others can just as easily pick up a few at a time from a fanned stock. Keeping alert and delaying the pickup of your cards until all have been dealt is your best protection.

Illustration

If you're in a game with a player who has the nervous habit of continually touching the cards of the stock, watch him like a hawk. If it appears that nothing is wrong but you still feel anxious, the best rule is stop the game and get out. There's no excuse for anyone to ever continually play with the stock.

The final and best assurance is to watch your opponent every time he picks up a card from the stock. It only takes an instant, doesn't interfere with or delay the game, and insures a fair game.

Some players are awfully clever about taking more than one card at a time from the stock. If the other party knocks or gins, they try to palm the leftover cards and put them back on the stock. But if really caught by surprise, they suddenly "notice" that they have one extra card, claim a misdeal, and try and get away with it that way. Of course, that may happen— one misdeal. But if it happens more than once in a game to you, you can be sure that your opponent is grabbing extra cards. Get away from him fast.

When I mention all these methods of cheating, and continually advise you to be alert, I don't mean to encourage a paranoid approach to gin rummy. If you're playing for small stakes with old friends, all right— you know your friends. But if you're playing for big stakes against a comparative stranger, being alert will save you money and the ignominy of being a sucker.

Kibitzers and Onlookers

When I play gin rummy, I don't like kibitzers. For the uninitiated, a kibitzer is an onlooker who comments about your game either while you're playing or after. I differentiate a kibitzer from an onlooker, who merely watches the game mutely. In any event, I don't want anyone watching my game. First, they may get a good idea of my style of play. Second, I just don't like anyone staring over my shoulder. I may unconsciously alter my play to please them rather than myself. And third and most important, the guy watching the game over my shoulder may be a confederate of my opponent and he may be signaling all my cards. You don't think this can happen?

I knew a brilliant player once who was born with short pudgy fingers. Try as he might to learn card manipulation, he just couldn't do anything with cards; they'd pop out of his hands. He was just not naturally endowed for cheating, but he knew how to play gin rummy with the best of them. However, playing for big stakes he was up against other equally good players, and he didn't want to play to while away the time; he wanted to win big money. He had a friend who was a professional kibitzer, always looking over everyone's cards. The friend was ingratiating, clever, always cracking jokes, and everyone liked him. But he wore glasses and he had this nervous habit of adjusting his glasses. He could signal more with those glasses than the average Morse Code operator. Everyone loved him, even the suckers. If they only knew.

Cheating in the Knock

When an opponent knocks, take a count of his cards. I have watched too many players who, after an opponent's knock, took a quick look at the knocked cards, saw there was nothing to lay off, and then began their own count of their points. And some players, when they hear their opponent say "gin," immediately assume without looking that the opponent actually has gin.

It only takes a moment to check out the count. And if you have gin or knock, don't accept a count from the closed hand. Have the opponent put down all his cards and count them yourself. If he protests, tell him you're willing to do it, and you expect the same from him. If he refuses to do this, get out of the game.

Scoring

Even after the play of the game, you can be cheated in the scoring. If possible, you keep the score. If you don't, check every count or total on the scoresheet. Anyone can make a mistake, and God knows there are a great many honest mistakes made in scoring. That's okay, but why lose by having added points thrown on your opponent's side, or taken off your side?

A Final Word

There are going to be ingenious cheats who will try to introduce marked cards or stripped decks, or who will wear contact lenses, or who will try anything at all to get an edge. You might find yourself cheated even with all your knowledge and alertness. But after reading this section and Chapter XIV, you should be able to stop most of it. And anytime you're in a game against an equal or inferior player who seems to win about eighty percent of the time, you have to be extra careful. If you just can't seem to beat someone, even though you get good cards and you know you're playing well, there could be something wrong. Remember, your manhood doesn't have to be at stake in gin rummy. Go and play someone you won't always lose to.

I recently read a rather interesting case involving a band of cheats who operated out of the Friar's Club of Beverly Hills, California. They played the members of the Friar's Club and won something like $400,000 at gin rummy over a number of years. That's an awful lot of money to be cheated out of.

How did they cheat? They had a wonderful method. Gin rummy was usually played on a certain floor. One of the men, or two of the men, would play gin against the members (or suckers). The other man would look through a hole in the ceiling, which had been drilled just for this purpose, and signal the players electronically.

Well, after a while the game was moved to a higher floor, and so new holes were drilled, and the confederate crouched in an airshaft to signal his confederates.

This story illustrates the lengths to which cheats will go. Anyone they play is a potential mark, or sucker. Don't you be that one. Don't take anything for granted when you sit down to play for any kind of stakes.

Irregularities

No Shuffle: If it is ascertained that the cards have not been shuffled, either player, during any portion of the game but prior to either one knocking or ginning, may declare it a misdeal, and both hands are dead.

Card Exposed During the Shuffle: Should a card be exposed, the card must be put back in the deck face down and the deck completely shuffled until it is impossible to ascertain the position of the formerly exposed card.

Faulty or Poor Shuffle: Should the nonshuffler decide that the shuffle has been faulty, poor, ineffectual, so that the cards are not properly mixed, he may call this to the attention of the shuffler and demand a better shuffle. Should the shuffler refuse to reshuffle the cards, the nonshuffler (nondealer) has the right to shuffle the cards himself, then hand them back to the dealer for the final shuffle. If the dealer does not wish to give them a final shuffle, the cards may be cut and the deal begun.

No Cut: If the cards have not been cut prior to the first play of the game—that is, either picking up a card from the stock, or picking up the upcard, or playing out the twenty-first card dealt to the nondealer—the hand can be called dead and a misdeal declared. After the first play, the game is considered valid and goes on.

Exposed Card During the Deal: If any card is exposed by the dealer during the deal, the hand is dead and it is a misdeal.

Too Many Cards Dealt: If either player has too many cards dealt and has already picked up and looked at any cards in his hand, the hand is dead and it is a misdeal.

If either player has been dealt too many cards, but has not yet looked at the faces of any one of them, then the excess card or cards can be taken away by the dealer and put at the bottom of the deck, face down.

Too Few Cards Dealt: If either player has been dealt too few cards, and the number of missing cards is more than one, it is a misdeal and both hands are dead.

Should only one missing card be noticed both a) prior to the upcard being turned over and b) prior to any play of the hand, then there is no misdeal.

Where the cards are still on the table, and the pack still in the dealer's hand, and either player notices that a card is missing by taking a count, the extra card may be dealt from the top of the pack to the player missing it.

Once the cards are picked up and the upcard seen, the hand is a misdeal if either player has been dealt too few cards.

If either player has too few cards in his hand and discovers this during the play of the hand, the hand is foul and play stops; it is a misdeal.

If one player knocks or gins and his hand contains too few cards, then the hand is foul and the deal void; a misdeal.

If the opponent of the knocking or ginning player has too few cards, his hand is foul, the game is void; it is a misdeal.

Too Many Cards: If either player has too many cards in his hand and discovers this during the play of the hand, or when he knocks or gins, or when his opponent knocks or gins, then the hand is foul, the game void; it is a misdeal. A WORD OF CAUTION: If playing against an opponent who does this several times, I would strongly suggest that you immediately end the game. Either you are playing a very sloppy player (to give him the benefit of the doubt), or he is cheating you by picking up more than one card from the stock at a time and was caught with the cards when you knocked or ginned. (See preceding section, *Cheating at Gin Rummy*.)

Dealing Out of Turn: If the dealer is dealing out of turn and this fact is discovered prior to the first play, it is a misdeal. Once the first play has been made, the game is valid.

A Face-Up Card in the Stock: If, during the play of the hands, a card is discovered face up in the stock, play immediately ceases and both hands are dead.

Discarding Wrong Card: Once a card has left the player's hand, it is considered a discard. If the player is still holding the card in his hand, but has put it on the pile, it is not a discard until his hand moves away from the card. Once discarded, even if the wrong card has been discarded, it cannot be retrieved, but must stand as the discard.

Knocking with the Wrong Amount: Should the upcard determine the knock, and a player mistakenly knocks with more than that amount, then he is allowed to retrieve his cards. But the card discarded as his extra, or eleventh, card must remain as the discard.

Should the player knock with more than ten points in the mistaken belief that he has fewer than ten points, the same rule applies.

Should a player declare gin and not have gin, but his knocking points are equal to or less than the amount he could legally knock with, then his gin declaration becomes a knock declaration; he cannot pick up his cards and go for gin.

If, in knocking or declaring gin by mistake, the player causes the opponent to put down his cards as well, then the player making the mistake of knocking or calling gin must play out the game with his cards exposed, while his opponent may pick up (retrieve) his cards and play with the cards in his hand.

Exposing a Card from One's Hand: Should a player inadvertently expose a card from his own hand, there is no penalty and the game goes on.

Exposing a Card from the Stock: Should a player pick up a card from the stock, exposing the next card which might be picked up by his opponent, he must show his opponent the card he has picked for his own. This is also the rule when he picks up two cards accidentally from the stock and sees both of them. He keeps the top card and returns the second card to the stock.

Picking Up a Card from the Discard Pile or from the Stock by Mistake: If any player picks up a card from the discard pile or from the stock and discovers that he has made a mistake in doing so, once the card is picked off the discard pile, or moved by his fingers from the stock, he must take that card into his hand.

Not Calling Gin with a Gin Hand: If a player has gin but doesn't realize it and his opponent gins, his opponent wins the gin, but gets no extra points from the gin hand that was not called. If the opponent knocks, then the gin hand undeclared would win, since it must now be considered an underknock, but not a gin off. A player cannot get extra credit for his mistakes.

Discarding More Than One Card: Should a player discard two cards, he may retrieve either one and put it back in his hand. However, should the opponent have picked up one of them, the mistake stands, and the player discarding two cards must then pick up a card from the stock or the new discard and not make a fresh discard.

V

K*nock* R*ummy**

♠ ♥ ♦ ♣

* This game is also called poker rum.

Rules of Play

Cards: It is played with a deck of fifty-two cards, without a joker.

Number of Players: Two to five may play. Each player is dealt seven cards, except, when two players play, each player receives ten cards.

Rank of the Cards: The rank of the cards is from king down to ace. King is highest, ace is lowest. The face cards and the 10 each count for ten points. Every other card's point value corresponds to the value of the card, with the ace counting as one point.

Object of the Game: The object of the game is to have the lowest possible point count, or to go rummy; that is, to have no points in the hand at all. The methods of reducing points is to form sets or sequences. These may be in groups of three or four cards; longer groups cannot be used, with one exception, a sequence of seven cards of one suit in order, such as ♠7 ♠6 ♠5 ♠4 ♠3 ♠2 ♠A or ♣J ♣10 ♣9 ♣8 ♣7 ♣6 ♣5. However, a sequence of ♣J ♣10 ♣9 ♣8 ♣7 ♣6 with an additional odd card is merely two three-card sequences, and the odd card is the point count. A sequence of ♣J ♣10 ♣9 ♣8 ♣7 with two additional odd cards can only be counted as one sequence of ♣J ♣10 ♣9 ♣8, with the ♣7 and two odd cards counting as points.

The groups, or runs, can either be in sequences of the same suit, or can be in cards of the same rank, such as three 5s or four jacks.

A sequence combined with the ace can only be 3, 2, and ace of the same suit, or 4, 3, 2, and ace of the same suit. A K Q is not counted as a sequence.

127

Play of the Game

The dealer shuffles the cards, then they are cut by the player to his right. If that player refuses to cut the cards, any other player may. The cards are then dealt in clockwise fashion, starting with the player at the dealer's left. The dealer deals himself last. If there are more than two players, the winner of the previous hand deals. If but two are playing, the same rule applies.

After each player receives seven cards, he sorts his hand, putting his sequences and matched sets in order. For example, dealt ♣A ♠5 ♦5 ♥Q ♥J ♠9 ♥4, the hand would be sorted to ♠5 ♦5 (with a potential for a matched set in 5s), ♥Q ♥J (with a potential for a sequence in hearts if either the king or the 10 is bought), and ♠9 ♥4 ♣A as odd cards. When discarding, it is preferable to discard the highest of the odd cards first, since the purpose is to reduce the point total of the hand. Thus, picking up a 2 and discarding the 9 immediately reduces the hand by seven points.

Unlike most other card games, in knock rummy the deal is not rotated in any particular order. The winner of the previous hand deals, since the dealer is at a disadvantage. Other players have the option of knocking, or picking up cards from the stock and reducing their hand prior to his turn of play.

A player can only knock when it is his turn to play. He knocks by either rapping his knuckles on the table or, preferably, by announcing his knock.

A player must knock *prior* to picking up a card from the stock (the pile of cards yet unplayed) or from the discard pile. Thus, the first player (the one to the dealer's left) on his first play has two options: he can either pick up a card from the stock, or knock immediately. Once he picks up the card from the stock, he must wait his next turn before knocking.

However, if he picks up a card from the stock or the discard pile and this gives him rummy, he can immediately disclose this after picking up the card.

The first player thus has a big advantage in knock rummy. First, he can knock immediately. Or, if he decides to pick up a card from the stock and discard a card from his hand, reducing it, he puts the other players at a disadvantage. They must then knock without reducing their hands, and have to be concerned with the first pick of the first player.

If the first player decides not to knock, he picks up a card and then must discard either that card or another from his hand, forming the discard pile. The second player now has three options: He can pick up the discard; pick from the stock; or knock. Again, once he picks up a discard or a card from the stock, he must wait his next turn before knocking. But if the card he picks up gives him rummy, he can announce that immediately.

After the second player picks a card from the stock and discards a card, the third player has the same options as the second player, and each subsequent player has those options: to pick a card from the stock, to pick the discard, or to knock.

Only the last card put on the discard pile can be picked up by the next player; all the other cards are, in effect, dead cards. If a player picks up a discard, he cannot immediately put the same discard back on the discard pile. He must wait one round until his next turn before discarding it.

After a player knocks, he puts out his cards, showing sequences or matched sets, if any, and his odd cards. Sometimes he may hold only odd cards. A player may hold A A 2 2 5 6 8 at the outset for a total of twenty-three, which is a good knocking total, and still not have any sequences or matched sets.

Let us assume that the knock is eight after several rounds of play. The knocker shows a sequence in hearts of Q J 10, a sequence in spades of 7 6 5, and an odd 8. Each of the other players now examines his hand, and if he has a point total of less than eight he announces it. Other players cannot lay off cards on the knocker's hand. Thus, if a player holds the ♥ 8 it cannot be laid off on the knocker's sequence, but must be counted as an odd 8, or eight points.

If any other player has less than eight points, he underknocks the knocker and collects double from the knocker, and the other players then pay the underknocker one unit. If the knocker has the low point total, he collects one unit from each player and then he deals the next hand. If he was underknocked, the underknocker, as winner of the hand, would deal.

If another player equals the point total of the knocker, the knocker wins.

If two or more players have a lower point total than the knocker, the player with the lowest count wins and is paid double by the knocker, and one unit by each of the other players.

Remember: Any matched set or three- or four-card sequence has no point value. Only odd cards have point value, and their total value determines the point count of the hand.

Scoring and Settlement

If a player knocks and wins, he collects one unit from each of the other players.

If a player has less points than the knocker, he collects double, or two units from the knocker and one unit from the other players.

When a player goes rummy, he collects three units or more from the other players, depending on the rules on payoffs agreed upon prior to the game.

Should a player have a complete sequence of seven cards in one suit, the payoff is either five or six units from each player.

Special Bonuses

Some players pay off double or quadruple if the point total of any player's hand, prior to the picking up or playing of any card, is fifteen points or below, or sixty-five and above. Examples: K K K 5 3 A A = 10; K K Q Q J 9 8 = 67. In some games, if a player has either of these totals he doesn't have to wait for his turn, but can immediately announce, show his hand, and collect from the other players.

Other Rules

If the game is played to the final card of the stock, the last player to put down a discard ends the game, unless the discard is picked up by the next player for rummy. Otherwise it is a dead card. Then each of the players shows his hand, and the player with the lowest point total wins, collecting double from each player.

If during the course of a game a player puts down a discard that is picked up by the next player, and then subsequently puts down another discard of the same rank, or in the same sequence, and the other player picks up that card and announces rummy, the player putting down those matching discards pays on behalf of all the other players in the game. For example: A player puts down a 7, which is picked up by the next player. On the next round, or any subsequent round, the first player discards another 7, which is picked up by the same next player, who announces rummy. The first player must then pay the necessary three units for all the players in the game to the player making rummy, because in essence he "fed" the player his rummy card.

A player must remember what discards are picked up by the player sitting left of him, since he is the only one who can "feed" that player discards and all other players are helpless in this situation.

The same rule applies in sequences. If a ♠7 is picked up, and on the next or subsequent rounds a ♠6 or ♠8 is discarded and picked up by the same player and rummy is announced, that player who fed the discard pays for every other player.

Strategy

The ideal strategy is to reduce the number of points in the hand, at the same time gauging the potential of sequences and matched cards. For example, a player may retain ♠Q J on the first round and discard an 8, because there is a potential sequence there. But if a ♠K or ♠10 is discarded by any player other than the one to his right, then the Q J should be immediately broken up.

Thus, it may be said that the wise play of the cards is to get rid of high cards and retain low cards, reducing the hand as rapidly as possible, even when the low cards may be odd cards. For example, picking up an ace and a 3 and getting rid of a ♠Q and ♠J immediately reduces the hand by sixteen points.

When three players are in the game, any hand holding in the vicinity of thirty-five to forty points is worth knocking on the first round if the knocker is the first player. If preceding players have picked up a card from the stock, a knock can be made only between twenty-five and thirty points. These are generally safe limits.

Of course, once a discard has been picked up, the hand has to be dealt with differently. In a four-handed game, if a discard has been picked up by a preceding player on the first round, a hand with twenty points might be risky to knock, but a hand with fifteen or less can still be knocked.

If a hand looks favorable for rummy, and a preceding player has picked up a discard and you fear that he may knock on the next round, while your point count is high (for example, you hold ♦7, ♦6, ♦5, ♦4 and ♥10, ♥9, and an odd card), it might be good strategy to pick up the next discard available to you. This would forestall the other player's knock and let you discard your odd card. Then wait a couple of rounds for the ♥J or ♥8.

If there is only one possibility of getting rummy—for example, you hold 3 3 3 and 7 7 7, and a 7 has already been played—it pays to knock rather than go for the rummy, since it is improbable that a low card like the 3 will be discarded. Far better to knock and win the hand than linger with these cards and see another player knock with one point or get rummy.

As to seating arrangements: Try to place yourself to the left of a poor player; his poor play and bad discards will be to your advantage. But the sportsmanlike procedure is to draw cards for seating arrangements, since it is so important in knock rummy.

Above all, watch the discards, learn the playing habits of your opponents, and reduce your hand in point total. By watching the other players' styles, you will be at an advantage. Some knock on the first round with any total; others are afraid to knock unless they have very low totals. Some never knock; they always dream of rummy. Study their habits and it will pay off in knock rummy.

VI

500 Rummy

♠ ♥ ♦ ♣

Rules of Play

This is a very popular social game in which the value of the melds are scored by each player, in addition to the points in the opposing hand when a player goes out.

Number of Players: Although some authorities suggest that the game can be played by as many as eight players, it is really a game for two to four players, and when four players are involved, they may play the partnership version of 500 rummy called Persian rummy.

The Pack: The usual fifty-two card deck is used, without the jokers.

Rank of Cards: In 500 rummy, the ace can rank as highest or lowest card, followed in order by the king (next highest), queen, jack, 10, and so on down to the 2. The ace is ranked highest when in a matched set of aces; otherwise, when used in the sequence 3 2 A, it is ranked lowest.

In 500 rummy, each card has a distinctive scoring value. The ace, when in a matched set, or as an odd card, has a value of fifteen points; but in a sequence of 3 2 A, it has a value of only one point. The king, queen, jack, and 10 each have a value of ten points. All other cards have the same value as their spots or numbers; thus, a 7 has a value of seven points.

Object of the Game: To score points by melds. Melds are either matched sets—for example, three or four of the same-ranked cards, such as four 8s, three 4s, etc.—or sequences of three or more cards in the same suit, such as ♣9 ♣8 ♣7 ♣6, ♥3 ♥2 ♥A, or ♦K ♦Q ♦J ♦10.

Points are also scored by laying off cards onto matched sets or sequences melded by the other players. For instance, when another player puts down a set of three 9s, you add the fourth by putting the other 9 on the table in front of the player.

135

Shuffle and Deal: After the dealer is selected, either by low or high card, he shuffles the cards and then gives them to the player on his right to be cut. If that player refuses to cut them, any player may exercise that option.

The deal is alternated when two players are in the game. If more than two, the deal goes clockwise around the table.

After the cards have been cut and returned to the dealer, he deals them face down, one at a time, starting with the player on his left and going clockwise around the table. Each player receives seven cards. The next card is turned up to form the discard pile. This is the upcard. The remainder of the deck is placed next to it, forming the stock.

Play of the Hand

Beginning with the player to the left of the dealer, who is called the "eldest" hand, each player may either pick one card from the stock, or take the cards forming the discard pile, or as many of the discard pile as he needs.

A word about the discard pile. Unlike other rummy games such as gin rummy or straight rummy, in which the discard pile should be squared so that only the top card is visible at any time, in 500 rummy the discard pile should be set out so that each individual card is clearly visible at all times. Even if there are twenty cards on the discard pile, each card must be easily identifiable to all the players.

Now, in order to take a card or cards from the discard pile, the player must have at least two others either matching, such as two 5s, or in a sequence, such as ♥8 ♥7. Thus, the card he picks from the discard pile will either form a meld or add a fourth card to a meld he already holds but has not yet melded. However, if a player picks up a card in the discard pile, he gets all the cards above that card as well, but he need only show that he can use the bottom card, the card originally taken, to form a matched set or sequence.

Here's how one takes cards from the discard pile. We'll assume the pile consists of ten cards. All are visible. As pictured below, the sequence of the ten cards are from the first to the last, the first being at the bottom of the discard pile, and the tenth on top, as follows:

♦K ♥Q ♠Q ♣8 ♠K ♥6 ♠10 ♦5 ♥J ♦9

You hold the ♣10 and ♣9. It is your turn to play. Since the ♣8 will form a sequence with the 10 and 9, you pick up the discard pile from the ♣8 onward. In other words, all cards from the ♣8 to the ♦9 are taken up by you. This still leaves the first three cards on the discard pile; those cards being ♦K ♥Q ♠Q.

Now, having picked up those seven cards, you must first show the matched sequence you sought and meld that. Thereafter, you may make any other melds you have in your hand or which have been formed by the other cards you picked up from the discard pile.

A player is not limited in melding. He may meld more than one set or sequence at a time. In fact, some of the strategy of the game has to do with withholding these melds and then melding all at once and going out. However, a player may only meld or lay off when it is his turn to pick from the stock or discard pile.

A player may go rummy, or go out (the same thing) at any time, by melding or laying off all the cards from his hand. He thus penalizes all the other players, who must subtract the odd cards remaining in their hands from their total score.

The particular game ends when either a player goes rummy or the stock is exhausted. When a player goes out, the remaining cards in each opponent's hand are counted against that opponent and subtracted from his score. When the stock is exhausted, all cards remaining in the players' hands are counted against them.

More about Laying Off

In 500 rummy, although the initial meld in a sequence may be three or four cards, thereafter, there is no limit to how far the sequence can extend. An A K Q J sequence may eventually run thirteen cards, all the way down to the 2. A player may lay off on any opponent's sequence, but may also lay off on his own. He may lay off two or more cards on a sequence as well as one card. For example, if a sequence shows ♠Q ♠J ♠10 and a player holds the ♠K, ♠9 and ♠8, he may lay off all three cards on the sequence.

When a player lays off cards he puts them in front of him on the table and must announce which cards he is laying off on. Suppose he lays off the ♦10 and there are already three 10s melded, as well as a sequence of ♦9 8 7. He must announce if he is forming the fourth 10 of a matched set or merely extending the sequence. Of course, when a player lays off an ace he should always lay it off on a matched set of three aces rather than on a sequence of 4 3 2, for with the matched set he'll get fifteen points credit.

In playing the game, a player must be careful and see what has been laid off, since there may be single cards in front of everyone. If there had been a sequence in clubs of 5 4 3, and subsequently a ♣2, ♣6, ♣7, and

♣8 had been laid off by various players, a ♣9 is not an odd card but may be laid off. All it takes is a careful examination of the table.

Scoring

The scoring total is made after one player goes rummy or the stock is exhausted. The total of each player's melds are added up. The player who has gone out has no subtractions, but all the other players subtract whatever cards they still hold, even if they failed to meld a proper sequence or matched set or failed to lay off. If the cards are in their hands at the end of play, they must be subtracted. The same thing holds true when the stock is exhausted.

Scoring is by point count, with the ace counted as fifteen in a set of three aces, but as one in a sequence of 3 2 A. If a player holds an odd ace in his hand, it is always counted as fifteen for subtraction purposes. If a player has laid off an ace on three aces held by another player, it is fifteen points. If it is laid off on a sequence of 4 3 2, it counts as one point.

A final score is then credited to each player and written down on a score sheet. For example, a player has melded four 10s, three 9s, and ♠8 7 6. He has 40 + 27 + 21 for a gross total of eighty-eight. However, another player has gone out and he holds in his hand a ♣2 A, and a ♥K. He holds 2 + 15 (ace) + 10 for a total of twenty-seven. He subtracts the twenty-seven from eighty-eight and his net total is sixty-one, which score is put down on a scoresheet.

If he had a previous net score of fifty-four, that is added to it for a total now of 115. The first player who gets to 500 wins the game. Thus the name, 500 rummy. A player may have 499 points, but he cannot declare 500 on his first meld in the next game. He must wait till the end of the game. If two or more players at the end of any game have a total of 500 points or more then the one with the highest total wins.

After the final score, if the game is for stakes the winner may be paid off on the difference in points between his score and the losers', or the winner may simply win a predetermined stake.

This is a very good game for social purposes, and the stake does not necessarily have to be in money.

Strategy

In 500 rummy, the best strategy is to keep a count of the important cards, such as the face cards and aces; and, when discarding, to remember how many of each card are already out or in use. This is not that difficult in 500 rummy, since the melds are out and viewable, and cannot be played from or used as in two-handed pinochle.

The main object of the player is not to go out, but to get points. Going out becomes important near the end of any particular game, and is also important when an opponent is dangerously close to 500 points. Then you may wish to go out in order to stop him from any more melds and lower his score by forcing him to subtract the cards he is holding.

If a player tries to go out too soon, he may meld out his hand and be left with two cards or three cards. He may then often find that no one will throw the cards he needs onto the discard pile, or, if one is played onto the discard pile and he picks it up, he will then have another meld but remain with two different odd cards in his hand. And with these cards all he can do is supply the others in the game with points.

An example of this: A player tries to go out early. He puts down a meld of four 10s. In his hand he holds two 8s and a 5. He hopes to get an 8 as a discard, pick it up, meld the three 8s, discard the 5, and go out. But if it is more than a two-man game, the chances of getting that discard may be slim. Perhaps he may get it from the stock. The player who is not immediately to the right of the player needing the 8 may discard it, and then the next player, to the right of and immediately before our player, discards a 9. Our player picks up the 8 and makes a meld of 8s. Our man is left with a 5 or a 9 in his hand. He must find a spot for it. If there are four players in the game and if, after the 8, two discards were made, the player melding the 8s will find himself with two odd cards and be stuck for the rest of the game.

At the beginning of the game, when there is little danger of anyone going out, the discards are usually low cards, since the players are hoping to make some sizable melds. If, at a certain point, there are few small cards left and only the big cards are falling, it is sometimes a good idea to "salt" the deck, or "prime the pump." This is done in the following way:

Suppose there are only low cards in the discard pile and now the player to your right has to discard a jack. You have a jack in your hand, but not two of them, and you are loathe to drop it. But you have been holding on to four 3s with the possibility of going out. You can now change your strategy, by picking up a card from the stock and dropping a 3. And now you can at any point, providing no one beats you to it, pick up the 3 to form your meld, and all other cards above it. You have "salted" the deck, putting down a card you know is fairly safe; probably no one will be able to use it but you. And as sometimes happens, if another player picks up the discard, he may drop down the small 3, to "salt" it unwittingly for you.

As a general rule, always play to increase your points rather than play safe. In other words, if you are near the end of the game, with the stock rapidly becoming depleted, and you can pick up a 7 to make a matched set of three 7s for twenty-one points, but at the same time will be picking up eight other cards from the discard pile, none of which can immediately help you, my advice is to pick them up. This way you take them out of circulation and increase your chances of being fed other cards, or getting other matching cards from those remaining in the stock. It is usually a worthwhile gamble.

What often happens is that if you do play safe, some other player gets the discard pile and proceeds to meld about eighty or ninety points, completely bombing you out of the game. In 500 rummy, play boldly. Safety is important at certain times—when playing to a score or if a player is in danger of going out while you hold a great many points—but the usual rule is *get points,* for that wins games.

Persian Rummy

Although 500 rummy can be played as a partnership game, with both players sitting opposite each other and combining their scores, a better form of partnership play is Persian rummy, for four players.

Forming the Partnership: The partnership may be determined before the game, or may be picked by the two low cards or two high cards.

The Players: Four play, two against two as partners. Each player sits facing his own partner. The players may not help each other verbally, but may help to form melds and to go out. The partnership's score is combined as one unit. When any one player goes out, the game is over and the scores are calculated.

The Deck: Fifty-six cards are used, the standard deck plus four jokers. It is important to get two extra jokers with the same back because most decks of cards come with only two jokers.

Value of the Cards: The joker counts as twenty points and can only be used in a matched set and not added as a sequence to other cards. The aces and all other cards have the same value as in 500 rummy. The big exception in scoring is that if all four cards of a matched set are put down in a meld at once, their value is doubled. For example, if four aces are put down at one time in a meld, their value instead of being sixty is 120. If three aces had been melded, it would have been for a value of forty-five points, and a fourth ace added to it later would be only fifteen additional points.

The four jokers melded together add up to 160 points; four 7s would be fifty-six points, etc. It can be seen that one of the objects of the game of Persian rummy is to get those four-card matched sets together, because of the increased points.

Game: Some games end after two deals, others after three deals. I prefer the three-deal games, since it gives more scope for strategy. After three deals the points are added up, and the winning team collects from the losing team.

An added twenty-five points is usually given to the team that goes out first.

After the final game, the winning team gets the difference in points between the total of its points and the opponents' points, and also gets a bonus of fifty to 100 points. The usual bonus in a three-deal game is 100 points.

All other rules are in conformity with 500 rummy. Each player gets seven cards at the outset, and the twenty-ninth card is turned face up to form the upcard. The game is over when any player goes out or when the stock is exhausted. Except for the jokers and the four-card-set double points, the scoring is the same.

However, it is important to remember that it's not 500 points, but the most points at the end of three deals that wins. So the strategy in the third game may be defensive, if your team is winning, or bold, if it is losing. The third deal is usually the most interesting and exciting, and that is why I prefer a three-deal game to the two-deal game.

Players may signal each other by the discards. It has been suggested that the signal of an ace calls for a partner to discard a joker if he has one; that the discard of a face card or 10 is the signal for the discard of an ace. However, unless a team has played as a partnership before, or the signals are exactly worked out, they should stay clear of them. The reason is that many times in Persian rummy a player has little choice of discards. It is unlike bridge, where, due to the bidding, a player has a good idea of what his partner is holding. There is no bidding in Persian rummy, and signals have to be carefully handled.

VII

Bridge

Introduction

Because of its wide popularity and the strong element of skill present, bridge is one of the few card games featured regularly in newspapers and magazines. Most of the major newspapers have regular contributors writing daily columns on the game.

Due to the partnership nature of the game, it has been possible to organize tournaments at all levels of the game. In small towns there are often weekly duplicate tournaments, and in the larger cities an enthusiast could play duplicate bridge nightly in tournaments if he or she were so inclined. The fact that a partnership team can participate regularly in these duplicate tournaments has added much flavor and interest to the game. By entering local, then regional, and then national tournaments, every player has the opportunity to match his skill against that of the finest players in the country, and often in the world, gathering master points as he goes.

Not only can bridge be played as a partnership game, but it can be played as a team game, a team-of-four contest. In these games, two partnerships are formed on every team; one plays north-south against the other team's east-west, while at the same time the first team's east-west pair is playing the second team's north-south partnership.

Played as a team-of-four game, the skill involved is at its highest. The element of luck in the deal is now eliminated. There is still some basis of luck, but it becomes negligible. Contract bridge played this way is the most skillful of all the card games.

With teams of four, the game moves into a new level of play. These

145

teams can represent cities, or schools, or factories, or any possible sponsoring group. These same teams can also represent nations, and most of the world championship matches are conducted in this way, with a score kept in IMPs (international match points).

For a long time, the great Italian Blue Team dominated modern world championships, but lately they have been broken up as a team representing their country, and the United States, with its vast array of top players, has once more come to the fore.

There have been a great many bidding and playing systems introduced in recent years, which I do not attempt to deal with in this chapter. It is recommended that the serious student of bridge examine the literature on bridge, which is voluminous. There are many fine writers in this field, and their works are general as well as specific. Many of the finest books deal with but a small part of the game.

What has been attempted here is a broad introduction to the game of bridge, from which any reader should be able to learn the basic game—learn correct bidding techniques and standard plays. As the reader will see, contract bridge can be played at many levels of skill. There is a great deal to learn and memorize, but sheer memory will not be enough. The game must be played seriously and often, but it is one course of study that any student will find enjoyable, because the excitement and pleasure this game affords is boundless.

Rules of Play

One of the unique qualities of contract bridge is the fact that it is a partnership game in which the partners, within certain limits, signal not only the bidding quality of their cards, but the play of the cards.

It is a game played by four players, forming two sets of partners—one partnership known as East and West, the other known as North and South. Any diagrammed bridge hand will follow that format, setting up the hands as follows:

$$
\begin{array}{ccc}
 & N & \\
W & & E \\
 & S & \\
\end{array}
$$

As can be seen by the diagram, the partners sit opposite each other. The result of the play is shared equally by the partners, and one score is kept for each partnership. Thus, if East and West bid and make one club, the score would be twenty points for East-West, not twenty points for East and twenty points additional for West.

Cards: The fifty-two-card deck is used, without jokers. Generally, two packs are used, one being dealt and the other, usually of a different color, being shuffled in readiness for the next deal. The standard method is to have the dealer's partner shuffle the other deck and then have the deck placed to the right of the player between the dealer and shuffler—in other words, next to the player who will deal next.

Deal: The deal passes clockwise, from player to player, so that each player in a partnership has one deal every four hands played. In this way, the deals are alternated between the partnerships.

A deal thus would pass from South to West to North to East. As South deals, North shuffles the other deck and places it to West's right. West, prior to his deal, has the deck cut by South, and as he deals, East is shuffling the cards.

After the cards have been cut, they are dealt face down by the dealer to each player, starting with the player at his left. Thus, if South deals, the first player to receive a card is West. The entire deck is dealt out, each player getting thirteen cards.

Players sometimes pick up their cards in the course of the deal, but this is bad practice. The cards should be left undisturbed until all have been dealt out. If there is a mistake, with one player receiving too few or too many cards, this can then be remedied, whereas, if they've looked at their cards, there is a misdeal.

Sorting the Cards: After the cards have been dealt, each player picks up his cards and sorts them according to suits. This is the only way to sort them, because in contract bridge the auction is in terms of suits, and the rules and strategies developed for contract bridge are based on suit length and suit strength. A typical hand should be sorted as follows:

♠A 10 8 6 ♥9 5 ♦J 8 3 ♣K Q J 3

In contract bridge it is important to remember that the suits have a definite value, both in scoring and in the auction.

Rank of Suits

The highest-ranking suit is spades, followed by hearts, diamonds, and then clubs. A one-bid contract made in the major suits (which are spades and hearts) is worth thirty points; in the minor suits (diamonds and clubs), twenty points. This figure, thirty or twenty points, is multiplied by the tricks bid and made. Thus, four spades is 120 points or game (game is 100 points), while four clubs is eighty points, twenty points short of game.

In the bidding, the same value system has to be observed. The bidding, in increasing order of suits, is clubs, diamonds, hearts, and spades. This becomes important because after a bid of one spade, the next suit bid will have to be two of any suit. If a player bids one heart, another player cannot legally bid one diamond after that, because diamonds are of a lower rank than hearts. The player who desired to bid diamonds would have to bid *two* diamonds. And after a bid of two diamonds, two clubs is not a legal bid; it would have to be *three* clubs if the player was inclined to bid clubs.

Bidding

In contract bridge, all bids may begin at the one level, but a bid of one establishes that the bidder and his partner expect to make seven tricks.

Book is the term used to describe the first six tricks to be made. These six tricks do not have to be bid. When a bidder starts at the one level, he is saying, in effect, "I can make, or expect to make, seven tricks." A one bid means *book plus one*. Since only thirteen tricks can be made in each game because each player must play one card at each trick, the highest bid is seven (called a grand slam). This is *book plus seven*, or all thirteen tricks.

Before going into the valuation of the hands, we will examine the possible bids that can be made. Unlike a game like pinochle, in which a trump must be established by the successful bidder, in bridge the game can be played in a trump suit or at no-trump.

And unlike pinochle, where the successful bidder does not name the trump suit until after the bid, the final bid in contract bridge determines the trump. If a player bids one diamond and this is the highest bid, the trump is established as diamonds. It cannot be changed subsequently.

Sometimes a bidder may determine that his hand is so distributed that it doesn't pay to bid a suit as trump. He may therefore bid no-trump. We have already seen the progressive order of the suits from clubs up to spades. No-trump is the highest possible bid at any level.

For example, the bidding in an imaginary case can go: One club, one diamond, one heart, one spade, one no-trump. After a one-no-trump bid, a one bid in a suit cannot be legally made. If the bid is two no-trump, anyone desiring to bid a suit thereafter will have to bid at the three level.

The highest bid, therefore, is seven no-trump. There can be no further bid, since there is no eight level in contract bridge (there being only thirteen cards), and a subsequent bid of seven in a suit cannot be made legally.

Also unlike pinochle, if a player passes his hand when it is his turn to bid, he can bid again at any other time when it is his turn. A player sitting North can pass the first time after a bid by West of one spade, let us say. Then, if his turn comes again, he may bid a suit or no-trump. Or he may double. Before we go into doubling, it should be made clear that the bidding must end at some time; it cannot go on indefinitely. And it must also be in order.

The first player to bid is the dealer. If we remember our diagram . . .

$$N$$
$$W \qquad E$$
$$S$$

. . . we can see the sequence of bidding, which is clockwise, the same as the deal and subsequent play of the cards.

A diagram is usually shown with one additional notation:

$$N$$
$$W \qquad E$$
$$S\,(D)$$

That (D) means that South is the dealer. He has the first bid, West the second, North the third, and so forth around the table. The bidding ends when there are three consecutive passes after the last bid, or if all the players pass on the first round of bidding.

Suppose South dealt and bid one heart; West passed; North bid one spade; East doubled (this is considered a bid); South bid two spades; West passed; North passed; and East passed. Since there are three passes from the last bid, which was two spades by South, the bidding has ceased. The hand is played in two spades and the North-South partnership must make eight tricks with spades as trump.

These bids can be notated so that it is simple to follow the progress of the bidding.

SOUTH	WEST	NORTH	EAST
One heart	Pass	One spade	Double
Two spades	Pass	Pass	Pass

The dealer is the player in the first column. If West had dealt, the columns would look like this:

WEST   NORTH   EAST   SOUTH

In the event that all the players had passed the first time around, the bidding would cease and the cards would be thrown in. There is no play after four passes on the first round.

Without going into the facts completely, a *double* by a player when it is his turn to bid may mean that he feels the hand cannot be made in that suit at that level. In the event that the game is played and lost, the losing team is penalized according to a particular system of points, which will be discussed later. This is called a *penalty double*. A *double* can also be used artificially as a takeout double. In the above bidding this would mean that the doubler had an opening bid but did not wish to announce his suit. This will also be discussed later in the section on doubles. If there is a double bid, the bidder of the suit doubled has the option to re-double (which again is treated as a bid, as is everything except a pass, for the purpose of keeping the bidding alive). If there is a redouble, the bidding eventually must return to the doubler, who can now put in another bid (not a double), or can pass.

An example: (East was the dealer.)

EAST	SOUTH	WEST	NORTH
Pass	One heart	Three diamonds	Three hearts
Pass	Four hearts	Five diamonds	Double
Pass	Pass	Redouble	

We'll interrupt at this point. West's bid of five diamonds was doubled by North, and then redoubled by West. North can make a new bid or pass. Then it is East's turn; then South's; then the bidding is over if all three pass. We'll continue:

EAST	SOUTH	WEST	NORTH
			Pass
Pass	Five hearts	Pass	Pass
Pass			

Since South bid five hearts, the bidding was kept alive and the double and redouble were past bids, not counting. The only bid counting was the last bid, which was five hearts. The game now would have to be played at this bid, book plus five tricks, with hearts as trump.

The options open for a bidder are: Any bid in a suit; no-trump; double; a redouble after a double; and pass.

Player of the Bid Hand

The final bidder does not necessarily play the hand. The original bidder of the suit that was the final bid suit plays the hand.

This may seem confusing, but it is not that difficult. Take a bidding situation:

NORTH	EAST	SOUTH	WEST
One spade	Pass	Two spades	Pass
Three spades	Pass	Four spades	

South had the final bid of four spades, but North originally bid spades, so North plays out the hand. Another example:

NORTH	EAST	SOUTH	WEST
One heart	Two diamonds	Two spades	Three diamonds
Four spades	Pass	Pass	Pass

North bid four spades, but South was the original bidder of spades; thus, South plays out the hand. He becomes the declarer, and North then becomes dummy.

Value of Cards

The value of the cards runs from the highest, the ace, to the lowest, the 2. (A K Q J 10 9 8 7 6 5 4 3 2.) The higher-valued card wins every trick, except where a card is trumped.

For example, if North plays the ♠Q, East the ♠10, South the ♠8, and West the ♠J, North would win the trick.

As already stated, there are thirteen tricks to be won on the play of the cards, which comes after the bidding has been completed, and the final suit bid determines the suit that will be trump. If the final bid is no-trump, then no suit is trump and each of the suits has equal value in the play.

The importance of trump is that the trump suit has precedence. If another suit, other than trump, is led and a player is void in that suit (that is, has no cards in the suit led), he may, at his option, play trump. A trump card, of whatever value, wins a trick against three cards of the original suit led. For example:

Spades are trump. North leads the ♥A; East plays the ♥6; South the ♥3; and West, void in hearts, plays the ♠2. West wins the trick.

Play of the Hand

Let us assume the following sequence of bids:

SOUTH	WEST	NORTH	EAST
One spade	Pass	Two spades	Pass
Four spades	Pass	Pass	Pass

After the bidding is completed here, spades are trump and the contract is four spades. Since South bid spades originally, he will play the hand. The first lead is then made by the player to the successful bidder's left. The successful bidder, in bridge, is called the declarer. So the first lead is by the player to the declarer's left. This player, West, will play in partnership with East, in an attempt to defeat the contract.

The declarer's partner, North, is now the *dummy*. In contract bridge, the successful bidders have only one of the two partners—the declarer— play out the hand. After the first lead, the declarer's partner puts his cards face up on the table for the whole board to see.

Dummy hand showing position of suits.

Each of the players has a full view of these cards throughout the play of the hand. The player doing this is the dummy. He has no further duties in regard to the play. He can get up and leave the table, in fact, until the play of the cards is over.

So, after the bidding is complete, the declarer plays out the hand against his two opponents, who retain the cards in their hands, while the declarer's partner displays his cards.

Taking in Tricks

After the first lead is made, let us assume a ♣6, the declarer looks over the dummy, which is now on display. Remember, the dummy is not displayed until the first lead is made. Otherwise, it might give valuable information to the player making the lead. Only after this player leads a card (which means dropping it on the table face up) is the dummy shown.

The dummy now plays a ♣2 (declarer plays out his dummy's hand);

the leader's partner plays a ♣J; and the declarer plays the ♣K. The declarer takes in the first trick. He puts all four cards together in front of him, face down. If he takes in a subsequent trick, he places each trick crosswise on top of the preceding trick so that he has a ready count of tricks made. In contract bridge, only the number of tricks count, not the cards inside those tricks, which have no value in the final count. Thus, if a declarer bids four spades, he must make *book plus four,* or ten tricks. He couldn't care less about the cards in those tricks, because if he makes ten tricks or more, his side wins. If he makes less than ten tricks, his side loses, and it is immaterial how many face cards, aces, black 7s, etc. are in those cards.

Since the declarer took the first trick, he is the first to play for the second trick. The rule is that the player taking in the previous trick makes the first play for the next trick. In other words, he has the next lead. And so the game goes on, until all thirteen tricks are played out. At the end of play a count is made of tricks to determine if the declarer made his contract or *went down.* Of course, the declarer and his opponents will know ahead of the final count whether or not the contract was made, since it is fairly easy to keep track of thirteen tricks. But a count is made to double-check the number of tricks claimed.

When a suit is led, players must follow suit. If a player is void in the led suit, he may play any other suit, or trump.

Scoring

The scoresheet used has two columns, simply stating "We" and "They." As was mentioned before, the partnership is credited with the point score, not the individual players. There are two parts to each column, the trick score and the overtricks of other scores. The sheet looks something like this:

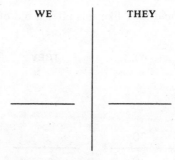

WE   THEY

Below that horizontal line is kept the trick score, or game score. One hundred points are needed for game. Above the line are credits given for overtricks and undertricks, slams, for doubling and redoubling, and for a previous game score. We will study each aspect separately.

Trick Scores

Spades and hearts are called the major suits; diamonds and clubs the minor suits.

To score below the line (that is, to count toward game score), the declarer receives only as many points as he bid. For example: Each trick made over book in spades is worth thirty points. Thus, making seven tricks in spades (or one over book) gives that declarer and his partner thirty points. If the bid was one spade, and one spade was made (seven tricks), the partnership would be credited with thirty points below the line toward game score. It would look like this:

WE	THEY
———	———
30	

One hundred points are necessary below the line to win a game. Two games win a rubber. Each rubber is a complete entity. After one rubber is won, another rubber can be played for.

Now, if the declarer bid one spade and made two spades (eight tricks), he would only get credit for thirty points below the line toward game, and an additional thirty points above the line for the extra trick he made (overtrick).

The scoresheet would look like this after a bid of one spade, with two spades being made:

WE	THEY
30	
———	———
30	

If declarer bid one spade and made four spades, it would look like this:

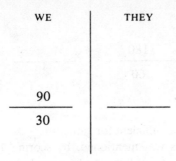

The declarer's team, though amassing ninety extra points, still has only thirty points toward game. We are now talking about rubber bridge. In duplicate bridge, extra tricks have a special significance.

It should be pointed out that rubber bridge is a game played among four people, in two partnerships, with a new shuffle after each deal. In duplicate bridge, as the name signifies, there are no new deals and each team of partners plays the duplicate hand played by all other partners sitting as they are (either East-West or North-South).

The following values are given to tricks by suits and No Trump. Note that hearts and spades have identical values, as do diamonds and clubs.

Suit	Value of Each Trick	Value of Each Doubled Trick	Value of Each Redoubled Trick
Spades	30	60	120
Hearts	30	60	120
Diamonds	20	40	80
Clubs	20	40	80
No-Trump	40 (first trick)	80	160
No-Trump	30 (per additional trick)	60	120

If a hand is doubled or redoubled, that score then goes below the line toward the game score. If the bid is two spades doubled, it is worth 120 points (sixty points multiplied by two). Thus, two spades doubled would be game if the contract is made.

If the bid was one spade doubled and the declarer made four spades (or ten tricks), the scoresheet would look like this:

WE	THEY
180	
60	

It would still not be sufficient for game.

Game is made, as was mentioned, by scoring 100 points. It doesn't have to be made at one time, but may be cumulative. For example, a contract of two hearts would yield sixty points, and on the next deal a contract of two clubs would yield forty points, for a total of 100 points. In between those two deals, the opponents may score with a contract of 2 no-trump for seventy points. That would be to their credit and not subtracted from the game score.

WE	THEY
60	70
40	

Since 100 points have been scored, "We" win the game. After the game is over, the seventy points would be subtracted from the 100 points, for a net total of thirty points to be added to the next game, since two winning games are necessary for a rubber. Prior to the first deal of the second game, the scoresheet would look like this:

WE	THEY
30	

This would merely reflect the net total of the previous game.

As can be seen by the trick values, a successful contract of four spades or four hearts makes game; a successful contract of five diamonds or five clubs makes game; as does a successful contract of three no-trump.

Being Vulnerable

After one team has won a game (100 points), it is said to be *vulnerable*. Should each team have won one of its games, each team is vulnerable as they play for the third game (or rubber game).

The purpose of vulnerability is to penalize the partnership that has won a game, by making it pay for its mistakes in bidding or play with additional points. It also enables the team that is not vulnerable to bid and play more aggressively, since they are not subject to additional penalties for their mistakes.

The next table shows the difference in scoring when a partnership is vulnerable and when it's not vulnerable.

Scoring of Vulnerable and Not Vulnerable Contracts

OVERTRICKS

For Each Overtrick	Not Vulnerable	Vulnerable
Undoubled	Trick Value	Trick Value
Doubled	100	200
Redoubled	200	400

Overtricks are those tricks made in excess of the bid contract. If four spades is bid and five spades (or eleven tricks) is made, one overtrick has been made.

UNDERTRICKS (Undoubled Contracts)

	Not Vulnerable	Vulnerable
First Undertrick	50	100
Each Additional Undertrick	50	100

UNDERTRICKS (Doubled Contracts)

	Not Vulnerable	Vulnerable
First Undertrick	100	200
Each Additional Undertrick	200	300

UNDERTRICKS (Redoubled Contracts)

	Not Vulnerable	Vulnerable
First Undertrick	200	400
Each Additional Undertrick	400	600

Undertricks are those tricks below the total necessary to fulfill the bid contract. If four spades is bid (ten tricks) but only three spades is made (9 tricks), this is one undertrick.

In scoring undertricks, the suit bid is of no importance; the penalties imposed are the same regardless of whether or not a major or minor suit was bid. However, in computing overtricks on undoubled hands, the respective trick values are used. But suits again are of no importance in overtricks where the contract has been doubled or redoubled.

Overtricks and undertricks are scored above the line.

Scoring Premium Points

SLAMS
Special bonus points are given for bidding and making twelve tricks— a *small slam*—or all thirteen tricks—a *grand slam*.

	Not Vulnerable	*Vulnerable*
Small slam	500	750
Grand slam	1000	1500

The slam must not only be made, but must be bid. A bid of four spades (ten tricks) making thirteen tricks is not a grand slam, but is merely counted as three overtricks. The bonus points are in addition to the regular score under the line, and bonus points are scored above the line. An example: Six hearts are bid and made, neither side vulnerable.

WE	THEY
500	
180	

Doubling or redoubling does not affect slam points.

HONORS (the A K Q J 10 of trump)
Holding four of five trump honors in one hand   100 points

Holding all five honors in trump in one hand   150 points
Holding all four aces in one hand at a
    no-trump contract   150 points

Vulnerability, doubling, and redoubling does not affect honor points.

RUBBER POINTS

Winning the rubber where opponents have won no game   700 points
Winning the rubber where opponents have won one game   500 points
Unfinished rubber—winning one game   300 points
Unfinished rubber—for having only part score   50 points

Doubling or redoubling does not affect the rubber points. Two games must be won by one side to win a rubber.

OTHER PREMIUM POINTS

Making any doubled or redoubled contract is fifty additional points, whether vulnerable or not vulnerable.

Point-Count Values

A method of point counts for individual cards was known for many years, but was publicized by Charles Goren, who based his method of bidding upon its use. The point-count system is today universally followed. Prior to the Goren method of point-count valuation, the Culbertson system of counting honor tricks was quite popular. Today it is largely obsolete.

The following are the point-count values of the cards: Ace four, king three, queen two, and jack one. There are ten point-card values in each suit, and forty in the deck.

In no-trump bidding, the valuation of these high cards is used exclusively, but in bidding a suit, other values may be added. They are called *distributional values,* and are as follows:

Void suit   three points
Singleton   two points
Doubleton   one point

A singleton is one card in a suit; doubleton is two cards in the suit. A void is no cards in a suit.

The above is the basic valuation; there are numerous variations that have been introduced and discussed and written about over the years, but basically most valuations of hands are based on this system.

Biddable Suits

A biddable suit may be a four-card suit, headed by an honor, and sometimes a five-card suit headed by a 10.

Although, as mentioned above, a four-card suit may be bid with an honor leading the suit, the usual practice today is to only bid major suits that have a length of at least five cards, and to bid minor suits with a length of four cards. This rule is predicated upon the fact that a four-card suit cannot normally be rebid. So in cases where there is a major suit with honors containing only four cards, many players open an artificial one-club bid, called the *short-club bid*. The following hand would indicate its use:

♠A973   ♥KQ64   ♦AJ   ♣865

The short-club bid should not be confused with a convention used by several systems which bids one club to show a very strong hand. Here it is used simply to facilitate a rebid.

Opening Bids of One in Suits

An opening bid is the initial bid made. If South had dealt and passed, West passed, North bid one diamond, that would be the opening bid. If, after North bid one diamond, East bid one spade, that is not considered an opening bid, but an *overcall,* which will be examined in the appropriate section.

To value the hand under the point-count method, both high-card (A K Q J) and distributional points are counted to arrive at a total.

If the hand has a value of fourteen points, it is mandatory that it be opened. Thirteen points is usually an opening hand, but sometimes, if the distribution is poor, such as 4-3-3-3, with no honors in the four-card suit, it is passed. (The 4 stands for four of a suit, and each 3 stands for 3 cards in one of the other suits.)

Opening bids may be made in a hand having a valuation of twelve points if the suit bid is fairly strong, having two honors and a length of five or six cards.

There is no fixed rule regarding opening bids, except that it is usually unwise to open a bid with less than twelve points.

Responses to Opening Suit Bids of One

In order to respond to an opening bid, the opener's partner should have a minimum of six points in cards. In some instances he may respond with less than six, perhaps with four or five points, but this is done only in certain unusual situations explained later. The basic thing to remember is that a minimum of six points is needed to respond.

There are four possible types of bids that a responder may make. They are in the following order:

1. Pass

A partner of the opener should pass unless his high-card point total is at least six. If below this figure, the best response is a pass, since a bid with less than six points may delude the opener. Generally, when a responder has less than six points he has a weak hand, and together with an opening bid of one, the partnership is going nowhere.

2. A Raise of One Over One

This is a bid of another suit at the lowest possible level. For instance, if the opener bids one club, any bid of one diamond, one heart, or one spade is a one-over-one bid.

A one-over-one response is a forcing bid; that is, it forces the opener to make another bid. Let us examine this situation:

SOUTH	WEST	NORTH	EAST
One diamond	Pass	One heart	Pass

Since South opened with one diamond and North responded with one heart, a one-over-one response, South must now bid again for at least one round.

If there is an intervening bid by an opponent, the response of one over one is no longer forcing, and the opener may pass or bid. The following is an example of this situation:

SOUTH	WEST	NORTH	EAST
One diamond	Pass	One heart	One spade

South, the opener, is not forced to bid because of the intervening bid of East.

In order to bid one over one, the responder is telling his partner, the opener, that he has:

a. Four or more cards in the suit bid.

b. Six to seventeen points in high cards.

Since the bid calls for a four-card suit, it doesn't necessarily mean that that suit has to be headed by an honor. In the following situation, the opener bid one diamond, and the partner held ♠A 6 ♥10 8 7 5 ♦K Q 4 ♣9 8 6 3.

The best response would be one heart. Although there are two four-card suits, it is preferable to respond in a major.

If you, as a partner to the opening bidder, hold two four-card suits, bid the lower of them if they are both major suits. The same principle holds true with two five-card major suits. If there is a four-card and a five-card suit, both major, bid the five-card suit.

3. Two Over One

This is a bid of two in a suit as the lowest possible bid when the opener has bid a suit. For example, the opening bid was one spade. A response by his partner of two diamonds would be a two-over-one response. A response of two clubs or two hearts would have the same effect. Again, as in a response of one over one, this is a forcing bid for one round.

In order to bid this, a responder must have:

a. Five or more cards in his bid suit.

b. At least ten high-card points, and up to eighteen points counting distribution strength.

Usually a two-over-one bid tells the opener that you are in a position to make another bid, but if you cannot make these two bids, a response of one no-trump might be more appropriate, as explained in the next section.

If your partner, the opener, bid one spade, and you hold ♠9 7 4 ♥A 3 ♦K Q J 5 2 ♣8 5 4, your response should be two diamonds, creating a two-over-one situation. You have a five-card suit, ten points in high cards. If your partner bids two spades, you can raise to three spades. If he bids clubs you can bid no-trump.

If you hold ♠5 3 ♥9 6 5 4 ♦A Q J 7 6 3 ♣8, and your partner has opened with a one-spade bid, respond with two diamonds. If your partner bids clubs next, you will have to rebid your diamonds, showing strength only in that suit and a hand unfit for no-trump. But should your partner bid hearts, you can raise the heart bid.

4. Raising Partner's Major Suit

If your partner has opened with a one bid in a major suit, you can raise in that suit if you hold the following:

A. For raises to two in the suit

1. Six to ten points.
2. Four trumps or three trumps headed by at least a queen.

B. For raises to three in the suit
  1. Thirteen to sixteen points, and four in the suit, headed by at least a queen.
C. For raises to four in the suit
  1. Seven to ten points in high cards.
  2. Five trumps.

A bid of four in partner's opening major suit is considered a shutout bid and indicates that the prospect of bidding till slam is negligible.

Those are the four types of responses. A raise to two in a suit is called a *single raise* and may be given with four or three trumps in responder's suit, but should not be bid with only two of the suit. Here is a good example of a single raise. Your partner has opened with one spade. You hold ♠K 9 6 5 ♥Q 9 3 ♦Q 2 ♣J 8 5 4. You have eight points and a four-card spade suit.

Remember that the six to ten points can be in distributional strength as well as high cards, so a single raise may be made with the following hand:

♠K 9 6 5 ♥J 9 3 2 ♦7 ♣10 8 6 4

Although there are only four points in high cards, the singleton adds three points when your hand is the dummy hand. (See page 159 on valuation of cards.)

A *double raise* is a raise to three in the opened major suit. It shows at least four cards in trumps headed by the queen, plus thirteen to sixteen points.

Since the point count is so high, a double raise in a major suit may be a prelude to a bid for slam. Thus, if your holding in the opened suit is four without an honor, you cannot bid three of the suit, since it would be misleading to your partner. A double raise in a major suit is forcing to game and, of course, is not a shutout bid as is a raise to four in a major suit.

A typical raise to three in a suit would be with these cards: Your partner has opened with one spade.

♠K 9 6 3 ♥A 8 5 ♦K 7 5 4 ♣5 4

You hold a four-card trump suit headed by the king, twelve points in high cards, and an additional point for the doubleton, for a total of thirteen points.

Another typical hand:

♠K 9 6 3 ♥K J 7 3 ♦A J 9 3 ♣6

You have a four-card trump suit headed by the king, thirteen points in high cards, and three additional for the singleton, giving a total of fifteen points.

A raise to four in the opener's suit is a *triple raise*. It shows five or more trumps and not more than ten points in high cards. When the raise is made to four, the responder is telling the opener that there is but a remote chance of making a slam, and, in effect, it is considered a shut-out bid.

After a bid of one spade, the following is a typical raise to four in spades:

♠Q 8 5 4 2   ♥9 8   ♦7   ♣K Q 9 3 2

This hand holds seven high-card points and five trumps and is perfect for a raise to four, shutting out the bidding.

No-Trump Responses

A response of one no-trump to partner's opening bid is made in those situations where the hand does not qualify for a one over one, two over one, or a raise in opener's bid suit. The responses can be one, two, or three no-trump.

One No-Trump: In order to bid one no-trump as a response, the hand should be weak, with six to ten points.

Two No-Trump: To respond with this bid the following is needed:
1. Thirteen to fifteen points in high cards.
2. Strength in each of the three unbid suits.
3. Balanced distribution.

Three No-Trump: For this bid, it is necessary to hold:
1. Sixteen to seventeen points in high cards.
2. Strength in each of the unbid suits.
3. Balanced distribution.

Remember, in no-trump responses short suits have no value, and therefore points are not counted for singletons or doubletons. Therefore, only count high-card points if you are going to make a no-trump response.

Examples of No-Trump Responses

Your partner has bid one spade, and you hold   ♠9 2   ♥K J 4 ♦Q J 8 7   ♣A Q 7 5.

With this hand, respond with two no-trump. There are thirteen points in high cards, strength in all the unbid suits, and balanced distribution.

♠9 2   ♥9 8 5   ♦K 9 5   ♣K Q 10 7 2

Here, bid one no-trump. There are eight points, but the hand is not strong enough for a two-over-one bid, and the one-bid response of one no-trump will be best.

Jump Response in a New Suit

This bid is forcing to game, and if there is enough strength shown in both hands it could very well lead to a slam bid. A jump response shows a very strong hand. The responder promises that he holds:

1. A strong suit, or excellent support for the opener's bid suit.

2. Nineteen points or better, counting high cards and distribution values.

The following are examples of a jump response:

Your partner has opened with one diamond. You hold   ♠K 4 ♥A K Q J 7 6 ♦8 7 ♣K Q 7.

Bid two hearts. There are nineteen points in high cards, and no support for the diamonds.

♠8   ♥A K J 9 2   ♦K Q 7 5   ♣K Q 6

Bid two hearts. But on a rebid you should show your strength in diamonds as well.

Opening No-Trump Bids

The use of *one-no-trump bids* in conjunction with the Stayman convention has made this bid popular and valuable.

There are three aspects that must be considered before bidding no-trump, and all three must be in harmony before one no-trump can be bid. They are: The strength of the hand; the distribution of the cards; and the location of honors, or high cards.

Unlike suit bids, in no-trump the valuation is not based on distribution plus high-card points, but on high-card points alone.

The standard range of high-card points is sixteen to eighteen. Some players stretch this to fifteen to eighteen points.

In a weak no-trump, players bid one no-trump with twelve to fourteen points, but this system is not discussed here. We concentrate on the normal one-no-trump opening bid, requiring sixteen to eighteen points, and possibly stretching to fifteen to eighteen points.

The following are the standard distributions of one-no-trump hands: 4-3-3-3; 4-4-3-2; and 5-3-3-2. In the latter instance the five-card suit is a minor suit. Some players open this distribution as one no-trump even if the five-card suit is a major suit, if sixteen points are held, but it may create rebid problems.

Where there are two doubletons, and the bidder desires to open one no-trump, each doubleton should be headed by a king or ace.

The high cards should be distributed among all four suits, which is not always possible, but in any event they should be distributed among at least three suits. A hand containing a weak doubleton, with high cards held in the other suits, may create problems both in the bidding and the play.

The use of a *two-no-trump bid* shows three things:

1. A balanced hand with a distribution (the same as in one no-trump) of 4-3-3-3; 4-4-3-2; or 5-3-3-2. In the latter, the five-card suit is a minor one.

2. Twenty-one to twenty-four points.

3. All four of the suits must be protected.

Unlike other opening bids of two, a two-no-trump bid is not forcing.

The requirements for bidding *three no-trump* as an opening bid are as follows:

1. A balanced hand.

2. Twenty-five to twenty-seven points.

3. All four of the suits must be protected.

Responses

To Opening One-No-Trump Bids

Two Clubs: This is the Stayman convention. See p. 167.

Two Diamonds, Hearts, or Spades: This bid usually shows a five-card suit with no interest in going to game.

Two No-Trump: Eight to nine points and a hand that is fairly balanced. However, a long minor suit with a little less high-card strength is sufficient for a three-no-trump bid.

Four of a Major Suit: With as few as seven to eight points and a long (six-card) major suit. When four spades or hearts is bid, this usually means the bidding is closed.

Four No-Trump: Fifteen to sixteen points with a balanced hand.

Six No-Trump: Seventeen to eighteen points with a balanced hand.

To Two-No-Trump Opening Bids

Pass: Less than four points.

Three No-Trump: Four to nine points.

Three of a Suit: It is forcing and shows the possibility of a slam with a five-card suit and at least ten points.

Four of a Major Suit: Eight points in high cards and a six-card suit.

Six No-Trump: Twelve to fourteen points with a balanced hand.

To Three-No-Trump Opening Bids

Four No-Trump: Seven points and a balanced hand.

Six No-Trump: Eight to nine points.

Seven No-Trump: Twelve points.

Stayman Convention

This convention, which is a standard one throughout the world, was popularized by Samuel Stayman.

Very simply, it is the response of two clubs by the opener's partner, asking the opener to bid a four-card major suit after the opener has bid one no-trump.

Should the opener not have a four-card major suit, he rebids two diamonds.

If the opener has a four-card major suit, he rebids the major suit.

If the opener has two four-card major suits, he can bid either one. Then, if the response is two no-trump, he can bid the other major suit.

The responder has a choice of various rebids, as follows:

Two of a Major Suit: This is usually treated as an encouraging bid, called nonforcing Stayman. The responder shows a five-card suit and indicates the possibility of game.

Two No-Trump: This is also an encouraging bid, showing the same values as an immediate raise of two no-trump. If the opener has bid a major, this shows possession of the other major. If the opener has rebid two diamonds, a bid of two no-trump shows control of one or both majors.

Three of a Minor Suit: In some systems this is forcing to game, with the responder looking for a minor-suit game or possibly a slam in a minor suit.

Raising the Major Bid to Three: This shows a four-card support for the major bid and is an invitation for the opener to bid game in the major suit.

Three No-Trump: Sometimes treated as a final bid and sometimes showing that the responder holds the unbid major. The opener can now bid the unbid major at this point if he has both majors.

There are other responses, but these are the basic ones, making use of the Stayman convention to go to game or slam, either in no-trump or in a suit.

Opening Bid of Two in a Suit

Where an opening bidder has a powerful hand and wants to force his partner to respond until they arrive at a game contract, the bid is two in a suit. In order to open with a bid of two in a suit, the following are necessary:

With a good five-card suit, twenty-five high-card points; with a second good five-card suit, one less point.

With a good six-card suit, twenty-three high-card points.

With a good seven-card suit, twenty-one high-card points.

If the game is in a minor suit, two more points are needed.

Responses to Opening Bids of Two in a Suit

An opening bid of two in a suit is forcing; that is, the partner must respond, no matter how poor his hand or devoid of strength.

Two No-Trump: A very weak hand. This is a negative response.

Three of the Same Suit: Shows adequate trump support and seven to eight points.

Other bids in the seven-to-eight-point range should be natural and are considered positive.

Three No-Trump: Nine points and no strong suit to bid.

Opener's Rebid

Usually, it is not difficult to find a correct opening bid, but the rebid is often a crucial test, requiring a great deal more thought than the opening bid.

After a One-Over-One Response

We remember that a partner's response has shown that he has length in his bid suit and a count of from six to eighteen points. He must rebid, since the bid is forcing for one round.

With thirteen to fifteen points and a balanced hand, a rebid of *one-no-trump* is appropriate where, for example, the opening bid was one heart; the response one spade; and the opener's holding is perhaps: ♠9 7 ♥K Q J 4 ♦Q J 7 4 ♣A J 6. This is a balanced hand with fourteen points in high cards.

With twelve to sixteen points, and at least a strong five-card opening suit, *rebid the opening suit.* If, for example, one heart was bid and one spade was the response, the opener now rebids two hearts with the following: ♠5 2 ♥A Q 10 5 3 ♦Q J 4 ♣A J 3. The heart suit is rebiddable, and with fourteen points it is close to a minimum holding.

When holding twelve to sixteen points and four cards in the responder's suit, give a single raise in the responder's suit. With three cards in responder's suit, the raise is appropriate also, unless the opener has a six-card suit of his own to rebid, or has a completely balanced hand, which would be suitable for no-trump.

The following is a good example of a single-raise rebid in responder's suit. Responder has bid one spade over opener's one-heart bid.

♠Q J 9 5 ♥A Q J 5 4 ♦A 3 ♣J 6

With that four-card holding in spades, a rebid in responder's suit would be superior.

With nineteen to twenty points and a balanced distribution a *two-no-trump rebid* should be made. If the hand held sixteen-to-eighteen points and the balanced distribution, it would have been opened with one no-trump. The following is a good example of a hand showing a two-no-trump response after an opening bid of one heart and a response of one spade: ♥8 4 ♥A Q 8 3 2 ♦K Q 9 ♣A K J.

A jump rebid in the opener's suit can be made with seventeen to nineteen points and a good six-card suit. Or with seventeen to nineteen points and a seven-card suit. The bid is encouraging and not forcing, and if the rebid jump is in a minor suit, it may suggest a final contract of three no-trump.

Jump-shift rebid: If the bidding has been one diamond, then a response of one spade, a bid of three clubs or three hearts would be a jump shift rebid. This bid is forcing to game and shows nineteen to twenty points.

A jump to game in three no-trump, or game in the responder's suit or your suit, shows twenty points. If jumping to game in responder's suit, the opener should have four cards in responder's trumps; if jumping to game in his own suit, he should have at least seven trumps, or a six-card suit headed by three honors such as K Q J.

After a Two-Over-One Response

The response of a two-over-one bid informs the opener that his partner has a good suit and ten to eighteen points, and will in all probability bid again.

If you have, as opener, twelve to fourteen points, then a rebid of the opening suit is the weakest bid, showing a minimum hand.

If you have twelve to sixteen points and a balanced distribution, bid two no trump.

If you hold twelve to sixteen points and another biddable suit, bid that other suit, and then await your partner's next bid.

If you have fifteen to seventeen points and good trump support for your partner, rebid his suit at the three level. It should not be done, however, with only twelve to fourteen points in the hand.

If your hand contains seventeen to nineteen points, you can make one of three bids:

A jump in your own suit, from one to three, if you hold a strong six-card or longer suit. If your partner now holds ten or more points, he should go to game.

A jump bid in the responder's suit. With this bid, you should have good trumps and a singleton or void suit. This is especially true since a four bid goes by three no-trump, which is game, and is preferable to a four bid in a minor suit. Thus, with the following bids and cards, a four bid would be proper.

SOUTH	WEST	NORTH	EAST
One spade	Pass	Two diamonds	Pass

It is now South's turn to rebid. He holds: ♠ A K J 7 3 ♥ 2 ♦ K 10 6 5 ♣ A J 4.

The singleton in hearts negates a no-trump bid, and the strong point count of sixteen points in high cards plus the singleton, and the good support for diamonds, makes this a natural four-diamond bid.

Three no-trump. With balanced distribution and a hand holding less than twenty points, this is the correct bid.

With twenty or more points, there are really only two alternatives: Either bid game or make a forcing bid to game.

If you had originally bid one spade to open and you have twenty points, a rebid to game wouldn't necessarily show high-card strength, but tells your partner that if he has only his response suit and nothing else, you can play your suit at game.

If, with twenty points, you want to show another good suit, and you bid it, that tells your partner that you are insisting on game, no matter what his holdings.

Responder's Rebids

The responder's rebids should be governed by the previous bidding. If the opener, your partner, has made a strong bid, then you, as responder, should count your points and his points; if they add up to twenty-six, bid toward a game, even if your hand is not that strong. Remember the important thing is the point total.

If your partner has given you an invitation to game by rebidding his suit after you have responded in that suit—for instance, one spade, response two spades, rebid three spades—then if the responder has nine points he should go to game. The raise of an opener's suit only promised six to nine points, and, with the maximum, it is well worth a game.

Preemptive, or Shut-Out, Bid

This is an opening bid of three or more in a suit. The bid is made with a hand holding a very long suit and with very limited high-card strength. It is best made in a minor suit, with less than twelve points in high cards.

Primarily, preemptive bids are used as defensive weapons. They upset the opponents' communications and may force them to overbid their hands at high levels, or may force them to bid inaccurately at a high level.

Sometimes, when a bidder of a preemptive bid has a self-sufficient suit and twelve or thirteen points, these bids are used as a trap for penalty points.

The best position in which to make a preemptive bid is sitting third at the table. There may have already been two passes, and you are fairly certain that the fourth player has a strong hand to bid. Sometimes, the dealer is in an advantageous position to preempt, with great length in a suit, but a weak hand.

Sitting second is a poor place for a preemptive bid, and the fourth player will very rarely make a preemptive bid, since he has little to fear from his opponents. If he does preempt, he should have a suit with honors; in other words, a strong suit.

Examples of Preemptive Bids

♦ Q 10 9 x x x x, with only ten points in high cards. Preempt with three diamonds.

♣ A K 10 9 8 x x, with ten points in high cards. Preempt with three clubs.

♠ A x   ♥ x   ♦ Q x x   ♣ J 10 9 x x x x   Preempt with three clubs.

♠ A Q J 10 x x x   ♥ x x   ♦ K x x   ♣ x   Preempt with four spades. The key to this hand is the very strong major suit of seven cards.

♠ -   ♥ x x   ♦ J x x x   ♣ A K J 10 x x x   Preempt with four clubs. Again, a strong club hand with a void in spades can go to a four level.

Examples of Preemptive Major Bids

♠ Q J 10 9 x x x   ♥ x   ♦ K J   ♣ Q x x   Preempt with three spades.

♠ K Q J 10 x x x x   ♥ x   ♦ x   ♣ A J 10   Preempt with four spades. An eight-card suit is usually a four opening bid when preempting.

All preemptive bids are bothersome to the opposition and should be made with extralong suits and a hand with few defensive high cards. These bids prevent the opponents from exchanging information about their hands at a low level.

Responses to Preemptive Bids

A Raise to Game in a Major Suit: Example, from three hearts to four hearts. Responder needs at least three strong-playing tricks, either in trump honors or in aces and kings of other suits.

Three No-Trump: If the preemptive bidder bid a major suit, it shows that nine tricks can be made without any strength in his partner's preemptive suit. They can be made even if the responder is void in his partner's bid suit.

If the original preemptive bid was a minor suit, it shows stoppers in at least two of the suits not bid, and may possibly show an honor in partner's bid suit.

Three of a Higher-Ranking Suit: Example, three diamonds, three spades. This is forcing to game and means that the responder has a strong suit of his own.

Four of a Lower-Ranking Suit: Example, three spades to four diamonds. This indicates a try for slam.

Defensive Bidding

Overcalls

An overcall is a bid made by the player immediately to the left of the opening bidder. For example:

SOUTH	WEST	NORTH	EAST
Pass	One club	One heart	

In this situation, West has made the opening bid, and North, to West's left, has made an overcall of one heart.

SOUTH	WEST	NORTH	EAST
One diamond	One heart	One spade	

Here, West has overcalled South's bid, but North is merely responding with his bid, since his partner and not the opponent to his right made the opening bid.

The proper use of the overcall is very important. If used incorrectly it can mean big losses. Thus, every overcall must have a very specific purpose. The various factors which determine this bid are discussed in order.

An overcall, with very rare exceptions, should not be made unless the bidder of the overcall has a five- or six-card suit. If there is an overcall at a two level, a six- or seven-card suit is usually mandatory.

An overcall should be equivalent to a minimum suit bid at a one level, and requires at least thirteen points in high cards. An overcall should not be made with more than sixteen points; at that strength, a double is preferable.

If the overcaller is vulnerable, or overcalling at a two level, he must not mislead his partner, who will consider the overcall to signify opening strength. At the one level, even though opening strength is preferable, there are times when, if the opposition is vulnerable and has opened a heart suit, the overcaller may step in with spades with a hand two or three points short of opening strength.

This factor of vulnerability must be taken into consideration, and it is correct at times to overcall with a slightly weaker hand if the overcaller is not vulnerable and his opponents are. But it must be done with care, for it can be punished badly with a double.

The following is an example of a bad overcall.

NORTH
♠ 8 6
♥ A Q 7 3
♦ A Q 4
♣ 10 9 8 2

WEST	EAST
♠ 9 2	♠ K 10 7 5
♥ K 9 5	♥ 8 6 4
♦ 8 2	♦ 10 9 7 5 3
♣ A K Q 5 4 3	♣ J

SOUTH
♠ A Q J 4 3
♥ J 10 2
♦ K J 6
♣ 7 6

The bidding went as follows:

SOUTH	WEST	NORTH	EAST
One spade	Two clubs	Double	Pass
Pass	Pass		

North opened the play with the ♠8, which was won by South's jack after dummy put on the 10. The ♥J was returned, and the contract was set by four tricks. Even worse would have been a saving bid by East of two diamonds, which, doubled, would mean a set contract by five tricks.

Here, all West had was a strong minor suit and twelve points in high cards, overcalling against a major suit. By bidding it as an overcall, he left himself in a bad position for a double. He should have passed and had no right overcalling.

A necessary factor was not present in this case—the ability to obstruct the bidding. Bidding a minor suit over a major suit at this level obstructs nothing. West did not have opening strength, and the use of an overcall in this kind of situation can be dangerous.

The following are examples of good overcalls:

1. Opponent opens the bidding with one club. You hold:
   ♠A K x x x ♥A J x ♦K 10 9 x ♣x
   One spade is a good overcall.

2. Opponent opens the bidding with one diamond. You hold:
   ♠x x ♥K Q J x x x ♦x x ♣A Q 9
   One heart is a good overcall.

3. Opponent opens the bidding with one heart. You hold:
   ♠A Q x x x ♥A x x ♦K x x ♣Q x
   One spade is a good overcall.

Weak Overcall: A self-sufficient suit headed by two high honors, and a hand slightly below an opening bid. This overcall can be used as a lead director and, at times, to force the opponents to higher levels.

Strong Overcall: A hand of opening strength, with a strong suit of at least five cards headed by two or more honors. The longer the suit, the better is the hand for an overcall, rather than a takeout double bid asking partner for his suit. When holding a strong major suit with opening strength, your partner's suit becomes relatively unimportant. If your opponent opened the bidding and you overcall, remember there are already twenty-six high-card points showing between both opening bids, leaving but fourteen high-card points among the other two players. So at this point you want to assert your suit, not be content merely to fit in with your partner's best suit.

The overcall is also often used as a competitive bid in a number of ways:

1. It may stop the opponents from arriving at a game contract.

2. It can be used to outbid part-score contracts or possibly game contracts.

3. It has nuisance value, depriving the opponents of the chance to exchange bidding information at a low level.

Don't use a weak overcall to defend a partial score; in that situation don't overcall unless you have opening strength.

If you have opening strength but don't have a five-card suit, don't overcall; a five-card or longer suit is essential in overcalling. A takeout double is the correct call without a five-card suit.

Takeout Doubles

A takeout double is not for the purpose of penalizing the opponents, but to announce to the doubler's partner that his hand is as strong as an opening bid. Thus, the doubler is forcing his partner to respond with a bid of his best or longest suit, regardless of his point count.

Since a double can be either for penalty or takeout purposes, the following criteria must be met before the double can be assumed not to be a penalty one:

1. It must be made at the bidder's first opportunity to double.

2. It usually doubles a suit bid below the game level.

3. The doubler's partner must not have bid yet.

Let us examine a few bidding examples.

SOUTH	WEST	NORTH	EAST
One heart	Double		

This is a very simple illustration of a takeout double. The bidder has made it at his first opportunity; the suit bid is below game level; and the doubler's partner has not yet bid.

SOUTH	WEST	NORTH	EAST
One heart	Pass	Two clubs	Pass
Two hearts	Double		

Here, two criteria are met—the double is made while the bid is still below game level and the doubler's partner has not yet bid—but since it was not made at the first opportunity, it is not a takeout double but a penalty double. In fact, it's a perfect example of a penalty double.

SOUTH	WEST	NORTH	EAST
One diamond	One spade	Double	

This is also a penalty double, because North's partner has already bid. Remember, any double after an opening bid by one's partner is to be considered as a penalty double.

A takeout doubler usually has either of two kinds of hands:

1. A hand with opening strength but no good suit to bid, yet with plenty of support for whatever suit his partner might bid. In other words, a good dummy hand.

2. A hand so strong that if he makes an overcall his partner might simply pass and leave him at a lower level than he wishes to play at.

A takeout doubler should try to foresee the suit his partner will bid; if the suit is going to be an unsatisfactory one, there is no point in doubling. If the response by partner is going to be in a suit in which the doubler has merely a singleton or doubleton without any honors, and the rest of his hand will not support no-trump, there is better strategy in passing an opening hand at the outset and waiting to see the results.

Suppose you are West and holding the following cards:

♠A 8 6 4   ♥A J 4 2   ♦9   ♣A Q 8 5

The bidding has been:

SOUTH	WEST
One spade	?

If you double, in all probability your partner is going to respond with two diamonds. Since two diamonds is going nowhere, there is a possibility of bidding two no-trump, but this is also going to be a very difficult hand to make two no-trump with if your partner has nothing. And remember, being forced to bid, he may very well bid with nothing. It is better for you to pass. In this hand, the bidding continues:

SOUTH	WEST	NORTH	EAST
One spade	Pass	Two spades	Pass
Three spades	Double		

This double was for penalty, and was very effective. Remember, a takeout double is forcing for one round.

If no-trump is opened as a bid by your opponents, a double of that bid is always for penalty purposes. There are some authorities who suggest a takeout double with sixteen points, but the better practice is always to treat a double after no-trump as a penalty double.

Responses to Takeout Doubles

Since a takeout double is forcing (that is, it calls for a response), the partner of the doubler must, no matter how weak his hand, make a bid. There is only one exception, and even that exception shows a response.

The bidding has been: One diamond; double; pass; and now it is your turn to bid. If you have six to eight points and length in the opponents' bid suit (diamonds), you can pass. This turns the takeout double into a penalty double, informing your partner that you believe the one-diamond bid can be beaten for a penalty score.

So, if the opponents have bid one diamond, and your partner doubled, and the third hand passed, you can:

1. Pass. It shows six to eight points and a long suit in opponents' bid suit.

2. Bid one heart, one spade, or two clubs, showing a very weak response at the lowest level and telling your partner that you have at the most eight points.

(If the original doubler had a minimum hand for a takeout double, he should pass either of these first two responses.)

3. Bid one no-trump, showing eight to ten points with a stopper in the suit bid (diamonds).

4. Bid a jump shift (two hearts, two spades, or three clubs), which is played as not forcing.

5. Bid a cue bid in the same suit (diamonds), showing the doubler that the partnership has enough strength for game but the suit has yet to be determined.

In the next example, the bidding has gone as follows:

SOUTH	WEST	NORTH	EAST
One diamond	Double	One spade	?

You are East. An intervening bid by the opener's partner relieves you of the obligation to bid, but you can still do so if you have moderate values and can bid at a low level. Here your bid would be a "free response," since it is no longer forced.

Penalty Doubles

Doubles of No Trump

To reiterate what was mentioned before in takeout doubles, all doubles of a no-trump bid are made for the purpose of penalty. Therefore, unless the bidder intends to penalize his opponents, he should not double an opening no-trump bid.

If Partner Has Bid

Any double after a partner's bid should also be considered as a penalty double.

When to Double for Penalty

Suppose the bidding has gone:

SOUTH	WEST	NORTH	EAST
One diamond	Double	One spade	?

You are East and you hold:
♠K 10 9 3 2   ♥J 8 5 4   ♦J   ♣Q 7 4

You have a good double because you have strength in the suit bid. Your partner's double was a takeout double. If he had bid two clubs, and North had bid two spades, you would have an even better penalty double. In either case, your logical bid would have been in spades. Since the opponents have bid it after your partner has shown strength, double for penalty.

If your partner has opened the bidding and the second player overcalls, there are many opportunities to pick up plenty of points by penalty doubles. Suppose the bidding has gone:

SOUTH	WEST	NORTH
One heart	Two diamonds	?

You are North and hold:
♠A Q 6 2   ♥6 3   ♦J 10 9 4   ♣K Q 7

You have a good penalty double as North. First, you have little support for your partner's heart bid. Second, although diamonds is not the suit you would normally bid, it is a wonderful suit to defend with because holdings of J 10 9 can pick up unexpected tricks in defense and are practically useless in offense.

A good rule to follow in deciding whether to double an overcall is to double if:

1. You have poor support for your partner's bid suit.
2. There is no strong and long suit of your own.
3. You have three or more trumps with middle strength, such as Q J 10 or Q 10 9 or J 10 9.
4. You have ten points and two tricks in trump; twelve points if you have one sure trump trick; above twelve points if the best you have is only a possible trump trick.

Never double under the following circumstances:

1. With four or more cards in partner's suit. If you have three cards in his suit, it is a close decision, dependent on the other factors such as your strength in the opponents' trumps.
2. If the hands will not fit well for you and your partner.
3. If the opponents are vulnerable and you are not. Borderline cases can be doubled more boldly than otherwise.
4. If you have length in your partner's suit. This is a very poor reason for doubling, since the opponents will be short in the suit and your main strength will be dissipated.

Slam Bidding

Good slam bidding is essential because there are large bonuses awarded for slam bidding, often in excess of those for winning a rubber. Thus, slam bidding can often make the difference between a winning and a losing night of bridge.

There are two essential elements involved in slam bidding: Strength and controls. These two elements must be present because a small slam requires the taking of twelve tricks and a grand slam all the tricks. Strength means a high-point count; controls refers to absolute domination of a suit or suits by either an ace or void.

Strength

There are forty points in high cards, and it is usually essential that the partners in a slam contract have at least thirty-three of them. This means that any time the opposition has eight or more points, there is a strong possibility that the slam will be defeated. If their eight points consist of two aces and they are able to take both of them, the slam will be defeated. The partnership bidding the slam may be void in a suit in which the opposing partnership has an ace, and will negate that trick. But if there are no voids, if the partnership bidding the slam must take it on power alone, then thirty-three points are necessary. If you have less, no matter how good the cards look, there is a good chance that the slam is going to be defeated.

If there is a good distribution, with a singleton or void suit negating the strength of the opponents' high cards, fewer than thirty-three points may be sufficient for the slam. If the distribution is particularly bad, with one or two suits vulnerable to attack, then even more than thirty-three points may be necessary.

Long, powerful suits are excellent for slam bidding because if there is enough length and strength, all the low cards of the trump suit are winners and this lowers the necessary point count.

Often, holding two powerful suits, the trump suit and another, is also a natural for a slam with fewer points than ordinarily required. In this case there will probably be a void in one suit and a singleton or doubleton in the other. It is quite easy then to see the possibilities of slam, regardless of the point count.

Controls

If the declarer could play the first card, instead of the opponent, it would be easier to bid more hands as slams. But in contract bridge the opposition plays the first card. And unless there are controls, if the opposition can make two quick tricks, no matter what else is held by the partnership that bids the slam, that slam is gone.

There are two ideal controls. One is the ace of that suit, and the other is a void in the suit. These are first-round controls and they are always necessary in slams. Second-round controls are also valuable in small-slam bids. A second-round control would be the king of a suit or a singleton.

Thus, it is extremely important in bidding a slam to examine just what controls you do have and what you are missing. If you hold all the controls, no sweat. But if one or more is missing, it is essential to find out just what controls your partner has, or if he is holding those missing controls. How to find out if your partner is holding them? The bidding should tell you.

Since aces are first-round controls, if you are missing any, the easiest way to find out if your partner is holding any is to bid the Blackwood convention. We'll discuss its basic elements here, but for greater depth see p. 182.

A bid of four no-trump, after the bidding has determined the trump, tells your partner that you are asking for the aces in his hand.

The responses to the Blackwood four-no-trump bid are as follows:

Cards Held	Response
No aces or four aces	Five clubs
One ace	Five diamonds
Two aces	Five hearts
Three aces	Five spades

Once a player has bid four no-trump, he takes control of the bidding and determines the final contract. He alone knows what controls are missing, and it is usually a wise move to let the strongest of the two hands ask for aces. If the four-no-trump bidder is missing two controls and his partner bids five diamonds, showing one ace, that bidder knows that they are still one ace shy of a grand slam and will stop at six. His partner must respect that bid and not bid over it.

If there are no aces missing but there is not full secondary control of the kings, the four-no-trump bidder, after getting his response for aces, may bid five no-trump. He is asking for kings, and is answered in the same manner:

Cards Held	Response
No kings or four kings	Six clubs
One king	Six diamonds
Two kings	Six hearts
Three kings	Six spades

The reason five no-trump doesn't show four aces, but five clubs does is that the original four-no-trump bidder would be foreclosed from asking for kings after a five-no-trump bid. Whether five clubs means no aces or four aces should be no problem from the previous bidding, and if the partner cannot figure it out he better put aside bridge for a while and learn his bidding all over again.

It is well worth remembering that the bidder of four no-trump controls the bidding after that and places the contract in its final suit. A top-notch bridge player pointed out to me a situation where he had bid four no-trump, asking for aces, and his partner, a novice, bid five diamonds, showing one. Thereafter the expert bid seven hearts. It was promptly doubled. His partner, the novice, thought long and hard and bid seven no-trump, at which point the expert nearly had a heart attack. That bid was promptly doubled and the hand was, of course, down and out.

"How the hell could you bid seven no-trump?" the expert wanted to know, wondering which form of murder would be quicker on this partner of his.

"I was blank in hearts. I was void."

"You mean you were void in your head! When I bid four no-trump, I was the captain of the team at that moment. I decide the final bid. I don't care if you're as blank in hearts as you are . . ." But rather than go on in a rage, the expert put down his hand, which was "cold" (a sure thing) for seven hearts.

What happened to his partner after that? No, he wasn't found dead. But he was found with his chin on his hand, contemplating the words of the wise expert.

Blackwood Convention

This convention, which was invented by Easley Blackwood, is a popular and standard one whose aim is to discover the number of aces in a partner's hand so that, if possible, the bidder of the convention can go to slam.

Blackwood is used by bidding the artificial bid of four no-trump. The response at the five level discloses the number of aces in partner's hand. A response of five clubs shows no aces or four aces; five diamonds, one ace; five hearts, two aces; and five spades, three aces.

If the original four-no-trump bidder bids five no-trump, that is also an artificial bid asking for kings in the partner's hand. The five-no-trump bid, which is an attempt to bid a grand slam, should indicate that the partnership holds all four aces.

The responses to five no-trump are in the same order as for four no-trump. Six clubs shows no kings or four kings; six diamonds, one king; etc.

In order to safely bid four no-trump, the bidder should have enough controls in his hand so that any response by his partner does not put him in an untenable position at the five level.

In the event that an opponent puts in an interference bid, the responder may still show the number of aces he holds by counting the intervening bid as the asking bid. That is, if the intervening bid is five diamonds, then a response of five hearts would show no aces; five spades, one ace; five no-trump, two aces; and six clubs, three aces. However, the responder should have a strong enough hand to enable him to start the bidding over the interference bid to show aces. If the interference bid is five spades, the level of five no-trump or six clubs may be too high, and a penalty double may be more appropriate.

A void should never be considered the equivalent of an ace in response to a Blackwood bid of four no-trump. Various methods have been worked out by leading partnerships to show a void. For example, a response bid of six clubs would show one ace and a void; six diamonds shows two aces and a void.

Cue Bids

The use of cue bids to show the way to a slam is used in those situations where a Blackwood convention is avoided. A cue bid shows a control, usually a first-round control of an ace, and it is made so that the intention to try for slam is communicated to the partner.

The following are typical bidding situations in which a cue bid is used:

NORTH	SOUTH
♠9 5	♠K Q 6 4
♥A Q J 10 7	♥J 9 3 2
♦Q J 9	♦K 4
♣A J 8	♣K Q 2

The bidding went:

NORTH	SOUTH
One heart	Three hearts
Four clubs	Four hearts

After South bid three hearts, North's bid of four clubs was a cue bid, showing the ace of clubs and asking his partner if there is a possibility of slam. South, having no aces, merely goes to game.

NORTH	SOUTH
♠A K 8 4 3	♠9 5
♥A Q J 8 6	♥K 7
♦K 9 2	♦A Q J 9 8 7 5
♣—	♣10 7

The bidding went:

NORTH	EAST	SOUTH	WEST
One spade	Pass	Two diamonds	Three clubs
Four clubs	Five clubs	Five diamonds	Pass
Five hearts	Pass	Six diamonds	Pass
Seven diamonds			

North had opened the bidding with a very strong hand just short of a two bid. South made a diamond response (two over one) forcing a rebid for one round. Then West, who probably had a tremendous club suit, entered the bidding with three clubs (an overcall). North's bid of four clubs after West's three-club bid showed a control in clubs, which could only be figured as a void. By making this cue bid and encouraging the try for slam, the partnership bid and easily made a grand slam.

NORTH	SOUTH
♠—	♠Q J 9 8 5
♥A K J 10 9 3	♥8 2
♦A 9 4	♦K Q J 10 7 3
♣A Q 4 2	♣—

The bidding went:

NORTH	SOUTH
Two hearts	Two no-trump
Three hearts	Four diamonds
Four spades	Five clubs
Six diamonds	Seven diamonds

When a player holds a void in an outside suit, the use of the Blackwood convention should be avoided for fear of bidding too high. The use of cue bids (four spades, five clubs) was necessary here in order to reach a grand slam. With the use of the Blackwood convention, South would show no aces, and only a small slam might be agreed upon, whereas a grand slam was "cold," (a sure thing).

Popular Bridge Conventions—Modern Bidding Techniques

In modern games of bridge, a number of bidding conventions have sprung up that have made the game more and more complicated. At one time there was a standard convention, embellished by Blackwood, Stayman, and perhaps one or two others.

I'll cover a number of the more popular of the modern bidding conventions in brief. My suggestion is that further study be made of any that might interest the reader, for they cannot simply be explained and immediately put to use. The more study, the better a player will become, and since bridge is a partnership game, it is best that not only the reader but his or her partner should be conversant with these bidding conventions.

The Jacoby Transfer Bid

This convention attempts to have the stronger of the two hands become the declarer, for the general rule is that the stronger hand as declarer has the best chance of making a suit or no-trump contract.

The convention is used after opening bids of one or two no-trump, and what the responder tries to do is get the no-trump opener to play the hand in the responder's long suit, if that is at all possible.

This is accomplished by the responder's bidding the suit beneath his long major suit, forcing the opener now to rebid in the responder's best suit. When this is done, the transfer is completed.

Here's how it works:

OPENER	RESPONDER
One no-trump	Two hearts
Two spades	

The responder's best suit is spades, so he bids hearts, just below the spades suit. Now the opener bids above hearts, and thus bids spades, which is responder's solid suit.

Another example:

OPENER	RESPONDER
Two no-trump	Three diamonds
Three hearts	

The opener knows that the responder's best suit is hearts because the diamond bid was just beneath it. Thus he bids hearts.

Generally, the Jacoby transfer bid will be used when the responder has at least a five- or six-card major suit. In effect, by using the JTB, the responder promises at least five cards in the major suit.

However, this bid shouldn't be used if the opening no-trump bid is overcalled or doubled.

Weak Two Bid

This is an opening bid of either two diamonds, two hearts, or two spades, and shows a strong six-card suit but only seven to ten high-card points.

The typical hand distributions are 6-3-3-1, 6-3-2-2, and 6-4-2-1. A weak two bid shouldn't be opened with a void, for the responder might misjudge the potentials of the hand.

The suit bid should have at least an ace and face card or two face cards, with 10 9 8 or any two of those three, such as A J 9 8, heading it.

When playing this convention, any hand with the potential to go to game, as well as no-trump hands in the area of twenty-two to twenty-four points, are opened artificially with a bid of two clubs. An opening bid of two no-trump shows twenty to twenty-two points, and an opening bid of two clubs then followed by a rebid of two no-trump indicates twenty-two to twenty-four high-card points and a balanced holding.

When in the third seat, after a partner has passed, a weak two bid indicates the partner's lead against the opponents. In this case a five-card strong suit is sufficient. The partner uses this bid strictly for leading purposes, since he probably has little strength.

The responder must keep in mind that the opening bid shows only seven to ten high-card points; therefore, unless he holds at least fifteen high-card points, the correct response is to pass. A new suit or two no-trump is forcing for a weak two bid opener.

The Weak Jump Overcall

This convention is similar to a weak two bid. It needs a solid six-card suit and seven to ten high-card points. By using the convention the responder skips over one level of bidding.

Suppose that the opponent to the right of the weak jump overcall bidder has opened with one club. With the following hand the bidder will go to two hearts.

♠63　♥AQJ962　♦842　♣93

Suppose you hold the following:

♠AKJ876　♥A108　♦32　♣86

You hold a good six-card suit with twelve high-card points, so after an overcall at the one-level, you can rebid this simple overcall, showing your partner that you hold twelve to fourteen high-card points along with a solid six-card suit.

The response to a weak jump overcall in a new suit is not forcing, but should the weak jump overcall bidder have support in that new suit, he should raise. For example, the bidding in a sequence might go like this:

EAST	SOUTH	WEST	NORTH
One club	Two spades	Pass	Three diamonds
Pass	Four diamonds		

The bid of four diamonds shows support in diamonds, with the possibility of going to game in diamonds.

Weak jump overcalls can be very tricky, and the partners must make certain they're handling the convention correctly.

Negative Double

This has become a popular convention among top players, who use it to replace the penalty double. It becomes a takeout double for the unbid suits, with emphasis on the unbid major suit or major suits.

Here's how it works. Suppose we have the following bidding sequence:

EAST	SOUTH	WEST	NORTH
One diamond	One spade	Double	

If the East-West partnership were not using negative doubles, then it would be assumed that West's double was a penalty double and that West had strong spades. However, with the negative double, this is a takeout double, showing at least four hearts.

If West had bid two hearts, he would already be in the second level, and would be promising five hearts in his hand. He might have only four, and by making this negative double, he gets into the bidding. Let's assume the following hand for West.

♠9 5 ♥A 10 9 8 ♦9 6 4 ♣A 8 5 3

By playing negative doubles, the partnership avoids being shut out of a situation where there might be a heart contract, even after the spade overcall by South.

What does a negative double bid promise? When it's made over a one-level overcall, as in the instance above, it shows seven to nine high-card points, and at least a four-card major in the unbid major suit.

If on the next round of bidding the doubler now bids his heart suit, it isn't forcing. He merely shows that he couldn't bid the suit directly because he didn't have a five-card major.

The reason for the popularity of this convention is that it enables players to adhere to only bidding five-card major suits. With the negative double they can show the strength they have in four-card majors.

When there is an overcall of one diamond, a negative double now shows strength not only in one major, but in both. This would happen in the following bidding sequence:

SOUTH	WEST	NORTH	EAST
One club	One diamond	Double	

With this bid the partner can assume that North has two four-card majors, with about seven to nine high-card points.

Negative doubles can be used at the two level as well. When using the double in this manner, you should have a hand with a four-card major, but still not be powerful enough to bid a suit at the two level.

The Lightner Slam Double

This convention is used in the special situation when the opponents have bid to slam level, and it has been doubled. Now the double directs a lead by partner against the slam contract.

There are four aspects to this convention.

If the player doubling has bid a suit: The partner can't lead a trump or that suit, and must lead from the other two suits, hoping to find a void or an A K or A Q in the doubler's hand in the suit bid by the opponents.

If the player doubling hasn't bid a suit: The partner can't lead a trump or the unbid suit. If there is more than one unbid suit, it is expected that the doubler has a void in dummy's bid suit.

If both the player doubling and his partner have bid a suit: The partner can't lead a trump, or either of their own bid suits. This is a clear indication to bid the fourth suit.

If the player doubling has doubled a no-trump slam: The partner must now lead the dummy's first bid suit.

The Responsive Double

This double is used after a takeout double followed by support. Suppose the bidding has gone:

NORTH	EAST	SOUTH	WEST
One heart	Double	Two hearts	Double

West's double, using this convention, tells his partner that he has no one suit of strength, but does have a good hand, and by doubling, he is inviting his partner to bid his longest suit.

In order to make a responsive double, where his partner can still bid at the two level, the doubler need have only seven or eight points. Where his partner's next bid will be at the three level, as in the above sequence of bids, then the doubler should have eight to eleven high-card points.

If the bidder has twelve or more high-card points, then instead of using a responsive double, he should make a cue bid forcing to game.

Suppose the bidding has gone, as before:

NORTH	EAST	SOUTH	WEST
One heart	Double	Two hearts	

West holds:

♠K Q 9 3　♥2　♦K 9 7 5 4　♣A 7 2

West will now cue-bid three hearts, forcing to game.

If your hand is basically a no-trump hand, you shouldn't use either the responsive double or a cue bid. In that case you must bid no-trump.

One final note. The responsive double, if used as a convention, should be limited to those situations in which the opponents have bid and raised in one suit only.

Michael's Cue Bid

The Michael's cue bid shows a two-suited hand. To show this, one bids in the opponent's suit.

When a cue bid is made in a minor suit, it shows major distribution of 5-5 or 5-4, but a hand lacking the high-card strength of a takeout double, with about seven to ten high-card points.

Responses to Michael's Cue Bid of a Minor Suit
A jump to the three level in a major is an invitation to game.

A bid of two no-trump shows no-trump distribution and about fifteen to seventeen high-card points, but is not forcing to game.

A response in a minor suit, such as two diamonds or two clubs, shows diamond strength, with no interest in a major suit.

If the responder makes a second cue bid in the opponent's suit, this is a very strong bid and asks the original cue bidder to bid his longest major suit.

Cue Bid of a Major Suit
When the initial cue bid is in a major suit, it shows strength in the

other major plus a minor suit. Now the distribution will be 5-5 between major or minor, or possibly 6-4 with the longer suit being a minor.

Here the cue bidder, bidding two hearts, will show five or four hearts, and between ten and thirteen high-card points.

Responses to Michael's Cue Bid of a Major Suit

Two no-trump asks for the minor suit.

Bidding the other major is not forcing, and is a natural bid.

Another cue bid in the opponent's suit is strong and forcing to game.

A three no-trump bid is to be taken as a natural bid.

A response in a minor suit is a cut-off bid, showing no interest in the cue bidder's second suit.

Two-Way Stayman

This version of Stayman is being used more and more in tournament play. However, if a partnership uses the Jacoby transfer bid, then they shouldn't use this convention, for they cannot coexist in bidding systems.

With two-way Stayman the opener starts the bidding with one no-trump in all sequences. The following are the responses and what they mean:

Two Clubs: This is an invitation to game but is not forcing. Responder is looking for a suit fit.

Two Diamonds: This is a definite forcing bid, with game in mind, and possibly a slam. The opener (one no-trump) must now bid at least to game.

Now it is the opener's turn to rebid. If he rebids two diamonds over the responder's two clubs, or two no-trump over the responder's two diamonds, he doesn't have a four-card major.

Suppose the bidding has gone:

OPENER	RESPONDER
One no-trump	Two clubs
Two diamonds	

The responder, by passing, has a weak hand with a void or singleton in clubs, but support for the other suits.

The responder, by bidding either major at the two level, shows either a five- or six-card suit in that major, with between five and eight points.

Suppose the bidding has gone:

OPENER	RESPONDER
One no-trump	Two clubs
Two diamonds, hearts, or spades	

The responder, by bidding two no-trump, shows eight or nine high-card points with no fit in opener's major suit.

By bidding a minor suit at the three level, the responder shows either a four-card major or five- or six-card minor.

Suppose the bidding has gone:

OPENER	RESPONDER
One no-trump	Two clubs
Two spades	Three hearts

The responder is showing a five-card major, but with only eight or nine points in high cards. This is not a forcing bid.

If the opener in the above sequence had rebid two hearts and the responder had rebid three hearts, it would be an invitation to game.

If the opener had rebid two hearts and the responder had rebid two spades, this would also be an invitation to game.

Likewise, a responder's bid of three hearts over opener's rebid of two spades is forcing to game.

Suppose the bidding has gone:

OPENER	RESPONDER
One no-trump	Two diamonds
Two of a major	Two no-trump

This rebid by the responder of two no-trump is asking the opener to show either a second suit or to rebid his five-card major suit.

On the opener's initial one no-trump bid, if the responder bids either two hearts, two spades, four hearts, or four spades, he is signing off the bidding at that level—either two or game.

The same holds true with a responder's initial bid of three in either minor suit.

However, if, after the first one no-trump bid, the responder bids three in either major, this is an invitation to slam, showing six or seven in the major.

Gerber rather than Blackwood is used with the two-way Stayman, so that asking for aces after an opening one no-trump bid will be a bid of four clubs by the responder, or the following bid sequence, which will also be Gerber, asking for aces:

OPENER	RESPONDER
One no-trump	Two diamonds
Two hearts, spades, or no-trump	Four clubs

However, if the responded rebids four no-trump to either an opening one no-trump bid or to a two-level bid as in the above sequence, this is a natural bid, and not Blackwood, asking for aces.

Bridge, especially at the tournament level, has become increasingly complex in the last twenty years or so, with more and more bidding conventions being used as standard procedure.

What we suggest to the reader is, as he or she becomes more competent as a player and attempts to play in tournaments with a regular partner, to study these conventions in depth, by getting a book such as Edwin B. Kantar's *Bridge Conventions*. We've tried to show some of the more popular conventions to acquaint the reader with the elements of modern bidding, and hope this will be used as a springboard to further study.

Declarer's Play

There are several tactical strategies available to the declarer as he attempts to make his contract. Some of these same strategies may be used by the defenders as well, should they gain control of the play of the hand.

Ruffing and Trumping

If a declarer is void in a suit, he can either trump the led suit (ruff it) or discard a card from another suit. Declarer can also lead a side suit (not trump), either from his hand or from dummy, and being void in the other hand, establish the trick by trumping it.

Crossruffing

This is a method of ruffing in both hands, leading a suit to one hand, trumping it, returning a different suit to the other hand, and trumping it in that hand. In crossruffing, there is a void suit in each hand. The following is an illustration of successful crossruffing:

NORTH
♠ x x
♥ J 10 x x
♦ x
♣ A Q 9 8 x x

WEST
♠ Q J x
♥ x x
♦ K Q 9 x x x
♣ x x

EAST
♠ K 10 9 x
♥ x x
♦ A x
♣ K J 10 x x

SOUTH
♠ A x x x
♥ A K Q 9 x
♦ J 10 x x
♣ —

East was dealer. The bidding went

EAST	SOUTH	WEST	NORTH
Pass	One heart	Pass	Two clubs
Pass	Two hearts	Pass	Four hearts

West led the ♠ Q, which was won by South's ace. He returned a small diamond to drive out East's ace. East returned a trump won by South, who played back a diamond, ruffing it in dummy. He then cashed (won the trick with) the ace of clubs, discarding a diamond, then ruffed a club. Declarer was then in a position of crossruffing back and forth between the two hands, making his contract.

Establishing Long Suits

In order to establish a long suit and take in winning tricks with the small cards in that suit, the declarer must make sure that the defenders cannot trump the long suit. As a precaution, therefore, he should play out trump, exhausting the defenders' trump holdings before running the long side suit.

The Finesse

This is one of the basic maneuvers of declarer play and is used for several reasons. The finesse itself may be defined as a lead or play toward a broken sequence of cards in order to take advantage of the favorable position of the opponent's card by playing the lower of the sequence cards so as to make the trick.

An illustration will make the concept simple. You are South, the declarer. Your dummy holds the ace and queen of a suit. You lead toward dummy with a small card, hoping that West holds the king in that suit. Here's how it looks:

NORTH
A Q

WEST
?

SOUTH
2

If West holds the king of that suit and plays low, your queen will be a good trick. You are trying to finesse the queen and establish it as a good trick. Of course, if East holds the king, your finesse fails.

If possible, avoid finesses unless they are essential to the making of the contract. There is the possibility that they will fail, costing you one or more tricks. If you have a long second suit that can be established to make the contract or a finesse, play the percentages and establish the second suit.

Entries

An entry is just what the name implies—a means of "entering" a hand by playing a card to the particular hand that can be won in that hand. For example, if dummy holds an ace in a suit, and you, as declarer, lead a low card to that ace, the ace is your entry into dummy's hand.

Often, a declarer finds that he cannot make a contract because of lack of entries into a particular hand. If he holds the following cards in dummy and in his hand . . .

NORTH
4 3 2

SOUTH (D)
A Q J

. . . and East holds the king of that suit, then theoretically, if South could get to dummy twice more, he could establish the A Q J as winning tricks. However, if he has no entries he is out of luck. A declarer should always ensure entries in both the dummy and declarer's hands. Conversely, the defenders often try to deplete the entries to stop the contract.

Probability of Breaks in Suits

In the play of the hand it is important to know the probable division of cards in particular suits out against you. Of course, the division will not always adhere to the odds, but it is a good guide to follow if you rely on a suit break to make a contract. All the percentages are approximate.

Cards in Suit Out Against You	Possible Division of Cards	Percentage
Two	one-one	52
	two-none	48
Three	two-one	78
	three-none	22
Four	three-one	50
	two-two	40
	four-none	10
Five	three-two	67
	four-one	29
	five-none	4
Six	four-two	48
	three-three	35
	five-one	15
	six-none	2
Seven	four-three	61
	five-two	31
	six-one	7
	seven-none	1

Declarer's Strategy

After the bidding is completed and the first play has been made toward dummy, and the dummy exposed, the declarer should take time to plan his strategy for the play of the hand.

First he should review the bidding in his mind, and weigh the information it has revealed. If only one defender bid, he must be assumed to have the high-card strength that is missing. This is not always true, but true often enough to be a definite consideration. Perhaps one of the defenders opened the bidding. If he opened with a major suit, it can be assumed that he holds five cards in that suit, and that his point count in high cards and distributional strength is at least thirteen. With this information, an appropriate strategy can then be planned.

If one defender doubled the contract, and there were no other bids entered by the defenders, the declarer would then have to surmise the reason for the double. Perhaps the doubler has the cards to stop the contract, or perhaps he surmises that his partner has such cards. In any event, an important consideration is the playing strength of the opponents. This is not always discernible in duplicate play, because you, as declarer, may meet them only once during the entire course of play. However, a double is a red flag shown to the declarer and he must adjust his play accordingly.

If neither defender bid, then there is nothing to be learned from the bidding, other than the fact that both players opposing the contract may not have biddable hands. If the contract is low, at a two or three level, it may be that the honors are evenly distributed between the two defenders, or that neither player has a biddable suit. Thus, even passes supply information to the declarer.

After the opening lead, the declarer should examine that lead before playing one of dummy's cards. Why that lead? Why that suit? Is it a lead from a short suit, or is it a lead hoping to find out if the partner has strength in that suit? Is it the correct lead for the situation, or is it the lead of a weak player? All these questions should present themselves to an intelligent declarer.

If the lead is correct, the declarer must then and there ask himself: In what hand does he want to take the trick? What will be his next play? Before answering these questions, the declarer must examine the cards in both hands and decide on a strategy.

He should count his absolute winning tricks, then decide on the course of play to follow to make up other tricks if the sure tricks will not fulfill the contract. If there are enough sure tricks to make the contract, a safe course of play would be in order. If there are not enough tricks for contract, the overall strategy should be reviewed at that first trick, not later in the game when pressures of play may cloud the thinking process.

If a declarer finds himself short one or two tricks, he must decide on a course of action. Should he establish a second suit, or try a couple of finesses? Should he attack trumps or another suit, hoping for a good break in the suit? Before he can do this, he should know roughly how a suit will split. For that reason he should know the percentage table of suits.

To summarize quickly, the declarer should follow three basic rules.

First and foremost, he must stay alert. He must remember the bids, the leads, the cards discarded. He must also keep track of the suits, and know precisely how many cards in each suit have been played. Without this knowledge he will severely handicap himself.

Second, he must plan his strategy before the first trick is over, or, at the latest, right after that first trick. He must know what he intends to do, and then follow through. In case of bad breaks, he must also have alternative courses to victory, to making the contract.

Third, he must play percentages. He cannot disregard the odds in any situation. If West, his opponent, opened the bidding, he cannot count on East to have all the high cards. If a finesse has only a fifty-percent chance of succeeding, while the chances of establishing a long suit are sixty-eight percent in his favor, he must establish that long suit, and not disregard a favorable opportunity.

Of course, there are other basic considerations to be examined by the declarer. He should know how to play out his hand correctly; remember to leave entries; remember to keep control of play. All these come from study and experience, and, together with alertness, strategical planning, and playing the percentages, will make him a better player.

Defender's Play

Since the object of the declarer's play is to make the contract and, if possible, overtricks, the first object of the defenders is to defeat the contract. If the contract cannot be defeated by best play, then the second object is to limit the declarer to the contract itself, without overtricks. This is important in contract bridge, and of the utmost importance in duplicate bridge.

The first problem confronting a defender is the opening lead. No matter what the contract, the defender is going to be faced with this problem. Often, an opening lead by a defender will determine whether or not the declarer can make his contract, and very often it will determine who will have control of the play.

As we know, the lead is made to dummy, who then puts down his cards. The declarer, in all contracts, is the fourth to play. This is important to remember, for if both the declarer and dummy have bid, the defender making the opening lead should have some idea of where their respective strength lies. If the bidding by declarer had been spades, and the dummy had bid diamonds, it would be foolish to lead a spade, since the lead would be to the declarer's strength and he may then control the hand.

Therefore, we must examine those principles which govern the opening defensive lead.

1. If your partner has doubled to indicate a particular opening lead, you should open the suit your partner has signaled for by his double. A perfect example of this is when your partner has doubled a slam contract and thus asked for an unsual lead. Lead that suit. In defending against no-trump contracts, if the doubler does not have the opening lead, he may be asking for the suit bid by the defenders if only one suit was bid, or, if both defenders have bid, the doubler's bid suit.

2. Where there has been no double directing a particular lead, the best lead is the suit bid by your partner.

3. If your partner has not bid, then you can lead your best suit if your partner has raised you in that suit. Leading your best suit otherwise may create problems, since you might lose control of the hand if you give away your strength at the beginning.

4. If a suit has gone unbid, it is a good idea to lead that suit, since it might be the weak point of your opponents. If there is more than one unbid suit, calculate from the bidding if the dummy has strength in that suit and lead through the dummy, if possible, rather than leading to the declarer's strength.

5. If you're unsure of what to lead, it is best to lead through dummy's strength since that gives your partner the perfect position (third) to play his strong cards.

6. If your opponents, and especially the declarer, have a very strong trump suit, avoid that lead at all costs. But if your opponents have weak trumps and expect to make their tricks by ruffing or crossruffing, lead a trump to deplete their holding in trumps and prevent this.

7. If you hold a singleton, lead it if you expect that your partner will be able to take in the trick and come right back so that you can ruff. Generally, this will be a lead in a suit that you have not bid and that the opponents have bid on, and your partner should recognize that it is an unusual lead. It is particularly effective if dummy has bid that suit, since your partner may be in a position to cover dummy's card.

8. If you have good trump holdings of four or more and a long side suit as well, it might pay to play the long suit, forcing the opponents to trump and weakening their trumps so that later you can establish that long suit.

9. Against no-trump, lead your longest and strongest suit. If you have a weak hand with no suit that looks inviting to lead, try to lead through dummy's strength if this is a suit you figure your partner has some strength in.

The following are leads suggested by particular holdings in suits. If partner has not doubled for a lead signal, but has bid a suit and you hold these cards, lead as directed.

8 6—Lead the 8, the general rule being to lead the top card of a doubleton holding. If holding a 10 9, or J 10, in each case lead the higher of the two cards.

A 9 4—Lead the top card here, the ace.

Q 7 5—Lead the third-best card. This is true where there is an honor heading a three-card holding. (The exception is where the ace is the honor.) Thus, holding J x x, or K x x, lead the lowest card.

Where there is a holding of four cards and the top two cards are in sequence, such as 10 9 or Q J or K Q, such as K Q x x, lead the top card of the holding, in this latter case the king. Again, there is an exception where the top card is an ace, such as A K x x, in which case the king is led.

However, where there is a four-card holding, the top card alone being an honor (such as J x x x, or Q x x x, or K x x x), lead the lowest card.

If your partner has made no bids and you lead from the following holdings, lead as directed.

10 9, or 9 8, etc.—Lead the top card of the two-card sequence.

A K—Lead the ace.

When holding a three-card suit with the top card being an honor, such as K 6 4, or Q 7 3, lead the lowest card of the sequence.

If you hold three honors, such as K Q 10 or K J 10, lead the middle honor.

When holding a four-card suit with an honor at the top, such as Q 9 7 5, lead the fourth card, or lowest, of the sequence.

When holding three honors in a four-card sequence, lead the best card, the highest honor. Example: If you hold Q J 10 6, lead the queen. Holding K Q 10 3, lead the king.

If you hold any sequence of three with an A Q at the top, do not lead this suit. These holdings are A Q x, A Q J, and A Q 10.

Rule of Eleven

For many years the customary practice was to play the fourth-highest card in a suit on the opening lead. Therefore, a mathematical calculation was developed which enabled the leader's partner and the declarer to figure out the number of higher cards remaining in the three other hands.

If each of the cards from 2 to 10 are assigned the value of their face markings (that is, the 2 is assigned the value of two, the 3 three, and so on), we are prepared to work out the calculation afforded by the Rule of Eleven, which is as follows:

Subtract the value of the card led from eleven, and that will give the number of higher cards than the one led remaining in the other three hands.

For example: If a 7 was led, subtracting that card's value of seven from eleven gives us four, and that is how many cards above 7 are remaining in the other three hands. Another example: A five is led. If we subtract five from eleven, that leaves six cards higher than the five remaining in the other three hands.

Let us suppose that we are the leader's partner. He has led the 6. We see the following cards of that suit: The 6 is on the table; dummy shows Q 10 4; we hold A J 8 2.

If we use the Rule of Eleven, we subtract the 6 led from eleven, and the number of higher cards in the other three hands is five. Since the dummy holds two cards higher than the 6, and we hold three cards higher, that makes a total of five cards higher than the card led. This means that the declarer has no cards higher than the 6. If dummy's 4 is played, we can play the 8 and win the trick. We also know that our partner, who was the original lead, holds the king of that suit, as well as the 9 and 7.

If the original leader gets in again and leads a card from the suit lower than the 6, the declarer is void in that suit. If, however, he leads a higher card and dummy plays the 10 or queen, either of these two cards will lose to our ace or jack.

The declarer, as well as the leader's partner, can gain valuable information from the opening lead by applying the Rule of Eleven.

Let us assume we're the declarer and the same lead of 6 is made. This is what we see on the table.

DUMMY
A Q 7 3 2

LEADER'S CARD		LEADER'S PARTNER PLAYS
6		5

DECLARER
9 8 4

Using the Rule of Eleven, we subtract six from eleven and find that there are five cards higher than the 6 that was led. Since dummy holds three of them and we hold the other two, the partner of the leader holds none. Therefore, the leader holds the king, jack, and 10, and two finesses can safely be made through the leader's hand.

The Rule of Eleven is based solely on the lead of the *fourth-best* card in a suit. If the card led is not the fourth best, the rule should not be applied. In recent years, if a small card is led it may indicate a return in that suit rather than fourth best. Also, many players do not blindly follow the custom of leading fourth best for the simple reason that a calculation by the declarer may make the lead too revealing. So the declarer must decide whether the lead is truly fourth best before applying the Rule of Eleven.

Leads Against No-Trump Contracts

Lead the fourth-highest card from your longest and strongest suit. This is especially true when you hold one or two high cards from other suits so that you can again retain the lead and keep playing your longest and strongest suit. Eventually, you will establish the small cards in your best suit as winning tricks.

The Rule of Eleven will serve your partner well as he will be able to take an immediate count of your holdings in your best suit. He then might be in a position, with the lead, of continuing the led suit in order to establish control of that suit and make your small cards into winning tricks.

When your partner has made an overcall or bid a suit during the bidding and you hold two or three small cards in that suit, play the top card you hold. If you hold an honor card heading a holding of three cards in your partner's suit, lead the small card; but if you hold an honor in a doubleton, lead the honor.

When your partner has made no bid, but dummy bid without a response in that suit by declarer, then lead that suit through dummy's strength in the hope of finding your partner with strength in that suit.

If your partner doubled the no-trump contract (especially three no-trump contracts) and neither of you has bid, lead dummy's first-bid suit. This is a conventional lead through dummy's strength.

Examples of conventional leads against no-trump games when your partner has bid:

If holding A x x x or K x x x, lead the fourth best.

If holding K x x, Q x x, or J x x, lead the third best or lowest card.

If holding x x, Q J, K J, A x, lead the top of the two cards.

If your team has made no bids and dummy has bid, play dummy's suit. If holding 10 x, play the 10; if holding J 10, lead the jack; and if holding 8 7 5, lead the 8. If holding Q x x x, K x x x, A x x x, or K Q J x, lead the fourth best. If holding K 10 8 6 4, lead fourth best. If holding Q J 10 x x or A K Q x x x, lead the top card from those suits.

Other Defensive Plays

Second Hand Low

As a general rule, the second hand plays low. This is a usual tactic which prevents the opponents from running or establishing a suit. An example: You hold A 8 3; dummy holds K Q 5 2. The 6 is led to you. If you play the ace, then dummy's king and queen are safe and will control the suit. If you play low, dummy must play either the king or queen, still giving you control of the suit with the ace. If dummy held K J 5 2, then your partner may hold the queen in that suit, and a decision will now have to be made by declarer whether to play the king or jack. If he plays the jack it might very well lose to your partner's queen. If he plays the king, you still retain control of the suit.

If you hold A 8 3 and a low lead is made to dummy's holding of K 5 3 2, again it pays to play low, rather than giving up the ace. Declarer may hold the queen and thus be in a position to run the suit. By holding up the ace, you retain control.

Of course, there are exceptions to this and every other defensive rule, but if you play low on second hand, nine times out of ten you are making the right decision.

Third Hand High

Just as you would play low as second hand, in third hand you must endeavor to play high, either to take the trick or to force out higher cards in the fourth hand. This is a general rule also and is correct most of the time.

An elementary example:

```
                    DUMMY
                    8 7 2
    WEST                        EAST
    K 10 6 3                    Q 5 4
                    DECLARER
                    A J 9
```

West plays the 3; dummy plays the 2; and now East puts on the queen, playing third hand high. If East also played low, then declarer could win with the 9 and still retain control of the suit. By playing the queen, East will win the trick or force out declarer's ace. If the ace is forced out, on the next lead by East any play through the same suit will cost declarer both the jack and 9.

Another example:

```
                    DUMMY
                    Q 8 4
    WEST                        EAST
    J 10 5 3                    K 9 2
                    DECLARER
                    A 7 6
```

West leads the 3; dummy plays the 4. Now East should play the 9. If he plays the king, he will allow the queen to establish a trick. What third hand is doing, in essence, is standing over the dummy, preventing it from taking control. If, instead, the queen was played from dummy, East would have to play the king, covering an honor with an honor. This will either force out declarer's ace and establish West's jack and 10 as winners, or, if declarer holds up the ace, another lead of the same suit by East will force out the ace or enable West to win the trick with either the jack or 10.

Covering an Honor With an Honor

As we saw in the previous hand, covering an honor with an honor (by putting the king on the queen) forced out declarer's ace, and declarer had to give up two honors to take in the king.

Bridge players generally make this percentage play of covering an honor with a higher honor. However, it is not always advantageous, particularly when dummy has a sequence of honors and the defender has only one covering honor. Let's take this example.

NORTH (*Dummy*)
Q J 9 3

WEST   EAST
10 8 4   K 7 2

SOUTH
A 6 5

North (dummy) plays the queen; East plays the 2, playing low; South plays the 5; and West plays the 4. The queen has been finessed successfully. Now the jack is led from dummy; East covers with the king; and South wins with his ace. This play enables West to win the next trick in that suit with his 10. If East had covered with the king on the very first play, South would have been able to finesse the jack and 9 through West's 10 and 8 and win every trick in the suit.

Another example:

NORTH
J 10 x

WEST   EAST
Q 8 x x   K 9 x

SOUTH
A x x

The jack is led from dummy. If East covers with his king, then South would win two tricks in the suit.

East should play low, for if he covers with the king, South will win his ace; then a return of an x, allowing West to win with his queen, would establish dummy's 10 as the second trick. The difference of one trick in this situation may well spell the difference between defeating the contract or permitting it to be made.

More Defensive Plays

If your partner plays a suit, it is usually a signal to you to return that suit at the earliest opportunity. This is certainly important in defending against a no-trump contract; there are exceptions in defending against a suit contract, for sometimes each partner may lead to the strength of the other partner. But in defending against no-trump, return your partner's suit.

Lead through strength and up to weakness of the dummy's cards. This is particularly important if you see that dummy has a holding led by K J or A Q, for the missing honor may very well be in your partner's hand and leading through dummy's strength in this way is to your partnership advantage.

If the dummy is weak, showing no honors and, perhaps, 8 6 4 2, and you are to dummy's left, lead up to the weakness of dummy, who will be fourth hand. This allows your partner, who is just before dummy, to take in tricks with his strength. By leading up to dummy's weakness, you are leading through declarer's strength, killing two birds, as it were, with one stone.

Signals

Since bridge is a partnership, signals are of utmost importance. Of course, we are referring to legitimate signals which are expressed through the play of the cards. One of the best is the high-low signal.

The first of the signals comes when your partner plays a 6 or higher card on a card led by you. He is telling you to continue the suit. If he plays a lower card than a 6, he is discouraging you from continuing that suit. This kind of signal is predicated on the fact that there are other lower cards that could have been played by your partner. Suppose you hold K 8 6 3 and you want your partner to continue that suit; it is better to drop the 8, which is a definite signal, rather than the 6, which might have been your lowest card.

In a no-trump contract, your partner opens with a lead of a queen, and dummy shows 5 3. You hold the K 9 6 2 of the suit. You would signal with the 9, telling your partner to go ahead and continue the suit. In this situation, if the queen takes the trick it is probably because the declarer held up his ace, and the lead of the queen was probably from a sequence of Q J 10 x or Q J 9 x. Another lead of the suit will force out declarer's ace and establish the suit for your partnership. Should the declarer again refuse the suit, the same suit should be played back. Eventually your partner's small cards will be winning tricks.

In defending against suit contracts, any high card played by a partner, followed by a low card of the same suit on the next lead, asks his partner for a continuation of the same suit. This signal shows either a high honor card, capable of winning the next lead, or shows that the partner is void in the suit, allowing a ruff to win the trick.

These signals also have another purpose—showing or indicating the rank of another suit. Let's suppose that your partner leads an ace toward dummy's king and has no reason to continue, and you follow with a high card of the same suit. This signal asks the partner to play to the highest-ranking of the dummy's suits. But remember, signals always omit the trump suit when used this way.

A good example now of signals in a no-trump contract.

North and South are in three no-trump. West's and East's holdings are as follows:

WEST	EAST
♠ A 7 3	♠ Q 8 4
♥ 9 7 5 4 2	♥ A K J

West leads his ♥4; dummy plays a queen from a doubleton holding of Q 6; East wins with the king and plays back his ace, on which West plays the deuce to signify a five-card suit (using the Rule of Eleven). This shows that the declarer started with only three cards in that suit. East cashes in his jack, dropping declarer's 10, and now West has the opportunity to show a suit preference by signaling with a card. By playing his 9 from 9 7 5 (all winning tricks now), he is asking for a shift to the highest-ranking suit of dummy's cards. Since it is no-trump, the highest-ranking suit is spades and his partner would make a spade lead as directed. He plays a small spade. West wins with his ace and cashes the two good hearts to defeat the contract.

Without the play of the 9, East would have had to guess what suit to lead on his next play, and might possibly not have picked the spade, thus giving declarer the contract.

The Trump Echo
In defensive play it may become important to inform your partner as to how many trumps you are holding. To do this, a high-low signal is used.

For example, if on the first trick taken in by your partner he ruffs with the 5 of trumps, and on the next lead he ruffs with the 3 of trumps, this is a high-low signal informing you that he has exactly three trumps.

A final and perhaps most important word on defensive play: It is mandatory that the defenders count their tricks. Sometimes the correct play will present itself naturally when the defender has counted his tricks and knows he needs one more to set the contract. If he is sure that he holds the setting trick, or that his partner holds it, then the correct play to insure a defeat of the contract is to at once make that setting trick. Too often, poor players delay doing this, for whatever reason, until, to their dismay, they see the declarer start to unload the losers in his hand on ruffs and cross-ruffs.

Cheating at Bridge

Rarely is anything written about cheating at the game of contract bridge. The *Laws of Contract Bridge* does not take cheats into consideration in their penalty section; the official attitude seems to be that it would be wrong to accord cheats any sort of status by acknowledging their existence and providing definite remedies for their activities.

Cheating can be done at both duplicate and rubber bridge. In the first, cheating can be for master points, prestige, or fame; in the latter, for money. There was a great scandal concerning two international players who were accused of cheating by allegedly holding their hands in a certain way to indicate heart strength, and heart strength only. This was allegedly done at the highest level of play. They were eventually acquitted of the charge, but it brought the possibility of cheating at bridge to the forefront.

It is certainly difficult for a cardsharp or cheat operating alone to make any difference in either duplicate or rubber bridge. The main deterrent is the fact that bridge, above all, is a partnership game, and this definitely militates against cheating. But a lone cheat, working with a partner who does not participate in the cheating, but merely acquiesces, can be quite effective.

We'll call the cheat about to be described Mr. C. (*C* standing for cheat). He was an excellent player, a potential champion who occasionally liked to play in the more important duplicate tournaments. He had a steady partner, his wife, but he played with her only in rubber games. She was as good as he was, and could cheat just as effectively, but in a duplicate tournament out of town (he was a New Yorker) what could be better than mixing master points with pleasure? And his pleasure was young girls or young women (his bridge pupils or acquaintances), who would take the trip with him, stay at the same hotel, and have the honor of being his partner.

It was quite an honor, because to play with him was an experience. It was having as one's partner the perfect player. He made no wrong bids; he made no wrong plays; he could gauge all the hands immediately by the bidding. He would gently guide your play by correct leads, by legitimate signals. I played with him in a couple of small duplicate games in Manhattan and I didn't even have to bid to get to the correct contract. He had that instinct that I've never seen in any other player. His name is not a household word—far from it—but in big rubber games he is a demon, and those who have faced him for large stakes will never forget him.

Mr. C is getting old, but age has not taken away any of his sharpness. Now he still has pretty girls around him (his pupils, not acquaintances), but they're near him for his charm alone. Alas, age has withered him that way. They still love to play bridge with him as a partner, and they love to listen to his anecdotes about the great players and the great and not-so-great hands he has held, and he has held a lot of them over the years.

He still plays, but not for big stakes anymore. A recent cataract operation has put him at a disadvantage and his eyes can't take the pressure of looking at the cards for too long. But for short intervals of play, he is still a master.

Mr. C, in his prime (and way past his prime as well, if you want to know the truth), would take a pretty girl with him to Chicago, Atlantic City, Los Angeles, wherever a big tournament was being held. There she would be, this young bridge buff, among the great names of the game, all of whom knew Mr. C, by sight or by reputation, and she would be introduced to this great player and that one. The men introduced were courtly and getting on in years, and bridge players of this caliber, away from the table, can be quite gallant.

The girl with Mr. C was an acquiescent cheat. What that means is that she would do whatever Mr. C told her to do. She would obey no matter what her holdings and no matter what her own inclinations. She trusted his ability to handle the game for both of them.

Mr. C's advice to her was, "don't do anything on your own. If you have thirteen points, open the bidding with your best suit. Open it, and then shut up. If you have sixteen to eighteen points and are the first bidder, open one no-trump. If you have more than eighteen points, open at a two level with your best suit. If I open the bidding and you have more than six points, bid one over one, and that's it. If you have opening strength after my opening bid, jump and shift to your best suit. In other words, if I bid one heart and you have opening strength, bid two spades, if spades is your suit; and three if your suit is a minor.

"Don't bid otherwise. Don't bid after your opening bid or your response. If I bid four no-trump, bid your aces in the Blackwood convention. No other bids. The best bid you can make is to shut your mouth. After your one bid, I'll handle it.

"If I lead a small card or play a small card and you get in, lead a minor suit; which one should be apparent to you. If you don't know which one, lead one of them but not a major suit. If I play a high card, lead a major suit. If I double a slam and bid a suit, lead that suit. If I double a no-trump and bid a suit, lead that suit. I don't care what you're holding, do as I say."

And there would be the girls, playing with this magician. They did very well, winning a couple of trophies, winning master points, even winning a tournament. He had one big advantage—he wasn't married to any of them. Imagine trying to tell a wife, "Don't do anything but shut up. Play and bid only as I direct."

I asked Mr. C how this could work against really good players.

"It worked best against the best players, believe it or not. Let me give you an example. My girl of the moment and myself sit down in a duplicate tournament against a husband-and-wife team, both good players. Both may or may not know me well, but they don't know the girl, haven't seen her around. Just watching her pick up the cards they know she's hardly ever touched a deck of cards in her life. Maybe I just taught her the game a couple of months before. But she follows instructions.

"They look at the conventions I put on the sheet. I show Blackwood. They ask me if I play Stayman. Worse, they ask my girl. She gives them a blank look. She knows as much about Stayman as I know about brain surgery. No, I say, we don't play Stayman.

"After this short exchange, they know she's a yokel, and they're already licking their chops. A good high score, they figure, against this pair. Here's old Mr. C with a dumb chick he had to take along, else how can he get away from the missus? That's their first two mistakes. First, I can get away from my wife any damn time I please. And second, they're getting overconfident. We pick up our cards and the bidding begins. I'm sitting West, and South opens with a pass. I look at my cards and have an opening bid, maybe twelve points in high cards, but with my partner I've got to get into the bidding. I bid any suit; it doesn't matter to me. I bid one club. I want to see what my partner has. I may not even have a club, but it's a low bid, and if my partner responds, we keep the bidding low.

"Right way the wife, who's about to bid, looks at the sheet to see if I put down artificial club or five-card majors or whatever. All it says is Blackwood. She looks at her hand, this witch, and bids one spade. An overcall. I know she can't be strong enough to double then, and now I wait for my partner to bid. She knows nothing about overcalls or doubles; she only knows what I told her. She's still busy counting her points and says two hearts.

"Now the husband has his turn. I know we have at least eighteen points in our hands, and they have at best twenty-two, so where's the contract going? Nowhere. He bids two spades, and I look over my hand. I got a singleton club, a few hearts, a few spades, and a strong diamond suit. I say three clubs.

"The wife doubles right away. My partner passes. She has no other choice because my instructions were to keep quiet after her one bid. The husband passes, and I bid three diamonds. Wifey doubles, and all pass, and there I am in three diamonds.

The hand was cold. My partner gave me seven points and three diamonds headed by the jack. I had six of my own headed by the ace king. Of course, our method of bidding threw them off, but they were too confident to begin with.

The husband and wife were stunned. Far from asking top score, they were screwed up by the deal. They started arguing with me, asking how I could bid one club with a diamond opening bid, but as nature took its course, they started arguing with each other."

" 'Why didn't you shift to clubs?' the husband wanted to know, and 'Why should I?' the wife replied, 'it would have made no difference.' And then they started arguing about the bids, and how could she double three diamonds. 'Why not?' she angrily replied, and so on and so forth. Meanwhile, we had moved to another table. My beautiful girl friend sat down, kept her mouth shut, and we came off with another nice score."

I asked Mr. C about other duplicate-bridge games which didn't involve pretty girls.

"I sometimes was paid by my pupils to enter duplicate tournaments with them. Some of them were fairly well off and would pay all my expenses, wherever it was. And of course they were sports in other ways. If they wanted a good partner, I played that way, perfectly legit. They enjoyed it; I didn't, but got a good weekend out of it, so it was fun anyway. Others were desperate for master points and they figured I was the perfect vehicle to get them, so off we would go. If they were very, very bad, I gave them the same pep talk I gave the cuties.

"Sometimes they were fairly good and wanted all the edge. If the players we were sitting down with were very strong, I would tell the partner, 'Sit up and pay attention this hand.' If the players were poor, I would say, 'Sit down and play well this time.'

"Sometimes I would show them little hand signals to indicate my card strength or a lead. If I touched the right-hand part of the deck, it was spades;

the extreme left was clubs; near the spades was hearts; and near the clubs was diamonds. Simple and easy. These partners were always perfect leaders.

"Just holding the cards up a little was a strong hand, and down, a weak hand. Sometimes I would hold the cards up and pass, and my partner knew I was ready to spring a trap. Things like that. I could go on and on, because, in a partnership game, with words and gestures and lighting of cigarettes and touching of glasses, my God, it's like being a coach at third base."

Mr. C told me about some rubber games he was involved in.

"I always played for high stakes, because what was the use otherwise? I would get sick of sitting on my ass and playing cards sometimes, and it was no fun playing a couple of dumb suckers and winning a couple of bucks. I'd rather be at the trotters, or trying to work my way into some girl's pants. But if the money was right, there I was. How did I do it?

"My wife, God rest her soul, was a great bridge player and a great . . . I hesitate to use the word 'cheat.' Let me just say she could play with the best of them. If I could, I'd play with her against a couple of suckers. It was better sometimes to play with a stranger, because if they knew my wife was playing and we were the only winners, even though we switched partners they would get suspicious.

"I had several partners, all topnotch players. In bridge, the game is so technical and skillful that if you're a cheat but not a good player, you might still be at a disadvantage. So I had a few good partners. We would be at some club where there were big games, and we'd take on two suckers— either they were strangers or they knew each other—and we'd play a rubber game for some big money. Of course, to the suckers, I didn't know my partner, and we'd play as partners or switch; it didn't matter.

"Either way, the suckers got it. If I had a sucker as a partner, sometimes with a big hand I'd pass, then throw them in if all passed. Sometimes I'd let the sucker win. Most of the time I'd try and be dummy and let the sucker play—a sure way for him to lose.

"The ideal game is to have only one sucker and three sharps in the game. That's the perfect setup, and here's how it's done. We could play at a club or, better still, in some hotel room we rented in one of the better hotels. We'd never use marked cards—they have little value in bridge— but we'd keep a stacked deck sometimes.

"In cheating, there are two things to remember. One, if the sucker has a little larceny, he's ideal for a cheat. Two, if he has to persuade you to play with him, it's an ideal situation. So, all of us strangers to each other perhaps, but known only as good card players, we'd set the sucker up. One of us would bring him along to watch—only watch. There'd be four of us, and since we would tell him we were all great players, he could only watch.

"Watching bridge is like watching someone get laid. You want to get into the act. Here we'd play a couple of rubbers in this hotel suite, with the sucker looking on, just drooling. Then one of the foursome would have to leave, and I'd say, 'Let's call it a night.' But the sucker would say, 'Wait a minute, why not me?'

"I was always the good guy. I'd say, 'No, it's a big game, and you're not up to it. You're really not. I didn't invite you up to lose your money.'

"Well, to a sucker's honor, the idea that he's not that good really hurts. He insists that he is up to us in skill, and so, reluctantly, we let him in. We often played steady partners or, better still, rotated. We'd rotate, telling the sucker we wanted to even things out.

"If you really put a sucker down as to his skill, he gets stubborn. He wants to play with only one partner. So we let him. After a few bad rubbers, in which we murder them, my partner and I leave the room. We go for a drink, or water, or a cigarette, and we leave the sucker with his partner, who tells him, 'Look, buddy, I'm losing a fortune. Why don't you pick another partner?' The sucker protests, then the partner says, 'Okay, play with me, but we need a little help. Now here's what we do. . . .'

"As he explains his cheating methods, nine times out of ten, or ninety-nine out of a hundred, the sucker is all ears. He wants to win, and so just a little larceny won't hurt anybody. And if he agrees, he's going to be doubly murdered. If he backs out, the partner says, 'Never mind. Take another partner. Take Mr. C, the good guy.' And so now I inherit the honest sucker. It still does him no good.

"But if he goes along with the partner's suggestion about cheating, he is buried. We don't even let him win twenty percent of the time, and we can even get a little reckless because he has no protest—he's a cheat himself."

I asked Mr. C about any advice he could give.

"Play in a legitimate bridge club, or among friends at home, and play for the love of the game. It's a great game, a skillful game, and the mere skill involved in this game should supply all the excitement you'd ever want."

Irregularities

The following are the most common irregularities in bridge; not all of the possible infractions of the rules can be listed here. The reader is advised to read the *Laws of Contract Bridge,* published by the American Contract Bridge League.

Failure to follow suit: If a player has failed to follow suit—that is, failed to play the same suit as led when he still holds a card of that suit—

this is called a revoke, and any player may call attention to the failure and demand that the revoke be corrected. A revoke is established if the trick is finished and the revoking player plays another card.

The offending player may correct his revoke without penalty, but this must be done before the trick is completed, which occurs when a new lead is played.

If a revoke is established, the penalty is two tricks. If, however, after the revoke occurs the revoking side does not make any more tricks, then the penalty is just the one revoked trick.

Exposed card: Any card dropped on the table face up becomes an exposed card and must be left on the table. If the lead is in the same suit, that card must remain on the table and be played.

If another suit is led and the player whose card is exposed is void in that suit, then the card exposed must be played to the lead.

If the lead is to a suit other than the exposed card's suit, the offender must play the correct suit, but must lead the exposed card if he subsequently gets the lead or play it at the first opportunity.

Lead Out of Turn: If it is one defender's turn to lead, but the other defender leads instead, the declarer may accept the lead, or demand that the correct defender play the same suit or play any other suit but that suit. The incorrect leader then returns the card to his hand.

Declarer Leading Out of Turn: Should the declarer lead from his hand instead of from the dummy when it is the dummy's turn to lead, he may replace the card in his hand, provided no other card was played by the defenders, and then lead a card of the same suit from dummy. He does not have to play the card incorrectly led, but must merely follow suit. Should the dummy be void in the incorrect suit led from his hand, any card may be led from dummy.

Lead Before the Auction is Completed: If a player makes a lead before the bidding is completed, the offender must leave the card face up on the table until the auction is completed. If the card led is an honor (jack, queen, king, or ace), then the offender's partner is barred from the bidding during the auction.

Should the card led be lower than an honor, it becomes an exposed card and is left face up on the table. If the auction is bought by the opposing team, the declarer can accept that card as a lead, or ask for the offender's partner to lead that suit. He may also ask for a different lead. Should he do this, the offender may replace the exposed card in his hand.

Pass Out of Turn During the Auction: Any player making a pass out of turn must pass when it is his turn to bid on the next round of bidding.

Bid Out of Turn: Any player making a bid out of turn (other than a pass) bars his partner from making any bids until the entire auction is over.

The offender, however, is not barred and may continue to bid if he desires.

Insufficient Bid: When a player makes a bid, or response, or overcall lower than the preceding bid of the opponents, he must make the correct bid of the same suit at a higher level. Should he decide not to, but instead bids another suit, his partner is barred from any bids for the entire auction.

Claiming All Tricks: When a declarer, during the play of the cards, claims the balance of the tricks, he must announce the manner in which he intends to play his cards out, and then must lay his entire hand, face up, on the table.

If he claims all tricks and does not announce the manner in which he intends to play out the hand, he must play all his top honor cards and take no finesses, unless the finesse was established on a previous play.

DUPLICATE BRIDGE

Introduction

Because rubber bridge is dependent upon the luck of the deal, duplicate bridge was devised to eliminate this element of chance. In duplicate bridge, identical hands are played by all participants, which usually consist of eight or more partnerships. In order for this to be done, each partnership plays either as a North-South team or as an East-West team, and each participant plays the identical hands held by the previous players sitting, for example, as North, if he is North. Thus the relative skill of the players manifests itself without the luck of the deal.

In order to do this, the equipment necessary is a duplicate board. (See Illustration.)

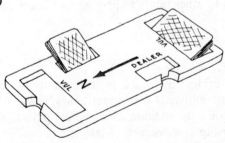

Duplicate board

This device holds four hands of a deal. The standard board is usually of metal. On it is an arrow pointing to the North hand. One of the sections designates the dealer, who is the first to bid. Also the vulnerability of any particular team is marked.

One of the advantages of playing duplicate bridge is that a player cannot afford either to bid or play sloppily since each deal is of the same importance as every other deal. Therefore, defending a one-diamond contract has as much validity as defending seven no-trump. It may yield more points to the defenders, since there is more likelihood that the seven-no-trump contract will be a cold, laydown hand, whereas the one-diamond contract might possibly be a mismatch.

Mechanics of Play

Each partnership is designated as either a North-South or East-West team, and is assigned a table and number at the outset of play. There will be a duplicate board at the table, with a deck of cards divided into four parts. The cards are put together, shuffled, and dealt out at random, thirteen cards to each player. Once each player gets his thirteen cards, he plays these cards, and all subsequent players at the same position during the session play the same cards.

In order to retain the same cards, when a trick is played the card played is not put into the center of the table but is put face up in front of the player, and then turned over after the play. If the trick was won, the longer edges face the partnership. After the play of the entire hand, the cards are picked up by each player and put into the slot marked for the player. The North player puts his cards into the North slot, etc. Then one team (East-West, for example) remains at the table, while the North-South team moves to other tables to play against other East-West teams.

Scoring

In duplicate bridge, there are no rubbers to be made. Each game played is a separate entity. If a contract below game is made, there is a premium of fifty points in addition to the actual points. This is so whether or not the partnership is vulnerable. Making game when vulnerable is an additional bonus of 500 points; when not vulnerable, it is 300 additional points.

To facilitate the scoring, a scoresheet is given to each team. On it is mentioned the board number (each board has one), the pair number (each partnership is given one), the final contract, whom it was played by, and the final plus or minus score and who scored it. After the scores are all in, the team scoring the highest or best score for one side gets the highest total. For example, if there are eight tables, the highest score will be seven (beating the other seven pairs), and so on. The highest total score of a partnership makes that partnership the winner.

The scoresheet is usually folded and kept with the board; it doesn't travel with the pairs. At the end of the game it is collected by the director of the tournament, and then the scores of all the pairs are totaled.

Laws and Rules

The laws governing duplicate bridge are put out by the National Laws Commission of the American Contract Bridge League and should be consulted.

A Final Word

For those players who have mastered bridge and wish to test their skill at higher levels, duplicate bridge is highly recommended. It is an exciting, competitive game, and through its competitiveness, the player with an open mind can only learn to play even better. It is best to have a steady partner to enjoy the game at its fullest.

VIII

Pinochle

♠ ♥ ♦ ♣

THREE-HANDED AUCTION WITH WIDOW

Rules of Play

The Pack: A pinochle deck consists of forty-eight cards. Each suit contains twelve cards. The only cards used are the ace, king, queen, jack, 10, and 9. There are two of each of these cards in each suit, so that a complete spade suit, for example, would contain two aces, two kings, two queens, two jacks, two 10s and two 9s.

Rank of the Cards: The ace is the highest-ranking, followed by the 10, king, queen, jack, and 9.

Number of Players: Three players are active in each deal, but the game may be played by four or five players, with only three participating at one time. The other stay out, but they are involved in the final payoff of the hand, whether or not they actively played.

If four players are in the game, the deal alternates around the table in clockwise fashion and the dealer stays out. If there are five players, the dealer and another player stay out.

Shuffle: The dealer shuffles the cards and gives them to the player on his right to cut. If he refuses to cut, any other player may cut the cards.

Deal: Each player is dealt fifteen cards, and the widow is given three cards. The widow consists of 3 closed cards, which are bought by the successful bidder. All cards are dealt face down by the dealer in clockwise fashion. The best practice in dealing is to deal three cards at a time to each player and one at a time to the widow. Some players deal four cards on the first three rounds and three on the last round, but this may cause a mix-up. The best way is to constantly deal three cards at a time until the pack is exhausted.

Although various rule books suggest dealing three cards at a time to the widow, again the best practice is to deal one at a time. If three are dealt at one time, there may be a possibility that all three are known to some player. Also, a dealer should never deal the last card in the pack to the widow; it might have been spotted by one of the players or the dealer himself, either on purpose or inadvertently, and a player knowing one of the cards in the widow has an enormous advantage.

After the cards are dealt out, the bidding begins.

Bidding

Each player in turn, beginning with the player at the dealer's left, bids for the contract. The first bid must be made by the player at the dealer's left. He must bid 300, or higher if he wishes. If the two other players pass, he can then throw in his cards and pay the kitty; he does not pay the other players. But if he wishes to look at the widow, and then throws in his cards—called *conceding*—he must pay all the other players.

After the initial bid of 300, each player in turn may bid or pass. The bidding is in multiples of ten points. Therefore, the next bid could be any bid at least ten points higher. For example, the second bidder may bid 310 or 350 or 400. Once a player passes, he cannot thereafter bid. Once two players have passed, the auction is over and the bidder has the contract.

Examining the widow: The successful bidder wins not only the auction but the right to examine the three cards in the widow. If, as stated previously, the initial bidder bids 300 and doesn't want to examine the widow, he simply throws in his cards and pays only the kitty. However, any bidder of 310 or more must look at the widow. After seeing these cards, he can use them either for melding, burying or in the play of the hand.

Object of the Game: The object of play is to make the final auction bid, either by having sufficient points in melds and playing strength and having the game conceded to the bidder, or by playing out the hand. The object of the opposition is to defeat the contract by play.

Melds

An A K Q J 10 of one suit is called a *flush* or *run*. Its value is 150 points. If a flush is melded, that suit becomes *trump*. In addition, each additional 9 of trump counts ten points more. The nine of trump is called the dix, pronounced "deece," after the French word for ten.

Thus, A K Q J 10 9 of trump is 160 points. With another 9 of trump it is 170 points.

A A A A of four different suits is called 100 aces and is worth 100 points.

K K K K of four different suits is called eighty kings and is valued at eighty points.

Q Q Q Q of four different suits is called sixty queens and is worth sixty points.

J J J J of four different suits is called forty jacks and is valued at forty points.

K Q of the same suit is called a marriage and is valued at twenty points.

K Q of trump, melded separately, is worth forty points. This is called a royal marriage.

The jack of diamonds and the queen of spades in one hand is a pinochle and is worth forty points.

A player can combine cards from different melds to add to the point total of his melds. For example, ♠K Q is worth twenty points, but ♠K Q with the ♦J is worth sixty points—twenty for the marriage and forty for the pinochle.

Combinations can go further. K K K K of different suits is worth eighty points. Now if there was a ♦Q and a ♠Q, that would be two additional marriages and be worth forty points more. A ♦J could then combine with the ♠Q for an additional forty points, making a total of eighty plus forty plus forty, or 160 points.

If a player holds the K K K K of different suits and the Q Q Q Q of different suits, it is called a *roundhouse* and is worth 240 points. Here is how the total is arrived at. The kings are worth eighty points; the queens are worth sixty points. Each king and queen forms a marriage, and since one of the marriages must be trump and is thus a royal marriage, that is valued at forty points. The total would be eighty plus sixty plus twenty plus twenty plus twenty plus forty, or a total of 240 points.

If a player melds a flush, the marriage in it (A K Q J 10) cannot be counted as an extra forty points. The flush is rated at 150 points, period. An additional K Q of trump would be forty points additional. This is possible, since there are two of each card of each suit in pinochle. The additional 9s count only toward trump and not to any other suit.

It must be remembered that the bidder must declare what his trump suit is before the start of the play. He doesn't need a flush in a suit to declare it trump, but if he melds a flush, it is automatically trump. Thus, if he says "Flush in diamonds" and shows it, the players automatically know that diamonds are trump.

A hand where there is no flush could be as follows:

A A A A 100 points; ♠K Q (spades declared trump), forty points; ♦J (combines with ♠Q), forty points; ♠9 9, twenty points; ♥K Q, twenty points. Total: 220 points in melds.

A successful bidder may declare any suit as trump, even if he doesn't meld anything in the suit. For example, in the above hand the player could declare clubs as trump, but he would lose twenty points from the ♠K Q, which would now only count as twenty points, not being a royal marriage; and he could not meld the two ♠9s, since only the 9 of trump counts as ten points. Thus, that hand with clubs as trump would have a value of only 180 points.

The other factor determining the bid is the number of points that can be made by playing out the hand. These are counted separately from the meld and are added onto it at the end of play. If the bidder made his game, he collects from the players and, if the bid is high enough (350 or more), from the *kitty* as well.

Value of the Cards

The following is the official, original count, used by the best players:

Each ace counts as eleven points
Each 10 counts as ten points
Each king counts as four points
Each queen counts as three points
Each jack counts as two points
Each 9 counts as zero points

If we total this amount we arrive at a figure of thirty points. Since there are eight of each card, the final total is 240 points. An additional ten points is awarded to the player who takes the last trick, making a grand total of 250 playing points in the hand.

If a player bid 300 and could only meld forty points, he could not win the game, no matter how strong his playing hand. This is because even if he took all tricks, he would be ten points shy, there being only 250 points in the deck.

Some players, to simplify the count, count the ace and 10 as ten points each, the king and queen as five points each, and the jack and 9 as zero. This kind of count takes the edge off the skill involved, for every trick and every card should be important in a finely played game of pinochle.

Some players simplify even further, perhaps because of difficulty in addition, or play, or both. They count the ace, the 10, and the king as ten points each, and the rest of the cards receive a zero value.

Either of these methods, together with the ten points alloted for the last trick, add up to 250 points. My suggestion is to use the original, official count. It makes the game more interesting.

Play of the Hand

After the successful bidder wins the auction, he turns over the widow's three cards in full view of the other players. After they have examined them, he may put them into his hand; if they later ask him what they were, before play begins, he must tell them. After the first card is played by the bidder, the players cannot ask about the widow.

Let us assume the successful bid is 310. The bidder exposes the widow, which has a ♣9, ♦10, and ♦J. He melds his cards after picking up the widow and putting it into his hand. He can use the cards in the widow for melds. He melds a flush in spades, A K Q J 10, with the ♠9, making 160 points. He puts down the ♦J next to the ♠Q for a pinochle, making a total of forty more points, or 200 points altogether. With the meld down, he now puts three cards away—called *burying*—before he commences to play out the cards; otherwise he would have eighteen cards. He cannot put away or bury any card he has melded, but he can bury an ace or a piece of trump without informing the opponents.

He now needs 110 points in cards, with spades as trump. One of the two other players, who now form a temporary partnership against him for this hand only, may remark, "One diamond," telling his partner to remember that the jack of diamonds was melded and is probably a losing trick for the bidder.

After burying three cards, the bidder makes the first play. He thus can control play right from the beginning, which is an enormous advantage.

On the play of the cards, an ace is the highest-ranking card. Since there are duplicates of each card, an ace followed by another ace of the same suit played by an opponent wins the opponent's ace; that is, the first ace has precedence.

Next in rank for the play is the 10, then the king, queen, jack, and finally the 9. A trick is taken in by the highest card after each round. A round consists of three cards played, one from each hand. The winner of the previous trick leads to the next trick.

Trumps have precedence over any nontrump card. The 9 of trump can take in an ace of another suit. Trumps can be played, if not originally led, only if the player is void in the suit led. If he has a card in the suit led, he must follow suit. Thus, if a heart is led and the other players have hearts, they must follow with hearts. If one of the players is out of hearts after it has been led, he must trump if he has trumps; there is no option. If he has neither hearts nor trumps, he can play any of the other suits. But if a 9 of hearts was led, and he is out of hearts and trumps and can only play the ace of clubs, the 9 of hearts, being led, has precedence over the ace of clubs.

If a trump is led, then the opposing player or players must play over it if possible. For example: If the bidder on the first lead plays the king of trump, the second player, if he has the ace or ten of trump, must play over it, and his partner must also play over it if possible. If one player holds the ace and 10 of trump, he must play one or the other over the king; but his partner, not having a card higher than the king in trumps, can play any trump. If he has no trump, he can play any card from any other suit. Since it is his partner's trick, he plays a high card, perhaps a 10. This is called *smearing,* or giving your partner a high-point card of another suit when void in the suit led.

Winnings and Payoffs

The usual payoffs are as follows for successful bids:

300	one unit
350	two units
400	four units
450	eight units

For every additional 50 points, the payoff is doubled. A player going bete pays double. Spades as trump doubles the payoff.

The Kitty

The usual practice in pinochle is to have a kitty, which is no more than a separate pile of money or chips contributed according to a pre-determined set of rules. The kitty belongs to all players in the game, and at the end of the session of play the kitty is split up among the players equally.

If it is a guaranteed kitty, this means that each player entitled to money from it must get the money, and if there is a deficiency, the other players must supply it. Thus, if a player bids and makes a 350 hand, and there is no money in the kitty, the other players must pay in lieu of the kitty. If a player leaves the game before the conclusion of the entire session of play, he is entitled to his share of the kitty.

The following are the payments normally made to the kitty:

An initial bidder of 300 who doesn't look at the widow pays one unit only. A player going bete (pronounced "bait" and meaning he failed to fulfill his contract) pays the kitty the same amount he pays to each of the other players. Any player who bids 350 or more and concedes the hand pays the kitty the same as he pays to each player. However, the kitty is not paid double for spades.

The following are the payments usually made from the kitty:

If a player bids 350 or more and wins, either by concession or by playing out the hand, he is paid the same amount from the kitty that he is paid by each player. However, the kitty does not pay double for spades.

Strategy in Bidding

Pinochle strategy is divided into two parts: bidding and the play of the hand. They are equally important to master, for an excellent bid is of little value if you cannot properly play out the hand and extract the points necessary to win the game. On the other hand, there are many excellent players who are either too conservative or too wild in their bidding, and thus they give up many valuable hands that otherwise could be made if bid correctly.

Generally speaking, a conservative bidder is much better off than a wild bidder. The conservative bidder, one who does not bid for the most his hand can produce when calculating his melds, his card strength, and the prospective value of the widow, is going to lose some hands that he could ordinarily make. But a wild player is going to lose most of them.

It is not too difficult to change from an ultraconservative bidder to a correct bidder; all it takes is proper knowledge of the odds. The main fault with most players, either through ignorance of the odds or undue optimism, or a combination of both, is not knowing when to stop bidding. Often, one sees a wild bidder who gets his share of good hands but comes out a loser in the end because of all the hands he had to throw away through overbidding. Probably he bid 350 when he had a cold 300 hand; or bid 400 with a sure 350 hand. It happens quite frequently in games at all levels. The expectation of getting needed cards from the widow buries many a player, who finds at the end of the evening that he is a loser despite the fact that he may have been the only player who was dealt decent cards.

To bid properly, the first and foremost thing a good player must know is how to value his hand correctly, both for melds and playing strength. These two factors were discussed previously in this chapter under *Melds* and *Value of the Cards*.

The next and really crucial aspect of bidding is knowing what the chances are of buying that card or cards a bidder so desperately needs from the widow. I'm sure that very few players know the exact odds against buying any particular card. They have hunches about it—they *feel* the card is there. But what are the odds? If they don't know this, how are they going to win?

Just as in any other game, if the odds are in your favor, you'll probably win if you bid boldly; and if the odds are not in your favor, there's no sense in making a big bid, which is suicide, or in bidding at all for that matter.

If the chances of getting a card were five to one against you and all you stood to collect was three to one, enough such bidding and you'd be bankrupt. And yet, too many players tempt these odds all the time. They bid 350 and then disgustedly throw in the cards, saying, "If I'd bought that queen of spades, it'd be a four fifty hand."

So before proceeding any further, take note of the odds against drawing cards in from the widow.

We are assuming a three-card widow, all cards hidden, and a regular forty-eight-card deck. The "openings" indicate the cards that must be bought in order to play out the hand.

Openings	Approximate Odds
One	five to one against
Two	two to one against
Three	even
Four	three to two in favor
Five	two to one in favor

Take a good look at those odds and memorize them, because knowing them is essential to winning at pinochle. I didn't say knowing them is essential to being a good player; I said "to winning." You can play well, memorize all the cards out and keep a running count, and know all about the play, but without knowing these odds, your bidding will ultimately make you a loser.

Now another factor enters into the situation. There are many players who bid, get the card they need, and then find that they either can't play out the hand, or go bete in the process. Make sure that the openings you are bidding for will enable you to successfully play out the hand; otherwise the openings are false ones. Here's a good example of this kind of delusion. The hand is as follows:

♠A K Q   ♥A K J 10 9   ♦A K J   ♣K Q J 9

Here we have a hand with a meld of 180 points (spades or clubs trump). If the player counts his openings, he might quickly count three: the ♣A, the ♥Q, and the ♠J. But this is nothing more than a mirage. On a 320 bid, getting the ace of clubs will increase the meld to 260 and it will be a laydown hand, a winner. Fine.

If the player bought the queen of hearts, the hand would have a valuation of 350, which of course is a sure winner. If he bought the jack of spades, his meld would now be 220 points, with the addition of forty jacks. But how is he going to make another hundred points with his hand? There are eleven losers in that hand, plus a short trump suit. The odds therefore are going to be two to one against his buying, because the only real cards available are the ace of clubs and the queen of hearts. Any other buy is going to lose.

If he doesn't buy, he's going to pay off three players plus the kitty in a typical four-man game. If he does buy, he collects from only three, because the kitty usually doesn't pay unless the bid is 350 or higher. With two-to-one odds against buying, you can see how readily a man can come out losing in pinochle with what he considers good cards if he doesn't know the odds.

Expect playing strength, rather than melds, from the widow and you will be on the right track. Bid for the widow to give you at least twenty points in playing strength, or as high as thirty—an average playing strength of twenty-five. Forget about bidding for openings unless it is even money and a spade hand that pays double, or if the odds are in your favor. If you follow this plan and your opponents don't, then, all other factors being equal, it will be hard for you to lose.

And don't hope for just forty more points with a ♦J for a pinochle, or a ♣Q for a marriage for an additional twenty. In the long run these cards will lose more than they gain if you rely on them, because they weaken your playing hand. It is better to have the goods, bid boldly, and wait for a 10—any 10—to strengthen your hand, which could give you that extra twenty or twenty-five points in playing strength. You might have only two 10s in your hand, which means that there are six that can be bought. Six openings for that 10 and you have the odds way in your favor. Usually, not only will a 10 give you that extra power, but a card in trumps or a long side suit will swing the balance in your favor. It is much wiser to bid for these than to wait for that magic forty points in a pinochle that paves the way for a bete hand.

Percentage Tables That Will Aid You in Your Bidding
The odds for or against your buying at least one card in trumps, when you hold five, six, or seven trumps, are as follows:

Number of Trumps	Odds
five	nineteen to thirteen in your favor
six	six to five in your favor
seven	three to two against

Of course, these odds not only apply to trumps, but to any side suit to which you're hoping to add.

With this in mind, it should be fairly evident that the way to insure wins from your bidding is never to buck the odds, and to bid for playing strength, not melds, from the widow.

More Strategy in Bidding

In pinochle, not only must the player know the percentages involved in buying help from the widow, he must know how high to bid up a hand that needs no help, that is playable as is.

Many times a player will bid a safe 300, only to find another player bidding 310. He then realizes that if he bids 320 and his opponent comes back with 330, he can't quite figure out whether or not to go higher. Or another player may have opened with 300, he bid 310, and the other player came back with 320. He knows he can make 310, but what about 330, which is what he's going to have to bid to win the auction?

This kind of thing happens so often at pinochle that the wise player must protect himself by knowing exactly what his chances are. If he doesn't, he will find himself either shut out of the bidding due to unnecessary caution, or, other times, bidding at a level where he can't make the hand, or has a good chance of going bete.

The best cure is to evaluate your hand immediately. If you have a meld of 180 points and you calculate that your playing strength is another 120 points for a safe 300 meld, you might expect an additional twenty or thirty points from the widow. Don't go above 320 and 330 with this hand.

If you just remember not to expect melds from the widow, you're already way ahead of the game. If, however, your hand is such that there are at least three openings, and filling any one of them will give you a hand worth 350 or 400; and if your trump will be spades, which will pay double (or, in some instances, hearts, which will pay triple), then go ahead and bid boldly. You don't have to pay the opponents double if you don't buy, but they'll have to pay you double if you do.

Competitive Bidding

There are times when your hand is enough for a 300 bid and it won't go much higher, but an opponent immediately bids 310. If you let him have it for 310 you might end up paying him, and possibly in spades, so you increase the bid by 320, forcing him now to go to 330 if he wants it. These are the kinds of competitive bids that could win you money, because at 330 the opponent might go bete.

In stretching a bid competitively, either to get the bid yourself or force an opponent up, keep to the rule that all you're looking for from the widow is playing strength. With this in mind, you can calculate almost exactly just where you want to end the bidding.

Another very important factor, as in most competitive card games, is your opposition. Gauge your bidding accordingly. You might easily bid a strong player up ten or twenty points because he gives himself that latitude. A weak player, after one bid, may get frightened, stop bidding and give you the auction.

It is important to know your opponents' playing strength. Thus, against two players, one of whom is weak, it may be possible to stretch your bid, counting on poor play to give you additional playing points. On the other hand, against players with more skill and experience in pinochle than you, it might very well pay to bid a little more conservatively. Against excellent play, the one trick you counted on may just disappear, and with it the margin of ten or fifteen points that was necessary to make the hand.

Also, in bidding there are some players who always want to see the widow. If you can get them up to a new level—let's say to 350 instead of 330—force them up. But don't just bid on nothing; have some reserve, so that at 330 you have a fighting chance to play the hand if you get some card strength.

Another clue to bidding up. If spades are double and you hold a stopper—let's say, both jacks of spades—and a player is bidding up, you know he's willing to take a chance, hoping for that spade. He may very well figure, "If I get that jack, I have 350, maybe 400, in spades. Why not go for it?" Why not indeed? Bid him up.

Sometimes a fake bid can be effective, but again you must know your opposition. A losing player who's been dealt bad cards all evening suddenly bids 350. Aha! Finally some good cards! A quick 360 bid will usually find a 370 response; after all this time, he's not going to let twenty points stand in his way. But those twenty points might very well be the difference between victory and defeat.

To Play or Concede the Hand

This is a decision that every pinochle player must face. The first problem is the fact that if he goes bete he pays double as a penalty to each player, and must pay the kitty as well. If the hand is a spade, the penalty exacted may be fourfold; and if hearts are triple, the penalty is sixfold. Quite a problem when the chances of making the hand are perhaps fifty-fifty, depending on breaks of suits, on a split in trump, and on the skill of the various players concerned in playing out the hand.

Before we go any further, an important table to know is the possibilities of breaks or splits in suits. See Chapter VIII, p. 187.

All the percentages are, of course, approximate, but some of the figures are well worth noting. For instance, with six cards against you in a suit, don't count on a three-three split; the best percentage is in favor of a four-two split. Knowing these percentages will help you decide whether or not to play out a hand.

For example, if you need a three-three split in trump, in order to make the hand, having only six yourself, and it is in spades, you'd better think twice about playing it out because you're bucking the odds and the chances are in favor of your going bete.

You can also see from the table that with only two cards out against you there is an almost fifty-fifty chance that they'll go either two-none or one-one. That can be very important at times.

And with three cards out against you, the odds are prohibitive against them breaking three-none, so if you can make your game only if they don't break this way, it pays to play out the hand.

The same is true of four cards out against you. The chances of them splitting four-none are only 10 percent, and if that's the only way you're going to lose, play out the hand.

To use the odds and percentages quoted above in deciding whether to drop or play a particular hand, it is best to calculate three identical hands and situations.

Let us suppose that the bid is 350. If you lose you pay each player double and pay the kitty also. If there are four trump out against you, you calculate that any break in trump worse than three-one is going to lose the hand for you. The chances of getting this split are 50 percent, or even. However, a side suit must also break in order for you to use your trump effectively and take last. In the side suit there are also five cards out against you, and with any split other than three-two you'll lose. Now, the chances are 67 percent in your favor that this side suit will split three-two, but together, the chances of both suits splitting three-two are 67 percent multiplied by 50 percent, or 33.5 percent.

Since the odds of winning are 33.5 percent or roughly one-third, if you play out three of these hands, with the splits as mentioned above, you theoretically will lose two and win one. Is it worth it?

If the bid of 350 pays ten chips, on the first loss (two players besides you, plus the kitty) you're going to pay out sixty chips; on the second loss, another sixty chips. (Twenty to everyone, including the kitty, because of the bete.) So far, your total loss is 120 chips. On the third hand, if you win, you collect only ten chips from each player, plus the kitty, for a total of thirty chips. Net loss is ninety chips.

All right. But suppose that instead of playing any of the hands with this one-third probability of winning, you conceded the hands. Let's see what would happen.

On the first concession, you'd pay out thirty chips.

On the second concession again thirty chips.

On the third concession, out another thirty chips.

Your total loss would be ninety chips, or the same as if you had played out three hands, winning one and losing two. What does this tell us?

If the chances are 33.5 percent of making the hand, or two to one against making the hand (the same thing), it pays to play it out. You have nothing to lose in the long run.

What about spades, where you are paying quadruple if you lose (twice for bete and twice for spades) and only collect double if you win?

Calculating the same way, with one win out of three, we find the first hand costs 120 chips; the second 120; and in winning the third, we collect sixty. Net loss 180 chips.

If we conceded each hand the net loss would be thirty plus thirty plus thirty, or ninety chips. By conceding each hand in spades we'd have saved ninety chips. Put another way, we doubled our loss by playing out the hands. Thus, if it's spades, you need better odds in order to play out the hands.

To play out a spade hand at 350 (where the kitty pays also) you need at least a fifty-fifty chance of making the hand, or else the odds are that you will lose more by playing the hand than conceding it. If the odds are not even, don't play out a spade hand at the 350 level.

In many games, a bid at 300 that is bete pays the kitty, but the player doesn't collect from the kitty if he wins. In these situations, don't play out the hand unless the odds are in your favor and the percentage is at least 60 percent. If it is spades, then you can play it with about 52–55 percent in your favor.

Burying Strategy

Once the player decides to play out the hand, he must make a decision that often is vital, especially in close games. He must decide what cards to bury. The successful bidder must bury three cards. This privilege of burying is to his advantage, and he should take full advantage of it, otherwise he may give away valuable points that will eventually ruin him.

To know what to bury, a pinochle player must first realize that the ideal hand to hold (other than those dream hands of all trumps and aces) is a hand with both a long suit in trump and a long side suit, or what is known as a two-suit hand. It is the best hand to play because he can use the long side suit to win tricks and drive out the opposition trump, after which all the trump and small cards in the side suit will be winners.

With this in mind, whenever there is indecision about what to bury, preserve the longer suits, if possible, and bury cards from the shorter suits.

Suppose you hold the following hand:

♠A K Q J 10 9   ♥A J 9   ♦A A K Q 10 9 9   ♣A 10

Your holding consists of eighteen cards because you are holding the three cards from the widow. Your meld totals 280, and you've bid 400. You need 120 in cards, and have to decide on three cards to bury now.

Using the principle enumerated before, retain long suits and get rid of short suits if possible. Since your diamond suit is your longest, you want to get rid of cards from your shorter suits.

Burying the ♥J and ♥9 is going to immediately save you forty points in losing tricks, and the ♣10 is a sure loser protected by nothing but the ace. A 10 in a doubleton in pinochle is a loser, and a 10 in a three-card suit headed by an ace is usually a loser as well.

Now you've buried twenty points and insured against over sixty points in losing tricks. You need 120 points. Can you make it?

If you remember the table on percentages, you will find that there are six trumps out against you, and an eighty-two-percent chance that they will split no worse than four-two. There are five diamonds out against you, and they will split no worse than three-two, sixty-seven percent of the time.

If you play three diamonds, therefore, on the third diamond you should be trumped. On the fourth diamond both opponents will trump. To play out this hand, you'd first play both singleton aces; then play the two aces of diamonds, which should hold sixty-seven percent of the time; then a ♦9, and, when you get the lead again, another ♦9. Then keep forcing out their trump, retaining your own for last and tricks.

Calculating this way, you can see how the hand then becomes wide open and everything is clearly in front of you. So, burying not only involves knowledge of the play of the subsequent hand, but of the probable break in suits as well.

Sometimes, and probably most of the time, you won't get two suits.

You might end up with a hand in which the suits are fairly well distributed. Although I mentioned before that a 10 in a three-card suit, such as A J 10, is a loser, this is true only if you have to lead that suit. Sometimes it is wiser to hold the 10, especially when you have melded a jack of diamonds to a pinochle and the opponents expect you to retain that as your long suit. In that case, it might be wise to bury three small cards from that suit and retain the ♣A J 10, since the opponents won't attack the diamonds but may attack the clubs as your short suit. In that case, after an ace lead, your ace and 10 are both good, and you've held onto enough clubs so that the opponents can't immediately attack your trumps.

This is a very good strategy to follow in cases where you have few trumps and no flush, and especially where the bulk and strength of your meld is 100 aces.

Strategy in the Play of the Hand

Each hand is different and involves a different strategy, but the elements remain the same. A quick analysis of the strategy to be followed is much better than a vague approach to playing out the hand.

Since the bidder chooses trump and makes the first play, he has control of the game at the outset and must endeavor to maintain this control throughout the play of the hand. Generally, he has the superior trumps if he melded a flush. If he has one or more long side suits, he plays those suits to force out his opponents' trumps. Then he is in a position to control play by retaining his own trumps and taking in last.

If a bidder has melded cards in a retained long suit, it is to his advantage to play those melds—usually a jack, queen, or king—right at the outset, rather than play lower or try to play from the top of the suit. This strategy might be different if he started the suit with double ace and 10, and is in a position to run out the entire suit. In that case, a wiser strategy would be to open with trump, usually a king, in order to force out higher trumps; then lead high trumps, driving out the rest; and then run the second suit, the long one, retaining a few trumps for last.

Of course, with a good trump suit and a really good second suit, there is no particular problem in strategy in the play. The difficulty comes when the second suit is not that strong. As mentioned in the previous paragraph, an effective method of playing out a second suit that contains melds is to play the melded cards at the outset. The opposition may feel that once the melds are played out, the suit is exhausted. If they play this way, their 10s and aces will drop on the melds, allowing the bidder full control of the suit thereafter. Once the top cards are out of the long suit, the bidder may continue with low cards from that suit, forcing out the trumps from the opposition and not allowing them to smear.

The opposition has the opposite strategy; they want to be able to force out the bidder's trumps, if he has a weak holding, and then take control of the game. The essential battle in pinochle is for control. They then immediately search for his weak suit, or void suit, and attack in that suit, driving out his trumps. Once the opposition has control, they play their best suits, retaining enough power to take in last.

This strategy would be effective where a bidder has weak trumps and needs a great many points. If he needs but a few points, playing to his void suit and permitting him to trump may give him just the points he needs. If he needs but a few or comparatively few points to win, he is not so interested in taking in last as he is in getting those points. A good play then for the opposition would be to drive out his trumps by leading trumps of their own, and then control the game from that point on in their strong suits.

As can readily be seen from the previous paragraphs, the essential elements to be considered in the play of the game are control, maintenance of trumps, establishment of side suits, and taking in the last trick.

Before any game is played out, the bidder must analyze his hand and his opposition. If he has weak trumps, he can be sure they will be attacked, either through his weak or void suit or by the opposition playing trumps. Therefore, it might be essential for him to pick up his points at the outset and then attack the opposition trump before they attack his. This often happens when the key strength in the hand is 100 aces with a weak trump holding. The aces are established as tricks, then the one long suit is run out as far as it will go until it is trumped. Then once the bidder's trump is attacked, he counters with more of the long suit, forcing out more trump.

If the bidder has strong trumps and no long side suit, he might purposely relinquish control of the lead and let the opposition play to his suits. If he holds A 10 K in a suit, he may make the ace and 10 if the suit is led to him; otherwise, the 10 and king are sure losers.

The opposition must also gauge their hands. They don't have the first lead, and must therefore, at the first opportunity, try and wrest control of the game from the bidder. If the bidder leads a melded queen (not trump) at the outset, they must decide whether that melded card is in a long or a weak suit in the bidder's hand. To guide them, they have their own hands, the melds, and widow seen. Sometimes this is a crucial moment. If a bidder melds a marriage and leads the queen and then the king, he may either be blanking himself in that suit, or trying to force out the 10s and aces to establish control in that suit.

From the meld and the cards in the opposition's hand, it can sometimes easily be seen which is the bidder's weak or void suit. That suit should be attacked as rapidly as possible to force out his trumps, especially if he is not touching them himself. Not only should they be forced out that way, but the player to the right of the bidder can lead trump through the bidder, forcing him to decide where the opposition trump strength is. Often a lead of a 9 under those circumstances will force out an ace.

If a bidder is trying to establish a strong side suit, it might be wise for the opposition not to take in a trick in that suit at the first opportunity, thus gaining time. With this additional time, trump might be forced out, and then smears by one of the opposition would be in order.

It is not possible to smear when trump remains, because the void suit must be trumped. Therefore, when smears are necessary, the player to the right of the bidder should play trumps through the bidder, rather than the bidder's void suit. This is to get out the bidder's trump, at the same time getting out his partner's. Then, when the right-hand player can, he should lead a high card in his best suit, permitting his partner to smear if he is void in that suit.

As one plays more and more, certain unspoken rules of play become apparent. If possible, give the opposition lead to the player to the right of the bidder. If a partner plays an ace, play your ace on it. The expression is "Ace calls for an ace." If a partner leads a low card of a suit toward his partner, he is asking that another low card be put on it, for he has the count on that suit and knows that the bidder must trump it.

Above all, the opposition should play as a team. Although they cannot openly discuss their basic strategy, it should become apparent from the play of the cards and must be respected at all times.

Counting Points During Play

No matter how brilliant the strategy of the individual player in the playing out of a hand, there will be situations where unless he has kept a correct count of the points taken in by tricks he will be at a disadvantage.

Sometimes, during the play of the game, and particularly near the end of play, there will be a good chance of making one of two tricks, but a slim or gambling chance of making both. Worse yet, by trying to make both a player may jeopardize both tricks. Without a count of points in this situation, it is as if he were throwing down cards with a paper bag over his head.

To play well you must count your points. You must keep a running count, whether you are the bidder or the opposition. This cannot be stressed enough. I liken the situation to a football team on the opposing four-yard line with twelve seconds to go in the game. The team knows they have only one more play left, but should it be a field goal or a try for touchdown? They have a good field-goal kicker, but a try for the six points is going to be rather risky. What should they do?

The first and obvious question is: What's the score? If they're behind by only two points, get that field-goal kicker in. If they're behind by four or more, they must try for the touchdown. But if they don't know what the score is, they'd be in roughly the same position as that pinochle player sweating out his play, not knowing the points he's already taken in.

Remember, in pinochle many games turn on one or two points, especially against strong opposition. The difference may not be in taking in a trick; it may be the play of a queen instead of a king; or trumping with a jack instead of a 9. It should therefore be elementary that anyone aspiring to be a strong pinochle player must keep track of his trick points.

Remembering the Cards and Suits Played

In addition to keeping those points in mind, a good player must know the cards played. It is beyond question that he must first remember the trump suit. He should also remember the other suits and the play of aces and 10s, so that he can pinpoint the card from the suit that has not yet been played. If you say this is too difficult, and if you are playing pinochle for sufficient stakes, your opponents are going to have this information and you are going to be at a tremendous disadvantage.

Knowing the cards played is not sheer memory. Often it is a logical extension of what has been seen and played. If you are the bidder, you know all fifteen of your cards, plus the buried cards—eighteen in all. The opposition cannot know what you have buried, nor do they know each other's cards. You are at an immediate advantage, and you also have the first lead.

If you are part of the opposition, you know even more cards, although you are not in control of the game from the outset. You see the bidder's melds, which may be as many as eight or ten cards; you've seen the widow exposed; and you see your own fifteen cards. At this point, with a little foresight and reasoning, you should be able to tell what is missing and where it is. For example:

You hold the queen of spades, and the bidder has melded eighty kings but no marriage in spades. Your partner has that queen. Or the bidder has melded a marriage in spades but no pinochles. Thus, you know your partner has both jacks of diamonds.

There are many other examples that can be mentioned, but the point should already have been made: By merely being observant you have a terrific advantage. Now, it shouldn't be difficult to follow the play of the cards, keeping track of the suits. If your partner hasn't played either of his jacks of diamonds, and two complete rounds of diamonds have been played, and you hold one, you have a good idea of where that diamond strength is. By playing out your diamond, then giving your partner the lead, you'll probably be in a position to force out the bidder's trumps.

Combining both the knowledge of suits played and particular cards in suits played is going to open up the game for you and allow you greater scope in your strategy. Keep track of the aces, 10s, and other cards, and after enough play and practice the hands could just as well be open because of what you know.

Irregularities

Since the exposure or disclosure of any card, either from a player's hand or from the widow, would give the viewer of that exposed card an inordinate advantage, the rules as to misdeals are quite strict in auction pinochle. When a misdeal does occur, the deal is void, and the dealer must gather in the cards, shuffle them again, have them cut, and redeal.

Exposed Cards
If, during the active shuffle, one of the cards has been exposed and its position in the deck can be ascertained, then if the cards are dealt out without correcting the shuffle, any player may demand a misdeal.

Should a card become exposed during the cut, or the replacement of the cut, it is a misdeal.

If any cards are exposed by being face up during the deal, it is a misdeal.

If the dealer exposes any card dealt, including his own, it is a misdeal. Generally, the rule in other card games is that a dealer is penalized for exposing one of his own cards, but in pinochle, another player may benefit to the detriment of the other players by seeing that exposed card. Therefore, any exposed card during the deal constitutes a misdeal.

Should any card be exposed in the widow during the deal, it is a misdeal.

Other Misdeals
If the cards have not been shuffled, then at any time prior to the first play any player can declare a misdeal. This can be declared after the bidding has been completed, the cards in the widow exposed, and the melds put down, since at that point it might first become apparent that the cards had not been shuffled.

If the cards have not been cut, a misdeal may be declared prior to the bidding. Once the bidding has started, the deal stands.

If, after the deal has been completed and the cards gathered up by the players and examined, any player has too few or too many cards, it is a misdeal.

If the widow has too few cards, it is a misdeal at all times after the deal is complete. It is illegal to take one of the player's cards which may be face down and add it to the widow. A misdeal must be called.

Should one of the players have too few or too many cards but this fact is not discovered until the play of the game is under way, at the point of discovery the hand is dead, and it is a misdeal.

No Misdeal

If there has been an incorrect deal and one player has too many cards and another too few, and none of the players has looked at his cards, the excess amount may be taken from the player having too many and given to the player with too few cards.

Should the widow have been dealt *too many cards,* the excess card or cards may be taken and redistributed to the player with too few cards, even if the players have looked at their cards. If any bid has taken place prior to this discovery, it is a misdeal.

Player's Mistakes Prior to the Play

Should any player expose one or more cards of the widow that he alone has seen, he is foreclosed from any further bidding.

If that player exposed the widow prior to the bidding; and if the other players, by his exposure, see one or more of the widow's cards, that offender must pay as penalty the value in money or chips of the minimum bid, to each and every player.

Should the bidding have begun and a player exposes the widow, he must pay each and every player in the game the amout of money or chips equal to the value of the last bid. He must also pay this amount to the kitty.

Should a player expose one of his own cards, there is no misdeal.

Bidder's or Bidding Mistakes

Should the successful bidder discover that he has too many or too few cards in his hand after the widow has been opened, his hand is dead and he is penalized by having to pay each of the players and the kitty the value of the bid.

Should he discover his incorrect hand after making a play from his hand, then he is bete and must pay each player double the value of the bid, and must pay the kitty as well.

If a player bids out of turn, that bid has no value, but there is no penalty to the bidder.

If a player passes out of turn, again there is no penalty, but he cannot thereafter make a bid other than a pass.

If a player in his correct turn makes an insufficient bid—that is, a bid either equal to or lower than the preceding bid—he must correct this bid and bid higher than the preceding bid, whether or not he meant to.

After the successful bidder has made his first play, if it is discovered that he has buried too few or too many cards, he is double bete.

Playing Mistakes

If the bidder leads out of turn, there is no penalty. The player whose correct turn it was may demand either that that card stay as the lead, or insist that he, the correct leader, lead a card. It is optional with the player whose turn it was to lead.

If one of the opponents led out of turn, it is a revoke. (See below.)

Should a trick be taken either by the bidder or his opponents, when in fact that trick was not won by the party claiming the trick, then, prior to the time that trick is mingled with the other tricks, the error may be corrected. Thereafter, it stands.

Revokes

If there is a revoke on the part of the bidder, he pays double bete. If the revoke is on the part of the opponents, the bidder wins. At the time the revoke is declared, all play ceases, the hand is void, and the offender or revoker immediately makes a settlement. A revoke may be declared at any time up to the actual settlement of the hand, since at times the revoke will not be immediately apparent. For instance, a diamond lead may be trumped by the bidder, and at the last trick it is discovered that he has a diamond remaining in his hand.

The following are revokes:

If a player fails to follow suit when he is able to.

If a player does not trump a suit he is out of, when there are trumps remaining in his hand.

If a player fails to play a higher trump when he is required to do so.

If a bidder buried a card included in his meld.

Other Errors

Should the bidder miscount his melds, either counting them too high or too low, a correction can be made at any time prior to the settlement.

If any player, including the bidder, examines the cards taken in previous tricks after the play of a card on the next trick, it is considered a revoke.

The same is true if any player, including the bidder, looks at any trick other than the previous trick before the play of a card.

TWO-HANDED PINOCHLE

Two-handed pinochle is considered the oldest form of pinochle (auction with widow considered the most recent) and is a fine game of skill. In recent years, gin rummy has become a more popular two-handed game, but there are still those adherents of pinochle who consider their two-handed game the more skillful.

The main differences between this game and the three-handed game is that trump is arbitrary, there is no bidding, and there is no widow.

Rules of Play

Deck: The regular pinochle deck of forty-eight cards is used.

Deal: The deal is alternated between the two players. The dealer deals out twelve cards to his opponent and himself, dealing them three at a time. The twenty-fifth card (the card after each player has received his twelve cards) is turned up. This is now trump.

If the card turned up happens to be the 9 of trumps, the dix, the dealer gets credit for ten points. Otherwise there is no scoring at the outset. The unused portion of the deck, called the "stock," is laid to one side, to be picked from after the first play.

The First Play: The nondealer, after he is dealt his cards, must play a card. He does this by removing a card from his hand and laying it face up on the table, just as in auction pinochle. The purpose of the play is to reduce the number of cards in the hand to eleven. This is because the final card of the stock and the up card are not played, each player getting one of the two final cards, and so the final play of the game begins with each player holding twelve cards. But we'll get into that later.

Meanwhile, there must be a first play of the cards. The nondealer can play any card from his hand. After he makes his play, the dealer can play any card from his hand as well. He doesn't have to follow suit and he doesn't have to play trumps if he is out of the suit led.

If he wants to win the trick, he must beat the card led in the game suit, or trump it. He doesn't have to be out of the suit led to trump it. *He can trump any card at any time.*

Taking in Tricks: The purpose of playing out the hand as the players go along is twofold. Each trick made is part of the score count of the game. If a player leads a ♦ 10 at the outset (spades being trump, for instance) and the dealer puts on the ♣ J, the nondealer gathers in that trick and puts it aside face down. He already has twelve points—ten for the 10 and two for the jack, (the same values as in auction pinochle). The second purpose is melding.

Melding

The player taking in the trick is the only one permitted to meld. After every trick is played, a meld is permitted.

Let's assume that after the nondealer took in the first trick with his ♦ 10, he melded the ♠ K Q, trump. That is a royal marriage and is worth forty points. He announces "forty points," but since the dealer had dealt out the 9 of trump and received credit for it, the net is "thirty." A running count is kept during the game. It is not necessary to record the melds; it is usual for the players to keep a mental count.

Another important point about melding in two-handed pinochle: A flush can be melded after a royal marriage, using the royal marriage in the flush. Thus forty points can be gotten for the royal marriage, and on the next meld (or at any subsequent time) he can add the A J 10 of trump and get an additional 150 points.

Still another important point: If the open card showing trumps (the twenty-fifth card dealt) is other than a 9 of trump, then at any time after winning a trick if either player desires to meld the dix (9 of trump), he gets credit for ten points. He also has the privilege of replacing the trump card showing with that 9. For example, if the queen of spades was showing as the twenty-fifth card and one of the players took in a trick and melded the dix of trump, he would replace the queen with the 9 and put the queen in his hand.

In two-handed pinochle, the importance of this move cannot be overestimated. In some situations, if the trump card (the open card determining trump) is important to the hand—let us say, an ace of trumps—a player may play the 10 of trumps to take in a trick. This is so that he can then meld his dix and take the ace into his hand. A good player always calculates this move, because if he holds the dix of trumps and can replace the trump card showing, he doesn't want to give up that opportunity. On the next play, the opponent might also get a dix of trump and beat him to it.

Now, after the first card has been played, the first trick taken, and the first meld laid down, the player taking the trick is first to pick up a card from the stock. The other player does so next.

Then the taker of the previous trick plays out a card from his hand, He goes first. If he wishes, he can play one of his melded cards instead. Again, after his play, his opponent can play any card from his hand. If he desires to win the trick, he must play a higher card in that suit or trump it. Whoever wins the trick can make another single meld. He could meld a marriage, but not a marriage and a pinochle at the same time or a marriage and kings. A player is limited to one distinct meld at a time.

A player can win a trick and not make a meld, having none to make. In any event, the winner of the trick has the option to make a meld, then pick up the top card from the stock, while the loser of the trick picks up the next card. Then the previous winner of the trick plays out another card. And so the game goes, down to the final cards. When there are two cards left (one closed and the other the 9 of trump, the dix), the winner of the last trick gets the closed card and the loser the dix of trump. All the melds that are on the table are picked up by their respective players, and the final aspect of the game begins (end play).

End Play

Now, each player has twelve cards in his hand, and there are no cards left in the stock; they were used up in the first half of the game. There can now be no more melds. The player taking the last trick makes the first play. We are back to playing out the hand in pinochle, where the usual procedure is followed.

Thus, in the last part of the game, if a player leads a card of a certain suit, the other player must follow suit, or trump if he is void. If he cannot follow suit or trump, he may play any other card, and the first player's card wins the trick. If the first player plays trump, the second player must play a higher trump. The winner of the previous trick during the last part of play leads first.

After all the cards are played out, the count is made. The count of the cards adds up to 250 points, just as in auction pinochle, the ten points for last going to the player who took in the very last trick in the end game. The point value plus the net meld determines the winner. If *A* melded 140 points and *B* 180 points, *B* goes into the last part of the game with a net forty points. If *A* has a count of cards amounting to 136 and *B* 114, the final tally will show *B* winning by eighteen points.

In deciding the winner, players may play for a gross total of 1,000 points, instead of calculating each hand individually as was done above. If the game goes to the first player to total 1,000 points, no net total is kept, but at the end of the first game, the score would be *A* 276 (140 meld and 136 cards), and *B* 294 (180 meld and 114 cards).

If a gross total is kept leading to a winning score of 1,000, it would be wise to keep a written tally. And of course then each meld should be written down, too. Otherwise, it becomes very difficult to keep a clear count.

Strategy

In two-handed pinochle, a player's knowledge of cards already played is the most important aspect of his strategy. Without this information the player is at a strong disadvantage. How to get this knowledge? Mostly by memory, but sheer exhaustive memory is not necessary. The actual play and melding of the cards enables the average player to have a good idea of which cards have been played and which haven't.

The first and most important thing to know at all times is the number of trump already played and out of the game. If no trump are played at the beginning of the game (that is, at the first part of the game when melding is permitted), then it is fairly simple to know just which trumps and how many of them your opponent has. Just count those in your hand, subtract that figure from twelve, then look at the gaps in your trump hand. Your opponent has every missing card in trumps.

Usually, in the normal course of a two-handed game, both players will try and preserve trump, both for melding, such as a flush or royal marriage, and for the end play. Thus, as a general rule, trumps are hoarded and not played out. Of course this strategy might change radically, especially with a hand holding a great many melds and nothing really in trump to meld. If a player has 100 aces, eighty kings, and a few marriages to meld, he may feel that the substantial points gained from his total will more than offset the losses in points in the end play.

If a player has 100 aces and eighty kings to meld, both at the same time, it is far wiser to first meld the 100 aces. He can use any of those aces, if the opponent leads a card, to take in the trick, and then meld the eighty kings. Then, buying other cards, such as queens, he can substantially increase the point total.

For the same reason, it is best to meld a flush or royal marriage before ordinary marriages and other melds; not only because of the point count involved, but because the player can then use the trumps for the taking in of tricks to ensure that he gets his melds down.

Where there are a great many cards to meld, it may pay to give up trump to get the points, but the calculation should be precise, and the points melded should more than obscure the subsequent loss of played points in the end play.

Back to memorization of trumps. Occasionally a player will play trump upon another player's lead in order to take in the trick. You must keep a running total of how many and what trumps have been played. It is not necessary to keep counting trumps in play; just count those which have already been used.

Players will also lead trump in order to get a trick, figuring that the opponent will not waste a higher trump just to stop that trick. Of course, count those trumps led. By the end of the melding and start of the end play, you should not just have an idea of what trumps are left, you should know exactly. If you don't, you are probably in for an unpleasant surprise in the end play, and also in the end result. If you don't master this, you are going to find it hard or practically impossible to win at two-handed pinochle.

After trumps the most important cards to memorize are the aces. Again, unless tricks are needed, aces are rarely played until the end play. However, if aces have been melded they may be used by a player to ensure his other melds, especially after a lead by his opponent. Just memorize those aces that have been played, not the ones on the table, in your hand, etc. If you concentrate on just those played, you can readily have a count when you pick up your cards for the end play.

Tens are frequently played during the meld, because it takes an ace or a piece of trump to beat them, and also because they have no value in melding. A running count can easily be taken of them, and you will usually find that they are almost depleted by the time the end play begins.

Kings and queens, used often in melds, are not played in the beginning of the game unless out of sheer necessity or desperation, or unless there are duplicate honors held by the player. Once they are melded, they are sometimes not played because a marriage can expand into eighty kings or sixty queens. In order to protect your melds, you must know what has been played in kings and queens, but this is often very apparent because these are cards you are looking to for your melds.

Jacks and 9s are not that valuable. The jack of diamonds is easily kept track of because of the pinochle, and the 9s of trump and jacks of trump can be counted in the trump count.

With a little practice, or maybe a lot of practice and much concentration, you should know every card in your opponent's hand prior to the end play. Not many average players know this, but the winners at two-handed pinochle certainly do. That's why they are winners, all other things being equal.

If a player has to guess in the end play in a close game, he might as well throw in the cards because he's going to lose against a good player who knows his cards. If you want to be an expert at two-handed pinochle, you're just going to have to train yourself to memorize the cards, and then turn that knowledge into winning play.

When to Meld

If you can meld, meld. If you have melds at the beginning of the game, get them out by winning tricks with 10s if you can. The more you have melded, the freer is your game. Having early melds of substantial points enables you to play defensively, forcing the opponent to give up good melds in order to take in tricks.

It is obvious that if you are going for a flush you should first meld the royal marriage, then add the ace, jack, and 10 to it. But the important thing is to get that royal marriage down as fast as possible if you are close to a flush. It is certainly more important than melding a pinochle or jacks.

Any time you are in a position to meld a flush, do it, even if you sacrifice a lesser meld. A flush is very difficult to meld, and that trick you passed by may be the last chance you'll ever get to make the flush meld. Your opponent may sense or fear that you have it and keep feeding you trump, which of course you might not be able to beat without destroying the flush. This often happens with the stock low in cards and but few chances to make a meld.

I know that a lot of games are lost because of the poor timing of melds. Very often a player just runs out of cards when he still has a couple of melds in his hand which he can't get on the table.

One of the best strategies is just sitting back and appraising your hand at the outset of the game. After a few plays you should have a good idea of where you're heading, what melds are forming or have formed in your hand. At this point, plan an overall strategy. Do you want to sacrifice a few tricks now because you don't have any big melds? Will your opponent be able to meld high, say 100 aces and eighty kings, and then play defensively? What stoppers do you have? Will you show him that you have stoppers, or will you delude him into thinking he can get certain melds that you know he cannot get? Or, with the shoe on the other foot, is he teasing you into thinking you may be able to buy that king of spades for eighty kings, or that ace of clubs for 100 aces, when all along he has both of them stopped? With a little foresight and patience, and a momentary pause to figure out your strategy, you should be able to play much more intelligently.

Remember, you can't save every card for a meld. You must play cards to tricks and you must take in tricks in order to meld. And sometimes this is going to mean sacrificing a lesser meld for a greater one. If you have to do it, do it. A sure way to lose is to save everything and then find out at the end of play that your opponent is not letting you take in enough tricks to get down all the melds. So you end up with losing points in play and all sorts of kings and queens and jacks in your hand for the end play, all poisonous losing cards. Don't be a hog. You have to give to get. But you must use your discretion.

Watch your opponent's plays. If he takes in your 10 with an ace, he might very well have that other ace, especially if it's done fairly early in play. If you have the other three aces, they may be dead cards for melding. At this point, you must realize that their value will be to take in tricks to meld with, or to use in the end play.

If your opponent plays the queen of spades or jack of diamonds early, you must also count on him for duplicates. If he plays a king or queen of trump you can figure the same thing. However, he might be just false-carding you, trying to make you drop those cards and prevent you from making those 100 aces, those pinochles, and those royal marriages. You can do the same thing, but it must be done carefully. Don't destroy your hand just to deceive your opponent if the points gained won't make up for the points deliberately given up.

Strategy in End Play

If you don't know all your opponent's cards in the end play you are going to be at a distinct disadvantage, unless you are playing a mediocre player.

Know those cards!

The first consideration is to take in last, especially in a close game. When a game is close, you should have not only a knowledge of all your opponent's cards, but an exact count of your points taken in, so you know just what you need in the end game.

Guesses in this respect are just losing guesses. After you memorize the cards, you should try to have a running count of just how the points stand in cards played—in other words, card points. I know it is almost an impossible task to keep two running totals, but a net total can easily be learned. For example:

On the first trick of the game (not the end play) the opponent throws a ♦10. (Spades are trump.) You throw on a ♥9, he's ten up. On the next trick he plays the ♦9, and you put on the ♣9. No change. On the next trick he plays the ♥J, and you take it in with the ♥10. You're plus two. And so on. You will find it rather easy to keep this count, and this, together with the knowledge of your opponent's cards, will give you a big advantage over any opponent who doesn't do this, enabling you to hold your own against some of the best company.

To play for last, it is best to maintain your trump position and force your opponent to exhaust his. If he is void in a suit, keep attacking that suit. Once he is out of trump, you will have a much better chance to control the end play and get last. Those ten points are often the difference between winning and losing, especially in those games played for score, hand by hand, where the payoff is after every hand. It makes for more skill than a cumulative score, where the tendency might be to be sloppy when you are far ahead or far behind.

Irregularities

No Shuffle

If the cards have not been shuffled, the hand may be declared a misdeal by either player at any time during the play of the hand when such nonshuffling becomes apparent.

No Cut

If the cards have not been cut, the hand may be declared a misdeal by the nondealer until the first play of the hand. Thereafter the deal stands.

Exposed Cards

If a card is exposed during the deal and that card was dealt to the dealer, he must accept it.

If a card is exposed going to the nondealer, he may accept it or demand a new deal.

If a card is exposed face up in the pack during the deal, it is a misdeal.

If, when the upcard showing trump is turned over, other cards are exposed, the trump card stands, but the stock must be reshuffled and placed back on the table face down.

If a card is found face up in the stock during the course of the game, that card is replaced face down, the cards in the stock are reshuffled, and play continues.

Should any player expose one of his own cards at any point during the course of the game, it is no misdeal since each player is responsible for his own cards.

Imperfect Deck

If the deck is not a correct pinochle deck, the hand played is void, as are all other hands prior to that one if played with the same deck of cards, in the event the scoring is cumulative. However, should the scoring and settlement be on an individual-game basis, then the previous hands are legal.

Incorrect Number of Cards

If either player has been dealt fewer or more than the correct number of cards and play has begun, it is a misdeal.

If play has not begun, and either player has too few cards, he may be dealt the difference from the top of the stock.

If play has not begun and either player has too many cards, but has not yet looked at them or picked them up, then the excess number is removed and placed on the stock. Should the player in the above instance have looked at his cards, it is a misdeal.

Should either player discover *during the course of play* that he has an incorrect number of cards, the following is the rule:

If he has too few cards, he must draw enough cards from the stock to correct his hand on his next turn of play.

If he has too many cards, he continues to play, discarding without drawing until his hand is correct.

Mistakes in Drawing from the Stock.

Should either player draw more than one card from the stock and see it, he must show it to his opponent and then replace it on top of the stock.

Should either player draw a card from the stock out of turn, his opponent may accept the incorrect draw, or may demand the card drawn, in which case the next card drawn from the stock by the offender must be shown to his opponent.

Lead Out of Turn

If a player leads out of turn, there is no penalty. His opponent may require him to pick up his card, at his option, and then play his own lead card.

If after a wrong lead the cards have been collected, the lead out of turn stands. Play goes on, with the taker of the trick leading the next card.

Revoke

A revoke occurs during the final play of the hand, if:

Either player does not follow suit when he can.

Either player trumps a card when he still holds that suit in his hand.

Either player does not win a trump lead when he has the higher trumps.

A player may correct his revoke before the play of the next trick, and if it is the turn of the non-offender to lead the next trick, the offender may have that lead retracted in order to correct his revoke.

Should the revoke stand, not being corrected, the offender scores no points for that game, and his melds are also wiped out. But play continues to the end, in order to determine the final score of the non-offender.

Incorrect Number of Cards Remaining in the Stock

Should there be three cards at the end instead of the final downcard and the trump, the winner of the last trick gets the downcard, the loser the trump card, and then each counts his cards, and the one with the missing cards gets the odd card. There is no misdeal as a result of this.

Error in Melding

Should a player announce a meld that is not a legal one, on demand he must replace the cards in his hand, and there is no penalty. This incorrect meld may be declared illegal at any time during the game prior to the last part of the game; in other words, until the stock is exhausted. Thereafter, it stands and is counted as a correct meld.

During the period of time that a player may have too many or too few cards in his hand he cannot meld.

Errors in Scoring

An error in scoring must be corrected on demand of either player before the play of the next trick. Thereafter, it stands. This is not to be confused with an illegal meld, which may be corrected at any time until the stock is exhausted.

If there is an error in stating the value of a meld, the same rule applies.

PARTNERSHIP AUCTION PINOCHLE

There are many variations of partnership pinochle, and it is played differently around the country, with rules varying from state to state and often from city to city. In this section, we'll deal with partnership auction pinochle, the most popular variation.

Rules of Play

Players: Four, forming two partnerships.

The Deck: Standard pinochle deck of forty-eight cards, with only the ace, king, queen, jack, 10, and 9 in duplicate in each suit.

The Deal: As in auction pinochle, the dealer shuffles the cards and gives them to the player on his right to cut. If that player refuses to cut, any other player may. After a deal is completed, the next deal is in rotation, commencing with the player to the dealer's left and going clockwise around the table.

The deal is made by giving each player three cards at a time, face down, commencing with the player on the dealer's left and going clockwise around the table. Each player thus receives twelve cards. If the players wish, the dealer shall only give one card at a time to each player during his deal.

Rank of Cards: Ace (highest), 10, K, Q, J, and 9 (lowest).

Forming the Partnerships: The players draw for partners; the two highest cards determine one partnership, and the two lowest cards form the other.

Object of Play: To win tricks. Also to win the last trick, called "last." The bidding team's object is to make sufficient points to match or surpass the bid.

Melds: The following table shows the value of the melds: (See Auction Pinochle melds for description of 100 aces, etc.)

A K Q J 10 of trumps is a flush	150
Double Flush	1500
Four Aces (100 Aces)	100
All Eight Aces	1000
Four Kings (80 Kings)	80
All Eight Kings	800
Four Queens (60 Queens)	60
All Eight Queens	600
Four Jacks (40 Jacks)	40
All Eight Jacks	400
Pinochle (♠Q♦J)	40
Double Pinochle	300
9 of Trumps (each)	10
K Q of Trumps (Royal Marriage)	40
K Q of Any Other Suit (Marriage)	20

As in regular auction pinochle, 100 aces, 80 kings, etc., refers to four of the same rank, such as ace, one from each suit. Also as in auction pinochle, melds may be counted as part of another meld. For example, the queen of spades can be combined with the jack of diamonds for a pinochle, and also combined with the king of spades for a marriage.

Melding: The actual melding takes place after the bidding is completed. Each player places his melds face up in front of him.

The scorekeeper makes a note of the total of each side's melds, but no final credit is given until a side wins a trick.

Bidding: There are two variations of bidding. In each variation, the player to the left of the dealer bids first and must bid 100 or more. Thereafter, each player in turn must bid or pass. All further bids over the 100 opening bid must be made in multiples of ten. In the first variation, the bid after 100 must be at least 200 and there is only one round in bidding. In the second variation, the bidding continues so long as there is a subsequent bid at least ten points higher than the first bid. If a player passes he can no longer bid, and the bidding may go several rounds, until all but one player has passed.

In each variation the highest bidder names the trump suit.

Play of the Hand

After the bidding is finished and the melds have been shown, the cards are replaced in each player's hand. The player to the left of the dealer (called eldest hand) makes the first lead, regardless of who won the auction. Then the players follow in rotation, going clockwise.

The winner of the previous trick leads to the next trick.

On any lead, a player must follow suit if he has cards of the same suit. If he is void in that suit, he must trump (play trump). If he is void both in the suit led and in trump, he may play any card in his hand.

The highest card of a suit always wins the trick, provided it is not trumped. If a suit is trumped, the trump always wins, unless two players are void and play trump, in which case the highest of the trumps wins.

If a card is led (example, ace of spades) and an equal card (the other ace of spades) is played, the first card led wins the trick.

If a trump is led, each player must, if he can, play a higher trump than the one previously played.

One player on each partnership team takes in all the tricks for that team, regardless of which player in the partnership won the trick.

Scoring

A scorekeeper should be selected among the players prior to the game. First the melds are noted, then, after a trick is won by a side melding, the total of the melds are credited to that side.

Although the standard scoring of cards taken in tricks may be used, the more common form of scoring in partnership pinochle is ten points for the ace and ten and five respectively for the king and queen. The jack and 9 have no value in scoring points.

The last trick of play counts as ten points, so that there is a total of 250 points in playing points. The melds are counted separately.

The scoring is done by sides, rather than individually. The bidder's side must win at least its bid in tricks and in melds. If it does, its score is the total of points and melds. If it fails to do so, the bid is deducted from its score. The opposing team scores whatever it melds and makes in tricks.

The first team to score 1,000 points wins the game. The bidder's total is counted first; if it totals 1,000 or more, the bidding team automatically wins.

Partnership Conventions

There are certain conventions used in partnership pinochle. The most popular of these are as follows:

200 bid: Shows a hand with about 100 points in melds and average strength.

210 or 310: Shows one strong suit.

250: Shows at least a flush.

260: Usually shows aces. Because of the additional playing strength of the four aces, it is a higher bid than the 250 showing a flush.

Bidding Strategy

First, a bidder should know the basic conventions which will guide him and his partner in the bidding of any hand. Then the score should be taken into consideration. If you are behind, it pays to give a more aggressive bid. If your team is ahead by a great many points, a conservative bid would be in order. This is because your team will get credit for all points made in tricks and melds, regardless of the bid, if the other team gets the bid. If your team gets the bid, your conservative bid should enable you to make the bid in points and melds.

If both teams are very close to the 1,000 mark, it pays to be more aggressive, for the bidder's team counts its score first and this often is the difference between victory and defeat.

In counting tricks for bidding purposes, each ten is worth about twenty points as a possible winning trick. Also count points for your partner, but be very cautious in doing this and expect little from him unless his bid shows playing strength.

The first bidder is usually conservative, but another bidder, having heard his opponent's bid, is in a better position to bid more aggressively. If you are not first bidder, try and bid to the full measure of your hand.

Playing Strategy

The melds give each player his first knowledge of the cards held. From these cards, and by looking at his own cards, he should try and picture the composition of the hands. The missing cards, if the melds are carefully examined, may be in your partner's hand, and this should guide you in the play.

In the lead, a player should cash his aces. In the partnership game, the distribution of cards may be quite uneven, and there is a good chance that an opponent may have a singleton in the suit in which you hold the ace. If your opponent plays an ace, then your lead of an ace may be trumped.

If a bidder has a strong trump suit, he should usually lead it. If he has a strong side suit but poor trumps, he should lead the strong side suit. If he does so, it will be trumped, and this is a good way to attack the opponents' trumps.

As in auction pinochle, it is better practice to play out the melds before the other cards in that suit. Your opponents already know these cards, and it is to your advantage to disclose as little as possible.

Irregularities

Most of the irregularities are the same as in three-handed auction pinochle. The following are peculiar to partnership pinochle.

Incorrect Number of Cards: If one player has too few and another too many cards, and none have been seen, the player with too few cards takes the necessary cards from the player with too many.

If the cards have been seen, all players meld, and then the player with too few cards takes his cards from the unmelded cards of the player with too many.

Revoke: If a player fails to follow suit, trump when void, or play over a trump lead when able to, he is said to have revoked. If a player revokes, his side scores no points for tricks taken in on that deal, but the melds count.

Erroneous Score: If the score has been incorrectly added or entered by the scorekeeper, it must be corrected if any player demands it prior to the completed game. After that, it stands.

IX

Casino

♠ ♥ ♦ ♣

Rules of Play

Casino, or cassino, as it is sometimes spelled, can be either a social or gambling game and can be enjoyed as a game of skill by children as well as adults.

Number of Players: It is best as a game for two, though it can be played by three. It can also be played by four players as a partnership game.

Deck: The standard deck of fifty-two cards is used, without a joker.

Rank of the Cards: Except for the scoring cards, there is no rank of cards in casino. The face cards, kings, queens, and jacks, have no distinct value. All other cards, for building purposes which will be explained later, have a value equal to their spots. Thus, a 5 has a value of five, a 2 a value of two, etc.

Object of the Game: The object of the game is to score the most points. In order to score points, the players attempt to take in the most cards, to take in scoring cards, and to win the most spades.

Scoring

The following are counted toward the score:

Cards: Winning the majority of the fifty-two cards   three points
Spades: Winning the majority of the thirteen spades   one point
♦ *10*: Called the big casino or Good Ten   two points
♠ *2* : Called the little casino or Good Two   one point
Aces: Each counts as one point   four points

There is a total of eleven points to be scored at the conclusion of each complete deal of fifty-two cards.

In the event that each player ends up with twenty-six cards, neither gets any credit for most cards, and the three points are not counted. In that event, only eight points are divided.

Play of the Hand

The dealer shuffles the cards, and his opponent cuts them. The deal is alternated between players. The nondealer has the advantage of receiving his cards first and making the first play. The dealer has the advantage of "last," which means that at the conclusion of play any cards remaining on the table go to the player who has taken in the last trick. The dealer can force last by retaining a picture card; that is, the king, queen, or jack.

Most books suggest that two cards at a time be dealt, but I suggest that the cards be dealt one at a time, for the fewer cards dealt out at one time, the less likelihood there is of artificial runs in the hand, or duplicates.

The dealer deals one card to his opponent, one to himself, and then one is dealt open on the table. This is repeated until each player has four cards and there are four open cards on the table. (See Illustration.)

Casino

At this point the dealer puts the unused stack of cards to one side.

After each player plays out the four cards in his hand, the dealer deals four more to each player, but no more are dealt open. Open cards are only dealt the first time. Before the last deal there will be eight cards left. Before dealing these, the dealer must announce "last," which has a special significance in casino since the player taking in the last trick collects all the cards remaining on the table. Since these cards may make the difference between winning or losing, there is a special strategy used at the last, and unless a player is aware that it is last he may not use this strategy.

After the first deal, the nondealer makes the first play. He has three choices available to him; he may either *take in, build,* or *trail.*

Taking In

Since the general object of the game is to take in as many cards as possible, as well as to take in cards having a special value, the player looks over the cards in his hand and the cards open on the table. A player may take in a card on the table having the same value as a card in his hand. For instance, if he holds a 5 he may take in any 5 on the table. In casino there is no such thing as suit sequences, and suits are generally immaterial, except that particular cards of certain suits (♦10 and ♠2) have a special value. Also, since holding the majority of spades adds a point to the final count, it is always preferable, if one has the choice, of taking in a spade rather than any other suit.

For example, a player may hold the ♠6 and the ♦6 in his hand, and a 6 has been played to the table. It is better to take in the 6 on the table with the ♠6 rather than with the ♦6. Of course, as you will see in the section on building, it is possible here to build 6s, but that will be discussed later.

A king, queen, or jack (face cards) can only be taken in by their respective matching cards. Face cards cannot be built as can other cards.

Taking in can be accomplished in another way. If a player holds a card that can take in the total of two or more cards on the table, he can put those open cards in a pile and take them in with the card forming their total.

For example, if a player holds an 8, and there are a 3 and a 5 on the table, he puts the 3 and 5 together and takes them in immediately with the 8. If there were a 2, a 5, and an ace (which counts as one point), he could also take them in immediately with the 8.

If there are two cards of the same value on the table (which occurs sometimes on the initial deal), a player holding the same-valued card can take both cards in. For example, if the player holds a 3 and there are two 3s on the table, he can take in both of them. However, with face cards, only one can be taken in at a time. Thus, if there are two kings on the table and the player holds a king, he can only take in one of them.

Building

Since a card equaling the total value of two or more cards can take in those cards, a player may *build* such a total to enable him to take in the cards. He does this by first putting a card on the table on another card and announcing he is *building*.

For example, a player holds a 6. There is a 2 on the table, and he has a 4 in his hand, as well as the 6. He places the 4 on the 2 and announces, "Building six." On the next turn, he takes in the 4 and 2 with his 6. Once the build is announced, the opposing player cannot take in either the 4 or the 2 from the built pile. If the opponent has a 6, however, he can take it in.

A build cannot be made unless the player holds the card necessary to take it in. A player cannot put a 3 on a 4 and announce a build of 7 if he does not hold a 7 in his hand.

Builds can also be made with cards of the same value. If a 6 is on the table and the player holds two or more 6s, he can build 6s. He puts one 6 on the open 6 and announces that he is "building sixes." Then, on the next play, he can take in the two 6s on the table. Of course, if his opponent has a 6 he can take in the built 6s.

After a player has made a build, he may do one of two things on the next play: he may take in another card or he may increase or duplicate the build.

Increasing the Build

If the player holds three 6s in his hand and there is an open 6, he may place one of his 6s on and announce that he is building 6s. Then at the next turn, he puts on another 6, and finally takes in with the third 6.

Another method of increasing the build is as follows: If a player has built 5s by putting a 3 on a 2, on the next round he may place a 4 on the 3 and 2 and increase the build to 9, announcing "Building nine." In order to increase a build, the player must, again, have the card necessary to take in the increased build—in this case a 9.

An opponent also has the privilege of increasing the build. If the original player has built 5s by placing a 3 on a 2, his opponent can now put another card on it to increase the build to a total that a card in his hand can take in. For example, if he holds an 8 in his hand, he can add a 3 to the build and announce, "Building eight." If the original builder has an 8 he can take in the increased build, or if he has an ace and a 9, he can increase the build to 9 by adding the ace and announcing, "Building nine." Now, if his opponent has an ace and a 10 in his hand, he could add the ace and announce, "Building ten."

It must be borne in mind that the original build determines future increasing of that build. For example: If a player places a 3 on another 3, and announces, "Building 3s," his opponent cannot add an ace to increase the build to 7, since the build is 3s. If the opponent has a 3 he can take it in, however.

Duplicating Builds

A player may put a 6 on an ace and announce that he is building a seven. If, on the next turn a card in his hand can be added to another open card on the table to duplicate the build, he can duplicate. For example, if there is a 2 on the table, he could add a 5 to it, increasing the build to seven. Once it is duplicated, it can be duplicated again, but not increased. For instance, if there is now a 6 and an ace, and a 5 and a 2, neither player can now add another card, let us say a 3, and build ten. This restriction occurs once there is a duplication.

Now, having built 6 and ace and 2 and 5, the player can duplicate again, if possible, by adding a 3 to a 4, or making any other combination of seven and adding to the build. Then, on the last play, he takes in the seven.

He can also duplicate from the board and take in at the same time. For example: If he has built 6 and ace and 5 and 2, and there is a 3 on the table, and his opponent throws a 4, he can take in the 3 and 4 and the previous builds with the 7. But he cannot add the 4 and 3 to his build, then duplicate another card and keep the build intact. The 4 and 3, being open cards, are separate from the build and must be taken in at the same time as the build.

A build, however, cannot be increased by using a card from the table. Thus, if there are a 4 and 3 built to 7, and there is an open ace on the table, the player, if he holds an 8, cannot add the ace to the build and take it in. The build is separate from other open cards.

Trailing

If a player cannot or will not (due to strategy) take in or build, he can trail; that is, he places a card from his hand on the table as another open card. Even if his card matches a card on the table, he may prefer to trail it rather than take in the card on the table. Thus, if he has a 4 and there is a 4 on the table, he may trail it and not take in the other 4. This may be done for a number of strategical reasons. There may be aces, 9s, and 10s still in play, and he may hope that the opponent builds with an ace to make a build of nine, enabling the original player to take in the cards with his 9.

A typical game might be played as follows on the first deal: The nondealer is dealt ♠K ♦8 ♣2 ♣A. The dealer holds ♥9 ♥6 ♦5 ♠2. The open cards are ♥A ♣J ♣K ♥5.

The nondealer has the first play. He takes in the ace with his ace, leaving the jack, king, and 5 on the table. The dealer now plays and takes in the 5 with his 5, leaving the king and jack on the table. The dealer now hold ♥9 ♥6 ♠2. Since the ♠2 is worth a point, he is reluctant to play it immediately, so he plays the 6. The nondealer puts his 2 on the 6 and announces, "Building eight." The dealer now plays his 2, the nondealer takes in the build of eight with his 8, and the dealer plays his 9.

On the next deal, the open cards will be the ♥9 ♠2 ♣J. Again, the nondealer has first play, after he picks up the four new cards dealt to him. This goes on till "last," in which round the remaining cards in the deck are played out. The points are then added up by each player.

Scoring

The game may be played separately on each deal, with the holder of the majority of eleven points winning, but the more usual rule is to play until one of the players reaches twenty-one points after several deals. To determine who has reached twenty-one points, the correct procedure is to wait until the last game has been completely played. For example, player *A* may have eighteen points going into the final game, and player *B* fifteen. If, at the end of the deal, player *A* gets three points and player *B* eight, then player *A* has twenty-one points and player *B* twenty-three points, and player *B* wins.

However, the players may agree that the first player to reach twenty-one points wins, so that if, during the deal, player *A* has already collected three points before player *B* collected any, player *A* can announce he has reached twenty-one and claim victory. However, I prefer the first method, since the total of points counts and there is less likelihood of disagreement or mistakes.

Strategy

Casino is an easy game to learn—even young people have no difficulty picking it up—but it can be a difficult game to play well. A skillful player has a big advantage, despite the game's apparent simplicity.

The ideal situation is to keep track of every card played, but this is an almost impossible task, involving a great deal of energy that could be put to better use. A good player should keep track of the four aces, the big casino (♦10), and the little casino (♠2). Also, it is to the advantage of a player to remember how many 10s and 9s have been played. These cards, in conjunction with the aces and ♠2, are the key cards in the game of casino; they become the ultimate builds and, at the end of a deal, are of vital importance.

It is not that important to remember the face cards. They play themselves, and, at the end of a deal, all will have been taken in since they cannot be built upon.

Another important thing to do in casino is to keep a running count of the cards you have taken in. Since the player holding the majority of cards scores three points, this is a critical area of the game.

Since holding the majority of spades yields a point, it is to the player's benefit to take in spades at every opportunity and to build so that a spade is saved, rather than possibly given to the opponent. An example of this: Suppose there is a ♣7 on the table and the player holds two 7s, the ♠7 and ♥7. To build sevens, he should first put down the ♥7, retaining the ♠7. Thus, if his opponent has the ♦7 and takes in the build, he will not have gotten the retained ♠7.

In the quest for the most spades, it must be remembered that this yields only one point, whereas having the most cards will yield 3 points, so it is better to take in three cards than two spades in most cases.

In trailing cards, it is wise to first play the face cards if they are odd cards. If there is a matching face card on the table, with odd cards not having any point value, take in the face card first. Force your opponent to commit himself first by building or playing another odd card that you might take in as a total of two or more cards. For example, if the board shows a 3, a jack, and a 5, and you hold a jack, 6, 9, and 10, first take in the jack. If you build nine, your opponent may take it in. Let him build first. If he has an ace and a 9, he may very well put the 5, 3, and ace into a nine build, and then you can take in his build.

If you hold the ♦10 (big casino or Good Ten), try and cash it in as soon as possible. If there is a build of 7 and 3 on the table, and a 6 as well, and you hold a 4, it is better to take in the 7 and 3 with the ♦10, rather than build another ten with the 4 and 6. If you built and your opponent took it in with a 10, then knowing you have a 10 he will play to avoid letting you build to 10. Thus you may not be able to make use of it in that round and might subsequently lose it.

If you hold the little casino (♠2) or any ace, it is not wise to play it as a trail card. It is best to retain it, in the hope that your opponent also holds a 2 or ace and plays it first. If you have the correct count on

9s and 10s and know a build with the ace or ♠2 added is safe, then of course, you can build with it immediately. But other builds might not be safe if you cannot overtake the build when it is increased. For example: You hold an ace, 7, and 10, having already played the jack, and the board holds a 4 and 6. It might be better to build a 7 with the 6 and ace, rather than trail the 7, if there is one 7 left with a couple of rounds to go. If the big casino is still in the deck, your opponent might have it, might build to 10 with a 3, and you could thus take it in. But the build is safer since you have a higher card, in this case the 10, to possibly take in an increased build.

Since the person who takes in "last" (that is, takes in the last trick on the final round of the deal) takes in all the cards remaining on the table, if you are the dealer and play last and hold any face card, retain it to the end. The open face card will remain in play and you will thus take in the remaining cards. Every dealer should remember this rule well.

Irregularities

The rules should be agreed upon beforehand to avoid any disagreement. For example, it has been written as a rule of casino that if the cards are not cut before the deal, the nondealer not only has the right to call a misdeal before the first card is played out, but may decide whether the dealer should lose his deal. I think this rule is too strict and the nondealer should only have the right to call a misdeal. If the cards are not shuffled before the deal, again I feel that the nondealer has the right to call a misdeal, either before the first play or at any time during the game when it becomes apparent that the cards are in the same sequence as the previous deal. If both parties agree beforehand, however, the penalty for a nonshuffled deck should be a losing deal for the dealer after the first card is played. If the first card has not been played, then the dealer should be required to redeal the deck without penalty.

If the dealer forgets to call "last," his opponent has the option of calling a misdeal and not counting the deal, or letting it stand. An even better rule would be to make it the responsibility of both players by putting the deck in full view at all times so that both players would know when the last round commenced.

If the dealer deals too few cards to himself or his opponent, the cards to make up the short deal should be taken from the top of the unused deck. If, on the first deal, a card going to a player is exposed, it should remain as an open card, providing there are not already four open cards dealt.

If there are already four open cards and a card is exposed, the dealer must take that card as his own and replace it by taking an unseen card from his own dealt cards and putting it on the top of the unused deck. If the dealer has already seen his four cards, that card remains as an open card and the dealer deals himself only three cards on the next deal.

If too many cards are dealt to a player and that player has not seen his cards, the other player draws the excess card or cards from the opponent's hand and replaces the card or cards on the unused deck.

If any player is dealt too many cards and he sees all his cards, he may choose the cards he wishes not to play and put them on the table as open cards. On the next round, the dealer is penalized by taking fewer cards in the amount of excess cards dealt to the player. If the dealer deals himself excess cards, the other player has the right to pick the unseen excess cards from the dealer's hand and put them on the table. On the next round, the dealer is penalized with fewer cards.

If, on the final round, there are fewer than four cards available for each player, the deck should then be counted. If it is found to have fewer than fifty-two cards, the deal is considered void and does not count. If there are fifty-two cards, then the dealer is required to take fewer cards than his opponent if that will make up the difference. If there are only seven cards left to deal on the last round, the dealer takes three and deals four to his opponent. If there only are six cards available, each gets three.

However, it may be predetermined by the players that any such irregularity be considered a misdeal when coming on the last round, and that if there are not enough cards to go around, the dealer loses the deal.

If a player takes in a wrong card—that is, a card to which he is not entitled—he must, on demand, restore the card to the table and leave his own card on the table as well. This demand may be made at any time prior to the next round of dealing. After a new round is dealt, the player making the mistake cannot be penalized.

The rule is that if a player builds, on the next play he must take in that build, or take in another card, or increase or duplicate the build. If he trails a card instead, he must take in the build if the opponent so demands, but the trailed card remains on the table. If he cannot take in the build, not having the card necessary to do so, the build is broken up, and the opponent shall have two plays to take in from the table. In some instances, if so agreed upon, such a false build will cost as a penalty one point from the offender's score.

If a card is played out of turn, it must remain on the table; it is counted as a trailed card, and the offender misses his next turn. If it is partnership casino, his partner is not permitted to take in this card.

If a player exposes his card in two- or three-man casino without partnership play, there is no penalty. But in partnership play, since a partner is wrongfully benefited, the exposed card must be put at once on the table, and the player exposing the card misses his turn. The partner of the player exposing the card may not take in that card.

A player in the game cannot look at any trick taken in other than the one just taken in. If he does so, he should be severely penalized since it is a bad habit that gives him undue advantage. For each such instance, he should lose one point from his total. If the player decides to count his cards before the last play of the game, he should likewise be penalized one point.

Partnership Casino

There are four players, and the partners sit alternately. Dealing and playing move clockwise. The cards taken in by both partners are combined and added, as are the point totals.

Although the partners help each other, they are still subject to the rules of casino, and these must be followed.

Ducking

The same rules apply to ducking as to casino, except the idea is to *not* get points or cards, so the strategy is completely the opposite of casino. The aces, big casino, and little casino are played or trailed immediately, and on the last deal an effort is made to avoid taking in the last trick.

X

Hearts

♠ ♥ ♦ ♣

Introduction

Hearts is a fine game of skill which can be played by as few as two or as many as seven players. There are several interesting variations of the game. Hearts is, at its best, a four-handed game, each player for himself.

Rules of Play

The Deck: The standard deck of fifty-two cards is used, without the joker.

Rank of Cards: The ace is the highest, followed by K, Q, J, 10, down to 2, which is the lowest.

The Deal: Each player deals in turn, the deal passing clockwise around the table, in rotation.

After the cards are shuffled by the dealer, they are passed to the player to his right to be cut. If that player refuses to cut, any other player may.

After the cut, the dealer proceeds to deal out the cards face down, one at a time, starting with the player on his left and going clockwise, so that each player gets an equal number of cards. The deck is completely dealt out, and in a four-handed game each player receives thirteen cards.

If there is an odd number of players, there will be cards left over. Any remaining cards are placed on the table, face down. The player winning the first trick takes in these cards, but they are not to be looked at by any player.

The Pass: After each player has picked up his cards and sorted them into suits, he prepares to pass three cards to the player on his *left* and to receive three cards from the player on his *right*. These cards are passed face down. A player cannot look at the cards passed to him before he passes his own cards. The purpose of the pass is to remove cards that will hurt the player's score.

A variation of the pass is that the cards are passed to the player on the right, and, if the game is six- or seven-handed, then only two cards are passed.

Black Lady

In hearts, the queen of spades is called the Black Lady or Black Maria and, in the usual scoring, is valued at thirteen points. Since the object of the game is to have the least amount of points, no player wants to take in the queen of spades as a trick, nor does he want to take in any heart, since each heart counts as one point. Therefore, on the pass, if a player does not have enough other spades in his hand to protect the queen of spades, then he should discard it at the first opportunity by passing it to the player on his left.

Object of the Game: In most heart variations, the object is to avoid taking in any heart tricks or the queen of spades, but in some variations the object is just the reverse.

Play of the Hand

The player to the left of the dealer makes the first play and he can lead any suit. Although hearts are referred to as "trumps," they really are not, and do not have any special significance in taking in tricks; their value is strictly in the scoring.

After the first card is played by the eldest hand (the hand to the left of the dealer), the suit he led must be followed by all the players in turn, beginning with the player on the first lead's left. If any player is void in the led suit, he may discard any card in his hand. Each trick is won by the highest-ranking card in the suit led.

For example, the lead plays out the ♦K. Each player must follow suit, and only the player playing the ♦A on that round can win the trick. If any player is void in diamonds, he can play any card from any suit. However, if he plays a heart, it is not considered a trump, and thus only a diamond could take in the trick. The winner of the trick leads the next trick.

The usual rule is that the ♠Q (the Black Lady) must be discarded at the first opportunity by any player holding it. It is generally stated that this rule does not apply in purely social games, but the rule adds strategy and excitement to the game.

Scoring

In hearts, there are various ways of scoring. The usual method is to have a separate count kept by each player.

Cumulative Scoring
With four players, there would be four columns, and each individual score would be based on the following points:

For each heart taken in tricks   1 point
For the queen of spades   13 points

At the end of the game, the scores of each player are added up, and a settlement is made by the players. The final figures might look something like this:

A	*B*	*C*	*D*
5	4	1	16
7	3	15	1
9	13	2	2
5	6	14	1
4	4	14	4
5	2	6	13
35	32	52	37

(Note that, reading across, each line totals twenty-six, and therefore the sum of the four totals is an aggregate of twenty-six.)

The usual method of tallying the score is to add all four scores, 35 + 32 + 52 + 37, for a total of 156; find an average score by dividing this total by four, the number of players in the game, which makes an average of 39; then calculate the difference between each player's score and the average. (Every five games works out to an exact division, because 4 into 156 goes exactly 39 times.)

Player *A* is −4 from the average, *B* is −7, *C* is +13, and *D* is −2. Thus, *C* pays everybody. He puts in thirteen chips, and player *A* collects four; *B*, seven; and *D*, two.

Sometimes two players are plus and two minus. Let's take another total. The following column shows just the total points, not the individual games.

Points		Average	
A	47	39	+8
B	64	39	+25
C	33	39	−6
D	12	39	−27

In this case *A* puts in eight chips, *B* puts in twenty-five, for a total of thirty-three. *C* withdraws six of those chips, and *D* the balance of twenty-seven.

A common variation in play is to go for a slam; to get all thirteen hearts plus the queen of spades. In this variation, the player who does this gets all twenty-six points.

Sometimes, hearts is scored after every deal, rather than cumulatively. In that case, at the end of the play each player puts into the pot one chip for each heart held, and the player holding the queen of spades puts in thirteen chips. All the chips go to the hand with the lowest score. If two players tie for lowest score, they split the chips. If there is an odd chip, it is kept in the pot to be added to the next round.

One popular variation that is played most often is called sweepstake. Here's how it works.

Sweepstake

For each heart a player has won, he puts one chip into the pool, and thirteen additional chips if he held the queen of spades after the play of the cards. Any player who was "clear"—that is, took in no hearts and did not take in the queen of spades—wins the total pool. If two or more players were clear, they divide the pool. If there is an odd chip, it is left for the next pool.

If, however, every hand was "painted"—that is, held at least one heart or the queen of spades—then the pool remains on the table till the end of play of the next hand. It now forms a jackpot or jack. If the next hand is played out and still no one was clear, the jackpot becomes bigger, until it is finally won by one or more players being clear.

Hearts Without the Queen of Spades

This game is played without counting the queen of spades as thirteen points, and assigning it no value and no special role in the game. Left for points are the thirteen hearts, and instead of twenty-six points there are only thirteen counted.

In this variation, there is no passing of cards before the play, and each player plays out the original thirteen cards he was dealt.

Scoring with this variation is usually done by the *Howell* method. For each heart won by play, the player holding that heart puts in as many chips as there are other players in the game. If a player has won six hearts and there are four players in the game (three besides himself), he puts three chips for each heart held, or eighteen chips, into the pot. Then he subtracts the number of hearts he holds (six) from thirteen and that leaves seven. He then removes seven chips from the pot.

Auction Hearts

The feature of this game is that there is a round of bidding to determine which player can name the suit to be avoided. In this variation, a suit other than hearts can be the penalty suit. The bidding starts with the player to the left of the dealer and goes on for one round only. Each player may make only one bid, or he may pass. If the first bid is four, the next bidder must bid higher or else must pass. The bidding is for the right to name the penalty suit, and the high bidder then puts that number of chips into the pot and names the suit.

The high bidder leads first, and thereafter play proceeds as in the regular game. At the end of the play each player puts a chip into the pot for each card of the penalty suit he has won.

In auction hearts, sweepstake scoring is used. The pot can only be won by a player who is clear (has no cards of the penalty suit). If two players are clear, then the pool becomes a jackpot.

On the next deal, the original high bidder has the right, without any bidding, to name a new suit as a penalty suit. At the end of play of this round, each player puts in a chip for each card of the new penalty suit he holds. If no one is clear, the jackpot just gets larger, and another deal is had. The original high bidder retains his right to name the penalty suit without further bidding until the jackpot is won.

Domino Hearts

The game may be played by two to seven players, and six cards are dealt to each. The remaining cards become the stock. The rules are the same as hearts, except that if a player cannot follow suit (that is, cannot play a card from the same suit as is led) he must pick up cards from the stock, one at a time, until he gets a card of that suit.

After the stock is exhausted, any hand unable to follow suit may discard another suit. The game goes on until all the cards have been exhausted (taken in tricks). Since different players will have different amounts of cards, as each player runs out of cards he drops from the game. If a player dropping out won the last trick with his last card, the player to his left has the first lead on the very next round of play.

If two players are left and one of them runs out of cards, the player remaining with cards simply adds them to his own pile of tricks.

At the end of play, each player adds up his heart total, with each heart counting as one point.

Usually, in domino hearts the queen of spades is not used as the Black Lady and has no particular value.

Spot Hearts

Each heart in this variation has a special value, and the points charged to the player, instead of being the same for each heart won, are as follows: Fourteen for the ace of hearts, thirteen for the king, twelve for the queen, eleven for the jack, and spot value for all the others.

This kind of scoring can be used in any of the games of hearts.

Cancellation Hearts

This game is best for seven or more players, with a maximum of twelve.

Instead of one deck, two are used. They are shuffled together and then dealt out as far as they will go, one at a time. Any cards remaining after the deal are placed face down to form a "widow." There is no pass.

In this game, the queen of spades is a Black Lady and has a value of thirteen.

The player to the left of the dealer (eldest hand) plays first. After that, the same rules as apply to hearts are in force. The winner of the first trick gets the widow, and it is added to his pile.

The unique feature of this game is that if two cards of equal value are played in the same suit, they cancel each other out and neither can win the trick. For example, if two kings of diamonds are played, they do not figure into the taking of the trick, and the next highest card in that suit would win, unless it, too, was cancelled out by an equal card.

If player *A* dropped the king (all the cards are the same suit), player *B* the king, player *C* the queen, player *D* the queen, player *E* the jack, player *F* the jack, and player *G* the deuce, player *G* would win the trick, since all the other cards cancel each other out. This is possible because two decks are used.

If all the cards in the playing of a trick are paired (this could happen with an even number of players), the winner of the next trick must take in all the cards of the previous cancelled trick.

The leader of the cancelled trick has the lead in the trick following it.

Scoring is the same as in hearts.

Omnibus Hearts

Although this game can be played by four to six players, it is best for four. It is called omnibus hearts because it takes features from other variations of hearts and combines them into one game.

In this game, the thirteen hearts count, as well as the queen of spades, which is thirteen points. The hearts and queen of spades are minus cards, but the 10 of diamonds counts as plus ten.

If a player takes all fifteen counting cards, the 10 of diamonds, the queen of spades, and all thirteen hearts, he scores twenty-six plus for the deal, and all the other players score nothing.

In all other respects omnibus hearts is the same as hearts, Black Lady.

Strategy

The most important thing a player of hearts must learn is to keep track of cards and suits, and to be an expert player he must practically keep track of all cards played. By doing this he gains information about the location of other cards that is vital to his correct playing strategy.

Another important strategy is in the lead from suits held. If holding a short suit, with cards such as A Q 3, correct strategy calls for the play of the high cards, with the 3 used as an eventual exit card. If a short holding consists of only high cards, such as K J 9, this suit must be played out as fast as possible because the other players will attempt to force these cards into the lead after exit cards have been played.

Protected suits, such as K 9 6 4 3, are preferable, since they can provide exit with small cards and might, because of the length, be able to avoid taking in any tricks.

In cumulative and Howell scoring, it pays to take in some heart tricks if that strategy will allow you to avoid taking in many more tricks.

Thus, holding ♥K 4, play out the king first, then the 4. You cannot avoid a heart trick, but by playing this way you will avoid taking in still more hearts.

In sweepstake scoring, if there is a possibility of being clear, play boldly and aggressively toward that end. However, if the hand is destined to be painted, or if by the play of the hand it has become painted, then the player's sole object should be to paint every other player and thus set up a jackpot. Usually in the game he will find himself the ally of other painted players whose object also is to paint those players who have remained clear.

If not holding the Black Lady (queen of spades), it pays to lead spades to force her out. Sometimes the Black Lady can be pinpointed. If a player takes in a spade trick with an ace or king and then doesn't follow with another spade, one can almost be sure that he has her.

If holding a queen of spades, the strategy is to play out a short side suit, voiding yourself so that you can discard the queen of spades. When a player is doing this and refuses to lead spades, it might again be possible to pinpoint him as the holder of the queen of spades.

Irregularities

Misdeal

If a card is exposed by the dealer at any time during the deal, it is a misdeal.

A misdeal is also declared if any player is dealt too many cards, or too few cards.

Should there be a misdeal for any of these reasons, the deal is void and the dealer loses the deal to the player on his left, the next player in turn.

Should any card be exposed by a player through his own fault, it is no misdeal, since each player is responsible for his own cards.

If any of the above errors occur during the deal, but no player requests a misdeal and the first trick is played and completed, a misdeal cannot be called.

Revoke

Under the rules of hearts, should a player fail to follow suit when he is able to do so, an immediate revoke is declared and the offending player is charged with all the minus points on that deal.

A revoke under these conditions comes into force only after the trick is completed and the cards gathered in. If the player realizes he has played the incorrect card by not following suit, he may, while the cards are exposed on the table, change his play by picking up that card and playing a card from the correct suit.

A revoke may be called at any time up to the point at which the cards are gathered together for a new deal, since the revoke can be established by checking the completed tricks. For this reason, each player must keep the tricks he has taken in separate and apart, not mingling them so that a revoke can be ascertained.

Each trick taken in must be kept face down in separate units by the player winning the trick. Should a revoke be claimed against a player who has mingled his cards so that the proof cannot be ascertained, he is penalized by being charged with all the minus points of the hand.

Should a claim of revoke be made against another player, and one of the players has mingled his tricks so that revoke cannot be proved or disproved, he is penalized the full amount of minus points on that hand.

When playing Black Lady, the failure to discard the spade queen at the first opportunity is a revoke. A violation of this rule costs the revoking player the full amount of minus points.

Play out of Turn

Should a player play out of turn, there is no penalty. If brought to his attention, he must retract that card and wait his correct turn. But should other players have followed suit or played to that trick, the lead and the trick stand as legal.

Any player in the game may demand the retraction of a play (or lead) out of turn, but until such demand is made, the play stands.

Incorrect hand

If a player has too few cards, he must take every trick he cannot play to because of his lack of cards. If he is one card short, he must take the last trick.

In the event that a player is required to take tricks because of lack of cards, the player who would ordinarily have won the trick plays the next lead.

If a player is discovered to have too many cards, he must take the last trick.

XI

Blackjack

CASINO GAME

Introduction

Blackjack, or twenty-one as it is also commonly called, has become a standard game in most of the casinos in the United States and the Caribbean. It has become so popular in American casinos that in many it rivals the game of craps in money volume.

Blackjack can also be played privately, but first we will deal with the casino game. There are some basic differences between the two, the most notable being that in a private game the deal alternates among the players, while in the game played in casinos the dealer works for the house, and all players play against the house.

Some of the other differences, to mention just a few: In a private game, the payoff for blackjack is two to one, and the dealer wins in all ties. In the casino, blackjack is paid off at the ratio of one and a half to one, and all ties are standoffs—all ties of point value of twenty-one or below, that is. If the player goes bust (over twenty-one in card values) and the dealer also goes bust, the dealer wins. This last rule also holds true in private games.

In a private game, the dealer has many options and can decide whether to draw or not, depending on the cards of the other players. In the casino game, there are hardly any options afforded the dealer. Basically, he must draw to a hand containing sixteen points or less, and stand pat on a hand containing seventeen points or more. The dealer is bound to do this, no matter what cards the players are holding.

In some casinos, when more than one deck is used and the cards are dealt from a device called a "shoe," the cards are dealt face up to all players, and the dealer gets one downcard and one face card. If he has sixteen and all the players opposing him have hands no higher than twelve, if they stand pat he must draw to his sixteen, even though by not drawing he would automatically win. This is not the case in a private game.

The dealer has one big advantage over the player in blackjack. If the player "busts" his hand and goes over twenty-one, and subsequently the dealer goes over twenty-one, the dealer still wins for the house or for himself. In fact, the moment the player goes over twenty-one, his cards are taken away and his chips are taken in. He loses immediately.

Other than this advantage for the dealer in the casino game, the player seems to have all the other benefits. He collects one and a half to one if he has a blackjack; the house merely wins on its blackjack. The player can split any pair. He can double down, that is, double his bet and receive an additional card when the first two cards dealt to him total eleven. In some casinos he can double down on two cards totaling ten; in still other casinos he can double down on any two cards; and in still other casinos he can double down no matter when he gets a total of eleven. All these privileges are to the player's advantage and are denied the dealer.

The player can also insure his bet in the event the face card of the dealer shows an ace. This means that he can make a bet totaling one half of his original bet and get paid off at two to one in the event that the dealer's hole card is a 10 or face card, giving him a blackjack. Thus, the player would be paid back his original bet in the event that the dealer had blackjack, and lose one half his bet in the event that the hole card was not a face card or 10. Though the value of insurance is dubious except under certain circumstances, it is a privilege granted to the player and not the dealer.

One other advantage. In most casinos, the dealer must treat his cards as "hard" cards. Since an ace could count as an eleven or a one, holding an ace and a 6 could give a count of seven or seventeen. Usually, the dealer must count the ace as an eleven, while the player can count his ace as either one or eleven. In those casinos where the dealer counts the ace 6 as seven and has the option of drawing cards to that hand until he reaches a total of seventeen or more, the house has an added advantage.

But there remains another advantage, one which the house enjoys, but which can be turned to the player's advantage. The player must bet before he sees his cards.

This advantage to the house can be offset by card counting, which will be discussed in a later section, and also by knowing the game, knowing correct play, and knowing when the cards are in your favor. By the end of this chapter, the reader should have acquired this knowledge.

It is possible to beat the game of casino blackjack. It is the only casino game in which the odds sometimes shift in favor of the player. Knowing when this happens and taking advantage of it is the quickest and surest road to winning at the game of casino blackjack.

Rules of Play

Casino blackjack is played with a standard deck of fifty-two cards or multiples of the standard deck. At one time the game was played with a single deck; then multiple-deck games were introduced up to four decks. Today it is not unusual, however, to see multiple-deck games played with six or eight decks. This is pretty much standard practice in Atlantic City and on the Strip in Las Vegas. The single-deck game has all but disappeared from Las Vegas, but it is still standard in northern Nevada.

In casino blackjack the suits have no value whatsoever, and a blackjack of 10 of diamonds and ace of hearts is as good as one containing both the ace and jack of spades. To value the points the player examines the spots on the cards. A two is worth two points, a three three points, and so forth up to the nine, which is worth nine points. The 10, jack, queen, and king are each worth ten points; from now on we'll refer to any of these cards as either a 10 or 10-value card.

The ace has a separate valuation; it is worth either one or eleven points according to how the player wants to value the card. If a player holds a 10 with an ace as his original card, it will have a value of 11 so that the hand will be worth twenty-one points as a blackjack. If a player has a 10 6 A, the ace will be valued at one point so that the hand doesn't exceed twenty-one points.

The object of the game is to beat the dealer and thus the house. In some situations this might mean drawing cards to get as close to twenty-one points as possible; in other situations it might mean standing with as few as twelve points in order to let the dealer draw first. If either the player's or dealer's hand exceeds twenty-one points, it loses. If the player goes over twenty-one, he loses immediately and both his cards and chips are removed from play. If the dealer goes over twenty-one, he loses and pays off only those players still involved in active play.

Thus, if a player goes over twenty-one, which is known as "busting," and a dealer subsequently goes over twenty-one and busts, the player still loses. This is the big advantage to the casino; the dealer goes last and players may already have lost before it in his time to draw cards. By then it's too late for them to win.

The player has a number of options open to him, which are to his advantage and which will be discussed in full in a later section; the dealer has no options. He or she must abide by the house rules. In most casinos this means standing on all totals of seventeen or higher, and hitting, or drawing cards to, a hand that is valued at sixteen points or less. In some casinos, notably in northern Nevada and in downtown Las Vegas, the dealer will stand on all hard seventeens, but must hit a soft seventeen. When a dealer does hit a soft seventeen, it is to the disadvantage of the player.

Let's now explain what a soft and a hard hand is. A soft hand is any hand containing an ace in which the ace is valued at eleven. The following are examples of this:

A 8	Soft nineteen
A 7	Soft eighteen
A 5 4	Soft twenty

In the above examples, all hands were valued by making the ace worth eleven points, and thus these were soft hands or soft totals. The terms are indistinguishable.

A hard hand, however, is one in which there is no ace, or if there is an ace present, it is worth only one point. The following are examples of this:

9 8	Hard seventeen
10 9	Hard nineteen
K 5	Hard fifteen

All the above had no aces and therefore were hard totals or hands. The following are hands with an ace valued at one point.

10 5 A	Hard sixteen
A 2 10	Hard thirteen
A 4 A J	Hard sixteen
8 3 A	Hard twelve

In all the above situations, if the ace were counted as eleven, the point totals would exceed twenty-one and thus the hand would be a bust. But with the ace worth only one point, the hands are valued at less than twenty-one and are still valid hands. With the A 2 10, we see how a soft thirteen (A 2) is turned into a hard thirteen by the addition of a 10, and the same thing holds true for the A 4 A J, which turns from a soft sixteen (A 4 A) into a hard sixteen by the addition of the jack.

The ace is the most important and powerful card in blackjack, and its chief virtue is that, when combined with any 10-value card, it becomes a blackjack, which is the best possible hand in the game and is paid off at three to two, instead of the normal even-money payoff on other hands.

If the player and the dealer have identical totals, no money is exchanged. It is a tie, a standoff, or, in the parlance of casino blackjack, a "push." But if the player's valid total is higher than the dealer's, the player wins.

How the Casino Game Is Played

When you enter a casino, you'll find a number of blackjack tables in operation, for this game is the most popular of all casino games. If you go to an empty table, where the dealer is standing with his or her arms crossed, waiting for a player, the dealer will immediately start shuffling the deck of cards (assuming now a single-deck game).

At this point, if you have brought cash, the dealer will change the money into casino chips. You can bet the cash, but if you win, you'll be paid off in casino chips, and if you lose, your cash will be dropped into a slot out of sight. The casino discourages cash action and wants the players to bet chips.

After the cards have been shuffled, they're given to a player to be cut. At a table with more than one player, if any gambler refuses to cut the cards, another player is given the chance. After they're cut and restacked by the dealer, the top card is "burned," that is, removed from the deck and either placed to one side in a plastic case or put at the bottom of the deck face up, but not seen by the players.

After this card is burned, the game is ready to begin. Each player at the table must make a bet by placing chips in a box in front of his or her place. The bet must be made prior to the cards being dealt.

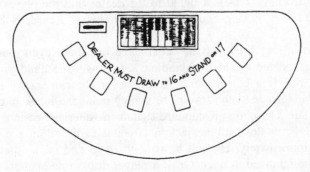

Casino Blackjack table

After all bets have been made, the dealer will commence dealing the cards, giving each player at the table one card face down, beginning with the player at his extreme left, facing him, and then giving the other players, in turn, one card face down in the same manner.

The first player to get a card is known as the "first baseman," and the last player is called the "anchorman" or "third baseman." After each player at the table has one card the dealer gives himself a card, also face down. Then a second round of dealing ensues, with each player in the same order getting a second card face down, while the dealer turns his second card face up.

The players see only one of the dealer's cards, while the dealer sees none of the players' cards. In multiple-deck games it is now the custom for all the players' cards to be dealt face up. Face down or up, it makes no difference, for the players are trying to beat the house, not each other, and even if the dealer sees the players' cards, he or she is bound by strict rules and cannot deviate from these rules even if the player can be beaten by changing the rules.

For example, in all casinos the dealer must hit a sixteen, hard or soft. If the dealer has a sixteen and the player against him has a twelve, he must still hit that sixteen by drawing another card, even though by standing, he would beat the player's twelve total with his sixteen.

After all the players have received their two cards, they now act on their individual hands in turn, beginning with the first baseman and ending with the third baseman.

Players have several options open to them, but the most important is standing or hitting the hand. By standing, we mean standing pat, not drawing a card to the hand. If a player decides to do this, he or she slides the cards under the chips and this is a signal that he or she desires no more cards.

If a player wants another card, he should scrape the cards on the felt surface toward him. This is a signal to the dealer that the player wants to get another card. Taking another card, or drawing a card, is known as "hitting."

In games that the cards are dealt face up, the players don't touch their cards, and the signal for standing is to wave one hand palm down over the cards. If a player wants to hit, he or she can scrape the index finger on the surface of the layout, or simply point the index finger at the cards for a hit. These are all standard signals in American casinos.

If a player is dealt a blackjack, a 10-value card and an ace, he turns them over immediately. He will be paid three to two on his bet and the cards will be removed at once. Or, if a player draws one or more cards (a player can hit the hand as often as he wishes, provided he doesn't go over twenty-one points) and "busts," that is, goes over twenty-one, he should turn the cards over immediately for the dealer to remove them, along with his chips.

After all the players have acted on their hands, it is the dealer's turn. He now turns over his hole card (the unseen down card) and displays both his cards. If his total is above seventeen, he must stand. If his total is below seventeen, he must hit. If his total is seventeen exactly, and it's a hard seventeen (without an ace), he must stand. But if the total is a soft seventeen, he hits the hand in northern Nevada and downtown Las Vegas, while in other gambling jurisdictions he must stand on that total.

If in doubt about the particular casino rules, look at the printed layout. If a dealer must stand on all seventeens, it will state "dealer stands on all seventeens." If he must hit the soft seventeen, it will so state.

After the dealer has acted on his hand, he pays all players who have a higher total than he has, collects the losing chips from those who have lower totals, and "pushes" those with identical totals. When there's a push, it's a standoff; no one wins or loses.

When a dealer has a 10-value card or ace as his upcard, he is required in most casinos to peek at his hole card to ascertain if he has a blackjack. If he has one, he turns it over at once, and collects from all players who are at the table, for they lose immediately to the dealer's blackjack. If any player also has a blackjack, it's a standoff. If the dealer doesn't have a blackjack, he starts play by turning to the first baseman, waiting for his decision.

If a dealer busts, he pays off all players still in the game. If a player busts, he loses immediately. If the dealer busts after a player busts, the player still has lost. In order to win in this situation, the player must have a valid hand remaining on the table when the dealer busts.

A player may play more than one hand at a time. Some players take a whole table to themselves. The usual rule is that if a player plays more than one hand, he must bet at least double the house minimum at that table. Thus, at a $5 table, each bet on each hand must be at least $10.

The table minimum is usually stated on a small placard on the table. In a casino, table minimums may be different from table to table. A casino may have $2, $5, $25, and $100 tables all in operation at the same time. At one time the maximum wager allowed was $500, but now casinos allow $1,000, $3,000, or even more, depending on the particular house. Sometimes the house maximum is also printed on the placard. If it isn't, ask the dealer if you're a really heavy roller.

At the present time most casinos have multiple-deck games, dealt from a shoe. A shoe is a gambling device that permits the dealer to remove one card at a time from a rectangular box by sliding it forward, unseen, along the felt surface of the table. Whenever four or more decks are used in a game, the shoe is in operation.

Player's Options

As mentioned, the dealer has no options, but must play according to the strict rules of the house. A player, however, has a number of options, all potentially valuable to him.

Hitting or Standing

A player may hit or stand on any total. He may stand with hands valued less than seventeen and hit soft eighteens (7 A) if he wants to.

Doubling Down

In Atlantic City and in Las Vegas a player may double down on any two-card total, no matter what the total. For example, if a player has a 5 3 for a hard eight, he could double down if he desired. Or if he held a 6 A for a soft seventeen, or a 3 A for a soft fourteen, he could also double down.

Doubling down means literally what it says. A player can double his bet, at his option. For example, in a game where the cards are dealt face down to the player, he can double down by turning over the cards and placing a bet equal to his original bet next to the chips in the betting box. If he had an original $10 bet, now it would be $20.

In those casinos where the cards are dealt face up, the player simply places the chips for doubling down next to his originally bet chips. When done correctly, doubling down is an enormous advantage to the player. In northern Nevada, with a couple of casino exceptions, a player can only double down on a hard ten or eleven. No other double downs are permitted, and thus this rule is much more inflexible than the Las Vegas and Atlantic City doubling-down option rule.

Splitting Pairs

Whenever a player is dealt two cards of identical rank, such as 8s, he can split them, that is, separate them and play each 8 as the foundation of another hand by placing another bet equal to his original bet on the table. When the cards are dealt face down, he turns the pair over; when dealt face up, he simply separates the cards and makes an identical bet.

Suppose that a player has been dealt 8 8. He now makes the additional bet and separates the cards. On the first 8 he is dealt a 10. Now he has 8 10 or eighteen and stands. On the second 8, he's dealt another 8. He can now resplit this 8 (except in Atlantic City) by putting down another bet. On the second 8 he gets a 5, then hits again and gets a jack. The hand 8 5 J is over twenty-one, so he loses this bet. Now he hits the third 8 hand and gets a 9. He stands with hard seventeen.

All 10-value cards are considered pairs for purposes of splitting. If a player gets a J, Q, K, he can split them as separate 10s, though splitting 10s is never advised. If a player splits aces, the rule is tighter. Once aces are split, the player can get only one additional card on each ace and no more. Suppose a player gets A A and splits them, always a good move. On the first ace he gets a 2 for a soft thirteen, a terrible hand. He's stuck. He cannot hit that hand again. In some casinos, such as the Horseshoe in Las Vegas, a player may resplit an ace if it is drawn on split aces, but this is the exception. In most casinos, even if an ace is drawn on a split ace, the player is stuck with that hand of A A, which is completely worthless.

Insurance

In Atlantic City and in the Nevada casinos, when the dealer shows an ace as his upcard, he will ask the players in the game if they want "insurance." Insurance is not quite the correct word to use, but it is in universal use. What the dealer is asking in essence is if the players want to bet that he has a blackjack, that is, a 10-value card in the hole.

If a player wants to make this bet, he or she puts out one-half the original bet as an insurance bet. If the dealer has a blackjack, the insurance wager is paid off at two to one; thus the player has not lost his original bet even if the dealer has blackjack. If the dealer's hole card is not a 10-value one, then the insurance bet is lost, and the game goes on.

Is it worthwhile to make this wager? Many novices and even dealers will tell you to always insure a blackjack. In that way, they state, you can't lose. Their point is this: If you yourself hold a blackjack and the dealer shows an ace, and you make the insurance bet at two to one, whether or not the dealer has a blackjack you will still get even money on your original bet as a pure profit.

Here's how that works. Suppose you have a $10 bet and get a blackjack. The dealer shows an ace as his upcard. You make a $5 insurance wager. If the dealer has a blackjack, he'll pay you two to one on the $5 wager for a $10 profit, while your blackjack and his are pushes. Net profit, $10.

If the dealer doesn't have a blackjack, he'll take away your $5 insurance wager, but pay you $15 for your blackjack. Net profit, $10.

But it doesn't pay to insure the blackjack you hold, because it isn't a good bet. Let's suppose that you're playing head-to-head with the dealer, just you and he at the table. On the opening round of play you get a blackjack and he shows an ace in a one-deck game. At this point you know three cards, two aces and one 10-value card. That leaves fifteen 10s (there are sixteen in a deck) and thirty-five other cards. The odds against the dealer's holding a blackjack are thirty-five to fifteen or more than two to one on a bet you will collect two to one on. Making this wager at this point gives the house about 8 percent as its advantage.

It's better to collect those three-to-two payoffs rather than to be cautious and only collect even money on your blackjacks when the dealer shows an ace. Many players will insure their strong hands, such as 10 10, but this is the worst thing they can do, because the two 10-value cards they hold are taken away from the dealer to use to form his blackjack.

When should you take insurance? Only when it's to your advantage, when the ratio of other cards to 10-value cards is less than two to one. The only way to know this is to count cards, and that method will be shown in a subsequent section.

Surrender
We mention this option only in passing because it has pretty much disappeared from casino play. At one time, especially in Atlantic City, the house allowed you to surrender half your bet if you didn't wish to play out your original two-card hand. This was valuable to card counters who, when facing a dealer's 10 or ace with a 10-rich deck or decks, surrendered when they held hands of hard fourteen, fifteen, and sixteen. But the casinos discontinued this option to thwart card counters, who were the only ones to fully understand its advantages.

Blackjack Rules According to Area

The following rules, pertaining to different gambling jurisdictions, are to be taken as a broad guideline. Rules change from time to time, and within jurisdictions and sometimes within a casino, the rules will vary from table to table.

Las Vegas Strip
Mostly multiple-deck games; a few single- and double-deck games, usually at higher limits.
Minimum bet $2.
Dealer stands on all seventeens.
Any pair may be split, then resplit.
Any two-card original total may be doubled down.
Insurance bet allowed.

Las Vegas Downtown
Mostly multiple-deck games, but some casinos still feature single- and double-deck games.
Minimum bet $1.
Dealer must hit soft seventeen.
Any pair may be split, then resplit.
Any two-card original total may be doubled down.
Insurance bet allowed.

Northern Nevada
Mostly single-deck games.
Minimum bet $1.
Dealer hits soft seventeen.
Any pair may be split, then resplit.
Doubling down only on hard tens and elevens.
Insurance bet allowed.

Atlantic City
Multiple-deck games only.
Minimum bet $2.
Dealer stands on all seventeens.
Any pair may be split, but not resplit.
Any two-card original total may be doubled down.
Insurance bet allowed.

Basic Strategies in Blackjack

Blackjack, though it has a strong element of chance, is basically a game of skill, and it is the only casino table game in which a skillful player can have an advantage over the house.

In order to have this advantage, a player must master two things: basic strategy and card counting. The first and most essential element is basic strategy—knowing in which situations you must double down, split pairs, stand or hit the hand. If you don't know this by rote, don't play the game. You'll end up losing. But once you have mastered basic strategic principles, you're well on your way to becoming a winner.

In the following sections we'll show you the correct plays that must be made, both for the single-deck and multiple-deck games.

Strategy—Hitting vs. Standing (Hard Totals)

In discussing hitting-vs.-standing strategies, we'll assume that all hands are hard hands; that is, they don't contain an ace, or the ace is valued as one. We're also going to use abbreviations, H for Hit and S for Stand. In the first column is the player's hand; in the second is the dealer's upcard; and in the third is the strategy involved, H or S. Since the player sees only one dealer's upcard as well as his own cards, all decisions must be made based on these factors. These strategies hold for single- or multiple-deck games.

PLAYER'S TOTAL	DEALER'S UPCARD	STRATEGY
12	2, 3	H
12	4, 5, 6	S
12	7, 8, 9, 10, A	H
13	2, 3, 4, 5, 6	S
13	7, 8, 9, 10, A	H
14, 15, 16	2, 3, 4, 5, 6	S
14, 15, 16	7, 8, 9, 10, A	H
17, 18, 19, 20	Any upcard	S

We never hit any hand totaling seventeen or more, if it's a hard hand, no matter what upcard the dealer shows. We don't hit a thirteen to sixteen if the dealer shows a "stiff card—that is, 2, 3, 4, 5, or 6.

We hit a hard twelve against all dealer's upcards except a 4, 5, or 6. The hard twelve, although a "stiff hand," that is, a hand that can be busted with the addition of another card, is least likely to bust of all stiff hands.

The reason we hit terrible hands with likely bust results such as fourteen, fifteen, or sixteen if the dealer shows a 7 or higher upcard is that the most prevalant card in the deck is a 10-value card, and we assume the dealer already has a standing hand, one that is 17 or higher. Thus, we don't want to forfeit our cards without trying to improve them.

Strategy—Hitting vs. Standing (Soft Totals)

The following table is useful only in the northern Nevada casinos and other casinos where no soft doubling down is permitted. A soft hand is any hand in which the ace is counted as eleven, such as A 4 (soft fifteen).

PLAYER'S HAND	DEALER'S UPCARD	STRATEGY
A 6	Any upcard	H
A 7	2, 3, 4, 5, 6, 7, 8, A	S
A 7	9, 10	H
A 8	Any upcard	S
A 9	Any upcard	S

The hitting of a soft eighteen (A 7) against a dealer's 9 or 10 is an expert play, since the eighteen is a loser if the dealer shows a 10 as his hole card. Never stand on a soft seventeen; it is the mark of a very weak player.

On totals below soft seventeen, always hit a soft hand, since it cannot bust with the addition of one card.

When playing against multiple decks, hit the soft eighteen against the dealer's ace.

Strategy—Hitting, Standing, or Doubling Down with Soft Totals

In those jurisdictions or casinos that allow doubling down on any two-card total, the following table should be followed. No longer will the player just have an option to stand or hit his hand; now he can double down as well. (D = double down.)

PLAYER'S HAND	DEALER'S UPCARD	STRATEGY
A 2, A 3, A 4, A 5	2, 3, 7, 8, 9, 10, A	H
A 2, A 3, A 4, A 5	4, 5, 6	D
A 6	2, 3, 4, 5, 6	D
A 6	7, 8, 9, 10, A	H
A 7	2, 7, 8, A	S
A 7	9, 10	H
A 7	3, 4, 5, 6	D
A 8	Any upcard	S
A 9	Any upcard	S

Again, in multiple-deck games, hit the A 7 against the dealer's ace. Never stand on a soft seventeen; it is either hit or doubled down. Study this table carefully; most players either never take advantage of soft doubling-down situations, or they do them incorrectly. Remember, whenever you hold a soft thirteen through soft eighteen, you're going to double down when the dealer shows a 4, 5, or 6 as his upcard, the worst upcards he can hold.

Strategy—Doubling Down with Hard Totals

In northern Nevada only hard tens and elevens can be doubled down. Study the table for those hard totals and use them when playing in Lake Tahoe or Reno. Otherwise, where you can double down on any two-card total, study those and the remaining totals. (D = double down.) When a hard total is not shown on this table, it can't be doubled down. Thus, a hard nine won't be doubled down against a dealer's 8; it's not on the table.

PLAYER'S TOTAL	DEALER'S UPCARD	STRATEGY
11	Any upcard	D
10	2, 3, 4, 5, 6, 7, 8, 9	D
9	2, 3, 4, 5, 6	D
8 (5 3, 4 4)	5, 6	D

Follow the above table and don't deviate. The hard-total double-down situations are correct and have been computer-tested. When the play calls for a double down, do it. Don't rely on hunches in blackjack; this is a game of skill and you must follow the correct basic strategy to be a winner.

Splitting Pairs

Practically all American casinos permit you to split any pair—that is, cards of equal rank, such as 8s. When you do split pairs, you play each split card as the foundation of a complete hand, and can draw as many valid cards to that hand as you wish. But if you split aces, you'll only be permitted to hit each one with one card. If you split aces and get a 10-value card on either ace, it's not a blackjack, just a twenty-one. It is only a blackjack—paid off at three to two—when dealt as the original two-card holding.

If pairs are split and an identically ranked card is dealt to the split card, that new pair can be split (except in Atlantic City). The rule is this: If the first split is correct, then resplit, because that will be correct play also. (Sp = split; DSp = don't split.)

PLAYER'S PAIR	DEALER'S UPCARD	STRATEGY
A A	Any upcard	Sp
2 2	3, 4, 5, 6, 7	Sp
3 3	4, 5, 6, 7	Sp
4 4	Any upcard	DSp
5 5	Any upcard	DSp
6 6	2, 3, 4, 5, 6	Sp
7 7	2, 3, 4, 5, 6, 7	Sp
8 8	Any upcard	Sp
9 9	2, 3, 4, 5, 6, 8, 9	Sp
10 10	Any upcard	DSp

The above table shows valid splits. If the dealer's upcard is not shown, that pair shouldn't be split against a different upcard. For example, you don't split 2 2 against a 9.

Always split aces, for an ace is counted as an eleven as the foundation for a new hand, and a 10 on it gives you an unbeatable twenty-one. Always split 8s, because they total sixteen, and it's better to have an 8 as the foundation for a new hand. Never split 4s or 5s. They form eights and tens, whereas if they're split they form a terrible foundation of four or five.

In some casinos a player may be permitted to double down after splitting. For instance, if he splits 8s and gets a 3 on the first 8, now he has an eleven and can double down against any upcard. In casinos that permit this option, use the following table for splitting. Note that you'll be more aggressive with splitting pairs.

Split 2s against a dealer's 2.
Split 3s against a dealer's 2 or 3.
Split 6s against a dealer's 7.
Split 7s against a dealer's 8.

The above splits are in addition to the normal pair splits. Thus, in a casino where doubling down is permitted after the splitting of a pair, 3s will be split vs. a dealer's 2 to 7 instead of the normal 4 to 7.

Winning at Blackjack

Blackjack is basically an even game. To play at your best, you must understand the principles discussed in the section on Basic Strategies in Blackjack. You must know which pairs may be split to your advantage. You must understand the principle of doubling down. If you understand all this, you are ready to progress from playing even with the casino to beating the casino.

But, and it is a very big but, if you haven't mastered the basic game, don't plod on here. Go back and study it and know it. Playing out the hands while looking at the strategy rules will make them easy to memorize. With a little more studying, the principles behind the decisions of when to stand or draw, when to split cards, and when to double down should become apparent.

The reason I am this insistent is that there are long periods of play when all you have is the basic game. You must know it perfectly. Only certain opportune moments come along in the course of a session of play where you'll be able to take advantage of the methods involved in this section. If you are sloppy about your basic game, you are going to take a beating, no matter what card-counting method you use. If you hold a fourteen and don't draw when the dealer's upcard is a 7, you're beaten before you start. If you don't split your 8s, or worse still, if you split 5s, there's very little chance that you're going to win. If you don't double down on an eleven, you're giving up one of your big advantages. Take away all the advantages of correct basic play and you're at such a disadvantage that even when the cards are in your favor, all you can hope for is to break even. Learn the basic game!

There are a number of basic methods of card counting, and I'm going to mention several here. Each one allows you to keep count of the cards and to find favorable situations. When these favorable situations occur, you must increase your bet, because at those moments the odds are in your favor, either by a small or large percentage.

Now, one thing should be mentioned before we progress further. All the card-counting methods and systems will come to nought if the dealer knows you are counting. If he is playing with a single deck, he will reshuffle every time you increase your bet drastically. We will later go into methods of betting to disguise the counting.

The first method of card counting is the count of 10s. This was discovered by Dr. Thorp, who used it as the basis of *Beat the Dealer*. What he discovered was that the percentage of 10s as against other cards determined whether or not the cards were favorable to the player.

One of the most important things to know is that there are sixteen 10s (cards of ten value) and thirty-six non-10s. Dr. Thorp discovered that when the ratio of non-10s to 10s is at 2.25 to 1 or less, the deck is in the player's favor. At the outset, the deck stands at 36 to 16, or 2.25 to 1. Therefore, the deck at the beginning is slightly in the dealer's favor (0.1 percent).

If the cards on the second round were 27 to 14, or less than 2 to 1, then the odds had shifted to the player. The player should increase his bet, but increase it slightly, because the percentage in the player's favor is slight. But if, after that round, the deck stood at 18 to 11, now the percentage was drastically in the player's favor, and the bet must be increased accordingly.

The principle was simple. Increase the bet when the odds were in your favor. When they were drastically in your favor, a drastic increase; when they were slightly in your favor, a slight increase. This, together with best play, would almost guarantee the player a winning session.

Before the casinos became wise to the counting methods, it was possible to bet the minimum, one dollar, and then suddenly increase the bet to $100, or even $500. But don't attempt it now, because the pit boss will come over and ask you to leave the casino.

The difficulty with this method of counting cards is that a double count must be kept. First, you must immediately ascertain how many 10s and other cards have been played on the first round, as the cards are turned over and collected by the dealer. Let's presume that you spotted three 10s and five other cards. Now you must subtract these from the 36-to-16 ratio with which the deck began. So now you have 33 to 11. It is difficult to figure with a 2.25-to-1 basic ratio, so for simplicity's sake it is better to calculate on a 2-to-1 ratio, which gives about a one-percent advantage to the player.

Here, obviously 33 to 11 is 3 to 1, which is a bad percentage; the deck is decidedly against the player.

As the odds are reduced from 2 to 1 to 1.75 to 1, the percentage doubles from one percent to two percent in favor of the player, and increases to nine percent when the deck has as many 10s as other cards. For a more thorough study of the odds and the 10-count method, it is well worth reading Dr. Thorp's book.

Since aces are important to the player and the number of aces remaining in the deck is to the player's advantage, another method was devised, this one by Allan Wilson. He gave a point count to the cards, counting aces as +4 points, 10-value cards as +1 point, and all other cards as −1 point. Thus, four aces equal 16 points; sixteen 10-value cards equal 16 points, and the other thirty-two cards add up to −32 points, and everything comes out equal. This formula was brought forth in his excellent book, *The Casino Gambler's Guide.*

In using this method, every time a card is dealt one point is added; every time an ace is shown, five points are subtracted; and every time a ten-value card is shown, another two points are subtracted. This is the same as deducting four points for each ace that has been removed from the deck and deducting one point for each 10-value card and adding one for each non-10 or ace.

Although I think Mr. Wilson makes an excellent study of the game of blackjack, and his mathematical skill and knowledge are very apparent, the method he follows becomes extremely complicated, and I feel that too much emphasis is placed on the aces. Why should they be four times as valuable as the 10s? The easiest answer is that by giving them a value of four, everything comes out even. I recommend study of Wilson's book, particularly his section on blackjack.

A "hi-lo" method of point count was developed by Mr. Harvey Dubner, in which only cards from 2 to 6 and 10 to ace were counted, the

7s, 8s, and 9s remaining neutral. The ratio of high cards to low cards remaining determined the percentage either for or against the player. For example, there are twenty low cards and twenty high cards and twelve neutral cards. If four high cards had been used up and ten low cards, then the ratio of high to low remaining would be 16 to 10, with an advantage to the player.

This has been perfected to a running point count, in which, using the same low and high cards, each low card is given a $+1$ value and each high card a -1 value. If six low cards have been used up, and five high cards, the point count would be $+1$. Each plus is to the player's advantage. The higher the plus, the more the player should bet.

If we examine a typical deal, we'll see how this works. The following cards were dealt in the first round of play: A 4 9 6 J 10 5 7 Q 3 7 4 K 6.

We have six low cards, or $+6$; five high cards, or -5; and three neutral cards (no value here). The hand is $+1$, to the player's advantage. With Thorp's 10-count method, the ratio of remaining cards would be 26 to 12, a little over 2 to 1, with a slight advantage to the player. (The first figure is non-10-value cards; the second figure 10-value cards.)

Let's try another random set of cards. 8 3 K J 4 9 2 10 A 3 6 2 8 K 10 A 4.

We have seven low cards, or $+7$; seven high cards, or -7; and three neutral cards (no value). Absolutely even.

With Thorp's 10-count method, we have a ratio of 24 to 11, with a slight advantage to the player.

I personally like the running count, rather than the 10-count method. First, it is quicker to calculate, because we immediately eliminate the 7, 8, and 9. It is expressed in the simple ratio of plus or minus one number, not in a ratio that first is calculated by subtracting, then figured. And remember, the dealer is dealing those cards at a very fast rate.

Secondly, it is fairly accurate, because even in the above situation the slight advantage Thorp would calculate is overcome by two aces out against the player. With a running count, you are going to spot those instances when the cards are in your favor, because any time you have a plus number, there are more small cards out than big ones.

To calculate the value of the aces, simply count them separately at the same time that you count them in the running point count. For example, in the above list of cards we would have $+7$, -7, or even, and two aces. That's not hard to do at all. When two aces are out of the deck, your chances of a blackjack are reduced considerably. Also, remember that the more cards you can keep track of, the better your chances of knowing what's remaining. For example, if there are three players and the dealer in the game, and those other two aces have not shown themselves, and there are about sixteen cards remaining with a count of $+1$, this means more than a simple count of $+1$. You can increase your bet accordingly, because the chances of getting a blackjack are considerably higher.

The Silberstang Method

Having analyzed the other systems and methods, I am now going to give my own method. It combines the best parts, in my opinion, of those methods previously discussed.

First, basic play must be followed, and again I refer to the strategy of drawing and standing. As the method is discussed, these will be modified, but you must first know the rules before embarking on the variations.

A point count is used, with the underlying principle being that the more tens and aces in the deck in proportion to the other cards, the more favorable it is for the player. These calculations have been worked out by many others, and I will not go into the mathematical computations. What I am going to show the reader has worked for me and others who have followed my method.

It must be remembered that the casino is not a living room; the dealer is not your close friend or your girl or your wife. There are no slowdowns of play so that you can recap the ratios or count the aces remaining in the deck. Remember, the casino is a place of business, and the losses of the players are the casino's profits. They don't want to jeopardize those profits. When the casinos speak of catering to gamblers, they mean giving them distractions, such as waitresses in hot pants, providing strong drinks for nothing, and easy credit. They don't mean giving them winning odds, percentages in their favor, or an atmosphere in which they can think clearly and take all the time in the world to make their bets.

Although other methods may be more involved, I have chosen a method that can be followed in the noise, the action, the speed of a casino. Here's how it works.

The Point Count
All cards from 2 to 7—that is, 2, 3, 4, 5, 6, and 7—equal plus one. All cards from 9 to ace—that is, 9, 10, J, Q, K, A—equal minus one. The 8 is neutral.

This gives us a count of plus twenty-four and minus twenty-four at the outset, or an equal amount, meaning a neutral deck.

Any time there is a plus score, it is in favor of the player; any minus score is against the player; and any neutral score of zero is also against the player.

First Point

On any neutral or minus score, bet the minimum amount. If we use one chip as the minimum, bet one chip.

With this method we take a running count, either during the hand or at the close of a round of dealing. It is ideally suited for multiple decks dealt from a shoe, where all cards of the players are open. It is also very effective and deadly against a one-deck dealer, in spite of all the other players' cards being closed.

Second Point

When the deck reads plus one or plus two after a round of dealing, bet two units; when it reads plus three or four, bet four units; when it reads plus five or six, bet six units. Above plus six, bet eight units as a maximum bet, but don't go from one to eight units at one time; it'll attract attention. I use a two-unit progression because it is natural and not conspicuous, and the dealers I have encountered took me for a systems player working a slow progression.

Third Point

Any time the deck reads minus six or more, do not split aces except against an upcard of 2 to 6. There are a great many small cards in the deck, and in this situation it would pay to draw to the soft twelve.

Fourth Point

If the deck reads minus six or more and the upcard of the dealer is a 7, 8, 9, 10, or ace, don't double down on a hard ten.

If the dealer's upcard is a 2 to a 6, then double down with a hard ten.

Fifth Point

If the cards have a count of plus six or more, don't draw to a hard sixteen against a dealer's upcard of 7.

You will find that these points are not always recommended by the authorities; that they may seem offbeat and unusual. But I have found in practice that the major losses I have endured have come from following blindly such rules as "double down on ten against any card 10 or below." When I have done so, with a poor chance of buying a 10, the results have generally been disastrous.

Sixth Point
With a point count of plus six or above, take insurance.

Other Suggestions
I suggest you play two hands, not one, but not more than two be-cause two hands are generally acceptable, whereas three make you con-spicuous. The advantage of two hands is, of course, that you see more cards. In some casinos, where one deck is used and the cards are dealt closed, the dealer allows you to look at one hand at a time. Avoid these casinos.

If you are playing against a multiple deck dealt from a shoe, all the cards in play are seen, since they are dealt openly. Play two hands if possible. You have a chance to quadruple your bet on favorable situa-tions, and can still bet the minimum on unfavorable situations, allowing your basic strategy to lessen your losses. You can even take advantage of unfavorable situations, by drawing more than in a normal situation if you have a minimum bet and want to finish off the deck and start anew. For instance, you are playing against a one-deck dealer, and the count is minus five, very unfavorable. You are dealt 10, 4 and 10, 5 and the dealer shows a 3.

You know that the deck is near the end, having, let us say, only ten cards left. If you stand with these cards, the dealer will draw and probably, with a minus deck, get to seventeen or above without busting. Then, once more, you have an unfavorable situation, with a minus factor of, let us say, three or four.

You can be bold in this situation. Draw to your fourteen and then to your fifteen. You will probably bust one and improve the other. More important, you will end a deal that can only be bad for you and limit you to an unfavorable minimum bet. It is far better to get a new deal, with a possibility of starting off with an immediate plus score, larger bets, and better winnings.

Generally speaking, and from my experience, dealers are reluctant to start a fresh deal with less than ten cards remaining in a one-deck situa-tion. If you find a dealer who is not afraid of dealing to the bottom of the deck, even better. Suppose, instead of a minus-five score count with fif-teen cards remaining and a minimum bet on your part, there was a plus-five score after the last round with fifteen cards remaining, and the dealer is going to deal to the end of the deck. In situations like that, with a maximum bet, you can stop working for a living.

Betting and Money Management

One of the two prime considerations in blackjack betting is the matter of preserving your capital. The other is disguising the fact that you are altering your bets according to some method of betting tied to a counting system.

Betting can be made in three basic units. You can use the one-dollar chip, the five-dollar chip, or the twenty-five-dollar chip. When you are using the one-dollar chip as a basic unit, make sure you play in a casino that pays $1.50 to $1.00 for a blackjack. Most do, but some Strip palaces are awfully fussy about small bets and don't pay off in change on a dollar bet.

Betting one dollar as a basic unit is recommended until you can play and count at the pace that is required in a gambling casino. If you can handle the action and find yourself ahead, switch to the five-dollar chip. In many clubs, the tables are divided into one-dollar- and five-dollar-minimum tables for blackjack. But remember at a one-dollar table you can still bet five dollars or more.

If you're betting five-dollar units, you can find plenty of action without attracting the attention of the house. The winnings are multiplied by five, but make sure that half dollars are paid out in winnings, because a blackjack should pay $7.50 to $5.00. Especially when on the Strip in Las Vegas, be certain that they pay off in half dollars. If not, you will get only $7.00 to $5.00. So take your business elsewhere, because otherwise you're giving up too much of a percentage for the privilege of playing there, which is no privilege at all. The name of the game in the gambling centers is competing for your play. That's why the big-name stars are on the marquees in front; that's why the drinks are free and the waitresses sexy.

If you're betting with twenty-five-dollar chips, you're going to be watched by a pit boss, no matter what game you're at, so be ready for scrutiny. But if you alter your bets according to my suggestion, no matter what game you're at, one dollar, five dollar, or twenty-five dollar, your method of play shouldn't be too obvious. You should be able to get your bets down without having the dealer reshuffle the cards every time a favorable situation develops. I say "should" because, as in all walks of life, paranoids abound. There are dealers who will reshuffle if you sneeze, figuring it's a signal for a conspirator at the table to make some kind of move.

I played in a game in Las Vegas where the dealer was a born re-shuffler. If I increased the bet, the cards were scooped up. All the while the dealer was giving me this knowing look. So, what better thing to do than to make a big bet right at the outset, with all the aces and picture cards and 10s intact, and the deck neutral. That baffled him. Then, if the count was favorable—boom!—double went my bet. If he reshuffled, I left the bet. Same situation. If the deck was favorable, I took out the winnings and left the original bet. If the deck was unfavorable, I left the original bet as well.

To make a long story short, after I started with this peculiar type of betting, any time the deck was unfavorable, a larger bet caused a reshuffle. Any time the deck was favorable, the same bet or a little larger one kept the deck going. I was making these bets because the deck was running well, and I was winning.

There are times, however, when the deck remains unfavorable, or, even if favorable, when you still find yourself losing. This happens occasionally, so don't get panicky and don't change your betting methods. Stick it out; the cards should turn because the odds are in your favor. Even the house, when it has the odds in its favor—let us say in a game of craps with place numbers—takes a temporary bad beating when the dice get "hot."

When you are increasing your bets because there are enough 10s and aces in the deck in proportion to other cards to make the deck favorable, you may still lose some of these bets, maybe even most of them, for a short interval. But in the long run, you're going to win. So, if the cards are "cold," and you are tired, get out of the game. Go back after a good meal, a good romp, whatever, but don't alter your method of betting. Losers alter their bets. We want to be winners, and if we have a winning method, we're not going to change just because the cards have gone wrong. Maybe the dealer has gone wrong. Who can tell? Either stick it out, or get out and return at another time, to another table, another dealer, or another casino.

In blackjack, the preservation of capital is very important. We want to preserve our capital because the odds will sometimes be in our favor and we wish to be in a position to bet heavily at that time. Remember, be bold when the odds are in your favor. That's not gambling; that's good sense. Why don't we bet all our capital when the favorable situation develops? Well, with one bet we might lose it all, no matter what the odds, but the long run is in our favor.

Thus, if we lose a fair-sized bet when the odds are in our favor, we can recoup again when the odds are again in our favor. But if we've blown the whole thing, all we can do is play with ourselves when the next opportunity comes. We want the real thing, right?

So here's how we arrange things. We take with us forty times our basic betting unit. If you're betting in one-dollar units, take forty dollars;

if betting in five-dollar units, take $200, etc. This gives us plenty of room to absorb some losses while playing for the favorable situations. There is nothing worse than running out of capital when the situation turns most favorable and 10s and aces are falling with abandon.

What happens if you lose your stake? Get out of the game and wait for another time. Limit your losses and let your winnings ride. But if you play my method, it's going to be very difficult, no matter how bad the cards are, to lose it all. When the deck is unfavorable, you still have, a minimum bet down. And secondly, you know the cards are unfavorable and that there are a lot of small cards out, so you can draw cards a little more boldly.

If you're winning, try to double your original stake. If you can't, but are winning and getting tired, get out with your winnings and call it a night. If you double your stake, let's say from $200 to $400, take $150 and your original stake, shove it in your pocket, and play with the extra $50. If you lose it, you're out of the game, but you still have a lovely win. If you increase that fifty to $200, put another $150 in your pocket and keep playing. Should you start making bigger bets? No. Because all your winnings are based on a method of forty times your stake. If, instead of five-dollar bets, you make twenty-five-dollar bets, a few bad turns of the card and you're out of money without $1000 behind you.

When to increase the bet? When you win enough, let's assume $1000, you can increase your basic bet to ten dollars with $400 in reserve. If you keep winning, increase your bets, but only as the beginning of another game with the correct stake ratio of 40:1 behind you.

Betting in Units

As was discussed in the previous section dealing with my method, the betting is done in units. All other things being equal (and with a dealer who will not reshuffle every time you raise your bet), when the deck is neutral or is unfavorable, bet one unit. If the deck is plus one or two, bet two units; plus three or four, bet four units; plus five or six, bet six units; seven or above, eight units. I would use a maximum of eight because it is not that conspicuous. I have also suggested increasing bets in multiples of two, because there are a lot of players who naturally use this kind of doubling method, since many play the Martingale or Grand Martingale System. Every time they lose, they double the bet—the surest way to bankruptcy.

We, of course, are doing quite the opposite. Every time the deck is more favorable, we're increasing our bet by two units. That's my method of betting. It's simple and, done carefully, won't attract the dealer's attention in a one-deck game.

Thus far I've dealt mainly with a one-deck game. But there are games using two or more decks, and many of the big casinos prefer four decks dealt out of a shoe. The advantage to the house increases with the use of added decks. The increase is very slight, but it swings the odds into the house's favor and puts the player in a position of playing an unfavorable game at the outset. Can we still play in this kind of game? Why not?

It's not the same as the other games, like craps, where the odds are *always* against the player. Here, very quickly, the odds can swing to the player's favor. And in a multiple-deck game, the dealer cannot touch the cards or reshuffle until the cards reach the point at which the shoe is considered used up. I'll explain this.

All four decks are shuffled by the dealer, deck by deck. Of course, they are not separate, complete decks; merely four sections of all the cards comprising four decks. Then they are put into the shoe, to be dealt out one at a time. A card, usually a joker, is inserted somewhere about three quarters of the way into the deck. As the cards are dealt out, they are face down and then turned over by the dealer. When the joker comes up, even though there are more cards to follow, that's the end of the shoe. The cards not in play are then reshuffled, replaced in the shoe, and dealt over again.

So, if the cards are running very favorably, you can increase your bet, keeping it at a high level, and there's nothing the dealer can do about it but deal the cards. Balanced against that good piece of news is the fact that in a multiple deck the odds are slightly against the player from the outset, and, at times, aces and 10s are dealt at the beginning with frequency, making a multiple deck unfavorable throughout the long deal. What do you do in that case?

That's right. Up off the seat, get a drink of ginger ale at the bar, look for a good-looking blonde, talk to her, get her number, whisper that you'll see her later. Much better than getting a calloused behind and losing your shirt.

XII

Blackjack

PRIVATE GAME

Rules of Play

The main difference between the casino game previously discussed and the private game is that in a private game the deal does not remain permanently with one person. There are other minor differences, but that is the basic one. Each player has a theoretical chance of becoming a dealer and thus stands to profit by betting against the other players, or he may lose in greater proportion because he is the banker (initial dealer).

Number of Players: From two to seven. More can play, but it gets cumbersome with too-frequent deals. The limit should definitely be seven players, including the dealer.

The Deck: A standard fifty-two-card deck is used, with a joker to substitute for the burned card.

Value of Cards: The same as in casino blackjack, with the ace counting as one or eleven, at the option of the holder, and all face cards (king, queen, and jack) counting as ten points. All other cards have the same value as their spots.

To Determine the Banker: At the outset of play, any player may pick up the cards and shuffle them, and any other player may participate in the shuffle if he so desires. Then the cards are cut by the player to the original shuffler's right and dealt out until one of the players gets an ace. He becomes the first dealer, or banker.

A variation is to deal out cards until one of the players is dealt a blackjack (an ace with a picture card or ten), but this often takes a much longer time.

Another variation is to have someone deal until one of the black jacks (spade or club) is dealt to a player. This method and the ace method are equally good, since the determination of the initial dealer is strictly arbitrary.

After a dealer has been selected under this method, he takes up the cards and prepares to shuffle and deal.

Shuffle and Cut: The dealer shuffles the cards and hands them to the player on his right to be cut. If that player refuses to cut them, any other player may cut the deck. The cards are handed to the dealer.

The Deal (First Round): After the deck has been shuffled and cut and squared by the dealer, he places the joker face up at the bottom of the deck. This is the burned card. Under the old rules, where the top card of the deck was shown to the players and then burned, the players had an immediate advantage over the dealer. By knowing just the burned card, the players could determine whether or not the deck was favorable. (See *Basic Strategies in Blackjack*, Chapter XI.)

Betting

In the private game, the dealer is given the right to determine the limits of betting unless all the players decide before the game what the limit will be (from one to five chips, for example). This is the better method, rather than having a continuous change in betting.

In private blackjack, although some authorities state that the bets should be made by the players prior to receiving any cards, I strongly recommend that the bets be made *after* each player receives one card. This is suggested because in the private game the dealer has a substantial advantage not enjoyed by the dealer in a casino game. In a private game, the dealer may draw to his cards to beat the players and is not forced to stick with seventeen, or forced to draw to sixteen.

Another great advantage to the dealer is that he may decide, at any time after receiving his first card, to double the bets.

The third and greatest advantage is that the dealer in the private game wins all bets on ties.

Against these factors, all a player has in the way of an advantage is that he is paid two to one instead of three to two on blackjacks. Without the option of making a bet after one card, the advantage would be all to the dealer. This balances it and makes the game more even and more interesting.

Blackjack played privately would, otherwise, merely be a game where the deal was all-important, and thus there would be continual auctions for the deal, slowing down the game.

The Deal

Each player, including the dealer, is dealt one card, face down. Some authorities suggest that the dealer's card be dealt face up, but that would put the dealer at a distinct disadvantage. The better rule: All cards for one round are dealt face down. Then each player looks at his hole card and decides what bet to make. He then places the chip or chips forward on the table, next to his cards. The dealer can now decide whether or not he wants the bets doubled. If he so decides, all the players must double their bets.

In the event the bets are doubled by the dealer, each individual player has the option of redoubling.

After all the bets are made, the second card dealt to each player (including the dealer) is dealt face up.

After both cards have been dealt, each player can now see if he has received a blackjack, which, as in the casino game, is an ace together with a picture card or 10 on the first two cards. In other words, a total of twenty-one on two cards.

If the dealer has a blackjack, he announces it immediately and collects double from each of the players. If another player has a blackjack also, that player loses his bet, but does not pay double. Remember, in private blackjack the dealer wins on all ties, including blackjack.

If any player has a blackjack, he is paid double by the dealer. More importantly, he wins the deal.

If no player has a blackjack, any of the players now may draw further cards or stand pat.

Drawing Cards

Each player may draw as many cards as he wants, providing he does not go bust (that is, over twenty-one). If he does, he loses immediately and must turn over his cards and forfeit his bet at once.

The player to the dealer's left has the first option of drawing cards or standing pat.

After he draws or stands, the next player draws or stands, and so on until it is the dealer's turn. If any player prior to the dealer goes bust, he forfeits his bet. This is so whether or not the dealer himself goes bust. If a dealer goes over twenty-one, he pays only those players who are still in the game (that is, who have not gone over twenty-one).

Pairs may be split by any player, and if aces are split, the player splitting them may draw as many cards as he wishes. If he gets blackjack with the split aces, he is paid double the bet by the dealer and gets the deal.

It is not customary to allow doubling down with totals of eleven, but if all the players agree, doubling down can be allowed.

Bonus Payments

In the private game, bonus payments for certain hands are common. The following prevail in a private game:

Five cards totaling less than twenty-one points: Double payment.

Six cards totaling less than twenty-one: Quadruple payment.

And so on, each doubling the previous one. Thus, eight cards would pay sixteen times the original bet. These are all very rare occurrences and generally favor the dealer, since the player may give up a good hand going for a bonus and, instead, bust and lose his original bet.

Any player receiving three 7s to form twenty-one gets triple the original bet as a bonus.

These bonus payments go only to the players, not to the dealer. When a player makes his bonus cards and collects for the bonus, his hand is now dead, whether or not the dealer beats or ties him. The payment of the bonus thus ends the participation by the player in that particular hand.

Losing the Deal

The deal is lost to any player getting a blackjack, providing that the dealer does not have one also. If two or more players get a blackjack, the player closest to the dealer's left wins the deal. To put it more simply, the first player to get a blackjack in order of betting wins the deal.

Auctioning the Bank

After the completion of any one hand, the dealer may sell the deal to any other player. The dealer is allowed to ask if anyone wants the deal, and then, after hearing how much will be paid for it, he may reject the offer and continue dealing. If the dealer decides to give up the deal voluntarily (perhaps as a result of a bad losing streak), then the deal is auctioned off to the other players and the proceeds of the auction are given to the previous dealer. If there is such an auction, the highest bidder gets the deal, and the previous dealer cannot refuse the highest bid.

If no one bids on the auction, the deal moves to the player on the dealer's left, who may or may not reject it. If he rejects it, the deal moves to the player on his left, and so on, till a player takes the deal.

Strategy

Betting

Since a player has an option to bet after seeing one card, he should always make the maximum bet on an ace and also a maximum bet on a

10 if the deck is rich in 10s. Card counting is just as applicable in a private game as in a casino game and can be a big advantage to the player against the dealer. If the deck is neutral and there is betting allowed from one to five units, four should be bet on a ten; three on a 9 or 8, and one on a 4, 5, 6, or 7. Two units can be bet on a 2 or 3 because of the bonus for five cards totaling not more than twenty-one. But if the deck is 10-rich, then make a minimum bet when getting a 2 or 3.

If a dealer is dealt an ace, he should immediately force all the players to double. If he gets a ten and most of the players have bet near the minimum, he should force them to double their bets. If they have all bet near the maximum, he then should not increase the bet.

If a dealer doubles and you hold an ace, it is always worth a redouble with a deck rich in 10s.

Drawing Cards

Since there are so many options open to a dealer, a player should not automatically draw in the same manner as in the casino game. Several factors may be present which could determine his draw. For example:

Is the dealer conservative or wild? If the dealer is always trying to see how close he can get to twenty-one, it might pay to stick at fifteen or sixteen if the dealer is showing a 7.

How many players are left in the game? If you are the only one left and show an 8, even if your total is twelve, it would pay to stand if the dealer has a 7, since he will try to beat you by drawing. Even if you're not the only player in the game, if the other players have high totals, they may be an umbrella for your low total, since the dealer will try and beat most of the players.

Has the dealer doubled his bet? If he did and shows a 7 or higher card, you must draw below seventeen, just as in the casino game. The odds are that the dealer has a 10 showing underneath.

Is the deck 10-rich? Is it 10-poor? All these factors can be taken into consideration, especially using the Silberstang Method (page 296), which will give you a good idea of your chances in drawing or not drawing.

The Dealer

The dealer can also determine his play in much the same manner, noting the upcards of the players and their original bets, which will give him a mine of valuable information. Also, if the dealer uses a card-counting method, such as the Silberstang Method, he can easily figure out just how the deck is stacked, for, as dealer, he can take all the time in the world to count the cards.

Buying the Bank

Never pay too much for the bank. If you can count cards, you stand a good chance against any dealer and the payoff of two to one for black-jack is going to work heavily in your favor in 10-rich situations. If you have an opportunity to buy the bank, never pay more than ten times the minimum bet for it.

It is hard to calculate exactly what a bank is worth because of the play of various bankers and players, but with best plays I have found that ten times the minimum bet is usually worthwhile and profitable.

XIII

Baccarat

Introduction

Baccarat was originally an Italian game called *baccara*, meaning zero. A version of the game may have been introduced into France as early as the fifteenth century, though some authorities claim the game was not played there until the seventeenth century during the reign of Louis XIV.

At first it was an illegal game, but after a while baccarat was legalized and a tax was imposed on the game for the benefit of the poor and sick. Its legality, plus the supposed good its profits were creating for the poor, soon made baccarat one of the most popular gambling games in France.

During its long run in France the game was out of fashion from time to time, particularly during the reign of Napoleon Bonaparte. It then was banned again for a period of seventy years, from 1937 to 1907, when all gambling games were declared illegal in France. Though banned, it flourished once more in illegal casinos, and once again the cheats who gravitate to illegal games were in evidence.

When it was legalized once again in 1907, baccarat regained its previous popularity, and casinos featuring the game sprang up throughout France. Some of the best-known of these were at Deauville, Nice, Cannes, and Biarritz. During the time Edward VII was Prince of Wales, he introduced the game to England, where it became the rage. Edward VII had first encountered the game in the South of France, had become smitten by its mystique, and played it avidly both as prince and king. To this day, baccarat, in the version known as chemin de fer, is still one of the most popular gambling games both in Great Britain and in Europe.

Eventually the game came to America, but it was a minor gambling pastime at best compared to the native games such as faro, poker, and craps. When gambling was legalized in Nevada, the game that was first played was chemin de fer, in which one player holds the bank. Eventually the game in Nevada changed to the present game of baccarat, in which the house is the banker and books all the bets on the table, whether made on Bank or Player.

Although it doesn't compare in popularity to craps and blackjack, the two leading table games in Nevada casinos, baccarat took its unique place as the game for high rollers—the game in which the stakes are highest.

The casinos work hard to keep the image of baccarat glamorous. The area where the game is played is roped off from the common chaos of the casino, the dealers wear tuxedos, beautiful young women are hired as shills to promote the action, and the stakes set for the game, both minimum and maximum, are usually the highest in the casino.

Many players avoid the game, fearing its glamour, but all players are welcome at the table. At one time the game was played with cash, but now it is customary to play with gambling chips. It is a simple game to play, with two chief bets available, either on Bank or Player. One can also make a disadvantageous bet on Tie.

That's all the participant need do, bet on Bank or Player. The dealers do the rest: call for more cards, declare the winner of that particular coup, or play, and make payoffs.

In the casino game of baccarat a 5 percent commission is collected on all winning Bank bets, and most gamblers think that this is the house edge. But it is much less than that—1.17 percent on the Bank hand and 1.35 percent on the Player hand.

In many ways it is a mindless game, but any game played for stakes —and in the case of baccarat, very high stakes at times—has its own excitement.

Baccarat has taken hold in American casinos, and its popularity is steadily increasing as gamblers recognize the small edge the house has, and systems players, who abound by the thousands, discover this is an ideal game for systems.

American Baccarat

The game was introduced into American casinos by Tommy Renzoni, who worked at the Sands Hotel and had known of this version of the game from his gambling days in Cuba. The year was 1959, and the game originally was played with cash. At the beginning the minimum bet was set at $20, for two reasons. First of all, there are $20 bills, and secondly, a 5 percent commission on a $20 bet is an even $1.

The game now, as played in both Nevada and Atlantic City, is no longer a cash game but one utilizing casino chips. It is still a big action game, and often the limits at individual tables are raised for the really high rollers.

Gamblers have won and lost millions in this game, and the high rollers like not only the action but the fact that they are pampered with roped-off areas, pretty women, dealers dressed to the nines, and the spotlight as they make their big wagers.

The game has evolved over the years into a set of complicated rules, which are printed on a card that anyone can study, but it is not necessary to know them to play the game. The dealer calling the game generally knows the rules by heart, and he runs the game smoothly and efficiently. The caller or callman makes it a swift and exciting game. After a while any player can easily pick up the fine points of the rules, for hands repeat themselves over and over, and anyone can become an expert player in a short period of time. But the important thing is whether to bet on the Player hand or Bank hand, for that determines who wins and who loses.

In many casinos, rules vary on games such as craps and blackjack, but no matter where you play baccarat, the rules are the same. Once you understand them, you can play this game in any casino.

Baccarat Table and Layout

The baccarat table is known as "the big table" and generally comes in two sizes, one seating twelve players and the other fourteen. The Atlantic City tables are of the bigger kind, while the Nevada tables sometimes seat twelve and sometimes fourteen. However, this doesn't affect the game at all.

The table and layout are shown in the following illustration.

Each side of the table is identical to the other, and the numbers shown (1–7, 8–15) represent the numbered seat of individual players. The 13 is usually omitted on these tables for superstitious reasons. It really doesn't matter where a gambler sits, for position means nothing in the final outcome of the game. What is important is how the cards come out, either for Player or Bank.

The game is played with eight decks of cards, totaling 416 cards, without jokers. The usual bridge decks are used, with cards of four suits (diamonds, hearts, spades, and clubs) having values or spots from ace to king. We'll go into their values in the appropriate section, but for now

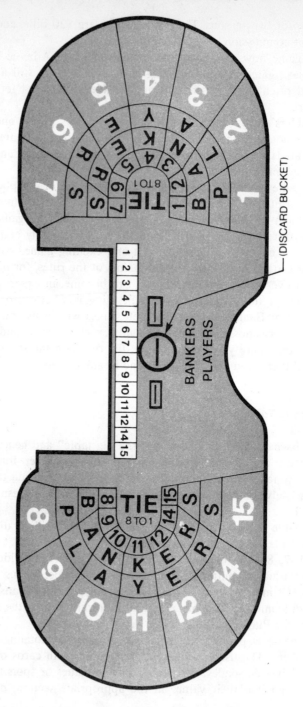

we'll mention that these cards are placed in a shoe, or device that enables someone to deal them out easily one at a time.

Each player may get a turn at dealing from the shoe, and the shoe moves around the table from lower-numbered to higher-numbered position. For example, after participant number 1 has finished dealing, the shoe goes to the player sitting in the number-2 seat, and so forth, all the way to position number 15.

In front of each numbered position are boxes allowing the player to bet on either Bank hand, Player hand, or Tie. The bet is made by placing chips in either the box marked for the Bank bet or the Player bet.

As we study the table, we see that there are two indentations, one small and rounded, the other rectangular. In the smaller rounded area stands the callman, the dealer who runs the game. Opposite him sit two dealers, one for each side of the table. They are responsible for collecting losing bets, paying off winning wagers, and taking in commissions on winning Bank bets.

Notice also three slots in the center of the layout. The center one, or largest, is used for discards, or cards that have already been played. The two slots flanking this one are used to drop cash or markers.

In front of these slots are two terms: Bankers and Players. The cards played on each round are put there in the correct area, Bank cards over Banker, and Player cards over Player.

The Dealers and Other Casino Personnel

Three dealers run a baccarat game. The callman is the standing dealer, and he calls for cards to be dealt by whichever player is holding the shoe. After he receives the cards, he places them in the appropriate area, the Bank hand's cards above the Player hand's cards. Then he announces the totals and determines if an additional card should be dealt to either the Player hand or Bank hand, or both.

He does this by knowing the rigid rules of baccarat. There are no options and no deviations from these printed rules. After the play of the round is finished, he announces which side, Bank or Player, has won, or if there is a tie.

If a winner is announced, the two other dealers, who remained seated, move into action. Each is responsible for his half of the table. First they collect all losing bets and place the chips in the chip trays in front of them. Then all winning bets are paid off. If the Player hand won the previous round of play, that's all that is necessary. But if the Bank hand won, they note the 5 percent commission due to the casino by placing this amount in marked disks or chips in the appropriate box matching the player's position at the table. These boxes are in front of the sitting dealers, and each handles one-half of this action.

In addition to these dealers, a third employee of the casino is involved in the game. In the baccarat area, this man, a casino executive, sits above the table action on a ladder, and is known as the ladderman. His duty is to supervise play and make certain that it is run correctly and fairly. All disputes or arguments are finally settled by the ladderman. Since the game has no options, most of the disputes have to do with bets or commissions owed or not owed to the house. In this case the ladderman's decision is final.

Card Values and Baccarat Totals

Many onlookers find the game incomprehensible because they don't realize that all 10s and face cards (jack, queen, king) count as zero (0). In most of the other casino games involving cards, these count as ten, but not in baccarat. They have no value in this game, and are merely zeroes.

All the other cards in baccarat are equal to the spots or pips printed on the card. An ace is worth one, a deuce two, a trey three, a four four, and so forth to the 9, which is worth nine points. In baccarat the 9 is the highest card one can have.

At the outset of the game, the Bank and Player hands are dealt two cards each. To determine the total of these cards, they're added together. For example, if the Bank hand were dealt a king and a 5, that total would be 5, since the king is zero and the 5 is worth five points. If the Player hand were dealt jack and 10, it would have a zero value, since each card, the jack and 10, is worth zero.

In baccarat no hand can be worth more than nine points, nine being the best possible hand or total in this game. Thus, if one hand is dealt 8 and 5, which normally would total thirteen, the hand is worth only three points. The first digit in any total of more than ten is removed to get the correct hand total. A hand of 9 and 7 would be a six rather than a sixteen, and a hand of 8 and 2 would be zero, instead of ten. This is the second important concept in baccarat, after the fact that all 10s and face cards are worth zero.

Once you've mastered these two principles, the game becomes simplicity itself in determining the value and totals of cards. At times a hand may contain three cards (but never more than three), and again, the same principle applies. Suppose the Bank hand is dealt 9, 3, 8. These cards add up to twenty, but since the first digit is removed, the hand is just a zero.

In baccarat the hand having the highest final total wins, whether Bank or Player. A one beats out a zero, and three is better than a two, and so forth in determining the winner of the round.

Let's recapitulate this information:

1. All 10s and face cards (jack, queen, king) count as zero.

2. All other cards, from the ace to the 9, have the same value as their spots or pips.

3. No hand can total more than nine points.

4. If the hand has ten or more points, the first digit is removed to figure out the correct total. A twenty-one becomes a one, a sixteen becomes a six, and so forth.

Let's now study a number of hands in baccarat to remember these concepts. For purposes of these examples, as well as their use throughout this section, the jack will be designated as J, the queen as Q, and the king as K.

CARDS	TOTAL
9 4	3
J 10	0
2 K 9	1
8 8	6
3 7	0
K J 4	4
7 3 Q	0
4 5	9
2 A 5	8

Rules of Play

The American game of baccarat is governed by a standard set of rules, which are the same no matter what casino you play in. When the bank holds a zero, one or two he must draw an additional card unless the player holds a "natural," an eight or nine. At the tables these rules are printed on cards that can be studied by the players, but the dealers know the rules by heart and rarely make a mistake in interpreting them.

We already know that the highest hand possible is a nine. This total beats any other total and wins for whichever side has the nine. The next best total is an eight, which beats all totals but a nine or eight (a tie). To make this point absolutely clear, a nine beats all lesser totals, and an eight likewise beats all totals less than an eight. A nine or eight dealt in

PLAYER RULES

HAVING	
1-2-3-4-5-10	DRAWS A CARD
6-7	STANDS
8-9	NATURAL. Bank cannot draw.

BANK RULES

HAVING	DRAWS WHEN GIVING	DOES NOT DRAW WHEN GIVING
3	1-2-3-4-5-6-7-9-10	8
4	2-3-4-5-6-7	1-8-9-10
5	4-5-6-7	1-2-3-8-9-10
6	6-7	1-2-3-4-5-8-9-10
7	STANDS	
8-9	NATURAL. Player cannot draw.	

Pictures and Tens do not count.
If Player takes no card, Bank stands on 6.

the first two cards is known as a *natural* and wins at once, unless the other hand contains a card higher or equal to it. For example, if the Bank hand has an eight but the Player hand a nine, the Player hand wins, even though the Bank hand has a natural eight. If both had nines or eights, it would be a tie, and a standoff, no side winning.

When players receive totals at the outset (first two cards) less than eight or nine, there are no automatic winners, and the rules card must be referred to. Let's see how this works. In all examples the Player hand acts first, followed by the Bank hand.

Looking at the card, we see that the Player hand *must stand* on all totals of six, seven, eight, and nine. No further card may be drawn. However, if the Player hand has any other total, one to five or ten, (0) it must draw one other card.

Suppose the Player hand totaled eight, having received an 8 K. This is a natural, and the Player hand would have to stand on this total. If the Player hand had received a 9 7 for a total of sixteen, it would likewise have to stand. However, if the Player hand was 3 2, totaling five, it would draw a card.

On the other hand, the Bank rules are determined not only by its original holding, but by what card the Player receives as its third card. Like the Player hand, the Bank cannot draw to naturals (eight or nine), nor can it draw to a seven. If the Bank hand totals six and the Player hand doesn't draw a card, it must stand on its six. For example, if the Player hand contained 5 A for a six total, and the Bank hand also totaled six, it would be a tie, a standoff, since by the Player rules the Player hand cannot draw and by the Bank rules, since the Player took no card, the Bank must stand on six.

The term used on the rules card is "giving" when examining the Bank rules. This is synonymous with "Player drawing a card." For example, if the Player hand is dealt a 3 2 for a total of five, and the Bank hand is dealt 5 K for the same total, first we examine the Player rules. Under these rules a card must be drawn to the Player hand. Suppose the Player hand's third card is a 6. The Player has drawn a 6 as its third card, or, with the same meaning, the Bank has "given" the Player hand a 6.

Now we look at the Bank card rules. It states that when the Bank hand totals five and it "gives" the Player's hand a 6, the Bank must draw another card. Therefore, the Bank hand now draws a third card. If the card is a 5, at this point the two hands would look like this:

Player 3 2 6 = one
Bank 5 K 5 = zero

The Player wins, one to zero.

Suppose we repeat the same two cards for the Player and Bank hand. Each starts once again with a total of five, but this time the Player hand (which always acts first) draws an ace, giving it 3 2 A, for a total of six. Looking at the Bank Rules, we see that the Bank hand, holding an initial total of five on the first two cards, doesn't draw another card when the Player hand receives a third card having a one total. The Bank hand must stand, and thus loses, six to five, to the Player hand.

Let's do one other example to make this point absolutely clear. The Player and Bank hands have the following at the outset:

> Player   4 K   =   four
> Bank   Q 3   =   three

Since the Player acts first, we see from the Player rules that holding or having an initial four total forces it to draw one additional card. The Player draws a 7 and now holds 4 K 7 for a total of one.

Now we look at the Bank rules. The Bank hand held an initial total of three, and the Player has drawn a 7 as its third card. Therefore, it must draw another card. Let's say the Bank hand draws a 10. Now it holds Q 3 10 for a total of three. The final hands would look like this:

> Player   4 K 7   =   one
> Bank   Q 3 10   =   three

The Bank hand wins, three to one.

Let's start with the same initial hands, with the Player holding 4 K for a four, and the Bank holding Q 3 for a three. Again, the Player hand must draw a card. It draws a J. Now it has 4 K J for a total of four. Since the Bank hand started with a three total and the Player hand drew a third card valued at 10, it must also draw a third card. It draws a 9. Now the hands in complete form look like this:

> Player   4 K J   =   four
> Bank   Q 3 9   =   two

The Player hand wins, four to two.

Remember that when naturals are dealt either to the Bank or Player hand, the other side doesn't take any cards, and the result is immediate. For example, Player is dealt 8 Q for an eight, and the Bank is dealt J K for a zero. The Player hands wins immediately, eight to zero.

Or if the Player hand is dealt 3 3 for a six, and the Bank hand is dealt 8 A for a nine, neither side draws and the Bank wins nine to six.

But suppose that the Player hand doesn't draw another card by its rules. What does the Bank hand do, since it hasn't given a card?

Let's assume the following:

$$\text{Player} \quad 6 \, K \; = \; \text{six}$$
$$\text{Bank} \quad 3 \, J \; = \; \text{three}$$

The Player hand doesn't draw a card under Player rules. Now it's the Bank hand's turn to play. Having a three, we see that Bank draws when giving a 6. What this really means is that the Bank hand, holding a three, will draw a card if the Player *stands on a six, or draws a 6 as a third card.*

This is true of all Bank hand decisions. For example, if the Player hand stood on a seven, and the Bank hand totaled four, it would draw another card, and so forth, according to the rules.

One final example to explain the last possibility that might be confusing. Suppose the following hands were dealt initially:

$$\text{Player} \quad 9 \, 2 \; = \; \text{one}$$
$$\text{Bank} \quad 4 \, Q \; = \; \text{four}$$

The Player hand must draw a card under its rules. It draws a 7 and now totals eight, a very strong hand. Can the Bank hand now draw a card? Yes. An eight or nine gotten by drawing a third card is not a "natural." We now must look at the Bank rules. It holds a four, and according to the rules it draws when giving a 7 (the third card drawn by the Player). Thus, another card will be drawn by the Bank.

Again, we emphasize that the dealers of baccarat know the complicated rules of play by heart and the player need not concern himself or herself with memorizing them. We showed these examples to explain and illustrate the game. The rules are complex because there was an attempt to make the game as close to equal as possible, but still the Bank hand has the advantage; thus the 5 percent commission rule, which gives the house an edge of 1.17 percent on Bank bets and 1.35 percent on Player bets.

Playing the Casino Game

If you sit down at the baccarat table when it opens for play, you'll see the dealers going through an elaborate ritual. They have eight decks of cards in front of them, and all three are busy shuffling the cards after removing and discarding the jokers, which are not used in baccarat.

After the cards have been thoroughly and randomly shuffled, a plastic card is handed to one of the players. All eight decks have been now brought together and stacked horizontally along the shoe. The player inserts the plastic card into the decks anyplace he or she desires. Where this inserted card is put, the cards are then separated and restacked along the side of the shoe.

The cards are now placed into the shoe, with the plastic card inserted about three-quarters of the way in. When this card is reached in the course of play, the decks are once more reshuffled, or new decks are placed into play, according to the individual casino's rules.

After the cards are in the shoe, the top card is removed by the dealer and placed face up for all to see. Whatever its value, that many cards are removed from the shoe at the outset of play. For example, if an 8 was the first card, then eight cards are removed. This is known as "burning cards," and has no impact on the game; it's just a ritual, and also prevents someone from stacking the decks so that he or she knows the value of the first few cards dealt.

These burned cards are placed in the discard slot and the game is now ready to begin. The shoe is given to the player in seat number 1, and thereafter it will be moved around the table according to the ascending order of player positions, moving from position 1 to 2 and so forth.

To refresh our recollection, the shoe is a rectangular box holding all the decks of cards, and it is built so that cards can easily be removed from it by a player one at a time by merely sliding them out.

As the game goes on, each participant at the table will get a chance to hold the shoe and deal. However, any player may refuse the shoe and the deal. There's no stigma or penalty for doing this. Some players feel unlucky with the shoe; others only bet on Player hands and don't want to deal cards.

Prior to the cards being dealt by the holder of the shoe, he or she must make a bet. The bet can be made on either Player or Bank hands, but the holder of the shoe acts as a nominal banker, and usually bets on Bank. All players who want to involve themselves in this round of play must also make bets, on either Player or Bank or Tie, or any combination of Player or Bank and Tie.

After all bets have been made, the callman will signal the player holding the shoe to start his deal. He does this usually by a nod of the head or other gesture or by saying "Please deal the cards," or some such phrase.

The player now slides a card out and pushes it face down to the callman. This is the first Player's card, since the Player hand gets and acts first in all instances. Then a second card is dealt and this is put to one side face down or slid under the corner of the shoe. This is the first Bank card. Then a second card is dealt face down for the Player hand and another card to the Bank hand. At this point each hand contains two cards.

If there are a number of players at the table, some will be betting Player and some Bank hands. This doesn't have to be the case, since there are times when all participants at baccarat will go one way, either Player or Bank. The casino doesn't care; it books all bets and has an edge on all wagers.

Ritual again enters the game after the cards are dealt. The callman will give the Player cards face down to the gambler with the biggest bet on Player. If no one has bet on Player, he'll turn them over himself. But if someone has bet on the Player hand, that person gets to turn the cards over and return the cards to the callman. The callman places the cards in the Player area in front of him. Now the person holding the shoe turns the Bank cards over and gives them to the callman, who places them in the Bank area in front of him.

All this ritual is time-consuming, but the game is based on mystique and ritual. For example, it is bad form for the player holding the shoe to peek at Bank hand cards before the Player hand is exposed. It is not prohibited, just not done in the best gambling circles.

After the cards are in front of the callman, he now calls their totals. Suppose Player has an eight and Bank has a total of three. He will call "Player eight, a natural, over three. Player wins." Now the other dealers spring into action, first removing all losing Bank and Tie bets and then paying off the winning Player bets. If the Bank hand had won, they'd have to figure the commissions and then note them in the appropriate player position box in front of them.

Most of the time the decision of win or lose is not made until a third card is drawn. For example, suppose the following hands were dealt initially:

Player   4 9   =   three
Bank   10 K   =   zero

The callman will now call for another card from the holder of the shoe for the Player hand. Suppose this is a 2. He will now call for another card from the Bank hand. When the Bank hand totals zero, one, or two, it will automatically get another card no matter what third card is drawn by the Player. The Bank hand will also receive a third card if the Player must stand pat with a 6 or 7.

Another card is dealt, and this is placed next to the original Bank cards. Suppose it is a queen. The final cards would look like this:

Player   4 9 2   =   five
Bank   10 K Q   =   zero

The callman will announce, "Player wins, five to zero."

A gambler at the table will hold the shoe as long as the Player hand doesn't win. He will hold it if the Bank hand has won or there was a Tie. If a Player hand wins, however, he relinquishes the shoe to the next player position, and the game goes on.

Again, all bets must be made before the cards are dealt. Suppose we have this situation: There are four players at the table and three are betting Bank, while one is betting Player. Let's assume that this is a high-limit game in a Strip casino, and there is a total of $15,000 bet on the Bank hands, while the sole bet on Player is $25.

The holder of the shoe deals out the following cards:

Player   A J   =   one
Bank   K 4   =   four

The betters on Bank breathe a bit easier, but they know that by the rules of play, Player draws another card. He draws a 2 for a total of three. Now the Bank hand must draw another card, even though it has a four to Player's three. How the bettors on Bank wish it could stand! But it can't. The callman signals for another card from the player-dealer, and it is slid to him and turned over: a 6. The Player hand wins, three to zero, and the dealers pull in $15,000 and pay out $25 to the only Player bettor.

These are the small moments that add so much drama to this game, especially when big money is at stake. It is this excitement, this jolt, that makes baccarat such a popular game with high rollers and premium players, the kind that will bet several thousand or more on the turn of the card.

When the game has reached the point where the plastic marker is reached, the cards are reshuffled, and there is a break in the game.

Commissions

Commissions are continually being totaled during the course of play, for whenever a Bank hand wins, the casino gets 5 percent of that win as its commission. Commissions are payable whenever there is a break in the game, such as when the cards are being reshuffled, but are not collected after each winning Bank hand.

The accumulated commissions are thus payable during the shuffling of cards or when a player decides to leave the game. At this point, if he or she has commissions owing, they must be settled up.

Toking or Tipping the Dealers

It is usually customary for winners to toke or tip the dealers at the end of their play, when they are leaving the table. This is not mandatory, and the dealers understand that losers are less likely to toke them than winners.

The Odds of Baccarat

The house advantage in baccarat is quite low, and is comparable to the line bets in craps, being less than 1.5 percent in favor of the casino.

Since the house takes 5 percent as its commission on winning Bank bets, many novices assume that this is the house edge, but the 5 percent commission only assures the casino of a small advantage, and on Bank bets it comes to 1.17 percent.

Here's how the odds are calculated in baccarat.

Bank wins 50.68 percent of the time.

Bank loses 49.32 percent of all bets.

Since the casino takes a 5 percent commission on all winning Bank bets, we calculate that the Bank hand wins 95¢ on each winning wager and loses $1 on each losing bet.

Bank loses $1 \times 49.32 = \$49.32$.

Bank wins $.95 \times 50.68 = \$48.15$.

The net loss on Bank bets is −$1.17. Thus, the casino has a 1.17 percent edge on all Bank bets.

There is no commission extracted from winning Player bets, but the Player bet wins less often than the Bank bet.

Player wins 49.32 percent of all bets.

Player loses 50.68 percent of all wagers.

Player loses $1 \times \$50.68 = \$50.68$.

Player wins $1 \times \$49.32 = \$49.32$.

The net loss on Player bets is −$1.36, which means that the casino has an edge of 1.36 percent on all Player bets.

If more gamblers knew the true odds and weren't worried about learning the rules of play, this would be a much more popular game than it is.

Chemin de Fer

Chemin de fer is the version of baccarat played in Europe or Great Britain. The game is named for the French term for "railroad," for chemin de fer resembles a slow railroad moving around the table, as the shoe or *sabot*, which holds the cards, goes slowly from player to player.

Unlike American baccarat, in which the house or casino books all bets and is thus the banker on all deals, there is no fixed banker in chemin de fer. Each player, when he or she holds the shoe, becomes the banker; bets are made between the players; and the temporary banker is responsible for paying off and collecting the wagers.

In chemin de fer the casino merely supplies the equipment and the personnel, and for this it charges a 5 percent commission on the winnings of the Bank hand. Other than this commission, the house is not involved in any other money transactions.

The equipment necessary to run a game of chemin de fer is the table, the cards, the *sabot*, and any other amenities, such as scorecards and pencils. The personnel for this game consists generally of a single dealer, who is known as a croupier. The croupier in effect runs the game, and makes certain that the rules of play are followed. These rules are slightly different from those of American baccarat, since there are a couple of optional plays available.

In Europe or elsewhere, chemin de fer is usually played with the French terms predominating. Every round of play is called a *coup*, the nine as natural is known as *la grande*, and the eight is called *la petite*, when dealt on the first two cards.

Instead of cards being handled by the dealer's own hands as in the American version, a palette is used by the croupier when giving the Player cards to the bettor wagering on Player.

How Chemin de Fer Is Played

There are usually six decks of cards used for this game, which comes out to 312 cards. After the cards are shuffled, cut, and stacked in the *sabot*, the Bank is then auctioned off among the participants at the table. The highest bidder becomes the Bank for the first round of play, which is known as a *coup*, as are all individual rounds of play.

By highest bidder, we mean that player who puts up the highest amount of money as the Bank. He or she is then known as the banker, and holds the Bank until the Bank hand loses. Thereafter, the Bank moves around the table in a counterclockwise fashion, which means that the player to the original banker's right next becomes banker.

However, the banker can relinquish the Bank after any particular coup, even if the Bank had won. If this is the case, the croupier will hold an informal auction and any bidder willing to match the money in the previous Bank will get the shoe. If the participant holding the Bank hand loses, then the *sabot* passes to his right, and this gambler now becomes the banker. But any player can pass up the *sabot* when it is his or her turn to become banker.

The holder of the *sabot* in chemin de fer is always the banker, and no one else can bet with the Bank hand. The others at the table must bet against him, on the Player hand.

Once the player has the Bank, he puts the money he is willing to risk as banker into the center of the table, where it is counted and verified by the croupier. This money in the center is, in essence, the Bank, and others at the table can now bet against the Bank by taking pieces of the action, or "fading the Bank." At times, one individual player may fade the entire Bank.

There are also times when the entire Bank will not be bet against by the players, and when this happens, that portion of the Bank not faded will be put aside and then returned to the banker if he or she loses the next coup.

After the Bank money is put into the center of the table, any player may cover or fade the entire Bank by crying "*Banco*." Once any player calls out *banco*, no other player may make a bet against the Bank. Should two or more players call out *banco* at the same time, then the player closest to the banker's right has precedence over the others in fading the entire Bank. This privilege of covering the Bank while sitting closest to the banker's right is known as *banco prime*.

If no one desires to cover the entire Bank, the other players, beginning with the one to the banker's right, can fade a part of the Bank. After the entire Bank is covered by Player's bets, no more wagers can be made.

Suppose the Bank is $1,000. Should no one call out "*banco*," then the player to the banker's immediate right has the first option to cover any part of the bank he or she desires to. Let's assume this player fades $400, and the next player $400, and the third player to the banker's right puts up $200. Now the entire Bank has been covered and the other players are out of action on this particular coup.

As we mentioned before, there will be times when the entire Bank isn't faded. When this happens, that unbet amount is put aside, and the only monies the Bank has at risk are those covered by the other players.

When a player calls *banco*, and thus fades the entire Bank, then loses his bet, he has the privilege of calling "*Banco suivi*," on the very next round of play. This call gives him the right to once more fade the entire Bank.

After all bets have been placed, the cards are then ready to be dealt. The croupier will instruct the banker to deal out cards; only two hands are dealt. The Player hand will go to the gambler who has bet the largest amount against the Bank, and the Bank hand will remain with the banker. Everyone at the table who has bet against the Bank will be affected by the Player hand, and will win or lose according to its value and according to the decisions made by the holder of the cards representing Player.

As in American baccarat, four cards only are dealt out at the beginning of play, with two cards forming each hand. The first card goes to the Player, the second to the Bank, the third to the Player, and the fourth to the Bank. If additional cards are to be drawn, the Player hand always acts first.

Chemin de Fer Rules

Although the rules of play are very similar to the American baccarat rules, there are a few optional plays open to the Bank and Player hands in chemin de fer.

The following are the rules dealing with drawing and standing by the Player hand:

POINTS	PLAY
0, 1, 2, 3, 4	Must draw a card
5	Optional play; may draw or stand
6, 7	Stands; no draw allowed
8, 9	Natural. The player's cards are turned face up immediately and the coup ends.

When the Player's hand holds an eight or nine, the hand must be displayed immediately and no further play is allowed either by the Player or Bank hands. If the Bank also holds a natural, the higher hand wins. If both naturals result in a tie, then the bet is a standoff and neither side wins. This same rule applies to all ties; they are standoffs and no money changes hands.

Both Player's and Bank's cards are dealt face down because of the optional play involved, when a Player hand may draw or stand on a five. In American baccarat the cards are also dealt face down, but since there are no options, they could just as well be dealt face up. However, by dealing them face down, the drama and tension are increased.

When a Player hand at chemin de fer totals less than five, another card must be drawn to it, and when a hand holds a total of six or seven, it must stand.

These rules allow the banker to ascertain the value of the Player's hand, to some extent. If the Player has drawn a card, then his total must have been less than six. If the Player hand stands, then his total could be five, six, or seven. Of course, a natural of eight or nine must be turned over at once.

If the Player hand is required to draw another card, or if the Player exercises the option of drawing to a five, this third card is dealt face up, next to the two closed cards of the Player.

After this is done, or if the Player's hand is such that he need not draw another card, then it is the banker's turn to play out the Bank hand.

The following rules explain the Bank hand plays at chemin de fer:

Chemin de Fer

CHEMIN DE FER–BANK RULES				
		DRAW WHEN GIVING	STAND WHEN GIVING	
HAVING	3	1.2.3.4.5.6.7. 10	8	9
	4	2.3.4.5.6.7	1.8.9.10	
	5	5.6.7	1.2.3.8.9.10	4
	6	6.7	1.2.3.4.5.8.9.10	

(OPTIONAL)

Although the totals of zero, one, and two aren't shown on the rules card for Bank, these totals force the Bank hand to automatically draw another card, whether or not the Player hand has stood or drawn another card.

There are two optional plays open to the banker, as against the Player's single option of drawing or standing on a five. The Bank can stand or draw when holding a three when the Player hand has drawn a 9 as its third card. The Bank can also stand or draw when its total is five and the Player has drawn a 4 as its third card.

On these two optional plays, the difference between drawing and standing affects the Bank's chances of winning by about 1 percent. If the banker, holding three and having given the Player hand a 9, stands on his total, then his chance of winning is approximately 60 percent. However, should the banker draw another card, then the chances of winning by the Bank are reduced to about 59 percent.

The situation is not quite the same on the second option. If the banker holds a five and gives the Player a 4, the banker's winning chances increase by about 0.5 percent if another card is drawn. This figure is involved with the drawing of a card to the Player total of five. If the Player always stands on five, then whether or not the Bank hand draws makes no real difference in the final result.

Chemin de fer is one of the most exciting games to play because during a long winning streak by the Bank, the money at risk can double and redouble. Here's what happens. By the rules of chemin de fer, the banker cannot skim off his profits and play with the balance. He must risk the entire Bank, and should this Bank be faded or covered fully after each win, the Bank increases by doubling after each win. Of course, the player holding the *sabot* can relinquish the Bank at any time, but should he decide to hold the Bank and the entire Bank is faded, the bets continue to double.

For example, if the Bank began at $1,000 and this was fully covered, after the first win the Bank would stand at $2,000. If this is faded, then another win brings the Bank to $4,000 and a win after that to $8,000 and one more win to $16,000. Now, if the players wish to fade the entire Bank, the banker cannot take any of the money off the center unless he decides to give up the Bank.

Again, this adds to the tension and drama of the game. It is one thing to play for $1,000 and quite another to suddenly have $64,000 at risk, all dependent on the turn of a few cards. It becomes even higher drama when there are optional plays to be made, either by Player or Bank, for so much is riding on the outcome. If the Player hand wins the last coup, all the Bank's previous wins have gone for nought, but should the Bank hand win, and should the banker decide to give up the Bank after the last successful coup, then he has $63,000 in profit, minus the 5 percent commission owed to the casino.

Some casinos give the banker the option of cutting the Bank total in half after three wins in a row. When this happens, the Bank will still show a profit even if the fourth coup loses for Bank. Should the Bank hand lose, the players who bet against the Bank are paid without any commissions charged against their winnings. After the Bank hand loses, the Bank automatically passes to the player to the banker's right.

In those cases when the banker decides to give up the Bank before he actually has lost a coup, the croupier will then hold an informal auction and the player willing to put up the amount of the previous Bank is the new banker.

The double-or-nothing feature has made chemin de fer the popular game it is in Europe and England, and it is an ideal game to show in adventure films; it has been featured in several James Bond movies.

It is much more popular than its American version, and several

Continental casinos feature chemin de fer as their main game, setting many tables aside for play—and the tables are crowded with gamblers anxious to get lucky, win a few coups in a row and possibly a small fortune.

XIV

Cheating at Cards

♠ ♥ ♦ ♣

Introduction

A motto whose truth has kept many card cheats in business for a long time is "There's a sucker born every minute, and two to take him." Barnum was a cynical man when he spoke those words, but they are as true today as they ever were. There are cheats in every walk of life and they seem to have no difficulty finding suckers. The world seems to be filled with "marks," the con man's name for suckers. Swindles of all sorts are pulled off on these marks, but one of the easiest and safest for the professional is card cheating.

Since most card games are played privately among men and women who like to gamble for stakes, there is a small likelihood that a card cheat, once exposed, will be prosecuted. Therefore, it is a rather safe field. The police have special bunko squads which deal with con games in general, but rarely is a card cheat arrested. If he is really good at sleight of hand, it is merely his word against his accusers'. If he is found with marked cards and is not among friends, he will probably have to return the money and be kicked out of the game. In a rare moment, he may get beaten up. But that is the cross he bears, and he accepts it stoically.

If we believe that for every sucker there are "two to take him," then the world may well be filled with more cheats than suckers, even though suckers abound. If this is so, the average cardplayer is going to be involved with cheats at some point or other; indeed he may be facing cheats in every game he plays. Why does he continue to play then? First, he may not know he is being cheated. And second, although he has a faint idea that perhaps the game isn't on the level, it's the only game around.

The cheat is not easily discernible. He doesn't wear a mustache, have shifty eyes, wear flashy clothes and diamond pinky rings, and he doesn't come in with a black hat on. His methods may be subtle or they may be gross; he may be an expert or a bumbler. In fact, cheats run the full spectrum of human looks and intelligence. This is so because, as was said before, cheaters abound in all walks of life.

Who is the cheat? We all are. Once that point is recognized, once it sinks in, we will then be in a better position to avoid being cheated and, more important, to avoid cheating ourselves. Am I being cynical by saying we are all cheats? Well, perhaps we wouldn't "stoop so low" as to cheat in card games, but which of us has not, when the opportunity presented itself, done a little cheating at something?

"Cheating" is the term commonly applied to extramarital relationships, among other things. We cheat every time we make a phony excuse, every time we apologize for ourselves, every time we say one thing and mean another. We go through life cheating so much and on so many different levels that after a while we lose contact with truth. We imagine that cheating is necessary, that it is a necessary fact of life. A white lie isn't bad, we reason, and what the other person doesn't know won't hurt him, and on and on.

Every time a man tells a girl he loves her so that he can sleep with her, he is cheating. Every time a woman goes out with a man so that she can get a free expensive meal, she is cheating. Every time she sleeps with a man to get some material thing, she is cheating. Sometimes one wonders what would happen to most people if the freedom to cheat were taken away from them.

A man's scorn for cheats is often a dead giveaway that what he dislikes are just those traits he finds in himself. I know many honest men who, if they found an old woman had just dropped her pocketbook, would run and give it back to her. How could one stoop so low as to run off with it? Yet, these same men will fake an expense account; will take a friend's wife to bed; will cheat on their income tax. Why? Well, that is something else. It's a good feeling to return an old lady's pocketbook. It reassures us that we are honest. And now we can cheat with impunity.

Everyone cheats at different levels. There are those desperate enough to cheat for a nickel, while others won't bother for under $10,000. But I don't believe anyone can honestly say, "I have never cheated," or "I would never cheat, even if the right opportunity came along." If we recognize this, we are on the right track. The first lesson to remember is that we all have a little larceny in ourselves. If we recognize this, we will be better equipped to cope with cheats.

The second lesson to remember is that our best defense against being cheated is our own self-control.

Any man who hungers for action, hungers for a game, is sure to be cheated. The very desperation of his interest in gambling forecloses any chance of his getting an honest shuffle. Cheaters recognize this compulsive trait immediately and take full advantage of it. It's like running through some low neighborhood with a handful of bills and asking where you could find a whore. Nine chances out of ten, you're going to end up on the ground in some dark alley, without your money and without your whore.

One of the easiest ways for cheats to operate is to get a man or group of men hungering for action and fleece them systematically. A man desperate for action cannot think straight, let alone examine cards. And there are enough fools running around looking for a game to make the cheat's life easy.

Up to now, we've examined those traits within us that may make us victims of cheating. Now, let's look at the methods employed by cheats. Cheats may work in several ways. They may be card manipulators, work with confederates, or they may take advantage of our own sloppy methods of play. They may introduce marked cards, or they may be merely bumblers, dropping cards on the floor and peeking at closed cards. Their methods and their abilities cover a tremendous range. Some of their tactics are easily discernible; others are so expertly done that the closest scrutiny will not uncover them.

Card Manipulators or Mechanics

These are the most dangerous cheats because their tactics, performed with great skill, are almost undetectable. A cardplayer who doesn't know what to look for will be cheated hand after hand, will find himself losing all his money and, at the end of the game, will still not know how it was done.

Card mechanics employ much the same sleight of hand as card magicians. The only difference is that the card mechanic uses these skills to cheat at cards, while the magician's purpose is to entertain. One of the basic tools of both the mechanic and the magician is the mechanic's grip. Although it is possible to use sleight of hand and control cards without this grip, the mastery of the mechanic's grip facilitates the control of the cards. A cheat may use the mechanic's grip or some variant thereof, or merely use the principles of the grip so that it is not easily detected. But a cardplayer who can recognize the mechanic's grip and knows what it implies will be able to detect cheats, while the average cardplayer, without this knowledge, has no method of detecting this type of sophisticated cheating.

Mechanic's Grip

The grip itself is rather awkward and difficult to master. It is a rather unnatural way of handling the complete deck of cards. This is what it looks like.

Mechanic's grip

Try to grip a deck in the manner illustrated. Note that it is hard to keep the pinky in place, and the entire grip feels uncomfortable. And remember, when you see someone holding a deck in this unnatural way, it is not an accident; it is as normal for him to handle the deck with this grip as it is to swing a golf club the first time with the overlapping Vardon grip. Both grips are completely artificial; both must be learned and practiced.

The cards, as seen in the illustration, are held in the left hand. Now, holding the cards as illustrated, press the top of the middle finger of the right hand against the portion of the cards held in place by the left index finger (the top edge of the pack), while pressing the right index finger against the long edge of the pack, and pressing, at the same time, the right thumb against the bottom edge of the pack.

Try the grip. Now you will notice that the right thumb and middle finger exert counterpressure, while the right index finger pushes the edge against the left palm. While holding the cards in this manner, exert pressure downward with the left thumb. (By downward, I mean against the top card of the deck, which the left thumb is touching.) Maintaining this pressure, remove all the cards but the top card by sliding the rest of the pack away with the right hand.

Done correctly, all the cards will move *en masse* except for the top card, which, allowed to fall, will drop onto the four fingers of the left hand. Try it and practice it a few times. This, in the most elementary sense, is the basis for control of the top card in the deck using the mechanic's grip.

Now, grip the cards again with the mechanic's grip and once more place the right hand in the correct position. This time, instead of just pressing down with the left thumb, press also with the ring and index fingers of the left hand, so that pressure is exerted against the bottom card as well. Now remove the pack with the right hand. What should happen is that the top and bottom card are retained, and the top card should fall gently on the bottom card, resting in the left hand.

With this grip, note how top and bottom cards are retained.

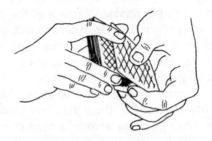

Retention of top and bottom card

This retention of top and bottom card at the same time causes a certain slapping sound to occur. This sound is usually a dead giveaway to the use of the grip to retain both cards. However, in the din of a noisy card game, it can't always be heard. And some expert mechanics can eliminate the sound with many hours of practice.

The Injog

We are still in the mechanic's grip. Now, having retained two cards, remove half the deck with the right hand. The pinky of the left hand should extend beyond the cards still held. Take the cards held in the right hand and using the overhand shuffle, shuffle them on top of the two retained cards, but use the pinky to separate the main body of cards from the two bottom cards. After the shuffle, the pack looks like this:

The Injog

This is the injog. Now, pressing the cards firmly with the right thumb so that the break between the retained cards and the rest of the deck is maintained, shuffle them all over again from the last position. But when you get to the break in the cards caused by the injog, simply put the retained cards on the top again. And that is how card cheats shuffle and reshuffle cards, retaining control of the top card or cards. With practice they can retain ten or more cards for use in games like gin rummy. All they do is have the break caused by the injog cover those additional cards.

Hopefully, you won't go on to become a card cheat from this simple examination of what can be done with the mechanic's grip. However, for those seriously interested in sleight of hand, there are some fine books on the market, notably Bruard's *Royal Road to Card Magic,* which can teach you a great deal about it. The point I want to drive home is what the mechanic's grip is all about and what you are up against when playing cards with someone who uses it. If you are in a game and see it in action, get the hell out. And if you've lost money up to that point, grab that mechanic and demand your money back. Of course, this last bit of advice is subject to time, place, and who you may be demanding it from. But if you are in what you thought to be a friendly game, with some of your friends present, get that bastard to pay you and all your friends back.

Having once mastered the mechanic's grip, a cheat at cards, to avoid being detected, may alter the position of his hands. But the principle remains the same—control of the top and bottom cards—and the injog permits him to form a break in the cards at any point in the deck he selects.

Dealing Seconds

Again, we have the same principle of retention of the top card, this time by the left thumb. There is a slight retraction of the top card as well,

so as to allow the thumb of the right hand to pull out the second card
while the thumb of the left hand squares the top card to conform with
the deck.

Dealing seconds

It is a coordinated motion and can be done with great precision by
trained card cheats. It is especially valuable in situations where the top
card is known and, for whatever reason, would not be dealt immediately,
or at all.

In what games can this be very valuable? Poker, certainly, and
blackjack. A good second dealer, working with a marked deck (one
that can be read from markings on the design), can achieve a thing of
beauty in his work. He can destroy an entire corps of opponents with
the help of a confederate and his own trained hands.

Dealing seconds can also be done without a marked deck. In a
game like blackjack, for example, the dealer can peek at the card or
have a confederate do the same. Or he can simply stack the deck, give
a few false shuffles and riffles, and then start to deal seconds. If a dealer
puts an ace on the top in a game like blackjack, deals himself a 10 or
picture card, and then deals seconds until it is his turn to get a card,
which by fortunate circumstance is that very same ace on the top of
the deck—well, what can the players do but pay, and pay dearly, for
this fleecing?

How to deter a second dealer? Break both his wrists. However, this
is not recommended if he is employed by a casino or a crooked mob,
because the old story of *quid pro quo* is involved; that is, you break
his wrists, and they break your head. So do the next best thing and get
right out of the game.

Remember, in order to protect yourself from a second dealer who
might just show up at a casino, you must make sure that 1) he is not using

a marked deck 2) he is not peeking 3) someone else is not peeking for him and 4) the deck has not been stacked.

So the prevention is usually the cure. If a dealer lingers over the cards picking them up, hesitates before dealing, seems to be using a lot of thumbs in his dealing, these are all sure signs that something is wrong. In a private game, examine the deck carefully for marked cards, but in a casino that may be impossible, so just get out, and if you've lost, get in touch with the Gaming Commission.

Palming

Palming a card is a simple art to learn. It is effective, it is simple, and after a while it can become almost automatic. It aids those cheats who may not be that proficient in second dealing or other methods of retaining a certain card. They simply palm it, and presto, when they need it, there it is.

What is palming? It is the retention of a card by putting it in the right palm. Here's how it's done, so you can be on the lookout.

The cheat holds the deck in the left hand, with his left thumb on the top portion of the cards, preferably at a forty-five-degree angle with the upper left-hand corner of the deck. Then, while the cheat's index, ring, and middle fingers are gripping the cards, he slides the top card out as far as it will go with the left thumb.

Palming, First Step

That's the initial motion, but where's the palming? Well, now he takes his right hand and, with four fingers (other than the thumb), covers the top of the deck. The left thumb remains on the top of the deck, so his right hand is covering most of his left thumb as well. The right thumb is pressing into the bottom edge of the deck, pushing it up toward his four fingers.

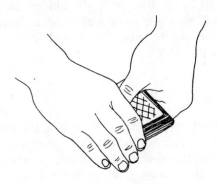

Palming, Second Step

Now, with his hand thus, with only about half his pinky over the top right edge of the deck, and the whole meaty portion of his right hand forming a cover, he slides that top card over as far as it will go with the left thumb.

Pushed out this way, the top card is hidden in his right hand. Now, the important thing is to remove it without attracting attention. So a good cheat moves his left hand away holding the pack of cards, the motion drawing attention to that hand. The right hand remains stationary for a moment, then it unobtrusively moves away. In it is the top card, out of view. This is what palming is all about.

And do those nasty devils keep the card palmed in the right hand? No; some of them remove it entirely and sit on it, drop it, or whatever. This is done in poker, where the confederate has a flush and that pesky queen is palmed by the dealer to insure that the guy who needs it for his full house won't get it.

How to replace the palmed card and get it ready for dealing? The dealer holds the deck in his left hand toward the right hand, and the right toward the deck, and finally the right hand passes over the deck and slides away. During this process, the top surface of the deck is kept clear of thumbs. With a pressing motion, the palmed card is returned to the deck.

False Overhand Shuffling

Using the mechanic's grip, a dealer can shuffle and reshuffle the cards till they look as though they have been mixed for ten years, and yet the cards will remain in almost the exact position in which they were before the shuffle. This is done with the aid of the injog, forming a crimp in the cards. One whole section of the deck is forever untouched, and the other section can be moved back and forth so that almost the original position of the deck is reached again.

False Riffling

A riffle, or riffle shuffle, is done by dividing the deck into two equal portions, or as close as possible to two equal portions, and then, with the thumbs, pushing from the bottom of each pile. This creates a tension so that the cards from the two piles, when they are close together, will fall so as to mesh together, a card from one pile alternating with a card from the other pile. (See Chapter I) It is very easy to learn this kind of shuffle, and it is the standard one used in most games. It is more difficult to intermesh the cards exactly one to one, but if that is learned, the first few cards can be shuffled to any desired position in the deck. This is enormously advantageous in a game like gin rummy. See *Cheating at Gin Rummy*, Chapter IV, to find out how this is done and how to watch for it and defend against it.

In a false riffle shuffle, an expert cheat, after the meshing of the two piles, with a swift motion removes the piles and puts the cards back in the same place they were originally. This is a difficult motion to get away with, and unless you are groggy from the long hours of playing, or drinking, or a combination of both, it should be easy to spot.

Some dealers can move the intermeshed cards right through and out the other side, and pick them up and start again. But this is also a very difficult maneuver, both to do and to get away with.

Cutting

After the shuffles in any game, a player other than the dealer has the right to cut the cards. Cutting is simply taking a portion of the deck from the top and putting it next to the remainder of the deck.

Most players try to cut about midway into the deck, and cheats take advantage of this by putting the cards they want dealt just below the middle of the deck, so that when cut, they are back in the original position again. And some cheats love to have confederates sitting next to them obliging them with the cut they want. If there is no confederate, a cheat will crimp the cards (see illustration).

Crimping

In this way he is assured of the correct cut. When you cut cards and find that they seem almost to divide of their own accord in a certain place, don't continue the cut, but replace the cards and try again. If the same place suggests itself, you are being handed a deck that is crimped, and the best thing is to announce this to the table. If you are losing, ask the fellow who handed you the deck for your money back.

It may happen that someone else, in a previous shuffle, crimped the deck and didn't straighten the cards out. But this is unlikely, because an easy way to get rid of a crimp is to square the deck and then push the deck against the direction of the crimp, arching the cards so that the crimp straightens itself out.

There are some dealers who don't even bother crimping the cards; after you cut they simply place the cut portion in the same position as before, rather than putting the cards cut at the bottom of the deck. If you see this, you are in a game with a rascal, and possibly more than one. Think of ways to get out if you are winning, and if you are losing, point out this maneuver to the offender. When he denies it, your anger should be controlled, but will still be a very effective force, especially with friends around.

Marked Cards

Cards have markings on their backs, usually in intricate designs. With the displacement of a white dot here and a small bar there, their values are easily discernible to one who studies these things. And, of course, a card cheat has nothing better to do all day than study markings and practice maneuvers with his hands. By the time he sits down for the nightly game in which you are a welcome guest, he'll know those markings so well he can read the backs almost as fast as you can read the faces.

This gives him quite an advantage, wouldn't you say? Now you wonder how he is going to get a marked deck into a game. First of all, as a precaution, when you enter a card game make sure that the decks are fresh and unopened and have the government seal on them. There is a government tax on playing cards and there is a stamp pasted over the flap under the cellophane.

But remember this, and this is of utmost importance: The mere fact that a deck of cards comes in its original box, with a revenue stamp and with cellophane neatly enclosing it, means nothing. The deck can still be marked, the cellophane and stamp having been removed and then replaced by the marking company, and all you see is a fresh deck of cards. I've seen them myself, looking all clean and unused although every card had been marked. That is one of the things you must guard against, especially in games like poker and gin rummy. It may be impossible at first glance to tell whether a deck is marked or not, but there are certain telltale signs.

When it is your turn to deal, take the cards and, holding them securely in your left hand, arch the top of the deck forward so that the cards, as they are released in quick order by the thumb, will snap back one at a time, in rapid succession. This is the same way you'd run through a deck of pictures to give them a sense of animation. (Remember those old picture cards?) As the backs of the cards move rapidly past your eyes, they should make no particular impression if they are honest and unmarked. If they are marked, however, they will seem to have jumping designs. This motion-picture effect is a dead giveaway that the cards are marked.

If they are, don't give them up, but ask who brought them and display them to the players. Again, as with all my advice on blowing the whistle, remember that if you are in a strange place among strangers and the whistle blowing can put you in danger, just get out of the game quietly. But get out.

Spotting marked cards

Sometimes, cards are marked by a luminous process that makes the mark distinguishable only when wearing certain glasses, or contact lenses. This is very difficult to ascertain, but look into your opponent's eyes, and if you are losing to someone who is wearing unusual glasses, or who stares at the backs of cards peculiarly, it is a clue. Generally, the kind of glasses necessary are the tinted variety. This situation, however, is not one you'll come across very often.

Other decks have high cards cut slightly wider than the others, or the lower cards are cut this way so that with one good tap, the wider cards fall out. So, in addition to looking for the motion pictures in a deck of cards, hold the cards upright, tap them hard, and lift. If four aces fall out, it may either be the most startling of coincidences, or you are playing with a cheat.

Confederates

Two or more men may get together (women are not immune from this kind of work either) and by the mere fact that they signal each other, they can have the other players in a bind.

For example, two men work together in a poker game in which there are eight players including you. If you get a good hand and are in the habit of showing your hole card to the player next to you, and if he is a cheat and you are playing against his confederate, a hand signal will tell the confederate whether to get out or stay in. That's simple.

If the cheat is the dealer and can manipulate cards, and if his confederate is to his right and thus cuts the cards, then a deck will be set up so that they will win hands they deal. Of course, they deal these hands so that most of the other players get very good cards too, so there will be big pots and much raising.

If you find that the same two men seem to be in pots to the end, together with another player or players, and that one of the two men had very poor cards, yet raised in a crazy and unusual fashion, it is a signal that he is merely building up the pot for the other player. I've seen this a couple of times.

I was once in a game with a player everyone thought was a wild man, a guy who raised and raised on nothing, on the wildest hopes, and on even less than that. He was going after cards in seven-card stud that seemed unbelievable. He would raise three of a kind with his possible garbage, and especially in a high-low game, where he had neither high nor low, he raised interminably. And there was another player at the game who kept insulting this raiser, laughing and antagonizing him, and who kept winning these very big pots. It was almost as if he were goading the raiser.

And all of us were losing.

Well, there was another player in the game, a very sharp poker player I knew well. After being raised by the wild man and having that raise reraised by the big winner, only to be reraised by the wild man *ad infinitum*, he waited for the last card to be dealt. The winner bet; the wild man raised; my friend called; the winner reraised; then the wild man folded. But my friend didn't call.

As the wild man gathered up his cards, my friend simply grabbed the cards out of his hand, and a hush descended on the table. It was seven-card stud, high only, and my friend opened the seven cards of the raiser. They showed a pair of fours and nothing else. The winner had two kings showing, and my friend had a three flush and a pair of 10s showing.

"How did you raise with this shit?" my friend wanted to know.

"Who the hell are you?" the raiser demanded. "I got a right to play my own game."

"Not when you're costing me money," said my friend.

"Screw you," said the raiser.

And the big winner, in the spirit of arbitration, said "Gentlemen, gentlemen."

But by this time my friend had dragged the raiser up off his seat, and holding him in a hard grip, he moved toward the big winner.

"Show me your full house," he demanded.

"Hey, what is this?" demanded the big winner. "You bet to see, if you want. And play a game. If you can't take losing, get out of the game, but don't be a child."

"Show me the full house."

The big winner looked around at us.

"What is this?" he asked. "What is this? You gonna let him get away with this?"

Blank faces greeted him.

I reached over and showed three kings full in his hand. I had been caught like that a few times that night, raised and reraised until my head was spinning, and then my straight lost to a flush in which three of the flush cards had been hidden.

The big winner, who was a squat, heavy guy, stood up.

"I'm not taking this crap," he said, trying by his indignant attitude to make us all feel guilty. He started to put on his jacket.

"You're going nowhere," I said.

The other guy, the raiser, tried with a sudden jerk to release my friend's grip, but landed on the floor from a hard right. When he got up, there was a trickle of blood on his chin, running down from a corner of his mouth.

"Empty your pockets," my friend ordered the big winner, who appealed to us with his eyes.

"Empty them," we all said, as if in a chorus. The bastard had won almost a thousand dollars.

We kicked them out of the place. The raiser threatened my friend as he was propelled to the door. "I'll get even with you," he said.

My friend answered so calmly that it amazed me. His voice was low and even.

"If I see you again," he said quietly, "I'll kill you."

The raiser got the message. They scrammed fast. Did they complain to the police? No, sir, they just disappeared out of our life and our game. One of the guys we played with had brought them into the game, but he was innocent in the matter. He was an executive in an electronics firm, and they were salesmen making a call. Talk had got around to a poker game, since they'd be in town only for the weekend. It was beginning to look like a very profitable weekend for them—until the shit hit the fan.

Other Methods Used by Card Cheats

Not only are those methods we have discussed so far used by cheats to fleece the unsuspecting public, but a whole variety of other methods are open to them.

The Stacked Deck

Instead of introducing marked cards, the cheat may have a stacked deck—that is, a deck already set up in a predetermined manner. This is often used by a cheat who has a confederate present, so that the confederate can cut the cards in the right place. Then the deck is dealt out, and in a game like poker there will be a rash of full houses, straights, and flushes. However, the four of a kind held by the cheat's confederate will somehow win the pot. This stacked-deck principle is often used in any card game, and especially where all the players but one (the sucker) are in cahoots and all are cheats. In this type of situation, there may be a whole series of stacked decks, and while the sucker's attention is momentarily drawn away, the new deck is introduced.

The stacked deck is, of course, the same kind of deck that has been previously used by the players, with the same color and design. It would be foolish to introduce a completely new deck with a different design —after all, even a sucker has his limits.

The best thing one can do to prevent stacked decks is to be observant. If suddenly everyone gets excited by his holdings, that is a danger signal. If you are playing against all strangers and seem to have a tremendous hand (four of a kind), yet face three raises, be careful. In fact, in any game with strangers, be careful. All of them may be partners looking for a good day's pay—your bankroll.

If, after playing cards for about an hour, you suddenly notice that the cards have a rather cool feel, that is a sure sign of a stacked deck. After much use, cards become warm to the touch. So if, after a night of garbage, you are dealt rather stiff, cold cards and you are looking at a straight flush, 10-high, that is not scaring anybody, watch out!

Even if stacked decks are not used, the danger of confederates in a game is always present. You won't even know they know each other, and they might not know each other (see *How Card Cheats Recognize Each Other*), but you're in for a bad time. If the game is big enough and some of the players are strangers to the general group, there's always the danger of confederates cheating.

An acquaintance of mine told me of a poker game he had played for years with the same players in which it was finally disclosed that two of them had been working together as cheating confederates. It is really difficult to know when you are being cheated this way.

Again—and it cannot be repeated often enough—be alert and observant. Sometimes a wrong move will give them away. If a player is too busy with hands and eyeglasses and cigarettes or cigars, watch him closely. There is a certain kind of busyness that is like a red flag waved in front of you.

Signals

Signals are not standard among cheats; if they were, everyone could study these signals and always spot them. Basically, the signals involve use of the fingers and cards. Pointing to a corner may indicate a high card or a particular suit. Watch for hands that are always full of pointing fingers.

In a game with strangers, watch the winners, watch their motions. Then watch yourself. When you are dealt a couple of cards, what do you do with them? Your movements are probably sparse. You put them down and then wait. If some other player is readjusting them, changing their direction, watch out.

In closed games, like pinochle and bridge, again test to see how you pick up and hold your cards. They should be fairly even. If an opponent always has a card or two sticking up, or is holding the cards in a peculiar way with his fingers, again watch out.

By telling you to observe, I don't mean you should be paranoid; just don't keep your head stuck in the sand. There is no greater scorn than that of a cheat for a sucker. Don't be the object of this bastard's scorn. Try and be one step ahead of him. These guys are not supermen; generally they are men of rather limited ability, else why should they be making a career of cheating? You should be able to handle them, to spot them and stop them. Use your powers of observation, and if something is wrong, immediately stop playing and get out of the game. If your friends are involved as well, get them out of the game.

No chapter on cheating will ever be complete, because new methods are being used every day, new techniques are constantly being devised, and with more and more electronic equipment available, the cheating methods may be more subtle.

But against this whole array of methods, your best defense is yourself. If you are losing steadily, if something "smells" wrong, get out of the game. Often, your instincts will protect you in a game. Keep your feelings and eyes open, and trust what they tell you.

How Card Cheats Recognize Each Other

I knew a couple of men who made a living as professional card players. They were expert at most of the big-money games, but preferred games like gin rummy and two-handed pinochle, games in which they had only one opponent. However, if they could get into a big poker game, that was just fine with them. They didn't know each other, and I, being their mutual friend, never did get around to introducing them to each other. But both had similar tales to tell about their methods. Each felt that his skill was enough in most games to win without any cheating. One was also an expert card mechanic who took advantage of any idle hours to practice his sleight of hand techniques. He was a marvelous trickster, and I would be entertained by aces falling out of the deck at his command. The other professional wasn't that good, but he knew the mechanic's grip and could use it effectively enough.

The one thing I was interested in was this: If they got into a game like poker with strangers and felt that the players were ideally set up to be cheated, how would they know if there were any other cheaters in the game? (I used the word "mechanics" with these gentlemen.)

There was a time, one of them told me, when a cheater would sit down at a card game and extend his left hand, putting it flush on the table. It was done unobtrusively, just as drinks were being served, the cards were being opened, the players were getting to know each other by introductions. The flat hand said, "I'm a cheat. Are there any others around?" If another man extended his hand in the same way, he was signaling back. Then the cheat could remove his hand, in which case they'd work together and split their winnings at the end of the session. Or he'd make a fist of his flat hand, telling the other cheat, "I want to work this game alone. Get out when you can."

These signals are not used much anymore. For one thing, there aren't the same old circuits as in the past, and a lot of the wide open places in Kentucky and Arkansas where cheats used to gather during resort time (Saratoga Springs was another place) aren't what they used to be. Luxury liners were fertile grounds also, but air travel has changed that.

Occasionally these cheats book themselves on junket flights to Las Vegas, or Puerto Rico, or London, or wherever the junkets are going, and start games with the gamblers on the junkets who can't wait the several hours the flight takes for "action." Sometimes the pickings are good, but generally they're slim on most flights. Usually some mob has their own men available and it's getting awfully difficult for the independents.

"So now that these signals are out, how do you recognize other mechanics," I asked.

"I'll tell you," one of them told me. "You know the way an ex-con recognizes another ex-con? There's a certain look about them. Or you hear how a queer can always spot another queer. It's the same with us. I can just spot the guy. I can go into any game and right away I know who's in the business. I don't need signals and I don't even got to look at the guy. I just know."

"What do you do?" I asked him.

"Nothing. Maybe I take a break, go into the kitchen for some coffee or a glass of water, and then the guy comes right in, and I offer him some coffee or some sugar, and we look each other in the eye and we nod. Later, I meet the guy at a nearby bar and we split up the money."

"How do you know what to split?"

"Well, I *don't* know, to tell the truth. So most of the time we just play the game, help each other out. He deals, I win. I deal, he wins. He's got the best hand, I do a little raising for him, and vice versa. Then we don't even meet. There's one guy I've been doing this with for five years, and I don't even know his name. I don't think I even exchanged ten words with him in all this time."

He paused.

"It's just the look," he said. "If you're in the same business, you can always spot the look."

XV

Craps

BANK CRAPS OR CASINO GAME

CRAPS—PRIVATE GAME

CRAPS—CASINO GAME

Introduction

Bank craps, or, as it is more commonly called, craps, is by far the most popular casino gambling game in the United States, and its success spread to the Caribbean, South America, and Europe. Craps can also be played as a private game and is quite popular as such, but this chapter will deal with the casino game, known as bank craps, and the private game will be discussed later in this chapter.

Craps is a game of pure chance. There is absolutely no skill involved in playing the game, and unlike poker and blackjack, reason does not enter into its play and has no effect on its outcome. But go into any casino in Nevada, and though the clamor at the slot machines will be louder, most of the excitement and interest will usually center around the crap table. The game is fast, it can be bet for high stakes, much money can be won and lost quickly, and a bet may be made with every roll of the dice.

The game is known as bank craps because, in effect, the house is the bank and plays against all the players, whether they bet with or against the dice. There is an old fallacy which says that to make money in craps at a casino, it pays to "bet with the house." What many a player thinks this means is to bet against the dice, or "wrong." It doesn't mean anything of the kind. If you bet "wrong," the house will book, or bank, your bet just the same as if you bet "right."

There is only one way to "bet with the house," and that is to get a gambling license, open a casino, run a crap game, and bank the players' bets. Otherwise, if you're at a craps table, your bet is against the house, no matter what bet you place.

In any gambling casino, the following equipment is necessary to run a game: First, there is the table, curved but otherwise rectangular, about ten feet long and about five feet wide. It stands about three feet off the ground, and its edges are built up another foot or so. Running around its edge is a wooden surface with grooves for holding chips.

The surface of the table is green felt, and on the surface is the "layout," a diagram of all the possible kinds of bets. The most popular are the pass line and don't-pass line. Also popular are the come and don't-come boxes. The area for field bets is very large, and the place numbers are given a prominent spot. There are provisions for betting on craps and eleven, and on any craps, on the 7, on the Big 6 and 8, on hard-way combinations, such as a 6 made by rolling 3 and 3. There are bets that can be made on the 12, and bets on any hard way. There is indeed a panorama of betting opportunities afforded the gambler.

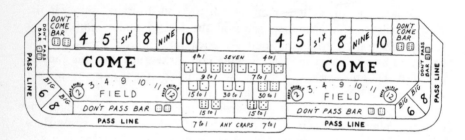

Casino craps layout

Running the game are four men, all employees of the casino, who are at the table during its use. Two are dealers, standing at the table and placing bets for players who cannot reach them, or placing bets for them on the place numbers. They pay off bets and collect losing bets. Between them sits the boxman, who is in charge of the table. He supervises the play, watches over the action, and usually collects all cash money and puts it into a slot which deposits it into a box buried inside the hollow part of the table. He has the right to extend credit by giving markers, and also to raise the betting limit above the house limit. Standing at the other side of the table is the stickman. He holds a wooden stick which he uses to push the dice to the players. He takes bets on the various proposition bets that can be made at the table and pays off those bets. He also calls the game.

On the table, close to the stickman, are the dice. They are perfect, or near-perfect, cubes, each having six sides. Dice come in pairs; one is called a die. Each die is made of some plastic composition, usually red or green, with numbers represented by dots imposed on its surfaces, usually in white. A typical set of dice would look like this:

Dice

Each die has six sets of dots—one set per side—representing the numbers one through six. Therefore, using two dice, the lowest number possible is 2; the highest 12; and there are thirty-six possible combinations of all numbers.

On the table there may be ten to twenty dice, but only two are used by a player. The same dice are used by the player unless he requests that they be changed, in which event all the other dice are shoved over to him by the stickman, and the player may select two different ones. Sometimes the house will demand a change of dice, particularly if, on examination, they find a flaw in them.

Each new shooter, or thrower of the dice, in turn has the right to select two dice from the many on the table. After he selects two, the others are pushed to one side, out of play, so that they don't come into contact with the dice being rolled.

Other than this equipment, all that is necessary for the house is chips. These are stacked up in piles according to their denominations. There are one-dollar, five-dollar, and twenty-five-dollar chips. These are the most popular denominations, although some houses use hundred-dollar chips as well.

The players (gamblers) stand around the table, and the only limit to their number is the amount of affordable space into which these people can squeeze themselves. Not all the table is available to them; the stickman occupies a great deal of space, and the area covered by the boxman and the two dealers may be almost one whole long side of a table. Usually, however, at least fifteen players can be accommodated at a table.

Each player participating in the game has the right to roll the dice at his turn. Generally, the dice may be given to anyone at the table when the game starts (usually, for purposes of gallantry, to a woman, if one is present), and thereafter the dice move clockwise around the table. Each player, when his turn comes, may roll the dice or skip his roll. No penalties are imposed and no fuss is made when a player declines to roll. Some players only bet "wrong"—that is, against the dice—and hate to bet against their own roll.

A player rolls the dice until he "sevens out" when attempting a point. That is, he might roll a 5, then try to make another 5 before he rolls a 7. Should he roll a 7 before another 5, the dice lose, and it is the next player's turn to roll the dice. That is the only time he relinquishes the dice other than voluntarily. The next roller then selects two dice from the pile, but before he can roll them, he must make a line bet.

The bets are made before each roll of the dice. In casino games there are no oral bets permitted; each bet must be placed on the table or handed to an employee at the table before that bet is valid. Some bets are for one roll of the dice; others await the outcome of several or many rolls. But as soon as a bet is won or lost, it is collected or paid off immediately.

Combinations in Dice

Since dice are cubes, they have six sides. Each side of each die is numbered by means of a white dot or dots, the numbers running from one dot to six dots. When two dice are used, the lowest number that can be rolled is one dot plus one dot, or 2. The highest number is six dots plus six dots, or 12.

Since each die contains six numbers, the possible variations that can be rolled are six times six or thirty-six. Here are the thirty-six possibilities.

Number	Combinations to Make	Ways to Make
2	1-1	1
3	1-2, 2-1	2
4	1-3, 3-1, 2-2	3
5	1-4, 4-1, 2-3, 3-2	4
6	1-5, 5-1, 2-4, 4-2, 3-3	5
7	1-6, 6-1, 2-5, 5-2, 3-4, 4-3	6
8	2-6, 6-2, 3-5, 5-3 4-4	5
9	3-6, 6-3, 4-5, 5-4	4
10	4-6, 6-4, 5-5	3
11	5-6, 6-5	2
12	6-6	1
Total		36

Because there are thirty-six combinations, the odds against rolling either a 2 or a 12 are thirty-five to one; against rolling a 3 or 11, 17 to 1.

All other numbers with the exception of the 7 are "point" numbers, which, when rolled initially must be repeated before a 7 is rolled for the shooter to win. Since the value or relative value of a point number must be measured against the 7, the odds against making any of the point numbers (4, 5, 6, 8, 9, 10) are figured by measuring their possible combinations against the combinations which can make a 7.

For example, there are six combinations that can make a 7. Translated into dice terms, there are six ways a 7 can be rolled. There are only three ways in which a 4 or 10 can be rolled. Therefore, the odds against making a 4 or 10 as a point are six to three or two to one.

Table of Point Numbers and Odds Against Making Them

Number	Odds
4	two to one
5	three to two
6	six to five
8	six to five
9	three to two
10	two to one

Now, if you are betting the pass or don't-pass line, the come or don't-come box, you must either give or take these odds as the correct odds on any odds bet that you make.

Although the odds against making a 2 or 12 in one roll are thirty-five to one, on the craps layout the odds given are only thirty to one, thus giving the house an edge of more than thirteen percent. Likewise, although the correct odds against making the 3 or 11 on one roll are seventeen to one, the house will only give fifteen to one, or an edge to the house of about eleven percent.

Other interesting things to observe on the crap layout. There are two huge boxes, Big 6 and Big 8, which pay even money. The odds against making either a 6 or 8 are six to five. Again, the house has insured itself a sizable advantage of more than nine percent.

All of these bets, plus all the possible bets on the table, will be discussed in their appropriate sections, but a player or potential player of craps should readily see that the house percentage varies drastically on different kinds of bets.

Mechanics of Play

The Come-Out

When a new shooter is about to roll the dice, this is called a come-out. The stickman will announce, "New shooter coming out." Before he rolls the dice, he must make a line bet, either a pass bet or don't-pass bet. This is done at the pass or don't-pass line. He may make other bets as well, but this minimum bet is required of him. All other players may make any other bets they wish.

The Line Bet: Pass or Don't Pass

This is the staple bet of the bank craps game. The pass line is used by those players who bet with the dice. The don't-pass line is used by those bettors who are betting against the dice.

Pass Line: A player wins his bet in the following ways:

1. On the first roll of the dice, if a 7 or 11 comes up.

2. If he rolls a 4, 5, 6, 8, 9, or 10 on the first roll and repeats the initial number before he rolls a 7. These numbers, on the initial roll, are called "points."

For example, if a roller initially rolls a 7, he wins his bet on the pass line. His next roll is now a first (initial) roll again. He rolls a 5. Thereafter he rolls a 6, 11, 2, 8, 8, 9, and then a 5. He wins his bet. Note that although he rolled two 8s, he would not win on the second roll of 8 because his initial roll was a 5. That became his "point." All other numbers had no value or interest to him after that on a pass bet. His only concern was a 5 or 7. If the 5 came up first, as it did, he won the bet. If a 7 had come up first he would have lost his bet. Thus, the 11 and 2 had no value in the middle of his roll.

Having made his point, he now begins another new roll. If he were to roll a 7 now, he would win because on the initial roll, a 7 or 11 wins.

A player betting the pass line loses in the following ways:

1. On the first roll, if he rolls a 2, 3, or 12. Those three numbers are known as "craps." Although the roller and all other players betting the pass line would lose on the initial roll of the 2, 3, or 12, the shooter does not relinquish his roll.

Note also, and this is quite important, that all other bettors at the table are bound by the roll of the shooter. In essence they are betting with him or against him. His roll determines whether or not they win or lose. Only one roller or shooter may roll at a time.

2. On the first roll, if a 4, 5, 6, 8, 9, or 10 is rolled (points) and a 7 is rolled before the point is repeated. Should the shooter roll a 6, then 8, 9,

4, 2, 5, 10, 5 and 7, he would lose, because the 7 came up before the point, which was 6, repeated.

Note also that rolling a 2, 3, or 12 in the middle of the roll has no effect on the roll. Only in the initial roll is it a losing bet.

This basically is the pass line.

Don't-Pass Line: This is a "wrong" bet. The bet is against the making of a pass or a 7 or 11 on the first roll. A shooter may bet against the roll even if he is rolling, by betting the don't-pass line.

The don't-pass bettor wins in the following ways:

1. If craps come up on the initial roll. Craps are the 2, 3, or 12. However, all casinos bar either the 2 or the 12 because otherwise the odds would be slightly in favor of the "wrong" bettor. By forbidding the don't-pass bettor to collect when either a 2 or 12 is rolled on the initial roll, the house insures that the odds will be in its favor, rather than in favor of the "wrong" bettor.

The 12 is generally barred at all casinos in Las Vegas. The 2 is barred in casinos in Reno, as a general rule.

2. If the shooter rolls a 4, 5, 6, 8, 9, or 10 (point) on the initial roll, and a 7 comes up before the first number, or point, is repeated.

Conversely, a don't-pass bettor loses if a 7 or 11 comes up on the first roll, or if the point is made.

This is basically the don't-pass line.

Odds Involved in Line Bets

One of the reasons for the popularity of the line bets is that the odds favoring the house are at their lowest, and may be made lower still by making a back bet, or odds bet, which will be discussed next. But first let us examine the odds on a line bet.

Pass Line: The percentage against the bettor on the pass line is 1.41 percent.

Don't-Pass Line: With the 2 or 12 barred, the percentage is 1.40 percent against the don't-pass bettor.

Note that both the pass and don't-pass bettors have approximately the same odds against them.

Taking or Placing Odds on Line Bets

To recapitulate what was discussed in the previous section, the shooter must make a line bet, either a pass bet ("right" bet) or a don't-pass bet ("wrong" bet). Other players at the table may also make these bets, and if they do, they are bound by the dice as rolled by the shooter.

No matter which line bet is made by the players, the odds are slightly in favor of the house. On the pass line, the percentage is 1.41 percent against the player, and on the don't-pass line, approximately 1.40 percent against the player.

There is one option open to both pass and don't-pass bettors (also come and don't-come bettors, discussed in a later section); they are permitted to give or take free odds. If you study a craps layout, you will not find any sign of this, nor do the dealers mention it to the players, nor do they encourage it, but they take the bets.

The reason the bets are not encouraged is that they are the only bets that are taken or placed at exact odds. In other words, on these bets the house has no advantage at all, and the player has no disadvantage. Since this is the only time (other than doing the same with come or don't-come bets) that the house, in craps, is going to have no advantage over the player, a bettor at the dice table would be foolish not to take advantage of it. Here's how it's done.

Suppose you are a bettor on the pass line. You have bet ten dollars. You hope the dice will pass, or win. Thus, you are a "right" bettor. The shooter throws the dice on his initial roll and a 4 is rolled. If we look at the table of odds we see that there are three ways to make it, either 1-3, 3-1, or 2-2. There are six ways to make a 7. Therefore, the odds against a 4 coming before the 7 are two to one. These are the exact, correct odds. The house, in most casinos, will allow you to make a bet of equivalent size on the odds. That is, you can bet an additional ten dollars at two-to-one odds that the 4 will come up before the 7.

By doing this, you have, as a bettor, materially changed the overall odds. Instead of collecting ten dollars for ten dollars bet where the possibility is two to one against you, you now stand to collect thirty dollars for twenty dollars bet. By betting odds and taking them whenever possible, as a "right" bettor you lower the overall percentage in favor of the house from 1.41 against you to 0.85. Quite a difference. Philosophically speaking, one might consider the house to be entitled to this small percentage for running the game, supplying the dice, etc.

In some gambling casinos (usually in Tahoe or Reno, but not in Las Vegas) the house will allow you double odds. This means that with a ten-dollar bet on the pass line, you can bet twenty dollars on the odds line. With the same point 4, you would stand to collect fifty dollars for the thirty dollars bet. This brings the house percentage down to a measly 0.61 percent in their favor. If you are a serious craps player and bet only the pass line, or make any line or come bets, it certainly would pay to get up to Reno and get those odds. You can't beat them in any casino crap game.

So far, we have spoken about taking the odds. If we were bettors at the don't-pass line, we would have the privilege as well of giving the odds.

Let's follow the same 4 as the point, only this time we are "wrong" bettors, betting on the don't-pass line. We have bet ten dollars. We can increase our bet with another bet on the odds. Since we are betting against the dice, we may lay twenty dollars to ten that the 7 may be rolled, which will win for us, and only three ways that the 4 may be rolled, which will be a losing bet for us.

We simply put twenty dollars behind the ten-dollar bet, and we now place, or give, the odds. By betting the correct odds and giving them whenever possible, the "wrong" bettor changes the house odds from 1.40 percent against him, to 0.83 percent against him.

And, if he is betting in a casino which permits him to give "double odds," or bet forty dollars to twenty in this instance, he further reduces those percentages to 0.59 percent against him, and this is rock bottom.

Thus, without belaboring the point, you should readily see that it pays to take and give the odds on all line bets and, if possible, to find a casino that permits the giving or taking of double odds.

The percentage will still be against you, but it will have been reduced drastically, more than fifty percent in the case of double-odds bets. But with these small percentages against you, you are in an almost even game, and you have the best chance in craps, of all the games of chance, to play a progression or other system. Doing it in roulette, where it is most popular to play these progressions, is almost fatal, because the percentages against you in American roulette is, at best, over five percent.

Come Bets

One of the areas on the table layout is devoted to come and don't-come bets. These are perhaps the most misunderstood bets on the table, other than odds bets. The main reason odds bets are misunderstood is that there is no place shown for them in markings on the table. That is because the house has no advantage when you make this bet. However, the house welcomes come and don't-come bets, because these give the player, and thus the house, action on every single roll of the dice.

On the initial roll of the dice, the bettor can make a variety of bets. But if he desires to stick to the bets that will give the house the smallest edge, he would be foolish to bet anything but the front line, either the pass or don't-pass bets. Anything else, the field, the place numbers, the proposition bets, the Big 6 and Big 8, any crap, all are nothing but bad bets. You'll see why later. The percentages involved in these other bets range from 1.51 percent to 16.7 percent in the house's favor.

Now, let us assume that the bettor is smart. He bets ten dollars on the pass line. The shooter rolls a 6. The bettor now lays an additional ten dollars on the odds line, taking six to five odds. Now, the smart bettor wants to continue betting "right," with the dice. Perhaps he feels lucky; perhaps he feels that the dice will get "hot"; or perhaps he feels that he wants to take a chance on making or losing a lot of money right now with the best possible odds.

Whatever the reason, he now puts an additional ten dollars in the come box. What he is doing, in essence, is betting on the exact next roll of the dice in the same manner as the previous roll. Since he is a "right" bettor, he will win if the next roll turns up a 7 or 11, lose immediately if a 2, 3, or 12 is rolled, and if a point number is rolled (4, 5, 6, 8, 9, or 10), that will be an additional point on which he can take odds.

It may sound a bit complicated, but you must remember that a bettor at the dice table can make a whole series of individual bets, all independent of one another.

When he bet originally on the pass line and the number 6 was rolled, the dealer took a large plastic disk and put it on place number six on the table (see layout). This indicated to all the players that 6 was the point. The shooter's roll was basically to either make the 6, or, if he lost, roll 7 before the 6.

Right now, at this moment, the smart bettor has his ten dollars in chips on the pass line, backed up by ten dollars more as an odds bet. The two stacks of chips are one behind the other in the space for the pass bet (see layout). Now he has ten dollars more in the come box. If the shooter now rolls a 7, he would lose the twenty dollars' worth of chips, since a 7 before a 6 is a loser to all pass-line bettors. However, since he has ten dollars in the come box, he would win on that bet, because, as we said before, it is a new, independent bet based on this new roll, and a 7 on an initial roll is a winner.

Let's now take as an example a longer string of rolls. The smart bettor bets another ten dollars on the pass line. Another shooter is coming out. (The other shooter relinquished the dice when he "sevened out.") This new shooter rolls a 10. The smart bettor bets an additional ten dollars on the odds line, and now gets two to one on this new bet.

Now he puts an additional ten dollars in the come box. The shooter rolls a 9. The ten dollars is taken away by the dealer and put into the larger section of the place area for number 9. Now, the smart bettor throws over ten dollars in chips and says, "Odds." These chips are put on top of the stack of chips he had bet in the come box, which are now in the place area for number 9. They are tipped slightly to show that these ten dollars in chips are at the odds, which are three to two.

The smart bettor now places another ten dollars in the come box. The shooter rolls an 8, the chips are moved to the place area for 8, and the smart bettor throws over ten dollars in chips, which again are tilted on the stack to indicate an odds bet. Of course, he will orally indicate that they are for "odds."

Chips

Right now, the smart bettor has ten dollars on the pass line, with ten dollars behind it on odds. The point there is 10. In addition, he has ten dollars on the 9 with ten-dollar odds and ten dollars on the 8 with ten-dollar odds. He puts ten dollars more into the come box.

The shooter rolls the dice. An 8 comes up. Before the ten dollars is moved to the place-8 area, the dealer pays the smart bettor a total of twenty-two dollars; ten dollars for the bet on 8, and twelve dollars for the odds bet on the 8 (six to five on a ten-dollar bet). Since the 8 repeated, he is a winner of this bet. In addition, he gives the smart bettor back his twenty dollars in bets on the 8. Now, the dealer takes the ten dollars from the come box and puts it into the place-8 area. The smart bettor gives him an additional ten dollars and calls out, "Odds." In effect, he has the same bets working, the 10 at the pass line, the 9 and 8 as "come bets."

The smart bettor now places an additional ten-dollar bet in the come box. The shooter rolls a 7. Here's what happens. Since the 7 came before a repeat of the 10, the pass-line bet is lost. Since the 7 came before the 9 was repeated, the 9 is a losing bet. Since the 7 came before the new 8 was repeated (remember, each bet is an independent one), the 8 is lost as a bet. But the ten dollars in the come box is a winner because each roll is considered a new one. The smart bettor lost sixty dollars in bets and collected ten dollars in winnings. He had already collected twenty-two dollars from the repeat of the 8 the roll before, so his loss is twenty-eight dollars in all on the roll.

Don't-Come Bets

The don't-come bet is exactly the opposite of the come bet. With each bet, the player is betting that the dice will be wrong, rather than right, as with a come bet. And, as with the come bet, the player can bet on each roll of the dice, which becomes an independent bet, and may continuously make don't-come bets until the point is made or the roller sevens out. After this happens, the initial bet is then on the pass line, but each succeeding bet may be a don't-come or come bet.

One important note: To make a come or don't-come bet, it is not necessary to first bet the pass line, but on the initial roll, or come-out, only line bets are allowed. The bet after the point is established is a come or don't-come bet. But the bet after an initial roll of 7 or 11, 2, 3, or 12 is still a line bet.

To illustrate: If a shooter rolls a 2 on the initial roll, it is craps, and all don't-pass bettors are paid off, and all pass-line bettors lose. On the very next roll, since no point was established, all bets are taken for and against the roll only on the line bets. If, after this, a point number is rolled, then the come bets and don't-come bets are in force. So, if you bet in the come or don't-come box on the initial roll, in effect it is a nullity.

Let us follow another smart bettor, who is a "wrong" bettor, and see how the don't-come bet is utilized. He bets on the don't-pass line for his initial bet, on the first roll of the shooter. The shooter rolls a 3, which is craps, and the bettor wins. Now, he again bets on the don't-pass line. He is betting ten dollars, or two five-dollar chips. The shooter rolls a 4. Now, the smart bettor gives two-to-one odds on the 4, by placing twenty dollars behind his ten-dollar stack of chips. He is giving twenty dollars to ten that the 7 will come up before the 4. Since there are three chances of making a 4, and six of making the 7, the odds are exact, and neither he nor the house enjoys any advantage in the odds bet.

Now the smart bettor puts ten dollars in the don't-come box, and the roll is a 5. The bettor's ten dollars is put on the place-number five on the table, and the smart bettor is now permitted to give the correct odds for this bet. He gives the dealer an additional fifteen dollars and says, "Odds." The fifteen dollars' worth of chips are put on top of the ten dollars' worth and tilted slightly to indicate an odds bet.

As the shooter prepares for another roll, again Mr. Smart Bettor puts down ten dollars in the don't-come box. The roll is a 6. Now, since the odds are six to five, after the ten dollars is placed in the box marked "6," the smart bettor hands the dealer twelve dollars' worth of chips, which are placed on the ten dollars after the bettor says "Odds."

Sometimes, bettors make only consistent bets, such as don't-pass, with odds, followed by a series of don't-come bets. In that case, once the dealer knows the action of the bettor, and if the table isn't that busy, the odds money can be wordlessly handed to the dealer.

Another ten dollars is put down on the don't-come line by the smart bettor, and a 7 is rolled. Since the 7 on an initial roll is a winning bet, he loses his last ten-dollar bet. But he wins his bets on the 4, 5, and 6, as a 7 came up before any of those numbers were repeated, which was what his bets were all about. Thus, he wins sixty dollars on those bets, loses ten dollars on his last bet, for a net total of fifty dollars.

Now, if any of those numbers repeated, the smart bettor would lose those bets. Here's how it would work out. Suppose after the 4, 5, and 6 bets, the shooter rolled a 6. The twenty-two dollars on the 6 would be lost by the smart bettor; his ten dollars in the don't-come box would be transferred to the place 6 spot again, and he could again lay twelve dollars to ten with an odds bet. At this point, he would still have his three bets in order, but would have already lost twenty-two dollars because of the repeat of the 6. Should a 4 be rolled now, he would lose his thirty dollars on the 4, but could again bet twenty dollars to ten, along with his ten-dollar bet put on the place 4. Since 4 was the point, the next roll is a come-out roll, and if the smart bettor wanted to bet against the dice, on the next roll his bet would be on the don't-pass line.

The don't-come bets, when the dice are "cold," or steadily wrong, can be quite lucrative because, should the bettor have down several don't-come bets on various numbers, one roll of 7 makes him a winner of all those bets. There are some big gamblers who only bet against the dice, using don't-pass and then don't-come bets, giving odds on every number. Nick the Greek, a legendary gambler, was a notorious "wrong" bettor. On the other hand, Harold Smith, Jr., one of the owners of Harold's Club in Reno, Nevada, said he only liked to bet the "right" way, for the dice to pass (win). He claimed that he was an optimist in gambling.

Betting "wrong" can make a gambler a lot of money, but the danger is that one "wrong" continuous roll of repeating numbers can be deadly and wipe him out.

Place Bets

These are a favorite with heavy gamblers, because these big bettors feel that their winnings with "hot" dice can be multiplied rapidly. They are the optimists who wait for the one big roll that will pay handsome dividends. Place bets can give the "right" bettor plenty of action and an outside chance of making a big killing, but for the most part they mean losses and heart-ache.

What are place bets? If we examine the craps layout, we see a series of numbers, with rectangular areas surrounding them and a line running across the area, splitting it. The numbers are 4, 5, 6, 8, 9, and 10, all the point numbers. The purpose of these place areas is to permit the bettor to place money on any or all of these numbers without going through the bother of making come bets.

If you remember, when a come bet is made, the money is placed on the number, but that number has to be repeated in order for the bet to be won. Place bets do away with that formality. If you make a place bet, the *first time* that number shows, you are winning a bet. Well, why not a mad dash to Las Vegas to get those place bets down? First, let's examine the odds given and the correct odds on these bets.

The 4 and 10, 5 and 9, and 6 and 8 are all matched, since each pair of numbers can be made with the same combination. A 4 and 10 can be made three ways; a 5 and 9, four ways; and a 6 and 8, five ways. The correct odds, therefore, against a 4 or 10, are two to one; against a 5 or 9, three to two; and against a 6 or 8, six to five. If a player makes a come bet and takes odds, that's what he'll be getting.

However, on place bets the odds are as follows: On a 4 or 10, nine to five; on a 5 or 9, seven to five; and on a 6 or 8, seven to six. Not quite the correct odds. What are house percentages, then?

If you bet a 4 or 10 as a place bet, the house has an advantage of 6.67 percent. On the 5 or 9, the percentage is 4.0; and on the 6 or 8, the house comes in with a 1.51 percent edge.

It should be immediately apparent that the odds are rather bad on the 4 or 10 and the 5 or 9, while the odds on the 6 or 8, though a little high, are not prohibitive. Why, then, do players bet the place numbers on the 4, 5, 9, and 10? And, an even better question, why do some so-called "authorities" on dice suggest that they make these bets?

The usual reason is that this is the fastest way to make big money at the craps table. Of course, the other side of the coin is that it is also the quickest way to lose big money at the crap table.

Before we go any further into the philosophy of these bets, it might be worthwhile at this point to discuss just how they may be made.

One of the advantages to the gambler is that place bets may be made at any time. This advantage has nothing to do with odds; just with timing. The bets can be made prior to the come-out roll, or after it, or at any time during the roll. They are not, like pass bets, come bets, don't-pass and don't-come bets, frozen. Place bets not only can be put down at any time, but removed at any time. They can be increased or decreased at any time.

Since the odds are paid off on the 4 or 10 at nine to five, the cheapest bet that is worthwhile is a five-dollar bet. (I'm eliminating those small-time places that permit quarter bets, even dime bets.) Since the odds on the 5 or 9 are seven to five, again a minimum bet of five dollars should be made. If you bet less, you'll be paid off at even money. So, if you want to bet on these place numbers without betting at least five dollars, why don't you just turn the money over to a worthwhile cause and save a lot of wear and tear on your feet and legs, standing around a crap table?

And since the 6 or 8 is paid off at seven to six, six dollars is the minimum bet here, unless the house pays off in half-dollars, in which case you can bet three dollars and get back $3.50. But the usual bet when betting the place numbers is five dollars each on the 4, 5, 9, and 10, and six dollars each on the 6 and 8. This totals thirty-two dollars. Some bettors bet ten dollars each on the 4, 5, 9, and 10, and twelve dollars each on the 6 and 8. This is a total of sixty-four dollars. Still other bettors bet in multiples of these amounts. I have seen players betting $100 each on the 4, 5, 9, and 10, and $120 each on the 6 and 8, steadily throughout an evening. That comes to a total of $640 in place bets on each sequence.

The way to make these bets is to tell the dealer that you wish to make place bets on all the numbers. If you give him thirty-two dollars or sixty-four dollars, he'll know how to spread it. If you give him multiples of these amounts, again he'll know what to do. Or, you may bet specific place numbers, or bet more on one place number than on the others. But if you do this, be sure and tell the dealer exactly what you have in mind.

After the bets are made (let us assume the sixty-four-dollar spread—ten dollars each on the 4, 5, 9, and 10, and twelve dollars each on the 6 and 8), the next roll of the dice counts toward these bets. If a 6 is rolled, the dealer will hand you fourteen dollars. This is seven to six, or fourteen dollars to twelve. The place bet remains on the 6. You may remove it, but if you say nothing, those bets remain until a 7 is rolled. What happens when a 7 is rolled? All the place bets lose.

And here's the rub. When you make these place bets, you are betting that enough of the numbers will be repeated before a 7 is rolled to make a profit for you. The moment a 7 shows on those dice, you lose the *entire* spread, or sixty-four dollars.

What happens, you might ask now, if on the initial roll after the place bets are made, a 7 is rolled? You lose the entire sixty-four dollars.

That is the terrible risk of place bets. They are not involved with the point to be made, the come-out, anything at all. All that matters is that these numbers come out before a 7 does. So, if you are collecting fourteen dollars on the 5, 6, 8, or 9 each time that number comes up, and eighteen dollars on the 4 or 10 each time those numbers come up, you can readily see that a roll of 6, 8, 10, 9, and 7 would give you sixty dollars, and since sixty-four dollars has been bet, there is a net loss of four dollars.

However, there are many times when that 7 comes up immediately, or after one number, or after no numbers have been rolled. For example, if a shooter rolls 2, 3, 12, and then 7, you still lose the sixty-four dollars.

It is quite interesting to see exactly what the odds are in favor of the house when all the place numbers are bet. To arrive at the total, we should examine exactly what is lost and what is won.

First, there are the following possibilities to be examined. We eliminate the 2, 3, 11, and 12, since they don't figure into wins or losses; they are strictly neutral.

On any roll the 7 can come up six times; the 4, three times; the 10, three times; the 5, four times; the 9, likewise four times; and the 6 and the 8 each five times. Thus, there are twenty-four ways in which the place bettor can make money on each roll, and only six ways in which he can lose. Sounds good so far.

Since the 4 can come up three times and pays eighteen dollars each time (nine to five on the ten-dollar bet), we collect fifty-four dollars. We collect the same amount for the 10. Total so far, $108. If the 5 comes up we have four chances of collecting fourteen dollars, or fifty-six dollars. Same with the 9. Total so far, $108 plus $112, or $220. If the 6 comes up we again collect fourteen dollars five ways, or seventy dollars. Same with the 8. Add another $140 to our total and we get a new total of $360.

The 7 comes up six times, but each time it comes up we lose sixty-four dollars (the total place spread), so we lose $384.

It can easily be seen that no matter which way we twist or turn those place bets, we stand to lose $384, theoretically, and stand to win only $360. The advantage to the house is 3.22 percent on any single roll. The odds are better on a field bet.

Some gamblers compound their bets by calling, "Press." They are asking the dealer to "press their bets," or increase them by the same unit. For example: A bettor has ten dollars on the 5. A 5 is rolled. He would collect fourteen dollars, but instead, he tells the dealer to press the bet. The dealer takes ten dollars out of the fourteen and adds it to the place bet on the 5. Now he has twenty dollars on it. The remaining four dollars is given to the bettor.

The only excuse for this type of betting is a wild belief in luck. Gamblers I have spoken to who did this informed me that they had a "hunch." What kind of hunch? That the dice were going to be "hot." How did they know? Just a hunch, that's all. I had a hunch that they were going to lose a lot of money. Compounding bets such as place bets when each roll may bring a 7 and hence a complete loss is almost suicidal. Sure, there will be instances of wild luck, but the inexorable odds will ensure an inevitable loss, because when that 7 shows on the dice, all is lost.

My advice about place odds? Bet only the 6 and 8 if you feel the dice are going to be hot. Bet pass and come line and take the odds. You'll be keeping the house's advantage real low. You'll be what they call a "tough" bettor, and smarter than most.

Field Bets

Prominently displayed on most dice layouts are the numbers comprising the field bet. The word "field" is spread across almost half the table, with a group of numbers underneath. The usual numbers are 2, 3, 4, 9, 10, 11, and 12. The 2 and 12 are often circled, with the 2 paying two to one and the 12, three to one if rolled.

This is quite an array of numbers, and often the novice gambler, and women new to the game, bet the field. Thus, the field is heavily played where the table is crowded with amateur or small bettors. In big games, when the action is heavy, the field is often left alone, despite the constant intonation of the stickman, yelling "Field. Who'll play the field?"

Two factors usually dissuade me from playing it. One is the fact that it is so prominently displayed and so constantly pushed by the casino. The other is that I can get much better odds on the front line and betting the come or don't-come boxes.

In most of the smaller casinos, the 2 is paid off at two to one, and the 12 at three to one. In most of the Strip casinos, both numbers are paid off merely at two to one. In each instance, the odds are in favor of the house.

Although there are seven numbers in the field, the four missing numbers are quite important. They are the 5, 6, 7, and 8. These four numbers can be made in twenty ways. The numbers in the field can be made in only sixteen ways. But since the 2 is paid off at two to one, we add another way, and two more for the 12, which is paid off at three to one. With these additions, we come up with nineteen ways for the field to be made. Twenty to nineteen is an edge of 2.564 percent in favor of the house, because the field is paid off at even money.

If the house only pays two to one on the 12, then the odds are twenty to eighteen against the player, or a percentage of 5.36 in favor of the house.

Amateurs and novices bet the field for two reasons. One, they don't know the odds. Two, many gamblers want an instant decision; they can't stand the anxiety of waiting for a point number to be either made or lost.

With field numbers, each roll of the dice determines a win or loss. If the roll is 5, 6, 7, or 8, a quick loss. Any other number and a quick win. These numbers can be bet at any time—on the initial roll or anytime thereafter—but the edge is 2.564 percent in favor of the house.

Now, these odds aren't the worst at the table, but they aren't the best either. It is quite interesting to note that they are better than any given at American roulette, and thus a systems player, who might want continuous action, would be much better off playing the field than any of the even-money propositions at roulette.

Should a player decide to bet the field, for whatever reason, it would be foolish of him to play in those casinos in which two to one is paid on the 12. Of course, some casinos may reverse the situation and give three-to-one odds on the 2 and two to one on the 12, but this doesn't change the basic odds one bit, since either a 2 or 12 can be made with only one combination of the dice.

To summarize briefly: Field bets are not the best bet on the table, but they offer better odds than roulette for those players working a system. There is really no other reason to play them. If a player suffers too much anxiety awaiting the outcome of a point bet, he might very well be better off watching a good movie, rather than risking money and high blood pressure on the roll of the dice.

Any Crap

As the stickman collects the dice and passes them back to the roller, he usually keeps up a continuous barrage of suggested bets, the most frequent being the field, any crap, and hardways. Although the field bet is of moderate interest to the house because the percentage is 2.56 in its favor, the other bets are much more lucrative to the casino.

By "any crap" the stickman means the player should place a bet on the numbers 2, 3, and 12, betting that any one of these three numbers will come up on the next roll. This is strictly a one-roll bet, each separate roll determining whether or not the bettor wins.

Since only one combination (1-1) forms a 2, and one combination (6-6) forms a 12, and two combinations (2-1, 1-2) form a 3, there are only four chances out of thirty-six of any of these numbers appearing on the dice in any one roll. The correct odds would be eight to one, but the casino pays only seven to one, which means that the casino has an advantage of 11.1 percent.

Since the house advantage is so prohibitive, there is no worthwhile reason to make this bet.

Hardways

In dice, when the word "hardway" is used it means the combination of 2-2 to form a 4; 3-3 to form a 6; 4-4 to form an 8; and 5-5 to form a 10. Each of these combinations can be formed in only one way.

When you make a hardway bet, you are betting that a hardway number will come up not only before a 7, but before any other combination of that number. For example, if you bet a hardway 6 (3-3), if a 4-2 comes up on the dice before the 3-3, you lose your bet.

Let's examine the odds on these hardways. The odds against making a hardway 4 or a hardway 10 are eight to one. The house pays seven to one and gets an advantage of 11.1 percent, the same as in any crap.

The odds against making a hardway 6 or a hardway 8 are ten to one (the odds are higher because there are more ways to make each of these numbers), and the house pays nine to one, for an advantage to the house of 9 percent.

Why should anyone make any of these hardway bets, with the odds so favorable to the casino? I don't know. This bet is definitely not recommended under any circumstances.

Proposition Bets

These are one-roll bets, in which the gambler bets that a number will come up on the next roll of the dice. He either wins or loses immediately.

These bets may be made on either the 2, 3, 11, or 12. The odds against making a 2 are thirty-five to one (one chance in thirty-six). The same odds prevail against a 12. The house pays thirty to one. The house's advantage is a nifty 13.89 percent.

The chances of making a 3 are seventeen to one (two chances in thirty-six). The same odds hold true for an 11. The house pays fifteen to one, for an advantage of 11.1 percent.

Proposition bets are therefore foolish bets, and are sometimes bet by a player for one of the dealers he intends to tip. Instead of tipping a dollar, for example, he puts it on the proposition bet, and if the number comes up, the dealer wins either fifteen or thirty times that original tip. The dealer, however, would be better off with the dollar tip in the first place.

Any Seven

If a player wants to bet a 7 for one roll, he gets odds of four to one. The correct odds are five to one. The house has an advantage with this bet of 16.67 percent, the highest on the crap table. I personally think that the house is foolish to exact so high a percentage. It would be better off cutting its percentage, or getting none at all, because a larger amount of money might be bet on place numbers and pass-line and come bets if the player could protect his bets by betting the 7 for a substantial amount.

But with the exorbitant amount the house extracts for playing this number, no gambler in his right mind ever bets it.

Big 6 and Big 8

As with field bets, these bets take up a prominent place on the crap layout. A player may place his bet on either or both of these numbers anytime, just as if he made a place bet. What he is betting is that the 6 or 8 will come up before the 7. Since the odds against this happening are six to five, and since the house will only pay off a Big 6 or Big 8 bet at even money, the advantage to the casino is a whopping 9.09 percent.

If a gambler wanted to bet on the 6 or 8, he would be much better off betting six dollars on either number as a place bet, which would be paid off at seven to six, with the percentage in favor of the house reduced to 1.51.

Why do gamblers bet the Big 6 and Big 8 then? Mostly out of ignorance. They may feel hot as shooters, or may feel that the shooter is hot, and want all the bets down they can put. They may be unfamiliar with place bets and too embarrassed to ask the dealer about them. So there, big as life, stare those two beautiful numbers. A better question might be: Why does the house keep these bets instead of referring bettors to the place numbers when they want to bet the 6 and 8? Greed, you say?

This same ignorance of the odds extends to private crap games. Many gamblers know that the odds against the 6 and 8 are slightly above even money, or six to five, but they don't realize that this *slight* advantage amounts to over 9 percent. I have seen crap games in which these players took bets against the 6 or 8 at even money, blithely insuring their losses. I knew one dice player who played in rather large private games. He would make a pretense of fading bets and rolling the dice for small amounts, but all night, like a hawk, he would shout, "Ten dollars you don't 6. Fifty dollars you don't 8." He got plenty of these bets at even money, and with an advantage of nearly 10 percent, had many a good night against so-called "smart money" players.

What causes these players to behave so stupidly? They want action, and they don't care about anything so long as they get it. That's why the casinos are pleasure palaces, all prettied up on the outside. They welcome the high rollers, those men who want big action and are willing to throw caution, common sense, everything to the wind to get it.

How to Bet at Dice

A final word. You must remember that craps is purely a game of chance. It is fast moving, and a lot of money can be won or lost in a very short time. The limit is usually $500 on a front-line bet, and with odds, the bet can be doubled, and sometimes tripled.

One of the attractions of craps is the excitement and action of the game. The dice tables are usually busy places in casinos, and it is certainly the most popular casino gambling game. It can be fun if played for moderate stakes and with good judgment.

Whether you decide to bet moderately or go all out in a frontal assault on Lady Luck, you should determine your strategy before participating in the game. You may decide to bet right (with the dice). If so, make a bet on the pass line, take the odds, make the come bets, take the odds, and don't deviate from this method. It'll give the house the minimum advantage over you.

Or you may, if you prefer, bet wrong by betting the don't-pass line, making continual don't-come bets, and giving odds in both situations. Or, if you bet wrong, you might be content if you can make three don't-come bets and then sit back and watch the results.

Or, to go a step further, you might feel that you want to follow the dice by betting don't pass after a player sevens out, and then pass after a point is made. It is all immaterial, because the myth of "hot" and "cold" dice should not be taken seriously. Dice do run in patterns, but the individual roll remains unpredictable. There might be a whole pattern of win, lose, win, lose, and win again; or a few wins, then a few losses. But no one can predict the next roll of the dice, whether dice are "hot" or "cold." Anyone who could predict just one roll occasionally would be a millionaire many times over.

Bet sensibly, within your limit. If you are winning, don't increase your bets, unless you want to start a whole new series of bets at a higher level. In other words, if you win at the pass line, don't just double your bet. Take away your winnings; otherwise, one win, one loss, and you lose all your money. The other way, one win, one loss, and you're even. If you want to increase your bets, wait until you have doubled your original stake. If you were betting five dollars, you can then raise to ten dollars. At least have control over your money and be consistent.

You must keep a clear head at the crap table. The action, noise, and discontent can throw anyone off. Unless you have planned your strategy and unless you stick to it, you might find yourself making desperation bets on proposition bets—anything. Don't do that. Set a goal. If you start with $100 and lose it, get out. Don't keep plunging. Just this simple strategy will save you grief and money.

When playing in Atlantic City and most of the Las Vegas casinos, expect to be at tables that allow only single odds on free odds bets. This is a disadvantage to you. The same holds true in northern Nevada and the Caribbean.

If you're in a jurisdiction where there are no double-odds games, you'll just have to play single-odds craps if you play the game. But when you have a choice, as in Las Vegas, play at a double-odds table, especially if you're betting with the dice.

In some Caribbean casinos the "Come" bet is eliminated from the table. This forces the player to make place bets at unfavorable odds if he or she wishes to have continuous bets going. If this is the case, you can lay place bets on the 6 and 8, giving the house only 1.52 percent as its edge. Don't make any other place bets. Increase your pass-line wager if you want more action, and be sure to take the free odds.

Recapitulation of the Odds in Craps

Here's a table showing the casino payoff and the house's advantage.

Bet	Casino Pays	Casino's Advantage (in %)
Pass	Even money	1.41
Don't Pass	Even money	1.40
Come	Even money	1.41
Don't Come	Even money	1.41
Pass Line + Single Odds	Even + odds	.84
Pass Line + Double Odds	Even + odds	.60
Don't Pass + Single Odds	Even + odds	.83
Don't Pass + Double Odds	Even + odds	.59
Field	Even	2.56
4 or 10 Place	Nine to five	6.67
5 or 9 Place	Seven to five	4.0
6 or 8 Place	Seven to six	1.51
Big 6 or Big 8	Even	9.09
Any Crap	Seven to one	11.1
Hardway 4 or 10	Seven to one	11.1
Hardway 6 or 8	Nine to one	9.09
11 or 3 Proposition	Fifteen to one	11.1
12 or 2 Proposition	Thirty to one	13.9
Any 7	Four to one	16.7

A Dice Story

I had a interesting experience once. I wanted to go on a gambling junket and found an acquaintance who got me into an organization that arranged these trips. For a whole year after joining I received all sorts of brochures from the organization, but nothing resembling a free trip, a true gambling junket.

All I would receive were endless illustrated brochures inviting me to go to Las Vegas, London, Monte Carlo, Puerto Rico, or Haiti. Generally the trip was from a weekend to a week, strictly a gambler's journey, with expenses running from $199 up. I emptied these gaudy papers into my wastepaper basket as fast as they arrived, and they were arriving at least once a week.

After a year's wait, I at last received what I was looking for—a trip to a Caribbean island. The scheduled trip was in August, a slack time in the Caribbean. Round-trip fare, hotels, liquor, breakfast, and dinner were all free. The only catch was that you had to deposit $500 with the organization, and for this amount, you received $500 worth of chips to gamble with. That was all you had to do.

I sent in my $500 and called up my father, who liked a little gambling. I sponsored him, and together we planned the trip. Before departing, I explained my plan to him, a scheme for going on a gambling junket and using up the necessary chips without the whole trip costing us more than thirty or forty dollars apiece. In a later section I'll explain this plan, which can come in handy for those who want to fly away somewhere and see a foreign or exotic place and not spend a fortune.

But, alas, after explaining it to my father, he said succinctly, "I'll tell you what, Ed, you gamble the way you want to, and I'll gamble my own way." He was adamant, so I decided that I'd have to wait and see about the gambling when I got there. I knew I had to use up those chips some way, but I didn't want to lose them all.

I decided that I would bet the don't-pass line, and then bet don't come continually, giving the odds with each bet. In this way, the house's percentage would be reduced to .83, and I should be able to run through the money at an expense to me, theoretically, of about forty-two dollars. Of course, I thought I might switch from don't pass to pass, and play come bets taking odds on all bets. In this way, the house would make a little more—.85 percent—but the difference would be minuscule. If I alternated I might avoid either a very good roll or very bad roll.

So we took off one cheerful day from Kennedy Airport. The plane was packed with men, and some women came along as well. The men seemed like an interesting group as a whole. Later, I found that one of them was a playwright who had been invited along by a member just to write a one-act play for commercial purposes about the trip.

Generally, I found the men to be lively, good sports, and the conversation on the plane was interesting. There was little talk of gambling, but much talk of a compound that housed Venezuelan prostitutes. So off we went, and arrived that afternoon on the island—which shall be nameless —and were driven to the hotel by bus. My father and I found ourselves in a luxury hotel. Our room was air conditioned, overlooking the Caribbean, and after we put away our things, we went down to the lobby and out to a large patio, covered with tropical plants surrounding an oval swimming pool.

I took a long, leisurely swim, then changed for dinner, which was served in a paneled dining room by tuxedo-clad waiters. I had papaya, then a native dish, a steak, wine, dessert, espresso. Everything beautiful, delicious, and free.

At nine the casino opened. It was actually no more than a rather small room holding a roulette table, four blackjack tables, and two dice tables. There was a bar in one corner, and several slot machines along one wall. There was also a mechanical blackjack player which took quarters.

Before going there, I had done some reading back in New York about the island. The casinos were licensed by the government and there were supposed to be government inspectors on the premises at all times. During my entire stay at the hotel, which lasted five days, I never saw anyone remotely resembling an inspector.

All the employees of the casino were natives, and that included the dealers, the bartender, the croupier, and the stickman at the dice table. Only one employee was American, and he was a rather heavyset man of about fifty or so who was the boxman at the dice table. He was obviously the boss. Only one dice table was in use during my entire stay, and he was always there, sitting and watching, giving credit to losers, taking their checks. He had alert eyes and terrific peripheral vision. A tourist entered the casino one night with a camera. She was to one side and almost to this man's rear, yet he immediately spotted the camera. He signaled to one of his employees, who politely told her that no cameras were permitted in the casino room.

We were all given our chips that night. They were bright green and in five-dollar denominations, much different in color than the standard five-dollar and twenty-five-dollar chips in evidence. The minimum bet was five dollars at the crap table and five dollars at all the blackjack tables but one, which had a one-dollar minimum. The one-dollar minimum bet was also in effect at the roulette table.

My pockets were bulging with a hundred bright green chips. I went to the crap table, which was immediately crowded with the men from our plane. I couldn't get near enough to bet, but I took a good look at the table. Something was different.

Then I realized that the table layout had been altered to exclude come and don't-come bets. There was no place at all for these bets. No place. I wondered why, and it quickly dawned on me that the only way one could bet continuously was by placing the bets in the place numbers, at percentages ranging from 1.51 to 6.67 in favor of the house.

The only way then to get the best odds was to strictly bet don't pass or pass, the line bets, and give or take odds. This was allowed, but an awful lot of money was going on the place numbers. The betting was hectic, with the fresh green chips burning holes in a lot of pockets. I had not been in that casino more than a half hour when men were already reaching in for cash or writing checks for more chips.

Another difference I noted between this place and the normal casino was that the stickman kept absolutely quiet after announcing the point and each roll of the dice. There was no mention of field numbers, craps and eleven, hardways. He just called out each roll as it was made. And the dealers were very inexperienced, sloppy, and slow, often to the house's disadvantage. Sometimes, when a player took odds on his line bet, he placed the bet at a tilt on the original bet to signify that odds were being placed, and the casino dealer would immediately straighten out the pile. If it was a pass bet, the player would protest, but on don't-pass bets, the player would just keep his mouth shut, since he now often had a bet more than twice his original bet against a point number.

It didn't take long, however, for the boxman, who ran the whole game, to see what was happening. He made a few corrections, and after that the players were instructed to place their odds bet behind the line bet, not on top of it, and the dealers were told to keep their damn hands off the chips.

Now, all my plans to bet come and don't come were out the window. I made no bets at all that night; just watched the action. It remained hectic until I went to bed about 1:00 A.M., after a few free drinks, and I was told the next day that the action went on till 3:00 A.M. There were many big losers and a couple of really big winners.

The next morning, after a sumptuous breakfast of papaya, french toast, bacon, and coffee, I went exploring the island on foot. The place was literally a shopper's paradise. Everything was of best quality—cameras, rings, diamonds, watches, porcelain—and prices were substantially lower than in the United States. I was tempted by a Miranda Sensorex camera at half the American price. I decided against it and, instead, went for a walk along the seafront.

That afternoon I swam in the pool and became friendly with a couple of the men. Both were from Long Island; one had his own hardware business while the other worked as a machinist. They were old-time friends who often went on these junkets together. They described trips to London, Puerto Rico, and other places, but to them the best place was Las Vegas. That was the star attraction. The machinist described his gambling adventures there, telling me that he won over $30,000 one night, and by six the next morning had blown it all back. I wondered how he could gamble at that pace on a straight salary.

I also met the playwright, and he told me he had lost almost all of the original $500. I asked him how he had done it, and he really didn't know. He was vague about the whole mechanics of dice games and had bet the way others bet, on the numbers. A few quick sevens, and most of his money was gone.

We all had dinner together and had some good wine and the conversation was cheerful. The next day, it was decided, we'd all take a trip to the compound and look over the Venezuelan women.

That night I was back at the casino. Again, I couldn't get near the dice table, so I sat down at the five-dollar blackjack table and the dealer began to shuffle the four decks. I was the only player there. He was a nice slow dealer, a real pleasure to play against. I took a count of the cards (see *The Silberstang Method* in *Blackjack*) and took away a little over a hundred dollars in profits before he mysteriously announced that the game was over.

I wandered back to the dice table and squeezed myself in. My father was rolling. For sentimental reasons I bet ten dollars on the pass line. Boom, 7, a winner. They paid me ten dollars in chips, but didn't change the green ones. I realized I'd have to make a thousand dollars' worth of bets in order to get rid of them. I left the twenty dollars on the table. Another 7. I took out thirty dollars and put it into my bulging pocket, and bet ten dollars on the pass line again. My father rolled a 5, then covered the place numbers. I took three-to-two odds by betting an additional ten dollars, and my father rolled a 5 right back. I left the money on the table. He rolled an 11. I left twenty-five dollars and pocketed twenty-five dollars. He rolled a 6, then an 8, then a 7. I had taken odds of thirty dollars to twenty-five dollars on the 6 and walked away from the table.

The days and nights quickly went by. On the fourth (next to last) night, it was not difficult getting at the dice table. I had spoken to a stockbroker who had come down with us, and he told me he was down about $5,000. "I like to get it out of my system," he informed me with a wan smile.

The machinist was ahead a little, and his friend was down only a few hundred dollars. But this night, a young man, whom I had not previously noticed, was there with his wife, who was in a white mink stole. He put down $500 on the pass line; rolled a 4; put down another $500 on the odds, getting two to one; then put $100 on each of the place numbers and $120 on the 6 and 8. He rolled a series of numbers and told the dealer to press his bets. The boxman nodded and watched, his eyes alert, sunk into a head that had seen an awful lot in its time.

The guy was really hot. He wore a mod suit, a bright tie, and had a rather handsome face. His wife was a beautiful woman, flashy and sexy. She shrieked every time he won a bet, and he was yelling at the dice also. "Come on, baby. Come on, sweetie, come on . . . four . . . a winner!"

Within about fifteen minutes he had won $10,000 or more, with the chips stacked up all around him. The machinist and his friend were betting with him, as was my father, and everyone was having a good time.

"Mike," the young guy yelled at the boxman, "how about raising the limits, baby?"

Mike nodded imperceptibly. He was examining the dice and returned them to the roller. The gambler shook them after placing a $2,500 bet on the pass line. He rolled a 9. He put another $3,000 behind the line and now placed $500 on the 4, 5, and 10, and $600 on the 6 and 8. He shook those dice and shook them, whispered to them, raised his hand above his head and shook them some more, as all the players rushed to get their bets down on the pass line and on the numbers. The chips were stacked on the table in huge piles.

Finally, he rolled the dice. A 6. The wife shrieked, the men yelled and catcalled. General merriment rang out. The table was truly alive. "Press it," he yelled to the dealer, as he pocketed $100 and left the $600 on the 6. He rolled again. Another 6. "Press it," he yelled again, pocketing the $200. He now had $2,400 on the 6.

Everyone went along with him. Everyone was pressing his bets. The young guy smiled, flashing white teeth, and shook the dice fiercely.

"Come on . . . bay . . . beeee. . . ."

The crowd hushed. He rolled a 7. Quickly all the chips were taken off. The boxman's expression didn't change. The young guy was disgusted. He cursed, shook his head, yelled at the world in general, and he and his wife walked away from the table to the bar.

A new roller came on, an older man who wearily picked up the dice and rolled them as his wife made his bets for him. She was betting with twenty-five-dollar chips, putting them on hardways, proposition bets of all kinds, as well as the numbers. He had a moderately successful roll. Then, on big bets, crapped out twice, rolled a 6, then sevened out.

The dice grew cold. The older man whose wife bet for him cashed a $5,000 check and received a fresh supply of chips. About 2:00 A.M. the young guy, whose name was Maurice, came back to the table with his wife. He started in with $500 bets on the pass line and on all the numbers. Then he raised them to $1,000 bets as he lost the roll.

I started making substantial bets on the don't-pass line and gave the odds on every point. The dice grew colder as the bets grew larger. Everyone was making huge bets, and checks and drafts were being written left and right. It suddenly dawned on me that I was the only wrong bettor in the bunch, and as the losses mounted for the right bettors, as their bets increased in size, the dice got colder and colder. Something smelled awfully fishy, but I was winning nine out of ten bets and suddenly I had over $1,000 in profits in my pocket.

The young guy, Maurice, screamed an insult at his wife after a bad roll, and she stalked away from the table. He continued to play and cashed a $10,000 check. He ran through that money by 3:00 A.M., closing time. I had won a small fortune, meanwhile.

The last night I decided not to gamble at all. That morning I bought the Miranda Sensorex camera. I also bought some gifts and took a long walk around the city.

That night, the whole place looked weary. The men in my group had, for the most part, taken an awful beating. The machinist and his friend were aimlessly betting twenty-five-dollar chips on 12s and field bets and hardways. They were losing as fast as they could bet. It became quite clear to me that night that I had joined a group possessed of the demon, all losers, all compulsively dropping their money. The whole scene was turning sick.

I had a few drinks with the playwright, and we talked at the pool till dawn about writing. Then I went up to my room for a few hours' sleep. The next day we left for New York.

Yes, we did visit the compound. A group of us—the playwright, myself, the machinist and his friend, and two men from Connecticut—rented a Ford and drove there. I drove, and we had no difficulty finding the place. We went into a fenced off area, with rows of shacks to one side and, in the center, a sort of meeting room, where you could get a Coca Cola.

The women were heavy, beat, and held no interest for me and the playwright. We walked out and watched the sea for a while, then came back about an hour later. All the men were waiting for us. We drove to another hotel and had ice cream and took a swim.

The next day the men wanted to go back to the compound before the rental on the Ford was due. I took my father along, but he didn't know where we were going. At the compound he was a big hit. All the women crowded around him, calling him "Poppa," and rubbed him as he smoked briskly on his cigar. It was quite a sight.

A Method for Limiting Losses on a Gambling Junket

If any reader has the opportunity to go on a gambling junket, this chapter should be invaluable if he merely wants to enjoy the trip, rather than try and win big money.

A gambling junket is a free trip offered to gamblers or potential gamblers. It usually is to a place like Las Vegas, London, Puerto Rico, or other areas in which gambling is permitted. The organization running the trip generally has a deal with a particular gambling casino. It delivers the players, is paid for its trouble, and since the players are deposited at a particular hotel, they are expected to gamble there.

To insure that they will bet a certain amount of money in return for the privilege of a free trip, they are given $500 or $1,000 in special chips for which they pay before the trip. The chips can only be bet and are not redeemable. Since they can only be used at a certain casino, this insures that the voyagers will play at that casino. These chips are different in color, and cannot be mistaken for the ordinary casino chips. They may come in denominations of five dollars or twenty-five dollars and are useless unless bet by the gambler.

Let's assume that we are invited on one of these junkets. We are delighted that the round-trip fare, hotel room, meals, and all incidentals are free. We have deposited our $500 ahead of time with the organization, and after checking into the hotel, we go to the casino and are given $500 worth of chips.

There are various methods of getting rid of the chips by gambling, but we may run into a short-term unfavorable streak and don't want to risk much of a loss. Of course, we may run into a favorable streak and win a great deal of money. However, we didn't come to this spot, wherever it is, to gamble; we came here to see the sights, to enjoy ourselves. But don't feel sorry for the organization that sponsored us. They'll make a fortune with the other members of our group, because there are a great many men and women who can't stop betting and will lose small fortunes. I've never heard of a junket that lost money.

Here's how we limit our losses. It is best to go with a friend, for two must be involved to pull it off. Each stands at one side of the dice table. One bets with the dice, and one bets against. Bets are made on the pass and don't-pass lines. A standard amount is bet. The best method, to make sure that the loss is strictly limited, is for each party to bet thirty dollars. However, should a 12 come up, the right bettor would lose, but the wrong bettor would not win, since the 12 is barred. It is possible in a short period of time for the 12 to come up several times. If it came up five times in the course of the betting, the partners would lose $150.

So here's what they do to avoid this. The wrong bettor puts down a separate dollar bet on the 12 on each come-out roll. Thus, one of the partners is going to win thirty dollars, and the other lose thirty dollars, or both will be even. If a 12 comes up, the right bettor will lose thirty dollars, but the wrong bettor will collect thirty to one on his one-dollar bet, evening it out. In about thirty-three or so rolls, their $1,000 in special chips will be used up. Each player will have theoretically broken even, since if one is ahead and the other behind, they can settle later. The total loss? The thirty-three bets of one dollar apiece. Not too bad a price to pay for this kind of trip.

CRAPS—PRIVATE GAME

Introduction

Private craps, as opposed to casino craps, is still a very popular game. It is often played as a game for men only, and can be played most anywhere a group of men can congregate around a shooter holding dice. It can be played for pennies or for thousands of dollars, and can be played as a friendly game, without anyone in particular running it, or as a big-money game, run by operators who are usually affiliated with the "mob."

If the game is played without an operator, there is no house cut and the amount bet on each roll is usually determined by the shooter himself. Such a game becomes a free and easy one. I've watched it played, or participated in games in back of lumber yards, on the street, in army barracks, in empty lots—any place a group of men find that is private. I've also participated in the game in private homes, with just about anything used for a backstop for the dice, from a Rice Krispies box to a set of Shakespeare.

The reason for its popularity is threefold. First, it is essentially a very simple game. Second, it can be played for cash stakes with instant payoffs. And third, the only equipment necessary is one pair of dice.

Betting

Unlike the casino game, there is no house banking all the bets. Each player has the right to shoot in rotation. The rotation is usually not rigid, and some players, because of lack of money or otherwise, voluntarily give up the privilege to roll the dice.

Also unlike the casino game, there are not a multitude of bets. There are very basic bets, either "right" or "wrong." In a private game of craps there is one definite advantage, and that is held by the "wrong" bettor. He has an edge of approximately 1.40 percent. In a casino, the 12 or 2 is barred, taking away this advantage, but it is there in a private game. The so-called "smart" bettors always bet "wrong" to gain this advantage.

Play of the Game

Here's how the private game is played:

Anyone can be the first roller. Usually it's the one who brought the dice. He put down an amount of money on the floor near his feet. Let's say he puts down twenty dollars. He asks, "Who'll fade me?" That means, "Who will bet against me on the roll?" All or part of the twenty dollars may be faded by one or more players. Any player may say, "I'll take it all." After the bet is faded, the roller shoots.

At this point, the roller is betting "right," and the fader is betting against the roll, or "wrong." To "fade the bet," the fader must put down cash. Although occasionally in private games an oral fade is permitted, it is up to the shooter.

The shooter (roller) then rolls the dice. If he rolls a 7 or 11, he wins immediately. A 2, 3, or 12, and he is an immediate loser. Any other number (4, 5, 6, 8, 9, or 10) is his point. If he makes his point number before rolling a 7, he wins and continues rolling. If he doesn't, he "sevens out," and a new shooter rolls the dice.

A roller is presumed to be a right bettor in a private game. If he is a wrong bettor, he shouldn't roll the dice.

After the point is established, the roller may offer to bet more money on the point, or any player may offer to bet against that point. Additional bets may then be made.

The fact that the roller has put down a fixed sum of money does not prevent other players from betting amongst themselves, betting either right or wrong, and then making additional bets on the point number, either for or against.

Thus the game goes on. The odds on point numbers are six to five against the 6 and 8; three to two against the 5 and 9; and two to one against the 4 and 10.

A great many players in private games, through ignorance, allow even-money bets to be made by wrong bettors on the 6 and 8. I was once involved in a big craps game where I could lay even money against the 6 and 8. In addition, I bet wrong all the time, and there wasn't one bet I made where I didn't have an advantage. Needless to say, I was a winner.

When involved in a private game, you should make sure that the dice are honest. This is very difficult to do by mere examination, because generally the crooked dice are going to be rather finely made. If the dice seem to hesitate in the roll, or make that one extra twist before stopping, watch out. Also watch out for men who can manipulate them. A backstop is a good preventative, but not a total one. Make sure those dice are shaken and thrown, not carefully rolled out of the hand to rest against the backstop. Also, watch for a "switch of dice" by a shooter, where crooked dice replace the regular ones. Private dice games are very tricky games, especially when there is big money involved. A player must stay very alert and take nothing for granted.

I would advise any reader to avoid private games where a cut is taken by the house on each bet. Not only will the odds (house cut) bury you, but you can be fairly certain that you are in a crooked game. In a big game, with mob operators running it, they'll rob you deaf, dumb, and blind, and if you protest, you may still end up deaf, dumb, and blind. Stay away from those games. They're for suckers and losers.

XVI

Roulette

Introduction

Roulette has an aura of European glamour. One envisions crystal chandeliers, dukes in tuxedoes, beautiful women hovering over the table, fortunes won and lost, the inevitable suicide on the Mediterranean. All this glamour is somehow lost in the average Nevada casino, where roulette may be played by tired, bored people just killing time and getting a load off their feet.

It certainly is not a popular game in the United States and I've noticed the roulette tables in casinos empty for hours at a time as a bored croupier spun the wheel dully, waiting for business.

One of the factors which inhibit serious players is the house advantage in roulette. In Nevada it is an even 5.26 percent on all but one bet, and on that bet it is higher. In Atlantic City the advantage drops to 2.70 percent.

It is still very popular in Europe, however, where the house's advantage is a mere 1.35 percent because of the single zero and prison rule. This permits a player to either withdraw half his losses if the zero comes up, or to imprison his total bet for one more spin. Thus, if he bet on red and zero came up, he could leave his entire bet, and if red came up next, his wager would be returned to him. This rule, however, is not known at all in America.

Roulette is a rather simple game involving expensive equipment. In Europe, several croupiers are used at each table, but in Nevada and the Caribbean, one croupier handles all the action. There is a wheel whose perimeter is numbered one through thirty-six, half the numbers in red and half in black. There is a zero and a double zero, both in green.

American Roulette

This is what the American wheel looks like:

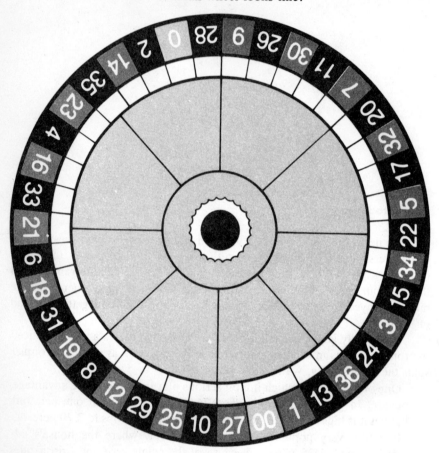

THE AMERICAN WHEEL

The numbers 1–36 come in two colors, red and black, whereas 0 and 00 are usually green. Because of the 0 and 00, the house edge on all bets is the same: 5.26 percent in Nevada casinos. In Atlantic City, where the *en prison* rule has been in effect, which imprisons the even-money choices for an additional spin without their automatically being lost if a 0 or 00 comes up, the edge is dropped to 2.70 percent. This rule will be explained fully in the section on American Roulette bets.

The wheel is usually about three feet in diameter, and spins freely. It is in constant motion during a game. The bowl of the wheel contains the thirty-eight numbers (1–36, 0, 00) in individual pockets. Above this area are metal buffers, some horizontal and some vertical, that slow down the rotation of the plastic ball, which is rolled counter to the spin of the wheel by the dealer.

As the ball spins, it loses speed and slides down toward the center of the bowl, hits the buffers and bounces before descending to the base of the bowl where it finally lands in one of the thirty-eight numbered pockets.

Each pocket is separated from its neighbor by a metal divider called a separator, thus trapping the ball in an individual pocket. The number of that pocket is the winning number, and all payoffs and collections are determined by that number.

The numbers on the wheel seem to be random, but not so. The 0 and 00 are on opposite sides, and each red number has two black neighbors, except where the 0 and 00 are placed. With two exceptions, if we add pairs of same-colored numbers running around the wheel in a clockwise fashion, they add up to thirty-seven, by adding the smaller number to the higher one. For instance, 25 and 12 are thirty-seven, as are 19 and 18, 21 and 16, and so on. The same holds true for the black numbers, starting with 29 and 8, 31 and 6, 33 and 4, and so on. The exceptions are the numbers to the left of 0 and 00; although they add up to thirty-seven, they run in consecutive order and are of different colors.

The wheels are built to exacting standards, but sometimes, because of wear or other factors, the wheel's spin is not perfect, and a "bias," or fault, is detected. When this occurs, a ball may land in a particular area of the wheel more often than random spins would dictate. Astute gamblers look for this bias, but it is rarely found.

The ball used in the spin is white and made of plastic.

The Dealer and Roulette Chips

A sole dealer can easily staff an American table, except when there are many players, in which case an assistant is there to stack chips. Payoffs are made by hand, and collections of losing wagers are also made by hand. The players use different-colored chips, different from those normally used in the casino, to facilitate play. Each player is given an individual color so that winning bets can be easily paid off. Occasionally standard casino chips are used for big payoffs.

There is usually a standard denomination for a roulette chip. If a player desires a bigger-denomination chip, then that is noted by putting that colored chip on the rim of the wheel with a button showing its denomination. Payoffs then reflect the higher value of the chips.

When a player leaves a roulette table, he or she is required to cash in the roulette chips, and the player receives the standard-denomination chips of the casino in return. But no cash will be given. The player must go to the cashier's cage to collect cash for these chips.

Roulette Layout
The following is the standard American layout:

American Roulette Bets

Roulette wagers can be divided into two basic types: straight bets and combination bets.

Straight Bets

Letter	Name of Bet	Odds Payout
A	Straight up	35-1

The letter A is on number 3. If that comes up on the next spin of the wheel, the player will receive 35-1 for his or her bet. Straight-up bets can also be made on the 0 or 00 as individual wagers.

B	Column	2-1

By betting on any individual column, the player covers all twelve numbers in that column, and should any one of them come up on the next spin, he or she wins the bet at odds of two to one. 0 and 00 are never column bets, and should either number come up, all column bets are lost.

C	Dozen	2-1

The previous two bets are known as "inside" wagers; now we have an "outside" wager outside the actual numbered area. Letter C covers the first dozen numbers, but bets may be made on any dozen, or two of the three dozens, if a player wishes to. 0 and 00 lose for the dozen wagers.

D	Red-black	1-1
	High-low	(even money)
	Odd-even	

These outside wagers pay off at even money, and since they come up most frequently, they are at the heart of roulette systems. In the Nevada casinos, if a 0 or 00 comes up, they are lost, but in Atlantic City, where the *en prison* rule is in effect, any even-money wager is "imprisoned" for another spin of the wheel, and if that choice then comes up, the bet is intact, with nothing lost. Or the player may surrender half the wager if 0 or 00 comes up, and then remove or leave the remainder as a normal bet for the next spin.

Where the *en prison* rule is used, the house edge on only even-money wagers drops to 2.70 percent. Of course, where no such rule is in effect, the house advantage is 5.26 percent.

Combination Bets

Letter	Name of Bet	Odds Payout
E	Split	17-1

A player who places his chip or chips on the line separating two adjacent or contiguous numbers on the layout covers two numbers with one bet, known as a split bet. If either number comes up, the payoff is seventeen to one. A split bet can also be made on 0 and 00 by placing a chip between 0-00, or by placing a chip between the line separating the second and third dozens, for those who can't reach the top of the layout.

F	Trio	11-1

This bet is made by placing a chip or chips on the boundary line separating the inside number from the dozen bets. The F chip covers three numbers: 13, 14, and 15. Any such three numbers, such as 1, 2, 3, or 34, 35, 36, can be covered in this fashion.

G	Corner	8-1

The G covers 14, 15, 17, and 18 by being placed at the corner where all four numbers converge, and this wager can be made at any such corner on the layout, such as 4, 5, 7, and 8, or 5, 6, 8, and 9.

H	Five numbers	6-1

This bet can only be made in one way, by placing a chip where the H is. However, although it covers 0, 00, 1, 2, and 3 and is paid off at six to one, the casino edge is higher than on any other wager, being 7.89 percent. It's the worst bet on the roulette layout.

I	Six numbers	5-1

I is placed on the outside line separating 22 and 25, and thus the bettor is covering six numbers, 22, 23, 24, 25, 26, and 27. If one chip were placed in another location, such as between 1 and 4 on the line separating the inside wagers from the dozens bet, then 1–6 would be covered at one time. Many other six-number wagers can be made on the layout.

A Final Note

Roulette is not recommended in Nevada because of the high house advantage of 5.26 percent. With the *en prison* rule in Atlantic City reducing those casinos' house edges to 2.70 percent only on the even-money propositions, it still isn't that good a bet. Preferred would be craps, in which the house edge can be reduced below 1 percent with free-odds bets, or blackjack, in which the player can hold an edge over the casino with correct basic strategy.

European Roulette

Roulette is a minor game in the American casinos, but remains a very popular game throughout the world, with its main popularity centered in England and Europe. The reason for this is the difference between the American and the French wheel; the French is the standard wheel everywhere but in the United States and its possessions.

Unlike the American wheel, the French wheel has only one zero (0), and this becomes a very important difference affecting the house edge, especially when it is combined with the *en prison* rule, which will be discussed in full later on.

In Monte Carlo, at the beginning of its rise as a casino center, the wheel contained both 0 and 00, but in the 1860s François Blanc formed the Société des Bains de Mer et Cercle des Estrangers, which bought the casino at Monte Carlo and installed the modern French wheel with its single zero. Since that time Monte Carlo, known as "the Big Wheel," has been the world center for roulette action. The casino has also been known as "the Factory," since it was a huge source of income for the Grimaldi family, including Prince Rainier and his late wife, the former motion-picture star Grace Kelly.

The Croupiers and Their Duties

The dealers staffing the European game are known as croupiers, and several of them are required to properly run the European game. In the American casinos, usually one dealer and at most an assistant to stack chips are used, but in Europe, with its more intricate layout and bets, and its double table in many casinos, which permits betting at either end of the wheel on identical layouts, the game becomes too complicated for a single dealer to handle.

In the European game one croupier, known as the *tourneur*, spins the ball and wheel and calls out the winning number, while on either side of him are other croupiers making payoffs, collecting losing chips, and also helping the players make their sometimes intricate bets.

In America the payoffs and collections are made by hand, but the European game requires the croupiers to use a rake. Losing bets are racked in by the croupiers, and winning chips are run out to the lucky players.

The chips used by the European houses aren't always the round disks used in American clubs. Often the higher denominations are in the form of rectangular plaques. In many casinos these plaques and other chips have standard denominations printed on them, and they aren't of different colors, so the players must keep track of their individual bets. Disputes occur when two bettors claim the same winning wager.

The European game is much slower than the American game; on average, there are barely thirty spins an hour as against the fifty spins a dealer can get in American roulette.

One of the major factors in the slow European game is the number of special bets, unknown in America, which the croupiers are called upon to make for players, such as *voisins, les tiers,* and *final.* These bets, which will be discussed fully in a later section, all take time and slow up the game.

In the American game the dealer doesn't announce when it is too late to make a bet, but simply disallows a wager if he or she thinks it has been made too tardily. In the European game players are permitted to make bets from the time the *tourneur* announces *"Faites vos jeux, mesdames et messieurs"* ("Make your bets, ladies and gentlemen") to the moment he announces *"Rien ne va plus"* ("No more bets").

In the American game the dealer will simply call out the winning number, such as "three." The croupier goes much further, stating *"Trois* [three] *manque* [low] *impair* [odd] *et rouge* [red]" after the ball lands in the 3 pocket. Roulette is a serious and traditional game in European casinos, often played for large stakes, and is dealt with much more formally than the American game, which is a minor table game in Nevada and Atlantic City casinos.

The French Wheel

The French wheel, holding the numbers 1–36, plus a single 0, has been so called since roulette was introduced in the late eighteenth century. There are thirty-seven numbers altogether on this wheel, and therefore it lacks the symmetry of the American wheel with its thirty-eight numbers, as a result of the 00. The players of the French wheel are more involved with the *voisins* (neighbors), or numbers adjoining one another, rather than with numbers at opposite sides of the wheel.

All the numbers are in alternate colors of black and red except for the 0, which is either green or light blue. Unlike the American wheel, where the numbers of equal color add up to thirty-seven going clockwise, the French wheel seems to be haphazard in its arrangement of numerals.

It is difficult to ascertain a specific pattern other than the alternation of black and red numbers. Odd numbers can be next to each other, as can even numbers, and high as well as low numbers can be *voisins,* or neighbors.

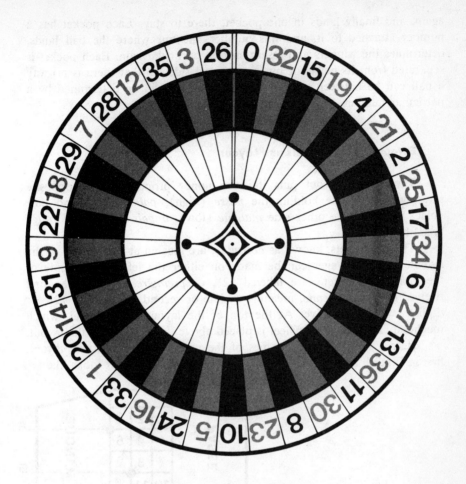

THE FRENCH WHEEL

The wheels used in European casinos are made to exacting standards and can spin freely for up to fifteen minutes at a time. They are ornate mechanisms richly embossed in wood and metal. The ball, once made of ivory, is now more often replaced by plastic.

Like the American wheel, the French wheel has a groove running near the rim where the ball is placed by the croupier, who spins it counter to the wheel's revolution, and as the ball loses momentum, it slides away from the groove and hits a series of the metal buffers alternating in horizontal and vertical configurations on the wheel.

After bouncing and sliding off these buffers, the ball moves deeper into the basin of the wheel, sometimes bouncing into one pocket and out again, and finally lands in one pocket, there to stay. Each pocket has a number attached to it, and this number, the one where the ball lands, determines the winners and losers on that particular spin. Each pocket is separated from its neighbor by raised metal sides so that there is no way a ball can be between two numbers. Each spin will be determined by a particular number.

European Roulette Bets and Layout

The French layout puts its even-money propositions on opposite sides, with one side holding the *passe* (high), *pair* (even), and *noir* (black) wagers, the other side *manque* (low), *impair* (odd), and *rouge* (red) bets.

The dozen bets, known as *douzaine*, are located at the bottom of the layout, and this wager can be made on either the left or right side of the table. The dozens are labeled 12^P, or *première*, meaning the first twelve; 12^M, or *moyenne*, meaning middle or second twelve; and 12^D, or *dernière*, the last twelve. At the top of the layout is the 0 bet, which touches 1, 2, and 3. The wheel is placed above the 0 wager on the layout.

Before we discuss the names of the possible wagers on the layout, first in English and then in French, let's see what the layout looks like:

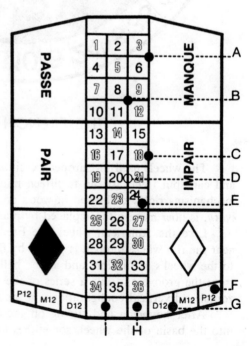

The European Layout

A. Transversale   6   numbers.
B. Carre   4   numbers.
C. Transversale   3   numbers.
D. Cheval   2   numbers.
E. Number, *en plein*   1   number.
F. Dozen   12   numbers.
G. Two dozens   24   numbers.
H. Column   12   numbers.
I. Two columns   24   numbers.

Straight Bets

American Bet	French Term	Odds Payout
Straight up	*En plein*	35-1

Because of the single 0, the house edge on this bet is 2.70, compared to the 5.26 percent on the American wheel.

Column	*Colonne*	2-1

A bet on the *colonne* covers twelve numbers, but never includes the 0.

Dozen	*Douzaine*	2-1
Red-black	*Rouge-noir*	1-1
Odd-even	*Impair-pair*	1-1
High-low	*Passe-manque*	1-1

The *en prison* rule comes into effect with these bets. Should 0 come up on the spin when these wagers are made, instead of losing the entire bet, the player has two choices. He can surrender half the wager (*partage*) and keep the other half, or he can imprison the bet for yet another spin of the wheel. When this occurs, the chips are placed on the line that borders the betting area, and if the choice bet on doesn't come up on the next spin, the wager is lost. If the choice shows, then the wager is freed, or liberated, and the player retains his original bet, but nothing is added to it. He or she may now remove it or bet it again.

With the *en prison* rule in force at a French table, the casino edge is reduced to 1.35 percent on all even-money propositions. All other wagers at the single-zero table give the house a 2.70 percent advantage. Therefore, it stands to reason that the best bets for any player to make at this game are the even-money wagers: red-black, high-low, or even-odd.

Combination Bets

American Bet	French Term	Odds Payout
Split (two numbers)	*À cheval*	17-1
Trio (three numbers)	*Transversale*	11-1

The *transversale* not only covers three numbers in any one line, but the numbers 0-1-2 or 0-2-3.

Corner (four numbers)	*Carré*	8-1
Six numbers	*Sixain*	5-1

This wager is made by placing a chip so that it covers two transversales, putting the chip at the boundary where the line separating the six numbers meets the outside of the numbers themselves. Thus a chip on the line between 21 and 24, placed at the corner where 21 and 24 meet the outside boundary, covers numbers 19 through 24.

There is no five-number bet on the French table, since the wheel has only a single zero, which is to the advantage of the player, for it is the worst bet on the American layout.

Special Wagers at the French Table

Unlike the American game, the croupiers are called upon more frequently to make wagers for the players, and some of these, because of the difference in the wheel, could only be made on the French wheel.

Voisins: This term means "neighbors," and as applied to roulette means the neighbors of the number that previously came up. For example, if 24 was the last winning number, then the *voisins* wager would include the four numbers that surround 24 on the *wheel* (not the layout). These would be 10, 5, 16, and 33. On *voisins* bets the winning number would also be included so that five numbers would be bet *en plein*, or straight up. Thus, five chips would be handed to the croupier for this wager. There is a smaller, modified *voisins* bet made only on the winning number and its immediate neighbors, in this case 24, 5, and 16, and this requires only three chips.

Les voisins du zéro: The bet can be literally translated as "neighbors of zero," and involves the numbers surrounding 0 on the wheel. It requires nine chips, and these bets are made on the splits (*à cheval*) 35-32, 29-26, 28-25, 22-19, 21-18, 15-12, 7-4; and two chips are placed on the *transversale* (trio) 0-2-3.

This bet is not a balanced one, for the numbers covered, counting clockwise, cover nine before and only seven after to 0.

Final: This bet covers all numbers ending with a particular digit. For example, a *final quatre* (final four) would be a bet on 4, 14, 24, and 34. All *finals* from 0 through 6, such as 0, 10, 20, 30 or 6, 16, 26, 36, call for four chips, while *finals* from 7 through 9 require only three chips. Usually this bet is made *en plein*, but it may be made *à cheval*.

If he wishes, the player may cover two *finals* at one time by making *à cheval* wagers. Final *deux-cinq* (two-five) is 2-5, 12-15, 22-25, and 32-35, easily made by the croupier on the layout.

Les tiers: This wager covers all the numbers on one-third of the wheel, and the French term for this bet is *tiers du cylindre*. By making this bet, the player covers the following numbers in clockwise order: 27,

13, 36, 11, 30, 8, 23, 10, 5, 24, 16, and 33.

Les orphelins: The "orphans" wager refers to those numbers not covered by either *voisins du zéro* or *les tiers*. They show on the wheel as 1, 20, 14, 31, 9, 17, 34, and 6. This bet involves five chips with four *à cheval* and one bet *en plein*. The 17, being between the 14 and 20 on the layout, is *à cheval* with both numbers.

Other French Roulette Terms

No matter where one encounters a roulette game outside the United States, it may be staffed by French croupiers and conducted in French. Therefore the following terms will be useful in understanding and betting.

French Term	English Term
Première	First
Moyenne (deuxième)	Middle, or second
Dernière	Last, or third
Premier-quatre	One-four (referring to numbers 1 and 4).
Quatre premiers	First four (numbers)
Trois derniers	Last three (numbers 34-35-36)
Six premiers	First six (numbers)

The *tourneur* may announce *"Rien ne va plus,"* which means "No more bets." The term printed on roulette cards *"Les mises sur paroles sont rigoureusment interdites"* translates to "No oral bets are allowed unless accompanied by chips."

The French wheel gives the player a much better chance than the American wheel, especially if the bettor sticks to even-money choices and uses the *en prison* rule. In this case the house edge is reduced to 1.35 percent, which is much better than the 5.26 percent generally prevailing on the American wheel without the *en prison* rule.

XVII

Betting on Sports Events

Introduction

At the present time, the only state where bets on sporting events (other than horse races) may be legally made is Nevada. However, millions of dollars are bet with bookmakers all around the country on the three major sports—football, basketball, and baseball. Also, in the near future, with offtrack betting becoming a possibility in other states besides New York, betting may eventually be allowed on sports events besides horse racing.

Generally

The first factor that any gambler on sporting events must overcome is the "vigorish." Vigorish is the difference between what you get if you win, and what you pay if you lose. Generally, if you lose a bet you pay the bookie eleven to ten; if you win the bet, you get even money. Suppose you bet $100 on team A to win a football game. If you win the bet, you get $100, but if you lose the bet, you have to pay $110. That's a big percentage to buck. And that's how the bookies stay well and financially healthy. They don't want to gamble; they just want enough bets balancing out so that the "vigorish" takes effect.

The second factor is the point spread. In football and basketball, the difference between the two teams is not shown in odds (team A four to one over team B) but rather in points. Thus, team A will be quoted as a four-point favorite over team B. If you bet on team A you give the bookie four points; if you bet on team B, the bookie gives you four points. To the bookie, which team you bet on is immaterial, for if the bets are balanced between team *A* and team *B*, he's going to collect his "vig" on half the bets. So, for the bookie, the more action the merrier he feels.

What happens if a lot of money is going on team *A* and very little on team *B*? The bookie raises the point spread to five, and if that doesn't bring in money on team *A*, he raises it still further. He may have to raise it to seven before enough money is bet on team *B* to balance out the bets. With the bookie giving away seven instead of four points, team *A* becomes a better bet, and more money will go on team *A*. It's simply the law of supply and demand. Or he may simply "lay off" the excess with bigger bookies.

Football

Football is divided into two main divisions: the college teams and the pros. To find the spread is as easy as buying a daily newspaper and looking in the sports section. There you will see a group of games, looking like this:

Slippery Falls	6	ENDZONE STATE
Pigskin U	13½	TWO FALLS TECH
GREASY HOLE	14	Ape School

In looking at these illustrious institutions, we first note that the favorite comes first, the middle number being the "point spread," or number of points by which it is favored over the other school. The capitalized school is the home team.

You will also notice that Pigskin is a thirteen-and-a-half-point favorite. This means that if it wins by fourteen, the bettors on Pigskin win; if it wins by thirteen or less, or loses, those bettors lose. This extra half-point spread avoids ties. If Greasy Hole, on the other hand, wins by the points (fourteen), it is a standoff, and the bookies get nothing. So they like the half-point gimmick.

That's about all there is to it. Pick your team and bet it. The same spread is involved in the pro games. These are played on Sundays, while the college teams play on Saturdays. Action is thus afforded the bettors on both days of the weekend.

In making the spread, the handicappers of football take a lot of things into consideration. They look at speed, the quarterback, the running game, the defensive and offensive lines, and the secondary defense of both teams. They look at the injuries, the factor of home game, and previous scores and records of the teams. It may be that these astute gentlemen have wrongly calculated the spread on a particular game, but generally they are very good at their business.

If you consider yourself a knowledgeable student of the game, you could match your wits on paper against the point makers and pick your own teams to win. Remember that you will be paying eleven for ten if you lose any bet, and see how you make out. If you can beat them, bet them.

Of all the sports events, I believe that college football is the best bet. Here's why. If you read the sports pages, there are a number of columnists who predict the football scores of the college games. They usually do this on a Friday. For the most part they go with the betting favorites, but they don't include point spreads. For example, if Notre Dame was playing East Hoboken Tech, the point spread might have Notre Dame the favorite by thirty-nine points. So your average columnist picks Notre Dame, and if Notre Dame wins, he chalks it up to clairvoyancy. With all this, some of these men barely have winning records, and this is due to the upsets. If a favorite, by whatever point spread, loses the game outright, it is a loss for those who bet on the favorite.

If I were to bet college football games seriously, I would examine the point spread of the last few years and see just how many underdogs won, not necessarily within the point spread. The figure should be quite high.

Then I would see how many favorites won by the point spread. I should think the figure would be less than fifty percent. Now, I would prepare a method of betting, as follows:

1. Bet only underdogs, for most games.

2. Bet on underdogs in games in which a rivalry exists, for these games are usually bitterly fought. Examples would be Notre Dame versus Purdue; Notre Dame versus Southern California; Michigan versus Ohio State (I would always bet the underdog in that game); Oklahoma versus Texas; Illinois versus Northwestern; Georgia versus Georgia Tech; Alabama versus Auburn; etc.

3. If teams going for national ranking are playing mediocre teams, bet on the top teams to win by the points. A lot of money these past seasons could have been made on Nebraska, Oklahoma, and Michigan.

4. Don't bet on bowl games. These games are often unpredictable, depending upon a team being "up" (psychological attitudes, etc.). Unless you travel with the teams involved, or know what's happening in their camps, don't bet the bowl games.

As to pro teams, they are more difficult because so much depends on the quarterback. This key player has an overwhelming importance in most of the games. The Jets, with Joe Namath well and hitting his receivers, are a formidable team. Without him, they are a mediocre and uncertain team.

If the quarterback is sharp and is improving and moving the team, that team is a good bet.

To bet the pros, you've got to pick one or two teams each Sunday, no more. Pick teams that are "up" for the game; that are improving; that have a good winning attitude, whether or not they are favorites or underdogs. And make sure that the quarterback is in good health.

But before betting on the pros, I would bet imaginary money for a whole season. If I could win consistently, only then would I bet the real thing.

Basketball

Like football, there is a point spread. Like football, there are the college teams and the pro teams. And there is the bookie with his "vigorish."

Basketball must be followed intensely to bet it on the college level. The teams must be studied; their attitudes must be known; the personnel must be examined thoroughly. It is a very difficult sport to bet, much more difficult than football. The points scored are higher, and the officiating has a great deal to do with the final result, as do the coaches' relations with the players. All this must be taken into account.

Unlike football, where I suggested concentrating on the college game, in basketball I would bet the pro game. There, an additional factor must be taken into consideration; the pros don't have to try to win every game. They can lose some and still make the playoffs and still win a championship. If you recognize this, you'll be an intelligent bettor.

One of the important factors in pro basketball is the travel. It wears out the players. A team traveling all around the country might need a rest. They can afford to relax against a team not in their division, a team that is not threatening them. If a team is weary, it is going to lose. Watch for the signs of weariness when they first come to town. Read about their attitudes. Know their schedule. If a team has to face team X tonight, but they are going against the champions in their own division tomorrow night, they might not pay any attention to team X tonight. Bet on X.

In pro ball, the teams all have brilliant players. Some teams go on hot winning streaks; others go on long losing streaks. If a team starts to get hot—starts to win big—go with it, whatever the point spread. If a team goes cold, bet against it. There may be dissension, injuries not reported, financial troubles plaguing a couple of players. Who knows? But bet against the losers and with the winners. It's as good a method as any.

Baseball

Baseball betting differs from basketball and football gambling in several ways. First, there is no division among college and pro teams. Generally speaking, only the major-league teams are bet on. College baseball is a very dull sport and there is little interest in it. Minor-league pro ball is not very popular either. The bets are made on the "big leaguers"—the National and American leagues.

In football and basketball, there is a point spread to measure the relative strengths of the two teams. In baseball, there are odds given to determine the strength of the opposing pitchers, rather than the teams themselves.

For example, if pitcher *A* on the Yankees is opposing pitcher *B* on the Red Sox, the Yankees might be seven to five favorites. If pitcher *B* was withdrawn as a starter and pitcher *C* pitched for the Red Sox, the odds might change to seven to five in favor of the Red Sox.

If you bet with a bookie on baseball games, you can either limit your bet to the pitchers for that day, or you can accept whatever the line will be for a different starting pitcher. The best practice is to cancel your bet if there is any change in starting pitchers, because the line quoted may not be to your liking, or may simply reflect the amount bet on each team to balance things for the bookie.

There is generally a small spread in odds given by bookies, because of the structure of the betting. If the Yankees were seven-to-five favorites over the Red Sox, the line would be seven even. This means that if you bet on the favorites, you gave the bookie seven-to-five odds, but if you bet on the underdog you only got even money. That's the way the bookie makes his money.

However, if a bookie quoted odds at that range he'd get little business, because the "spread" of seven to even money is too great. More usually, odds might be quoted as 1.40 to 1.20. This might be the regular line. If you bet on the favorite you'd give the bookie 1.40 to 1.00. If you bet on the underdog, you'd get $1.20 for each dollar you bet.

These odds become more refined for the "nickel line" or "inside" line. The odds may then be 1.40 to 1.30. It often depends on the relationship of the bookie and the bettor. With a small spread, the bookie first figures the correct odds on the game. As another example, he may think the Yankees are 1.25 to win. He thus uses the 1.25 as his guide. The regular line would be 1.35 to 1.15, the inside line 1.30 to 1.20.

Relationships between bettors and bookies are rather simple in regard to lines. If a bettor regularly bets $100 or more, he will get the inside line. Smaller bettors must be content with the regular line.

If you make small bets, the percentage the bookies take is too prohibitive to make any real money. Unless you can win on paper and maintain a large winning percentage, don't bet baseball games. Of course, there is a lot of action on baseball for several reasons. For one thing, during the summer it is the only sporting event around, while basketball and football often compete with one another. For another, it is a rather dull game unless there is a bet going. Also, there are relatively few teams to follow, and interest in the few games may therefore be high.

Since baseball depends so much on pitchers, you should study pitchers and their records thoroughly if you bet baseball. Also study and follow just a few teams. If a team is considered a strong pennant contender and loses several of its early games, it may start to pick up and win. Catch it then, because if the team is strong enough (Baltimore of 1971) it can really start to roll.

Another important factor. All that the team you bet on has to do is win. Scores otherwise are immaterial. You must pick a winner to collect that bet. If you have a hot team with a winning streak, and a good pitcher going against a mediocre or poor team, bet the good team, no matter what the odds. In baseball, the best bet is to go with favorites because you must get that win.

Intelligent Betting on Sporting Events

It is very easy to place a phone call and bet with a bookie. You can bet $500 on team *X,* hang up the phone, and wait for the results of the game that evening. You don't have to take that $500 out of your pocket and hand it in cash to the bookie. And that's the real danger of betting on sporting events. Because after a couple of big losses, he's going to call *you* and ask for the money. One way or another, you've got to settle accounts with him in cold cash.

To bet intelligently, therefore, is a prerequisite of this type of betting. It is too easy to place bets; too easy to lose. Don't fool around with sports events unless you know what you are doing. Here are a few tips that might help the average bettor.

1. Don't be sentimental. If you graduated from Fairyland U and they're playing Jockstrap Tech, and Tech has the better team, don't bet on Fairyland for sentimental reasons. Watch the game if you want to; it should be exciting enough without the bet.

In betting on anything, you must not be ruled by emotions, but by hard facts, by good information. Do this and you're on your way to winning.

2. Concentrate on a few teams and follow them and know them well. You can't make money by running down a sheet, or by calling the bookie and getting the "line" and then betting on ten teams you know little about. Know a few teams—study their personnel, their attitude, read hometown papers about them, or college papers. If you're going to concentrate on

Stanford, Oklahoma, Georgia, and Penn State, get hold of their college papers and hometown papers. You'll find a lot of inside information about them and a great deal about their attitude, things that may not have been picked up by the big newspapers or oddsmakers.

3. Don't bet parlays and don't bet on three or four teams in pools. If you assume that each bet has less than a fifty-percent chance of winning (because of the vigorish), to estimate the chances of winning several events, all it takes is a simple calculation. If we even the odds to fifty percent, to win one game you have an even chance (forget about vigorish for a while). To win two games you multiply fifty percent by fifty percent, or $\frac{1}{2} \times \frac{1}{2}$. This gives you one chance in four, or three-to-one odds against you winning both games. To win three games, your chances are fifty percent times fifty percent times fifty percent, or 12.5 percent, or one chance in eight. The odds are now seven to one against you. And picking four teams is fifty percent times fifty percent times fifty percent times fifty percent, or one chance in sixteen, or fifteen-to-one odds against you. They're awfully tough odds to overcome. You may be offered parlays which pay much less, because no bookie is going to pay you *more* than the odds.

The same is true in pools. These are conducted by passing out sheets in which you are given the spread on a whole series of football games. If you pick three of them correctly, you get four to one. The correct odds are seven to one. If you pick four, you get eight to one. The correct odds are fifteen to one. A sure bet for suckers to guarantee their bankruptcy.

4. Don't bet more than you can afford. If you have to sweat out a game because of a big bet, don't make that bet. Bet to add a little excitement to the venture, or bet to make money. If you bet to make money, know those teams cold, and know the situation and all the factors thoroughly. The oddsmakers are not fools, and neither are the bookies. They're pros in their business.

5. If you can't win by making imaginary or paper bets, don't bet money on sporting events. Your luck isn't going to change because real money is being bet. If anything, it will get worse because you might find yourself under pressure after several losing bets and bet heavily to recoup. Don't do this. If you can't stay cool, don't bet at all on sporting events. Scores seesaw back and forth, and there is enormous pressure on anyone making a bet. You must be able to withstand the pressure, and the easiest way is to win your bets. If you can't win the paper bets, you're not going to win the money bets.

XVIII

Horse Race Betting

Introduction

Horse racing is certainly an important sport in the United States, and the improvement of the breed is helped by literally millions of spectators and bettors at race tracks. This is one of the few sports in which betting is legal in many states, and the reason for this legality is the huge sums the states take in revenues.

It would be interesting to see how popular the Sport of Kings, as horse racing is often called, would be if no betting were allowed. In all probability, the tracks couldn't give away tickets to watch these horses run. The excitement, except for a few exceptional races involving champions, is in betting on a horse to win. There is very little pleasure in watching an ordinary horse race otherwise, unless you own one of the horses in the race.

Horse race betting is facilitated by pari-mutuel machines, an automatic totalizing system that computes the odds every thirty seconds or so, as bets are made. Usually, the odds are calculated after the money for state taxes, other taxes, the track's breakage, its share, etc.—all amounting to a whopping eighteen percent—is first deducted. The adjusted odds are then flashed automatically onto a board or boards in the infield of a track, showing the odds on each horse to win. The horses, though designated by name and number on the racing program, are designated strictly by number on the boards. A board would look like this:

1.	5	6.	7	11.	30
2.	9-2	7.	35	12.	25
3.	10	8.	8-5		
4.	15	9.	9-5		
5.	5-2	10.	12		

By looking at the board, we see that the number one horse is five to one, and the number 8 horse is eight to five. This means that a five-dollar bet on number one will pay back twenty-five dollars plus the original five dollars bet, while a five-dollar bet on number eight will pay back eight dollars plus the five dollars bet. Why the difference in odds? The betting public has determined that number eight is a better horse than number one.

The bettors are guided by the past performance record of the horse, the trainer, and the jockey, the breeding of the horse, the condition of the track, the kind of race he is running in, his opposition, his latest workouts, and a great deal of superstition—hunches, omens, and various other mysterious factors. In fact, there are so many factors involved that it is next to impossible to handicap races (pick the winner) with any degree of consistency.

If you disagree with me, show me any professional handicapper in the United States who has a winning record on his picks for win alone during any year. Pick up any newspaper, or one of the racing sheets, and follow the selections of the handicappers for about a month. In fact, just follow their best bets and you'll see what I mean. They can't pick winners consistently, even though they get all kinds of information, attend clockings, speak to trainers, owners, and jockeys. And if they can't do it, how can the average bettor, who can't afford to spend most of his time at the racetrack gathering information?

Not only is it next to impossible to pick winners by handicapping, but the eighteen percent that the state, track, county, etc., take out of the pari-mutuel handle (total of bets) makes the bucking of these odds almost prohibitive. How can any horseplayer seriously think that he can bet the races and beat them? Yet, there are literally dozens of "tout" sheets, booklets, pamphlets, books, and articles on how to beat the races and make a fortune.

Why this optimism in the face of so many disheartening facts? And they are disheartening. In the general public's mind, the image of a horseplayer is that of a deadbeat, a fool; a man betting his children's food money on horses and going broke, borrowing, owing money to shylocks, eventually losing everything, and on and on. And in many respects the image is correct. There are compulsive horseplayers, as there are compulsive players and gamblers in every sport or game. But the horseplayer is more pathetic and more capable of huge losses, because he imagines that he is doing something skillful by betting on horses. He reads the papers, examines the past performance charts, studies speed ratings, and goes through a whole ritual of handicapping before he makes a bet—and ends up losing anyway. Why? Because he thinks that studying those paper records as a skillful surgeon studies his medical books virtually assures success. It's just not so.

The horseplayer cannot know the exact condition of the horse; cannot know how it ate that day, or how it feels. He can know the past, but not the present. And that's not enough.

Often, in any given race, even someone not connected with the sport can see that there are several horses that could possibly win the race. Who can guess which horse is in the best condition that moment? You can't ask a horse how he's feeling. It becomes a matter of guesswork.

What I'm going to discuss in this chapter is what horse racing is basically all about; the mechanics of betting, etc. This is the only kind of worthwhile study, in my opinion, one that can give the bettor at least a fighting chance to win at races if a serious study is made. Otherwise horse race betting should be pursued as a pleasant pastime. If a man or woman or family wants to have a day of excitement at the races, betting a minimum amount on each race and getting the flavor of the track, the paddock, the general excitement that pervades a racetrack, that is fine. The final cost, if bets are made at a low level, will not be more than for any comparative day of entertainment.

I have taken my family to Saratoga, where the feeling of the old-time track still remains. The atmosphere is colorful, with the candy stripes on the awnings and the wide areas in which to roam. And Saratoga is a pleasant town. We made a few bets, walked around, watched "our" horse being saddled, and had a rather pleasant day.

I remember going to the old Jamaica track some years back. There, the track was strictly for business, and everything was concrete and steel. The stands were inadequate, and you were always being pushed and jostled. It would be unthinkable to spend a day there with your family, unless you wanted to punish them. But of course the old track has been torn down.

An old friend of the family, who was quite a devotee of the horses, told me that he went to Jamaica one Memorial Day. There were about 60,000 people there. (Jamaica started to bulge with about 15,000 in attendance.) I asked him how he made out.

"I came out winning," he said, "but I'll tell you the truth, I was praying to lose. There was such a mob there that it took almost a half hour to cash in winning tickets, and to stand on those lines . . . and then to have to stand on another line and bet. And it was hot, and I was sweating and had to take a leak, but there were lines a mile long to go to the bathroom . . ."

A pleasant day at the races.

A person who goes to the track once or twice a week, betting moderate or substantial money, or one who bets with a bookie or the newly founded OTB, must come out losing. *Must* is the word used. First, the odds are reduced by the various taxes and bounties taken out, so that the payoff is about eighteen percent less than it should be. Second, there is no handicapper who is consistent enough to come out ahead.

I have recently looked through all sorts of books and pamphlets dealing with ideal racing systems, picking overlays and dark horses, picking winners with such consistency that I wondered why the author bothered to write the pamphlet at all and wasn't, instead, out at the track cleaning up. Perhaps he just wanted to benefit mankind.

More probably, he realized that it just couldn't be done. If any reader wants to become a serious handicapper, I would first suggest that he pick up any edition of the *Racing Form,* study it, and pick those horses he thinks will win the next day. The papers will explain most of the details of handicapping, telling the reader what a speed rating is, what the various types of races signify. They will show the past performance charts of each horse and explain all the factors that are mentioned, such as date of race, post position, distance of race, time of race, condition of track, the race run by the horse at various points, his finish, his jockey, his trainer, his dam, sire, and many, many other things. It's all in the paper. In addition, several handicappers will select winners, as well as place and show horses. For the uninitiated, in a horse race there are three payoff spots: First (win), second (place), and third (show). A winner pays for win, place, and show; a place horse pays for place and show; and the third horse pays for show. It looks like this:

A	10.90	4.30	2.80
B		4.10	2.40
C			2.60

A, having won, pays $10.90 for win, $4.30 for place, and $2.80 for show. All these winnings are based on a two-dollar bet. *A* went off at odds of 4.45 to 1, for the two-dollar bet is included in the payoff. A bet for win, place, and show on any horse is called an across-the-board bet. You will notice that the payoff for place is less than the payoff for win, and the payoff for show is also substantially less. This is because the win pool, or all money bet on each horse for win, is not divided. The place pool is divided twice, and the show pool three times.

In handicapping horses, there are a great many factors to consider, so many that it would be hard to put them all down. But some of the most important are the horse's consistency of performance, his condition, and the horses he is running against. Also, the weight assigned to him, the condition of the track, his jockey, and his post position. Most of the handicappers who write books on the sport specialize in just a few of these factors, and show the reader how, by past handicapping of these few variables, they have selected winners.

So far, I have neglected two critical, and to me the most important, factors of any race. The first is the odds the horse goes off at, which is the total bet on that horse in proportion to the combined total bet on all the horses in the race. Second is the morning line, which is how the track handicapper rates the horses in the race. The morning line is shown on the racing program, and not in the racing sheets. Generally, a program can be bought at the track for about twenty-five or thirty-five cents. The program, as well as the racing sheet, will show the number of the race, what kind of race it is, the distance of the race, and the weight assignments, as well as the breeding of the horses, and who their jockeys and trainers are. Leaving out most of this and just concentrating on the morning-line odds, it looks like this.

PROGRAM

Post Position	*Horse*	*Odds*
1.	A	10-1
2.	B	8-1
3.	C	6-1
4.	D	5-2
5.	E	6-1
6.	F	15-1
7.	G	8-5
8.	H	3-1
9.	K	4-1
10.	L	15-1
11.	M	5-1
12.	N	9-2

The odds quoted above are not the official odds, but the morning-line odds. These odds are established by the track handicapper as a guide to the bettors. In this race, the track handicapper feels that *G* will win, *D* will come in second and *H* will come in third, and he believes that the horse will go off at approximately the odds that appear in the program. In the actual race the odds may radically change. Any horse may go off as the favorite, and there is no assurance that the horses selected to win, place, and show by the track handicapper will be the same as picked by the general public making the bets.

All this leads to what I consider the correct study of horse racing for the serious bettor. Before placing any bet whatsoever, anyone considering betting large stakes on horses should try and handicap them. He can read all kinds of books on the subject, either buying them or getting them from the library. He then should buy a racing sheet, such as the *Racing Form*, and make imaginary paper bets on those horses he has selected, without regard to the odds at the track. If he can successfully handicap horses, then he can make serious bets and attempt to win money.

My feeling, however, is that he will not be able to do this. He will find rank outsiders winning; horses that have had dreary finishes suddenly waking up; horses that were consistent in the past now folding in the stretch. However, I am not consigning to failure all handicappers or students of horse racing. It may be possible, perhaps with a computer, to examine all the variables and arrive at a winner.

Picking Winners

My method of picking winners would be much different. I have had one successful experience and will explain it a little later. Suffice it to say that my method would not involve handicapping at all; it would merely involve favorites.

In the following chapter on systems, I explain how various systems of betting on favorites are foolhardy things. I am referring to *indiscriminate* betting on favorites. Favorites come in approximately thirty-seven percent of the time. All favorites, that is.

Suppose these favorites were broken down as follows: All odds-on favorites (horses going off at less than even money); even money to seven-to-five favorites; eight to five to nine-to-five favorites; two to one to five-to-two favorites; and all favorites above five to two. The odds quoted would be actual odds, established by the betting public, not morning-line odds.

Any student examining a complete year's racing at any track would make some immediate and startling discoveries. He would find that odds-on favorites come in over fifty percent of the time, and that favorites of five to two or better come in much less than thirty-seven percent of the time. He might find more favorites at eight to five coming in (winning) than even-money favorites.

Therefore, before I would make a serious bet at any track, I would go to a library having back copies of the *Racing Form*. I would write down the final odds of every favorite in every race and calculate the percentage of times the above groups won. I know I would find that if, in betting on favorites, I eliminated all those at five to two or higher, the percentage of winning favorites would jump dramatically above thirty-seven percent.

Having done this, I would then divide the races into various groups, such as claiming, maiden races, allowance, handicap, and stakes racing. Claiming races are for the cheapest horses at the track; maidens are for horses that have never won a race; while stakes races are for the best horses at the track. Allowance and handicap races are for generally good horses.

Now I would calculate what percentage of favorites won at maiden races, etc. I would probably find that favorites in certain kinds of races won more times than in other races. Probably, though I am not certain of it, a favorite in a stakes race would be more consistent than one in a claiming race.

After doing this, and knowing exactly what percentage of favorites won each kind of race, and dividing them still in terms of odds-on, etc., I would go to the track and try to see every program of the races for the last year. It is possible to buy them, but it is also possible to look them up. (I personally did this at two trotting tracks.) I would then write down the morning-line odds of the three favorites in each race (first, second, and third selections) of the track handicapper.

Now, I would correlate the morning-line favorites with the actual favorites. What percentage of wins did they have? Did they go off at better or worse odds? If a morning-line favorite was not a track favorite, what percentage of times did he win?

Having this additional information, I would then prepare a study of the favorites and try to find the grouping that won most of the time. It might be morning-line favorites going off at less than eight to five in all races but claiming and maiden races. If that were so, and the favorites in this category won about forty-five percent of the time, we would have the beginning of a method of selecting winners. With further study, that figure could be increased. What about outside post positions? Track conditions? Number of horses that went off at three to one or below in any race?

As you see, a mass of information will be gathered, making the student of this method much more knowledgeable than any addict of the track, betting on hunches and handicapping methods.

Trotters and Pacers

So far, I have dealt with flat, or thoroughbred, racing. There is a great deal of harness racing as well, which involve standardbreds. The main difference is that a thoroughbred, in flat racing, runs with a jockey on his back, while a standardbred, in harness racing, races with a sulky tied to him, in which sits the driver.

Harness racing is usually conducted at night, on smaller tracks. The usual race is a mile, while in thoroughbred racing the distances vary from (usually) five furlongs to two miles. Harness horses are either pacers or trotters, depending on their gait.

There are a great many differences between flat racing and harness racing, but the important one for our consideration is post position. Since the horses in a harness race have sulkies attached to them, they are slower and have much less mobility. Therefore, a horse in an inside post position (near the rail) has a distinct advantage. He runs the shortest distance around the oval, and another horse, to get that rail position, must lap or run around him and then get in front.

In handicapping trotters and pacers, the other important factor is the "break." These horses must run at a certain gait, either a pace or a trot, involving a special coordination of leg movements. If they gallop, they go off the gait and are said to "break." The rider of a breaking horse must pull him back until he goes on the gait again. Thus a "break" is usually costly and generally means a losing race for that horse.

The serious handicapper can get the advance program and handicap the horses in a harness race by post position, past performance, conditions of the race, etc. But he will find, just as with the thoroughbreds, that it is almost impossible to do.

Therefore, again, a study of the past performances of favorites over the past year at a particular track, a study of morning-line favorites—the same general method of examining favorites as was done in flat races—is warranted, with the added factor of post position. At flat races, this factor is often negligible, but in harness racing it is all important.

A student will find that the number one horse (the horse in the inside post position) will win more often than any horse in any other post position. Or, to put it another way, a record of wins by post position will usually show the number one position winning most of the time, followed by two, three, four, five, six, seven, and finally eight. Sometimes five may win more than four, but number one is almost sure to win most of the time.

He will also find that favorites win about thirty-five percent of the time, but horses with odds under nine to two in the number one position, regardless of whether or not they are favorites, also win about thirty-five percent of the time. Thus, favorites in the number one position win more than thirty-five percent of the time, as a rule. Armed with this knowledge, the student has the basis of a method of betting.

One year, when there was a twin double at Roosevelt Raceway and Yonkers Raceway, I made a complete study of programs and the past performances of each track. I could find no pattern at Roosevelt, but at Yonkers it became apparent that certain events occurred with frequency.

Before going any further, I should explain what a twin double is. A bettor could bet on four races in a row, and if he won all four (the sixth, seventh, eighth, and ninth races) he would win a substantial amount, usually in the thousands for a two-dollar bet.

This interested me because, by betting four races in a row, I was not bound to pick only one horse per race, but could pick several. I therefore went to Roosevelt Raceway, where the programs of both Roosevelt and Yonkers were kept, and wrote down the morning-line odds by post position. I copied all the races for the previous year in which there was twin-double betting.

Then I correlated them with the winners of the actual races as studied in the *Daily Mirror,* which was still in business then. I then decided that in order to make the system work, I would have to pick the winner of the sixth race and make certain that I had a winner at least fifty percent of the time in that race.

To bet the twin double, you bought a ticket on the sixth and seventh races combined, and then, if you won both, you traded in this ticket for the eighth and ninth races combined. This meant that on the sixth and eighth races I could watch the actual track odds bet by the public. But in the seventh and ninth races I could only count on the morning-line odds, because the tickets had to be bought before the sixth race, and then before the eighth race.

I found that in order to win the sixth race fifty percent of the time, I had to bet on odds-on favorites in the sixth, or on the first three betting choices. These were the only chances I had to win fifty percent of the sixth races. I then bought 150 tickets, combining this horse with the first five morning-line favorites in the seventh race if it was odds-on. For example, if the number two horse went off at four to five, I would buy thirty tickets on number two combined with the first morning-line choice in the seventh race, and thirty tickets with the second, etc. Now, if the number two horse won the first race, and any of the top five morning-line horses won the seventh race, I had thirty active tickets to exchange for the eighth and ninth races. I would then take the first five betting choices in the eighth race (usually) and combine them with the six top morning-line horses in the ninth race.

This is just one aspect of the method I employed. I also used another method, betting the top three choices in the sixth race and combining them with the three morning-line choices in the seventh race. The important thing is that I had calculated this. I knew that I had a good chance of winning that twin double, without ever caring about the speed of the horses, or what their past performance records were.

On the first method, one times five, then five times six (the favorite in the sixth race with the five morning-line choices in the seventh race, the five betting choices in the eighth race with the six morning-line choices in the ninth race) once I won the sixth race I was almost sure to win the twin double. In fact, there was only one time I lost it that way. Did I end up ahead with this method? Certainly. But eventually the twin double was discontinued. And even before then, the strain of this kind of betting (I had to wait till the last odds showed before the race began to make my bets) caused me to call the whole thing off. But I saw then and there that it was possible, with intelligent calculations, to have a fighting chance in horse racing.

To summarize quickly: If you can handicap horses, that's fine, but don't kid yourself. Handicap them as though you were betting on them. If you can't make money (paper money) with practice, don't bet real money.

If you want to try to really pick winners and are serious about betting, try the study of favorites I mentioned. It is not a guaranteed method of beating the races, but it will make you a more intelligent bettor.

XIX

Systems

Introduction

A system is a special plan of procedure in betting, whereby the bettor bets in a formulated and predetermined way, no matter what the odds are. In fact, the basic use of a betting system is to try and beat a game in which the odds are in favor of the house, and unfavorable to the player.

Systems abound in most gambling games. There are volumes on systems to beat the races, for instance, because in horse racing a system can be tied to a method of handicapping, and thus have a semblance of legitimacy. But it is awfully difficult to devise a system to beat a game where the percentages are about eighteen percent in favor of the house, as they are in horse racing.

With an unfavorable percentage that great, there are long periods of poor results, and that is the ultimate kiss of death for a system. A system works best when wins and losses are about even over a long period of time, without any streaks going one way or the other. In horse racing, with many thoroughbreds in each race and various factors entering in, such as consistency, breeding, track conditions, weight, jockeys, *ad infinitum,* there can be long periods where the best handicapping in the world is going to produce nothing but losers for days on end. And if the system requires a progression—that is, a continual increase in the amount bet—bankruptcy may finally hinge on one horse race.

Systems are ideally suited for those games in which pure chance is involved, such as roulette and craps. In other games, such as poker or blackjack, there is no need for a system because the skill a player brings to the game or a knowledge of the odds involved will enable him to win. There is no such guarantee in a game like roulette, where no matter how you bet, you won't find a bet on the table with less than a 5.26 percent advantage to the house. That's what you have to buck when you devise a system to beat roulette, and although it's not as horrendous as the eighteen-percent advantage in horse racing, it still is a lot to swallow.

In craps, systems can also be used, because there the advantage to the house on single line bets can be reduced to 1.40 percent, which is substantially better than the house's advantage in roulette. However, the multitude of possible bets that can be made at craps often attracts and dooms the systems player; he tends to bet on those possibilities, such as a field bet, in which an instant decision is made with each roll of the dice. These bets are generally not at the best odds.

Now let's analyze some of the more common systems and see how they fare.

Progressive, Doubling Up, or Martingale System

This is generally the first and simplest system that any player will explore when he decides that he will never again work for a living, but will simply rake in the money with a surefire system at a casino or racetrack.

As the words "doubling up" signify, the system is that simple. After a losing bet, the gambler doubles his bet. If he loses again, he once more doubles his bet. What is the final result when he wins?

With a double-up system, the inital bet made is the ultimate win for the player. If he started with one dollar, no matter how high the progression takes him (and believe me, it can take him to dizzying heights) he wins that first bet. Here's how it works.

Bet Number	Amount Bet	Amount Lost (Total)
One	$1.00	$ 1.00
Two	$2.00	$ 3.00
Three	$4.00	$ 7.00
Four	$8.00	$15.00

Now, on the fifth bet, the gambler bets sixteen dollars and wins. Since he has lost fifteen dollars prior to this bet, his win totals one dollar.

A logical question right now might be: So what's wrong with this? Well, there are a few things wrong with it. For one thing, a penny doubled in this manner will add up to a million dollars in less than thirty doubles. If you don't believe it, try it on paper.

The same thing is true with that initial dollar bet. I know that after four bets the gambler is only betting $16, but by his tenth bet he will have to bet $512. Since the house limit is generally $500, he can only bet that amount and since his losses up to that point are $1,023, even if he wins he'll still be down $23. And if he loses that $500 bet, he's really in a bind, because another $500 bet won will still leave him down $523. Now he'll have to make a succession of $500 bets to win . . . yes, that $1. If that isn't madness, you tell me what is.

"Wait," you might say. "How often is a player going to lose nine times in a row? The odds against that are enormous." Yes, they are. But the odds of losing nine times in a row, where the house has a percentage, let's say, of 5.26 in its favor in roulette, are greater than winning the amount of money you have to win ($1,024 in a long succession of wins) to withstand that bad streak.

The best way to test a progressive doubling-up system is to simply take a coin and toss it, heads or tails. Here, we don't even have a house edge, just a strictly fifty-fifty chance. Bet any way you want to—heads, tails, heads and tails alternating, betting on the same side as the previous toss, etc. See how often you can win that $1,024 before you lose those nine bets in a row. It's a much cheaper way to test this system than putting that same money on red or black at roulette.

Doubling Up, Plus One

There are those who have even greater foolhardy courage than the doublers. They want to win faster, so they not only double up, but add an additional dollar to the bet. On the first bet, they bet one dollar. If they lose, instead of betting two dollars, they bet three dollars. And if they lose again, they bet seven dollars (double plus one again). Here's how this looks on paper.

Bet Number	Amount Bet	Amount Lost (Total)
One	$ 1.00	$ 1.00
Two	$ 3.00	$ 4.00
Three	$ 7.00	$11.00
Four	$15.00	$26.00

On the fifth bet, they bet thirty-one dollars, and if they win, the total win is five dollars. Note that with each bet the win increases by a dollar. After ten bets they would have won ten dollars (because of that plus-one factor).

However, by the ninth bet the total bet is $511, which is eleven dollars over the maximum. And since they've already lost $502, a win of $500 will bring a loss of two dollars. This is a slightly quicker method of going bankrupt than the pure doubling-up system.

Cancellation System

This system was discussed at length in the section on roulette. However, there are a few more things worth mentioning about it.

Instead of doubling up, there is a cancelling of bets. With each loss, one number is added; with each win, two numbers are crossed out. Therefore, theoretically, only one out of every three bets has to win to finish a cancellation setup and win. What do you win? The total of the numbers you start with. The most common is 1-2-3. When you finish the entire cancellation, you win the total of these numbers, or six dollars.

Well, sounds good so far. We don't fool around for one paltry dollar in winnings after betting $500 nine times in a row. Here we knock off six quick dollars.

The 1-2-3 cancellation system works as follows. Three numbers are put down, 1-2-3. The two end numbers are bet. Thus one and three equals four, or a bet of four units. If you win, you cross off the numbers so it looks like this: 1-2-3. Then you bet the 2. If you win, you cross it off also. Now you have won the total of the numbers, or six units. Any time you finish cancelling or crossing out all the numbers, you win the six units because $1 + 2 + 3 = 6$.

However, should you lose a bet, you add the lost bet to the end column and then bet the end numbers. Thus, on the initial bet, 1-2-3, you bet the two end numbers, or four. If you lose, your column now looks like this: 1-2-3-4. Now again you bet the two end numbers, which add up to five. If you win, you cross off the two end numbers just bet. It would look like this now: 1-2-3-4. Now you bet the total of end numbers, but since 2-3 remain, you bet five. If you lose, the column looks like this: 2-3-5. Now you bet seven $(2+5)$. If you lose, it looks like this: 2-3-5-7. Now you bet nine $(2+7)$. If you win, you cross off the 2 and 7, leaving 3-5, which is 8. You bet eight, and if you win, you cross off the 3-5 and your total winning from this column is six, the original total of 1-2-3.

It seems as though the numbers couldn't go too high, but let me show you how they easily can. We start with 1-2-3. We bet four dollars and lose. Now we have 1-2-3-4. We bet five dollars and win. Now we have 1-2-3-4. We bet five and lose. 1-2-3-4-5: We bet seven and lose. 1-2-3-4-5-7: We bet nine and win. 1-2-3-4-5-7: Now we bet eight and lose. 1-2-3-4-5-7-8.

Let's just follow the numbers remaining. We have 3-5-8. Now we bet eleven and lose. 3-5-8-11: We bet fourteen and win. ƶ-5-8-ɟɟ: We bet thirteen and lose. 5-8-13: We bet eighteen and lose. 5-8-13-18: We bet twenty-three and win. ƶ-8-13-ɟƶ: We bet twenty-one and lose. 8-13-21: We bet twenty-nine and lose. 8-13-21-29: We bet thirty-seven and win. ƶ-13-21-2ƶ: We bet thirty-four and lose. 13-21-34: We bet forty-seven and lose. 13-21-34-47: We bet sixty and lose. 13-21-34-47-60: We bet seventy-three and win. ɟƶ-21-34-47-6ƶ: We bet sixty-eight and lose. 21-34-47-68: We bet eighty-nine and lose. 21-34-47-89: We bet $110 and lose. 21-34-47-89-110. We bet $131 and win. 2ɟ-34-47-89-ɟɟƶ: We bet $123 and lose. 34-47-89-131: We bet $165 and lose. And now it's 34-47-89-131-165, and our next bet is $199, and we're still pursuing the six dollars.

You can see how perilous this system can be with a bad streak. The premise here is that since each winning bet cancels out two numbers, and each losing bet adds only one, one win out of three bets and we win. But when the bad streak comes, you can find yourself betting hundreds of dollars and finally going over the $500 limit. This bad streak comes sooner or later, and all it takes is one to wipe out all the winnings accumulated over the short winning streaks.

Remember one thing, and remember it well; it's very easy to spin the wheel at home, or roll dice against the wall and work out these systems with chips and monopoly money. But when you get to that casino, you are betting real money, and it is with considerably less bravado that you throw down $500 in chips and feel your heart jump a beat.

Raising and Lowering, or Up and Down System

This system is so slow that it will take a very, very long time to reach the maximum $500 bet the house allows, but when you do reach it, you're in deep, deep trouble. Here's how it works.

You start with a low figure, let's say two dollars. If you lose, you add another dollar and bet three dollars. Every time you win a bet, you simply reduce the next bet by one dollar. If you win twice and lose twice, you'll be ahead two dollars. The progression is at a snail's pace, but it's still there, and once more you must realize that one single win won't make you even. I knew a gambler who used this system and swore by it. I met him in Reno and he was calmly making these bets on the pass line at dice. How could he lose? he asked. The next time I saw him was over a cup of coffee at one of the cheaper places off Virginia Street. He asked me for five dollars to stake him on a new system.

No matter how slowly these systems move in their inexorable progression, they do move up, the bets increase, and eventually you are losing a great deal. It takes many, many wins to overcome one big losing streak. And there's no way to stop a losing streak unless you are clairvoyant, and if you are, there's no need to fool around with dollar systems in casinos.

The principal reason that all the above mentioned systems fail, and others as well that will be mentioned later, is that we are working with a negative factor in the first place. The odds are against the bettor, and all his millions of bets are not going to alter those odds one whit. It is like owning a huge department store and selling everything at a slight loss. You can have the biggest day in your history, with the volume of sales at an all-time peak, and you're still going to end up losing money. It's the same with these systems. You're selling at a loss, and all the sales in the world aren't going to help you.

Waiting or Patience

In this system, the gambler waits for a particular run in the game he is betting on. In roulette, for example, he may wait for five reds in a row to show up. At that point, he bets black. In dice, after a series of don't passes, he bets the pass line. His theory? One, he believes that the odds are in his favor, for everyone knows that the odds against getting six reds in a row in roulette are prohibitive. The same is true of any six events in any game. Why not then make the bet when the odds are in one's favor?

Secondly, not only are the odds in your favor, but the events must balance themselves out. After six reds, there must come blacks to balance the odds which theoretically are fifty-fifty as to red and black appearing.

All right, this is his premise. He, and many others like him, sit all evening at roulette, or stand all night at the crap table, waiting for this series of events to occur, and then they make their bets. Will they necessarily win? No, not in the long run. Is their reasoning correct? Again, no.

The first fallacy: That because five reds have appeared, the odds are in favor of a black appearing. Absolutely false. Unlike the gambler, who must have many bitter memories of past defeats, the roulette wheel and the dice have no memory. The past means nothing to them. The next roll of the dice, the next spin of the wheel, is not governed by what happened before. Each new event is independent of every other event. The odds are absolutely even on the sixth spin of the roulette wheel as to whether red or black will appear. That is, absolutely even with the factor of 5.26 percent in favor of the house because of the 0 and 00.

If the gambler could be permitted to bet that there will not be a run of six reds in a row before the wheel has spun off these first five reds, that would be a different matter. Since the odds would be so greatly in his favor at that moment, he would have to give odds against its occurring. All he is now doing is betting on one spin of the wheel. How could he possibly figure that the odds would be in his favor?

As to the events balancing, another fallacy. The wheel, or the dice, is not going to balance on any short series of numbers. The whole theory of odds is based on large numbers, numbers running into the millions and billions. Five reds coming up doesn't mean anything. How would this gambler know just what the balance is at that point? It could be 1,456,903 reds to 1,399,609 blacks, with more reds still to appear in order to balance out the numbers. All that will happen eventually is that the more times the event occurs, the closer red and black will move to showing up fifty percent of the time. However, the wheel may be spun eight billion times, and there may be ten million more reds than blacks, or vice versa, and the odds are very close to fifty percent at this point. How can anyone stop time to contemplate this balancing act? It cannot be done.

The only thing that is tested by this patient way of betting is the patience of the bettor, who, having wasted time waiting in vain for events to occur, will not find himself waiting long before losing his money.

The Impatient System, or Hot and Cold Bettor

Here is the opposite of the patient bettor. Does he wait for the five reds to appear? No, sir. Once that first red appears, he's on the band wagon betting those reds, so that by the time the patient bettor moves to make that first bet, the impatient, or hot and cold, bettor is already winning those other bets. If the dice have won the last time, he bets the pass line. If they lose the next time, he switches to the don't-pass line.

If you tap this fellow on the shoulder and ask him what he's up to, he will tell you that he's waiting for the streak to begin and once it begins, he's going to ride it. And furthermore, to protect himself, whether the dice go wrong or right, whether the roulette wheel shows red or black, he goes with those events that are actually happening. Does he tie himself down to an inflexible bet at the pass line? No! If the dice are cold, he goes along with the don't-pass line. He's not in love with any bet, he just wants to follow the streaks.

Does he win doing this? Of course not. All he can think about is streaks of wrong bets or right bets, or red or black in long series. What he forgets is that everything is a streak. A streak can be red, black, red, black, red, black, or pass, don't pass, pass, don't pass, etc. And what happens when this occurs? It is the whiplash principle, but instead of a sprained neck, his bank account is fractured and his credit is put on the critical list.

One-Shot Place Number System

This kind of bettor walks to the dice table, bets the maximum on all the place numbers, and, once a number is thrown, collects his bet and walks away a winner. What a system! One bet and a day's pay. Does it work? No. Because, if you look at place-number betting in the chapter on craps, you'll see that the odds are against the bettor by more than 3.22 percent. In reality, every bet on place numbers, when betting all the numbers, is the same as any series of bets. The odds don't vary. That single-place bettor can be hit with a 7 as well as a point or place number, and a series of these, with maximum bets being made, will bankrupt him.

Systems at the Track

The racetrack is the system-player's paradise. For one thing, he can lose his shirt sitting down, with the racing form shielding his lap from the sun. For another, he has a pause between bets of twenty to thirty minutes to watch the race. What better way to nourish the ulcer, pump up the blood pressure, and keep our medical profession in Cadillacs? And with these system players, it is not all cold dice and plastic roulette balls. No, much more interesting, it is living, breathing things, horses. As though any of these men could appreciate a horse as a living thing without a number on it and a starting gate to shove it out of. I wonder how many horseplayers have ever ridden a horse, or fed one, or stroked one. As far as they're concerned, bacteria could be racing around a one-millimeter oval, as long as as there was pari-mutuel betting.

Betting the Favorites

Since favorites come in between thirty-five and thirty-seven percent of the time, on the average, at most tracks around the country, the systems player bets only the favorite in each race. All he wants to make is a living wage, which he estimates at about forty-five to fifty dollars a day. To do this, he wants to win five dollars a race on nine races and keep carrying it over to the next day. There are fifty-four races a week, and he'll thus earn about $270 a week. Not bad pay for doing nothing but taking the train to the track, paying an admission, buying a racing sheet and program, and then sitting there all day and watching the races, rain, shine, snow, or sleet. What a racket!

Yes, some consider this is an ideal way to make a living. The question is, can a living be made this way? Can this system of betting on favorites work? The answer, simply, is no.

For one thing, when we speak about favorites, we speak about odds on horses, three-to-one shots, eight-to-five shots, anything that has the lowest price in a race. To make five dollars a race, the horseplayer would have to add an additional five dollars to his bet for every race he loses. For example:

Race One: The favorite is five to two. A two-dollar bet. A loss.

Race Two: Favorite two to one. To make ten dollars, we have to bet five dollars, but since we lost two dollars in the first race, we have to make twelve dollars. No sweat. We bet six dollars—and lose.

Race Three: Favorite is three to one. Now we have to make fifteen dollars, plus our loss of two dollars, plus six dollars, or twenty-three dollars altogether. We bet eight dollars—and lose.

Race Four: Favorite is even money (one to one). We must make twenty dollars, plus our losses of sixteen dollars, or thirty-six dollars. We lose.

Race Five: Favorite is seven to five. We must make twenty-five dollars, plus our losses of fifty-two dollars, or seventy-seven dollars. We bet fifty-five dollars and lose.

Race Six: Favorite is three to two. We must win thirty dollars, plus our losses. The bet is ninety dollars. We lose.

Race Seven: Aha! The feature race, and the favorite is one to two. A sure thing. Now we'll make up our losses in one fell swoop. We must make thirty-five dollars (seven races times five dollars), plus our losses. Since we have already lost $197 in bets, we must bet $464 on this one to two sure thing. We lose.

Race Eight: Now the favorite is even money. We lost $464 in our last race, plus $197 previously, and must make $40 for a total bet of $701. We make a $700 bet and lose.

Race Nine: The favorite is eight to five. Thank God we're not at a casino where we would be limited to a $500 bet. Here we can make any bet we want, which is $1,000 to make up that $1406. And again we lose. Well, just one of those bad days at the track. Total losses, $2,361. Tomorrow will be different. Tonight we'll sell the car, hock the furniture, and borrow the rest from a shylock, and tomorrow we'll be at the track bright and early, because in the fifth race there's this sure thing . . .

The above horrible example points up the flaw in all the progressive systems. To earn a small amount, the amounts that must be bet become larger and larger. It is quite possible that the next day the favorite will win in the first race, or second race for that matter, but it is one thing to bet $2,500 on paper, and another thing to make a bet of that size on a particular race and then watch the race being run. And after all that aggravation, heartache, and heart-stopping tension, the gambler will be ahead about fifty dollars.

The systems tied to favorites at a race track don't take into account one important aspect in their blind appraisal of a "favorite." A favorite can be a one-to-ten shot or a four-to-one horse. It all depends on the race, the horses the favorite must face, and, most important, why a certain horse is the favorite. To blindly bet favorites is as foolhardy as betting on points at a crap table, with the theory based on the supposition that such and such a percentage of points will be made.

Any fool will realize that the points 4 and 10 will not be made as often as the points 6 and 8, and it could be very possible that by betting a series of 4s and 10s a long losing streak will ensue. The same thing is true at the racetrack. The first calculation that should be made by any serious systems bettor is the breakdown of "favorites." How many win at five to two or higher odds? How many win at two to one, at even money, and odds on? For a further analysis of this factor, see *Horse Race Betting*.

A more dangerous system than betting favorites is betting second choices. The same method of betting is used, with an ideal goal of making five dollars per race. In every race, the second choice is bet to win. Since they come in approximately eighteen percent of the time, there are even longer losing streaks, but the payoff is higher per win than favorites. A second choice, by the very nature of its being a second choice, goes off at higher odds than a favorite.

An old-timer swore to me that he made over $40,000 one season at Saratoga with this kind of progressive system, betting nothing but second choices to win. Of course, how he ever made $40,000 by earning about fifty dollars a day for a thirty-day racing system I'll never understand. I asked the inevitable question: "What happened to that $40,000?" He explained that he deviated from the system at the end and lost it all, but insisted it was surefire. So I tried it in my own fashion, buying the *New York Times* every day, following second choices in the racing section, and calculating on paper just how much I would have won. There were wonderful days of winners, and the streak carried along for a while, until the inevitable losing spell, which lasted almost four full days. Four days! Not only would I have lost all my paltry winnings, but I would have had to mortgage my soul to avoid financial ruin.

Betting the Favorite for Show

Since favorites can only win about thirty-seven percent of the time, why not bet them for show, where they come in a little more than fifty percent of the time? This sounds better, and the bettor will get more winners and have less likelihood of extended losing streaks, but the catch is that the payments for show are often $2.10 to $2.00, or $2.20 or $2.40 for $2.00.

At those low odds, one to twenty to one to five, a fortune has to be bet to have any kind of streak going where you can make some real money.

A gambler I know, using his own skill in handicapping, started with $2,000 and bet it only a couple of times each racing day on favorites he liked for show. He tried to pick only sure things. He went along and won, then raised his original stake to about $6,000 and lost it all on a few bad bets. Betting $2,000 and getting paid $2.20 for $2.00 nets a bettor $200. A hard, dangerous way to win.

The System Players

In one of my visits to the Nevada casinos, I came across a couple of young men who were piling up chips at a roulette game. I sat down, bought a couple of dollars' worth of ten-cent chips, and watched them. They were betting with dollar casino coins and five-dollar chips.

They were a study in contrasts. Both were in their middle or late twenties; one was big and broad with a broad face as well—a plain, honest face; the other was small, intense, given to quick movements. The smaller one had a notebook at his side and, after each spin of the wheel, would tell the other what to bet.

The bigger man, Zeke, watched the wheel impassively, but the shorter one, whose name was Robert, couldn't bear to look at it. He seemed to shrivel up as the wheel spun. The bigger one, however, kept counting the chips, making the bets, and watching the wheel.

From their betting I could see that they were using a cancellation type of system. Many bets would be just one dollar more than the previous bet, a sure sign of that system. I watched them for a little while, lost about forty cents, left the table, and went to play craps. When I went by the table about an hour later, they were still there, and their winnings had mounted considerably.

I waited until they cashed in, then went over to them and started a conversation. They told me they were going to get a buffet supper at the Silver Slipper on the Strip. I offered them a ride, which they accepted. We had one of the $1.49 specials there, a hodgepodge of junk, and the men told me they were from New Jersey and had driven out the other day.

"I notice you have a system," I said.

"You could call it that," Robert answered. He could hardly eat, since the tension of his session at the roulette table was still with him. But Zeke was gobbling down the food and went to get another plateful.

"I know it's a system," I said.

"How do you know?"

"You were making a lot of notations in a book. It was pretty obvious."

"Yeah," said Robert, as Zeke came back to the table, "the croupier asked us about it. I told him nothing. I hate those bastards."

"Why?"

"I just hate them. It's like a war. A battle between them and us."

Zeke and Robert had been in the army together and now were room-mates in Newark, where they both taught school. It was early June, and they had just gotten their summer vacations.

"We were working on this thing for months," said Zeke, who, despite his appearance, was rather soft voiced and articulate. "We got this little roulette wheel, some chips, and practiced. We've been doing it literally for months."

"And it works?"

"It works."

"It always wins?" I asked.

"No," said Robert, "but nothing wins all the time. Actually, to win at anything all you have to do is win fifty-one percent of the time."

"Not at roulette, you don't," I said. "The house advantage is 5.26 percent. If you win fifty-one percent of the time, you'll be a heavy loser."

"I know the odds," said Robert. "They're pretty easy to figure out. But all we have to do is win thirty-five percent of the time at roulette."

"Can I ask you if you're ahead?"

"We're way ahead," said Zeke.

"You really think a system can beat roulette?"

"I know it can," said Robert. "We set a goal for ourselves. We're going to reach it, take off for San Francisco, take a vacation, come back, and work it again."

I was drinking my coffee. They wanted to leave, said something about two girls waiting for them at their motel.

The next day I didn't see them until late in the evening. They were at one of the downtown places, the Fremont, at the roulette table. They had a stack of chips and coins in front of them, but it was difficult to tell if they were winning or losing.

"How's it going?" I asked.

"So, so," said Zeke. Robert was busy writing a whole series of num-bers into the book.

Zeke made a fifty-seven-dollar bet on red. The wheel spun. Black came up.

"Eighty-two," said Robert.

"Eighty-two?"

"Yeah, come on, on red."

Zeke pushed over the chips. Black came up again. He looked over to Robert.

"A hundred and seven. On red."

"Jesus," said Zeke. He counted the chips. "We only got seventy-two."

"Here, then," said Robert, taking out some cash. "Bet it on red."

The wheel spun, the little white ball bouncing around. I looked at Robert's face. He was looking away, his face caught up in a wild grimace. I looked at Zeke. He was not looking at the wheel either. His lips were pressed tightly.

Red came up. Both men sighed in relief. "That's a way, baby," said Zeke.

Their next bet was back down to fifty-nine dollars. They lost it. Now they were betting on black. Another big bet was lost. Then they won, and lost two more. Their last bet was for $154. They couldn't seem to reduce their bets in the system.

They again tensed up, waited. All the money was on black. The wheel spun, the ball gobbled about. Boom!

"Double zero," said the croupier, impassively raking in the chips. He had wiped out the two young men.

"Come on," I said. "How about dinner at the Desert Inn?"

"I'm not hungry," said Robert. Zeke wasn't hungry either. He excused himself and ran to the bathroom.

We went to a bar instead, over at the Golden Nugget. Over scotches we talked.

"We're still ahead," said Robert, the liquor relaxing and loosening him up a little.

"About a thousand," said Zeke.

"No, not that much. About eight hundred."

"You must have really been ahead," I said.

"A little over two thousand."

"What was your goal?"

"Five thousand."

"How do you feel about the system now?"

"I don't know," said Robert. "It worked for us in Jersey."

"You're using a cancellation system, aren't you?"

Robert looked surprised. "How did you know?"

"From the betting. Are you using a 1-2-3?"

"Yeah."

"That's pretty steep."

"Yeah, we just realized it tonight."

"When you're winning, it's easy," I said.

"We got to win. We only have to win about thirty-five percent to be ahead."

"But you can't afford really bad streaks, Robert," I said. "You have to get wiped out sooner or later with 5.26 percent against you." I suggested the dice tables and 1.41 percent.

"I can't think clearly there. I look conspicuous with my book."

"Then why don't you quit?"

"We can beat it, man."

"You're ahead. That's beating it."

They told me they'd be at the Flamingo the next day, and I met them there and watched them play. Within an hour they were up to about $1500 in winnings. Then the tide turned. Their bets increased. They ended up with six out of seven losing bets, each one over $200. They went completely down the drain and lost all their winnings. They got up, their backs drenched with sweat despite the air conditioning.

I treated them to lunch at the Desert Inn, then we walked out and sat near the pool, watching the lovelies lounging around.

"It's a bad scene, man," said Robert.

"You can't win with that system," I said.

"I want to change it to 1-2, maybe 1-1. I can win with 1-1."

"Any cancellation system is going to bury you," I said.

"We're giving it one more try this afternoon."

I took them back to the motel. I felt that perhaps I was unlucky for them, so, though I knew they were trying the Sands, I didn't meet them. That night I went to their motel to ask how they made out. They had checked out. There was no note.

XX

Chess

Introduction

"Chess," wrote the Russian master, Tarrasch, "like women, like music, has the power to make men happy."

Chess does have that power, as is attested to by its popularity and the hold it has on its devoted players. It is a simple game to learn and can be taught to a child, but the ability to play well, to make the best moves, can only come through a profound study of the game.

Unlike all the card games, chess is a game of pure skill. Some authors who have played contract bridge on a professional level have likened bridge to chess, but there can be no such comparison. Bridge is a partnership game; chess is the supreme individual effort. In rubber bridge, the players are dependent upon good cards. A series of bad hands and even the best players in the world must lose. In duplicate bridge, in which skill manifests itself more clearly, percentages and odds are still important. Suit "breaks" often determine the winner.

But chess has none of these chancy elements. Chess is played on an open board, with all the pieces in view to both players at all times. There are no hidden pieces involved, no percentages, no odds. The more skillful player will invariably beat the less skillful one. Of course, players have their off moments, or occasionally play inferior games for whatever reason, in which case an inferior player may occasionally beat a stronger player. But when one loses, it is not by luck. There is absolutely no luck involved in chess.

Of all the games that can be played between two players, in my estimation chess is the best. When two players of equal strength, who have given some study to the game, play a game or a match, their absorption is total. There is the chessboard and there are the pieces. And the opponent. Nothing else intervenes; no extrinsic situations intrude.

One other factor may exist, but even this involves the player's skill. The introduction of a chess clock, limiting the time in which players must make a predetermined number of moves, certainly has had an impact on the game. Before the introduction of the chess clock, a player could win sometimes by just sitting tight, or, as the Germans express it, having superior *sitzfleisch*. His exasperated opponent could do nothing but wait for the next move, and might resign in disgust.

The chess clock, however, gives both players an equal amount of time to make their moves, usually forty moves in two and a half hours, although the number of moves may vary, depending upon the match or the tournament. Many players run into desperate time pressure during a game, for they know that if they do not make the required number of moves within the time limit imposed, they automatically lose the game.

I believe that one of the reasons that chess has such allure to the players of the game is its history. By "history" I don't mean in what country it was first played, or the origin of the pieces. I mean, rather, the history of the modern game; its players, its champions, its greats and near greats.

When a player sits down at the chessboard, he has before him a standard number of standard pieces in their standard positions, the same setup that confronts all the great players. He is not dependent on a bad shuffle of cards or a poor hand, and only his knowledge and skill will determine whether or not he will win. If he understands the game and its profundities; if he has studied the openings, knows the positional strength of certain moves; if he can think in terms of space and time, he will be prepared for his opponent.

Thus, any player, with enough study combined with a certain type of intelligence, has the potential to be a world champion. The kind of intelligence necessary has never been truly defined. Certainly, the ability to perceive spatial relationships is part of it, and many of the great players were mathematicians and engineers.

Of course, we know that a great deal more is needed. But in the basic sense, the game is all before the player's eyes, and theoretically, taking into consideration the time element of the clock, all possibilities may be made absolutely clear.

Of course, man in not a mere machine. A man, with all his intelligence, perception, memory, and skill, is still only a man. And being a man, he is not perfect and must make mistakes, whether they be outright blunders or slight misjudgments of position. And that, too, is part of the lure of the game. The search for perfection in chess will always go on; no matter how strong the player, he knows he can be still better. The game is there at all times, opening new vistas, new challenges, new opportunities.

As was mentioned before, when a player sits down at the board, he carries with him the whole history of the great names of chess. Any standard opening that he may make bears with it the full weight of chess thought and history. It is a game with great traditions, and these traditions manifest themselves in every move. It is a game in which one must study the past. Without the past in chess, as in life, the present is meaningless.

One cannot then, merely approach the game and say, "Well, I have learned the moves, I know the openings, I know how to mate the opposing king. That is enough." One must, instead, immerse oneself in the game, in its history, in the history of its great players, their games and ideas. Without this background, a player can only develop so far.

Chess, as a game of pure skill, is a game of ideas. The average beginner will have little conception of the four principles that govern the game. These are time, space, pawn power, and force.

Essentially, time in chess is measured by tempo. A player may gain or lose a tempo by his play. If he develops a piece and attacks an enemy piece at the same time, he gains a tempo, since he is accomplishing two things at once. Likewise, his opponent loses a tempo, because he must defend the attacked piece and postpone development of his offense for a move. Time is a crucial factor in chess, and often the only difference between winning and losing is an extra tempo.

Space in chess is basically the sixty-four squares of the board. This is the ultimate measurement, and the player controlling the greatest area of the board is said to command more space. It is, like time, an essential element. The player with space can expand, attack, and control, while the player with less space must be constricted, underdeveloped, tied down, and in a purely defensive position.

Pawn power is the strength of one's pawn position and its ultimate use in the end game (the stage of the game following serious reduction of forces). Pawns, which are rather dormant defensive pieces through most of the game, come into their own in the end game, where they are a constant threat because of their inherent ability to be queened. Without an appreciation of their power, a player might find himself helpless against their threats.

Force is the ability to cause an opponent to make a predetermined move or series of moves. This is done usually by direct threats, forcing the opponent to meet these threats. Generally, a player who has command of time and space is in a position to create the force necessary to secure the win.

A Short History of the Great Players

Although the first analyst of the game was Ruy Lopez de Segura, who lived in the sixteenth century, the first really profound thinker in chess was François Philodor, whose book *Analyse des Eschecs* was published in 1749. The modern era of chess is said to have begun with him.

It was not until the nineteenth century that a series of great players came to the fore. Although the English and French had representatives among the premier players, an American, Paul Morphy, emerged on the European chess scene in the mid-1800s and completely overwhelmed all the other players. Born of wealthy parents in New Orleans, he took up chess at an early age and at the age of twenty-three was no doubt the strongest player in the world. He crushed all those he played.

Morphy was the ideal romantic player, forceful and brilliant. He swept all honors and was the unofficial champion of the world. Then, at the height of his career, he suddenly returned to the United States, gave up chess completely, and eventually went insane. All this within the span of a few years. Truly, he was a meteor that had burned out. But the impact he had on the game will always be remembered. Although by today's standards his opponents played poorly, his games are full of brilliancies, profound ideas, and daring skills.

Toward the end of the nineteenth century, Wilhelm Steinitz, a German who had studied the game carefully and played what is known today as "positional chess," emerged as the strongest player in the world. He moved chess away from the wild gambits and fierce attacks popularized by Morphy, and instead looked at the game as a positional struggle, in which the player who commanded space had the advantage. To get this advantage, placement of pieces, rather than attacking moves, was all-important.

Steinitz eventually lost his title to Emanuel Lasker in 1894. Lasker also was German, a mathematician by profession. He won the title at an early age, twenty-five, and was a great champion, able to hold his own against the strongest players of his era, which lasted from the end of the nineteenth century all the way into the 1930s. In the 1935 Moscow tournament, he finished undefeated against a generation of the strongest players in the world, many of whom had not yet been born at the time he won his championship.

Lasker published little. His games were not marked so much by brilliance as by soundness, and he carried Steinitz' conception of positional play to its ultimate end. He was champion for twenty-eight years, finally losing, in 1921, to another great champion, the Cuban José Raoul Capablanca. Capablanca was cool and assured, amassing a brilliant record that may never be surpassed. Many authorities consider him to be the greatest player who ever played the game.

While still a student at Columbia University in New York, he challenged the brilliant American champion, Frank Marshall, to a match. Marshall, an experienced player at the highest levels of competition, was the overwhelming favorite, but was completely crushed by Capablanca, eight to one. Thereafter Capablanca was invited to an international tournament and won easily. In the greatest tournament held up to that point, the 1914 tournament in St. Petersburg, he played an epic game against Lasker, who was a half point behind Capablanca in the final round. Lasker, by psychological cunning and skill, beat Capablanca and won the tournament.

Then the war intervened. After the war, Capablanca amassed one of the most fabulous records ever. For five years he did not lose a game, while playing against the greatest players of his time in match and tournament play. He won the title from Lasker in 1921 by winning four games, losing none, and drawing thirteen.

In 1924, another great tournament was held, this time in New York. Among the participants were the champion Capablanca, the former champion Lasker, and the future world champion, Alexander Alekhine. Capablanca lost his first game in five years in this tournament, to Richard Reti, and finished second to Lasker. Alekhine was third.

In 1927, Alekhine challenged Capablanca for the world championship and defeated him. Alekhine had studied for years for this match, while Capablanca, who was known as the "chess machine," did not take Alekhine seriously. Up to that match, Alekhine had never defeated him.

After Capablanca lost his title, Alekhine never gave him the opportunity to regain it, which is one of the low points of championship chess.

Alekhine lost his title in 1935 to the Dutch champion, Max Euwe, but regained it again in 1937. He held the title from then until his death in 1946. He died in a Lisbon rooming house, in disgrace, having allegedly collaborated with the Germans during the Second World War.

After the war, a tournament was held in 1948 to determine the new champion. It was won easily by Michael Botvinnik. He held the title for a short while, lost it to Vassily Smyslov, regained it, lost to Mikhail Tal, and thereafter a succession of Russian players held it. Today another Russian, Boris Spassky, is the world champion.

Meanwhile, the American, Robert (Bobby) Fischer, has made his mark in world chess. An international grandmaster at fourteen (the youngest ever), he established himself first as the best player in the United States, and then in the world. However, he would not compete in the Interzonal Tournaments for personal reasons after failing in one of them. Since the Interzonals are held to determine a challenger for the world champion, it was not until 1971, finally competing again, that Fischer won the tournament and was able to enter the final matches to determine the challenger.

After the tournament victory, Fischer beat two of the greatest players in the world, Mark Taimonov of the Soviet Union and Bent Larsen of Denmark, by identical scores of six to zero, a feat unprecedented in the history of chess at that high level. He then beat Tigran Petrosian easily in the final match before the world championship battle with Boris Spassky.

This match was held in Iceland in the spring of 1972 and was marked by complications and tense moments when Fischer threatened to withdraw because of playing conditions. But in the end he destroyed Spassky and was world champion.

In 1975, however, because of a dispute with the Fédération Internationale des Échecs (FIDE) or World Chess Federation on very minor matters of scoring, Fischer refused to defend his title against the legitimate challenger, Anatoly Karpov, and forfeited his title. Since that time he has not been seen in public, nor has Fischer played tournament or match chess on any recognized level. Perhaps the greatest genius the game has ever known simply dropped out of sight and to all purposes ended his brilliant chess career.

Karpov took the title by forfeiture, defended it twice against Victor Korchnoi, then, in a controversial match with Gary Kasparov in 1984, defended it yet again. Leading by a score of five to nothing, needing but one more victory to retain his title, Karpov faltered, then tired. When the match stood at five to three in his favor, with Kasparov having won the last two games, Florencio Campomanes, the Filipino president of the FIDE, in a strange move, stopped the match. At this point there had been forty draws and the match had lasted five months.

Controversy swirled over this action, but both men met again in the fall of 1985. Kasparov decisively beat Karpov and emerged as the new champion, but was obligated to defend his title within a year against the ex-champion. They battled for the crown again in 1986. After Kasparov took a decisive lead of three points, Karpov battled back in the middle of the match to tie it, but Kasparov then once again took the lead for the final time, and retained his title by a narrow margin.

Gary Kasparov, twenty-three, is half Armenian and half Jewish and a citizen of the Soviet Union. He is a dynamic and adventurous player, unlike Karpov, whose reputation for caution and careful play made his games seem pedantic and boring. Certainly Kasparov with his dashing style, both on the chessboard and in life, has brought a breath of fresh air to this ancient game.

The Game

Players: Two.

Equipment: A chessboard consisting of sixty-four squares, alternating between dark and light squares, with a light square in the lower right-hand corner. Each horizontal row of the board is called a *rank*; each vertical row is called a *file*. The diagonals are utilized as well.

The only other equipment are the pieces, or men. Each player has sixteen. There are eight pawns ♟ , two rooks ♜ , two knights ♞ , two bishops ♝ , one queen ♛ , and one king ♚ .

The next illustration shows the positions of the chessmen on the board at the outset of a game, before the first move has been made. Note that the queen is always placed on the square of her own color (black queen on black square).

The Moves of the Chessmen

Pawns: There are eight pawns on each side, occupying the second rank. Each pawn can advance one or two ranks on the initial move; thereafter they can only advance one rank at a time. A pawn, in advancing, can only move in a straight line on the particular file it occupies.

Although a pawn can advance in a straight line only, it can take another piece or pawn only on the diagonal. Thus, in the following illustration, the pawns are blockaded; they cannot advance, nor can either capture the other, since a pawn can only take diagonally.

In the next illustration, either pawn may capture the other, since each opposing pawn is on the other's diagonal.

The pawn is unique in that although it moves forward on a straight line, it can only capture or take diagonally. A pawn, moving diagonally, can capture any piece on the board. It is also the only piece that can only move forward. It cannot retreat.

A pawn can also capture another pawn *en passant*. If a pawn has advanced to the fifth rank, it can take an enemy pawn that, on its initial move, advances two ranks, thus moving past the sixth rank, where it would have been in take.

Although the pawn has limited power during the opening and middle game, its full strength comes in the end game, for if a pawn is moved to the eighth rank it can be *queened*. This means that it can be exchanged for a queen, and has the full power of a queen from that move on. It can also be exchanged for any other piece, except a king, whether or not a similar piece is in play, but it cannot remain as a pawn on the eighth rank.

In end games, with this potential power, the specter of a passed pawn, a pawn on its way to the eighth rank to be queened, very often determines the strategy of both players.

Rook: Often called a castle, but in the English notation, it is given the symbol *R*, for rook. They come in pairs.

A rook can move in any direction, either on a file or on a rank, in a straight line, traversing the entire length of the board on one move if it wishes, so long as the file or rank is open. It can, like all the other pieces except the knight, be blockaded by its own men or enemy men. If it is blocked by an opposing piece or pawn, it may move into that square and take the enemy piece. See illustration for the possible moves of a rook.

The rook is akin to an artillery piece, best used at the rear since it controls an entire file or rank. One of the strategical aspects of chess concerns the opening of files and the placement of the rook in that open file to control it. The rook is a very powerful piece, second only to the queen.

Bishop: The bishops, like the rooks, come in pairs. However, as can be seen by the next illustration, each player has one "white" and one "black" bishop; that is, one bishop operating on light squares, and one operating on dark squares.

Since a bishop can only move on a diagonal, it is important, especially in an end game, to know the diagonal squares it controls. For example, if a pawn is moving to the eighth rank and is on a light square, and the white enemy bishop is operative, it can effectively control that pawn. But if the bishop operates on the dark squares, it may be powerless to stop the pawn.

The following shows the potential movement of a bishop.

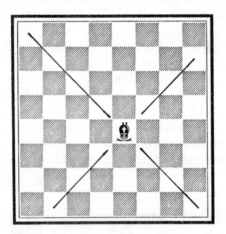

Queen: The queen is the most powerful piece at the disposal of the chess player. It combines the power of the rook and the bishop and, combining their power, is greater than both of them together. Whereas the rook is limited to moving on files and ranks in straight lines, and the bishop on diagonals, the queen can move both on files, ranks, and diagonals. And unlike each bishop, she can move on both dark and light diagonals. The queen is thus the most potent piece in the game. Like the rook, she is often not moved at the beginning of a game, since her power may be more effectively used to control files, ranks, and diagonals. The following is an illustration of the potential moves of the queen.

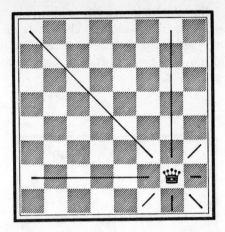

King: The king, like the queen, can move diagonally on a rank or file, but he can only move one square at a time. This gives the king limited mobility and makes him vulnerable to attack.

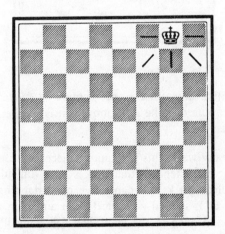

If any other piece is captured by the enemy, the game may still go on. If the king is captured, however, the game is over. The whole purpose of chess is to remove or take the opposing king. When any other piece is threatened with capture, the opponent need not be made aware of the threat. But a player, by custom, should be warned if his king is threatened. When a king is directly attacked, the player threatening to take the king should call out "Check."

When a king is attacked and cannot escape, it is "checkmate." The game is over. The next illustration shows a checkmate of a king. Note that he is checked by the queen, and there is no free space within one square into which he could move to escape her. Nor can either pawn be placed between her and the king.

The king, unlike any other piece, cannot be moved into a position where he will be captured. If he is so moved, it is an illegal move, and the move must be taken back.

Knight: In many ways, this is a unique piece, and the knight gives the game of chess that extra tension that makes it so difficult to fully master. Unlike all other pieces, a knight can move over standing men. Its moves may be described as L-shaped—forward once and then twice to the side, or twice forward and once to the side. The following illustration demonstrates the possibilities of a knight's move. The knight is able to capture all of the pawns in the illustration. It does not, however, capture any men it may pass over in the process—only the man it displaces.

Castling: This is the term used to describe the process of bringing a king into safety. The rule is: When the king and the rook have not yet moved; when there are no pieces on the same rank between them; and when no enemy piece is attacking any of the squares through which the king must move to castle, castling is permitted.

Castling is a regular move; after one player castles, his opponent then has the next move. Castling can be done with either the queen's or king's rook. The following illustration shows the position of the pieces immediately preceding castling on the king's side, and then the castled position.

In the next illustration, we see the final position after a queenside castling.

Notation Systems

There are two common notation systems in effect throughout the world.

Algebraic System: Used outside the United States and Great Britain. The board is marked as follows:

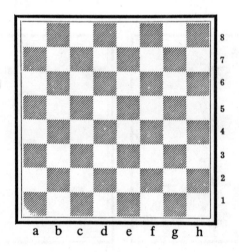

The pieces are listed as follows:

K	King	R	Rook	N	Knight
Q	Queen	B	Bishop		

The pawns are simply their position on the board. For example, the pawn move at the outset by the King's pawn, moved two spaces, would be e4. If the pawn moved forward one more space, it would be listed simply at e5.

Thus the first two moves of the Ruy Lopez would be listed as follows:

1. e4   e5

When a piece or pawn is taken, the first notation is the taker of the piece or pawn. If it were a rook, then it would be listed as R. If the rook took a bishop on c6, the listing would be simply Rxc6. The square is used rather than the piece or pawn taken.

Check is listed as a +. Thus a queen check might be Qc8+. This means that the White queen on the c8 square gave check to the Black king.

Since the algebraic system of notation is more precise and has become the standard notation system, it is the one we'll use throughout this section on chess.

Other notations using the algebraic system:

O-O   Kingside castle
O-O-O   Queenside castle

Pawn takes pawn en passant (e.p.).
A strong or best move is marked by !
A brilliant move is !!
A poor move is ?
A very poor or losing move is ??
A speculative move is !? or ?!

English or Descriptive System

This has been superseded by the algebraic system, but since many older books still have the system, we'll describe it thoroughly so that the reader can fully understand it.

Each piece has a particular symbol. They are as follows, under the English system of notation:

King   = K
Queen = Q
Rook   = R
Bishop = B
Knight = N (preferable) or Kt (little used today)
Pawn   = P

In the English notation system, each file belongs to a particular piece. For example, there is the queen rook's file, the queen's file, the king bishop's file. Counting the back row or rank as 1, the ranks are numbered from 1 to 8. The ranks are numbered according to the particular color of the pieces. For example, White's back rank is White rank 1, but is Black rank 8. See illustration.

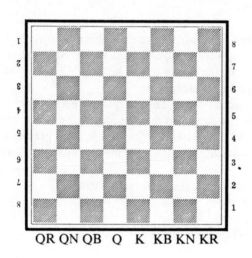

QR QN QB Q   K KB KN KR

Each move is numbered in the notation system. Since White makes the first move, that is 1. In this way an entire game can be studied, move by move.

Additional Notations

When a pawn or piece takes an opposing pawn or piece, the notation is marked by an x. Knight takes pawn would be marked as follows: NxP.

A check is ch.

Castling kingside is O-O.

Castling queenside is O-O-O.

Pawn takes pawn *en passant* is PxP e.p.

A best or unexpectedly best move is marked by ! after the move. Example: QxP!

A poor or weak move is marked by a ?. Example: NxP?.

A move with speculative possibilities that are not easy to immediately fathom is marked !?. Example: R-K1!?.

Notating a Game

When a game is reported, usually the opening used is placed at the head of the column, followed by the colors and names of the players. For example, a notated game might look like this after the first few moves:

RUY LOPEZ
WHITE: Smith   BLACK: Jones
1. e4   e5
2. Nf3   Nc6
3. Bb5   a6

Let's follow the first three moves of each player to follow the notation system.

1. e4 is the king's pawn moving to the fourth rank. 1. . . . e5 is the Black's king pawn moving up two spaces as well.

2. Nf3 is the king's bishop moving to the square f3, attacking the Black king's pawn at e5. 2. . . . Nc6 is the Black queen's knight moving to the square c6 to protect the king's pawn at e5.

3. Bb5 is the White king's bishop pinning the Black queen's knight. 3. . . . a6 is the queen's rook's pawn moving up one square to attack the White bishop, forcing it to either retreat or take the knight.

The Center

The initial struggle in a chess game takes place in the center, as a general rule, although there are openings which put off the struggle for the center until a later period. But the center cannot be permanently ceded without a poor and possibly losing position.

Theoretically, the center consists of the third to sixth ranks on the king's and queen's files. See illustration.

Rules of Play

1. The first move is made by White, and thereafter each player alternates, one move at a time.

2. The object of the game is to capture the enemy king. Once a king is checkmated, the game ends.

3. A player need not wait until he is checkmated to lose. He may resign at any time during the game, at which point he loses and the game ends.

4. A piece or pawn is captured by an opposing piece or pawn moving into the square the piece or pawn occupies. After a piece or pawn is captured it is removed from the game.

5. A pawn that reaches the eighth rank must be replaced by another piece, other than a king. This is called queening, or pawn promotion.

6. In non-tournament or match games, each player may have unlimited time to make his moves, unless the players, by prearrangement, decide otherwise. If time is to be measured, a chess clock is to be employed. In tournament and match games, a definite time limit is imposed, usually forty moves in the first two or two and a half hours of play.

7. A game may be "drawn" if agreed to between the players. It is a drawn game if there is not sufficient material for either player to force a win. A game is automatically drawn if there is a stalemate. A stalemate occurs when the king alone can move, and, while not in check, all of its moves would put it in check.

A draw can be claimed by either player if there is a perpetual check, if the same position is repeated three times in succession, or if during fifty consecutive moves no capture has been made and no pawn has moved.

8. In tournament or match games, under official rules, a player who has touched a pawn or piece of his own must move it. If he touches an opposing piece or pawn, he must take it if legally possible. If a player touches several men, his opponent has the option of choosing which piece or pawn is to be moved.

A player may adjust his pieces without penalty, however, providing that he first informs his opponent by saying "J'adoube," or "I adjust."

9. A move that is completed may not be retracted. A move is complete when the player removes his hand from the piece or pawn moved; or, if an opposing piece or pawn is captured, when it is removed from the board.

10. If an illegal move is made, the move must be retracted upon demand by the opposing player, and another legal move made with the same piece, if possible. If the illegal move was a capture, the capture must be made legally, if possible.

11. Should a position be reached due to an illegal move that was not

retracted, the position should be adjusted to that which existed prior to the illegal move, and the game should then continue from that point.

The Openings

A detailed knowledge of the openings is essential in chess. The greatest players have always concentrated on the openings, since such study saved them precious time in deciding the best moves over the board during a game. Today's grandmasters' knowledge of openings is almost complete, and many games between players of world class reputation follow established lines, the first ten moves of which take no more than a few minutes to complete.

A player should acquaint himself at the outset with the major openings used today: The Ruy Lopez, the Sicilian, and the French Defenses among the King's Pawn openings; and the Queen's Gambit and Queen's Pawn games among the Queen's Pawn openings. Thereafter, he may branch out into other openings, used less frequently. As White, he should concentrate on a few openings that he knows thoroughly and that suit his style.

He may be an attacking player and play the Ruy Lopez, or he may prefer a purely positional game, in which case the Queen's Gambit would be more suitable. The openings presented in this section will be the more popular ones—the standard ones used in tournament play today.

The opening moves will be shown in both algebraic and English notations, but thereafter, the variations will be listed in the algebraic notation, which is now the standard notation for chess games, used worldwide.

Openings in Which the First Move Is 1. e4 (P-K4)
RUY LOPEZ

This opening gives White a lasting initiative, and at one time was the most popular of all chess openings in master play. Because of this initiative, Black can avoid defending against this ancient opening by making a move other than 1. . . . e5. In fact, the whole point of the Sicilian Defense, with its first reply 1. . . . c5, is avoiding the passive defense that Black is often delegated to, instead allowing counterattacking possibilities.

The modern use of the Ruy Lopez, as far as Black is concerned, has to do with Morphy's move, 3. . . . a6. This pressure on the attacking White bishop is by far the best third move available to Black.

The standard opening moves are:

1. e4	e5	1. P-K4	P-K4
2. Nf3	Nc6	2. N-KB3	N-QB3
3. Bb5		3. B-N5	

Variations:
Morphy Defense: 3. . . . a6
Modern Steinitz Defense: 3. . . . a6 4. Ba4 d6
Closed Defense: 3. . . . a6 4. Ba4 Nf6 5. O-O Be7 6. Rel b5
Tarrasch or Open Defense: 3. . . . a6 4. Ba4 Nf6 5. O-O Nxe4

SICILIAN DEFENSE

This defense, beginning with the move c5 on the part of Black, is considered Black's best answer to White's opening move, e4. There are several modern variations of the Sicilian used in present-day grandmaster games, notably the Najdorf, the Taimonov, and the Richter-Rauzer Attack. Both the Taimonov and Najdorf were great favorites with Robert Fischer, and are currently used by the new champion, Gary Kasparov. The Richter-Rauzer Attack was very much in evidence during the Spassky-Fischer world championship match in 1972.

Against the Dragon Variation, Fischer had relied upon the Yugoslav Attack, with strong results. The Sicilian is a fighting defense, which allows the Black player to counterattack, putting pressure on the White queen's file.

The standard opening moves are:

1. e4	c5	1. P-K4	P-QB4
2. Nf3		2. N-KB3	

Variations:
Najdorf: 2. . . . d6 3. d4 cxd4 4. Nxd4 Nf6 5. Nc3 a6
Taimonov: 2. . . . e6 3. d4 cxd4 4. Nxd4 Nc6 5. Nb5 d6
Paulsen: 2. . . . e6 3. d4 cxd4 4. Nxd4 Nc6 5. Nc3 d6
Scheveningen: 2. . . . d6 3. d4 cxd4 4. Nxd4 Nf3 5. Nc3 e6
Dragon (Yugoslav Attack): 2. . . . d6 3. d4 cxd4 4. Nxd4 Nf6 5. Nc3 g6 6. Be3 Bg7 7. f3 Nc6 8. Qd2 O-O 9. Bc4
Richter-Rauzer Attack: 2. Nf3 Nc6 3. d4 cxd4 4. Nxd4 Nf6 5. Nc3 d6 6. Bg5 e6

FRENCH DEFENSE

This is a classical closed opening, which was much favored by Botvinnik, the former world champion, as well as by Viktor Korchnoi, who recognized its possibilities as a solid defense.

However, it is defensive from the beginning and leaves the Black defender with a cramped position.

The standard opening moves are:

1. e4	e6	1. P-K4	P-K3
2. d4	d5	2. P-Q4	P-Q4
3. Nc3	Nf6	3. N-QB3	N-KB3

Variations:
Classical: 4. Bg5 Be7 5. e5 Nd7 6. Bxe7 Qxe7
Winawer: 3. . . . Bb4 4. e5 c5 5. a3 Bxc3 6. bxc3 Ne2

Other King Pawn Openings

There are a great many openings, some regular and most irregular, beginning with the first move, e4 (P-K4). The following are the more interesting, showing but the main opening moves. For a more formal study of openings, it is strongly recommended that the reader study the latest edition of *Modern Chess Openings*.

The following openings all begin with e4, e5 (P-K4, P-K4):

GIUCCO PIANO

It is a strong attacking opening, and its variation, the Evans Gambit, was once feared at all levels of play. Today it is little seen in opening repertories of grandmasters, but it is a favorite of chess hustlers, who love its steamrolling possibilities against players who are unfamiliar with correct defense.

The standard opening moves are:

2. Nf3	Nc6	2. N-KB3	N-QB3
3. Bc4	Bc5	3. B-B4	B-B4
4. c3	Nf6	4. P-B3	N-B3
5. d4	exd4	5. P-Q4	PxP
6. cxd4		6. PxP	

EVANS GAMBIT (VARIATION OF GIUCCO PIANO)

Another favorite of chess hustlers. This strong attacking opening can easily crush those unfamiliar with correct defense.

The standard opening moves are:

2. Nf3	Nc6	2. N-KB3	N-QB3
3. Bc4	Bc5	3. B-B4	B-B4
4. b4	Bxb4	4. P-QN4	BxP
5. c3	Ba5	5. P-B3	B-R4
6. d4		6. P-Q4	

ALEKHINE'S DEFENSE

This opening was named after the great world champion Alexander Alekhine, who introduced it into master practice in Budapest in 1921. Although it was immensely popular for a while, especially with the hypermodern school of masters, it is little used today. Fischer has, however, taken advantage of its exploitation of White's extended center with some notable wins, and chess hustlers sometimes use it against weaker players, enticing their White pawns into indefensible positions.

The standard opening moves are:

1.	Nf6	1.	N-KB3
2. e5	Nd5	2. P-K5	N-Q4
3. c4	Nc6	3. P-QB4	N-N3
4. d4	d6	4. P-Q4	P-Q3
5. f4		5. P-B4	

Openings in Which the First Move Is d4 (P-Q4)

For a long time after its introduction in the fifteenth century, the use of the queen's pawn as an opening move was held in disrepute, being considered irregular, unusual, and not quite correct.

For many years it was considered a move made only by the most cautious of chess players. That fallacy no longer exists, however, and the first move of the queen's pawn is the most popular opening move in most grandmasters' repertories. In the last world championship match between Kasparov and Karpov, the majority of openings were d4. It is highly recommended that the reader acquaint himself or herself with openings beginning d4 in order to get a well-balanced game.

Most players at the grandmaster level open either d4 or e4, depending upon the opposition. However, Bobby Fischer throughout his long and controversial chess career considered d4 inferior, and rarely used it, though he knew how to defend against it. He was a notable exception among players of the highest order, many of whom rely on the d4 opening move.

Queen's Gambit Declined

This is still one of the most popular of all openings, for it gives White a strong initiative and poses problems for the Black player's queen's bishop. The opening has been analyzed and reanalyzed by generations of players, but still maintains a dynamic interest.

Although it is called a gambit opening, meaning that a pawn is sacrificed at the beginning, in effect there is no true sacrifice, for White can easily regain the pawn. The Queen's Gambit Declined is still a great favorite with most of the modern leading masters, in its several variations. The standard opening moves are:

1. d4	d5	1. P-Q4	P-Q4
2. c4		2. P-QB4	

Variations:

Orthodox: 2. . . . e6 3. Nc3 Nf6 4. Bg5 Be7 5. e3 O-O 6. Nf3 Nbd7

Exchange: 2. . . . e6 3. Nc3 Nf6 4. Bg5 Nbd7 5. cxd5 exd5 6. e3

Tarrasch: 2. . . . e6 3. Nc3 c5 4. cxd5 exd5 5. Nf3 Nc6 6. b3 Nf6 7. Bb2 Be7 8. O-O O-O

Ragozin: 2. . . . e6 3. Nc3 Nf6 4. Nf3 Bb4

Treated separately are the variations of the Queen's Gambit Declined that form the Slav and Semi-Slav Defenses. Whereas the previous variations utilize the move 2. . . . c6. This move eventually frees the queen's bishop, and was used by Tal and Petrosian, among other grandmasters. The main variations are:

Slav: 2. . . . c6 3. Nf3 Nf6 4. Nc3 dxc4 5. a4 Bf5 6. e3 e6 7. Bxc4 Bb4 8. O-O O-O 9. Qd3

Semi-Slav (Meran): 2. . . . c6 3. Nf3 Nf6 4. Nc3 e6 5. e3 Nbd7 6. Bd3 dxc4

Anti-Meran Gambit: 2. . . . c6 3. Nf3 Nf6 4. Nc3 e6 5. Bg5 dxc4 6. e4 b4

Queen's Gambit Accepted

The immediate acceptance of the White's queen's bishop's pawn by Black, although it takes away Black's own center pawn, allows Black to advance his queenside pawns while White is wasting tempo recovering the lost pawn.

The standard moves are:

1. d4	d5	1. P-Q4	P-Q4
2. c4	dxc4	2. P-QB4	PxP
3. Nf3	Nf6	3. N-KB3	N-KB3

Queen's Indian Defense

This opening was popularized by the hypermodern school, and especially the late master Nimzowitsch. The purpose of this opening, which Black uses to fianchetto on his queen's side, is to control the square e4 with both Black's queen's bishop and king's knight.

The standard opening moves are:

1. d4	Nf6	1. P-Q4	N-KB3
2. c4	e6	2. P-QB4	P-K3
3. Nf3	b7	3. N-KB3	P-QN3
4. g3	Bb7	4. P-KN3	B-N2
5. Bg2	Be7	5. B-N2	B-K2
6. O-O	O-O	6. O-O	O-O

Nimzo-Indian Defense

This defense is named after Nimzowitsch, who wrote of it in his monumental work *My System*. It exerts indirect pressure on the White center, and the move 3. . . . Bc4 is an attempt by Black to prevent White's e4 as well as open a counterattack.

The standard opening moves are:

1. d4	Nf6	1. P-Q4	N-KB3
2. c4	e6	2. P-QB4	P-K3
3. Nc3	Bc4	3. N-QB3	B-N5

Rubenstein Variation:

4. e3 O-O 5. Bd3 d5 6. Nf3 c5

King's Indian Defense

This defense leads to complicated struggles in which White's strength is on the queen's side, and Black has the edge on the king's side. The main feature of this opening is the fianchetto of the king's bishop, without any attempt on Black's part to stop White's e4.

The standard opening moves are:

1. d4	Nf6	1. P-Q4	N-KB3
2. c4	g6	2. P-QB4	P-KN3
3. Nc3	Bg7	3. N-QB3	B-N2

Samisch Variation:
4. e4 d6 5. f3 O-O 6. Be3

Classical Line:
4. e4 d6 5. Nf3 O-O 6. Be2 e5 7. O-O Nc6

Queen's Pawn Games

This term describes openings that begin with d4 (P-Q4) without moving into the Queen's Gambit or the Indian Systems. The Modern

Benoni and the Grünfeld Defense have both had a resurgence because of Fischer's important victories using these defenses.

MODERN BENONI

The main idea behind this defense is to allow White to advance his center pawns and occupy the center, so that Black can later attack these vulnerable outposts.

The standard opening moves are:

1. d4	Nf6	1. P-Q4	N-KB3
2. c4	c5	2. P-QB4	P-B4
3. d5	e6	3. P-Q5	P-K3
4. Nc3	exd5	4. N-QB3	PxP
5. cxd5	d6	5. PxP	P-Q3
6. Nf3	g6	6. N-B3	P-QN3
7. e4	Bg7	7. P-K4	B-N2

GRÜNFELD DEFENSE

Like the Modern Benoni, this defense, invented by the Austrian master Ernst Grünfeld, encourages White to storm the center, only to be attacked later on. Fischer was an important exponent of this defense.

The standard opening moves are:

1. d4	Nf6	1. P-Q4	N-KB3
2. c4	g6	2. P-QB4	P-KN3
3. Nc3	d5	3. N-QB3	P-Q4

Bf4 Variation:
4. Bf4 Bg7 5. e3 c5 6. dxc5 Qa5

Exchange Variation:
4. cxd5 Nxd5 5. e4 Nxc3 bxc3

Smyslov Variation:
4. Nf3 Bg7 5. Qb3 dxc4 6. Qxc4 O-O 7. e4 Bg4 8. Be3 Nbd7

Tactical Maneuvers

The following are some of the chief tactical maneuvers used in chess.

The Pin

A pin is a maneuver whereby the opponent's piece cannot be moved without allowing a major piece, such as a queen, to be taken by the piece causing the pin. Where the piece pinned protects the king, it cannot be moved, for it is illegal to move a piece and allow a king to be taken.

The following is an illustration of a pin.

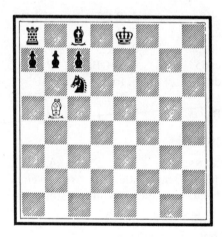

A pin can be broken by interposing a piece between the pinned piece and the king or major piece attacked. In the above illustration, moving the Black queen's bishop to d7 breaks the pin

Discovered Check

This comes about when the removal of one's own piece from a particular square will allow another piece to attack or check opponent's king directly. Since the enemy king must move or be immediately defended, the piece moved to create the discovered check can then capture or attack an enemy piece with devastating results. In the following illustration, by moving the White knight, White has a discovered check with his rook. Should the knight move to d6, it will capture the Black queen on the next move, for the king must move, or be defended, and the Black queen cannot move to protect the king.

Knight Fork

Since the knight controls many squares, eight in all, when it is strategically placed in the center or near the center of the board, it is often in a position to attack two pieces at once. When it is in a position to attack a king and queen at the same time, the enemy queen must be lost, for the king, when attacked by a knight, must move. No piece can be interposed in defense against a knight, because the knight moves *over* pieces. The following is an illustration of a knight fork. Note that both the king and queen are attacked, being on the same color squares.

Often, especially in an end game where an opponent has an active knight, it is important to keep one's major pieces on different colored squares to prevent a knight fork.

Mate on the Back Rank

Generally the king, during most of the game, remains on the first, or back, rank. After castling on the king's side, he is usually guarded by three pawns—the king's rook, knight, and bishop's pawns. If none of the pawns has been moved, the king cannot be removed from the back rank in one move, and thus he is susceptible to attack, should an enemy rook or queen penetrate to the back rank and check him. If no piece can be safely interposed, or if the interposed piece can be taken off by the attacking rook or queen with impunity, there is a checkmate. In the following illustration, the king, once checked by the rook, is doomed.

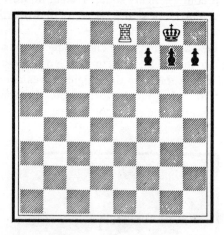

Combinations

A combination is a series of moves which force the opponent to react with set moves in order to defend his position. Finally, after a few or many moves, the point of the combination is discovered. It may be mate, a pawn queened, heavy loss of material. The art of the combination is basically what separates the master from the average player. To form a combination, it is necessary to "see ahead" in chess. Sometimes these combinations are "deep," involving twelve or more moves. The following is a mating combination from the game, Alekhine-Tartakower, London, 1932.

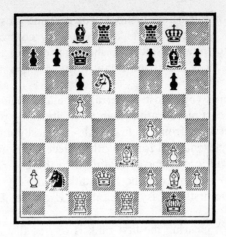

From here, the game continued:

White	Black
23.	b5
24. cxb5 (e.p.)	Qxd6
25. Qxd6	Rxd6
26. bxa7	Bb7
27. Bc5	Rdd1
28. Bxf1	Kxf1
29. Bxc6	Bxc6
30. Rxc6	Ra8

The last seven moves of Black (Tartakower) were virtually forced.

| 31. Rb6 | Rxa7 |
| 32. Rb8 Mate | |

Opening Principles

1. Open with 1. e4 or 1. d4 if you are White. This strikes at the center, prevents the opponent from dominating the center, and frees your other men.

2. Once having moved a pawn in the opening, don't move it again. It is better to develop your pieces. There are exceptions to this rule—the pawn may be under attack, or an enemy piece may be susceptible to an attack by your pawn—but as a general rule, move a pawn once and don't move it again.

3. Develop knights before bishops. The best and most natural position for the knights is on the third rank. There, they control the center and support your center pawns. Since a bishop can control a whole diagonal from the first rank, it is not as important to move them at the very outset of the game.

4. The queen is your most powerful piece and, being so powerful, is best used as a support piece, rather than as an attacking piece in the opening. If you move it away from the first rank, it is easily attacked, and since it cannot be evenly exchanged for any other piece but a queen (sometimes two rooks), you will lose tempo retreating it to the first rank.

5. Clear your pieces from the first rank as rapidly as possible. Any piece moved off the first rank is "developed." Example: Be2 is a developing move.

The reason for clearing the first rank is to free the king and rook so that the king may castle early. After the king has castled, the rooks can then work in tandem on the first rank, protecting each other from attack.

6. Do not relinquish control of the center. Protect it from encroachment by enemy pieces and support your own pawns there.

7. If White, try and maintain the initiative. Your pieces should be developed so that they carry an aggressive intention. This goes for the pawns as well. For example, the Ruy Lopez opening maintains initiative. If White opens, however, with 1. e4, then 2. d3, gives away his initiative by taking a purely defensive posture.

8. If a pawn or piece is to be captured, try to capture with a pawn moving toward the center. If there is a choice of capturing with a pawn that would be doubled (two in one file) or with a piece, all other factors being equal, avoid doubling your pawns.

9. Don't make any unnecessary pawn moves at the outset which will weaken your pawn structure and open the way for attack of a weak point. For example, if the knight is pinned by an enemy bishop, if possible put your bishop behind the knight, rather than advancing the KR pawn to relieve the pin.

Middle Game Principles

1. The pieces on your side must work in a coordinated fashion. If they cannot work together, they are subject to attack and cannot mount an attack of their own. Strive to move your pieces so that they can work together.

2. The rooks cannot utilize their power without open lines. Either open lines for them, or, if the lines have been opened by the enemy forces,

post your rooks along these open lines to control them or to offset enemy control.

3. Bishops can be quite effective on the diagonals of their color, but only if they have the mobility to operate. If you have blocked off the dark squares when you have a bishop operating on the dark squares, you are limiting its potential, and sometimes, when you have blocked a bishop off with immovable pawns, you have made it impotent. Don't neutralize your own bishops.

4. Knights are most effective near the center, where they occupy and control great areas. Putting a knight at the end rank or end file, or near it, greatly limits the knight's effectiveness. Try to keep the knight near the center.

5. If your game is cramped, exchange pieces to open up your side. If you have an ineffective piece, such as a blocked bishop, or a knight with nowhere to move, try to exchange.

6. If you are on the attack, working with coordinated pieces, avoid any exchange that will neutralize your attack. If, however, such an exchange will expose the enemy position for a mating attack, by all means, exchange.

7. If your opponent's pawn structure is weak, attack the weakness. This will force him to take strictly defensive measures, keeping his men back for defense, while you are able, by attacking, to control more and more space on the board.

8. If your opponent has a hole in his position—that is, a pawn structure that is not united—you should take advantage of this and post a knight or bishop there if possible, preferably deep in his position, where it cannot be removed, except at great loss of tempo on your opponent's part.

9. If your opponent's position is susceptible to attack, try to open up files so that your heavy artillery, the rooks and queen, can move in for the kill.

10. If you have the lead in development, keep opening up the position in areas where your forces will command time and space. Conversely, if you are behind in development, try to close up the position so that the enemy forces cannot penetrate.

11. If you are attacking on one wing, insure, if possible, that the other wing is not open for attack. Sometimes, a preparatory move, protecting the wing not attacked, is necessary before beginning your own attack.

12. If you find yourself under attack on one wing, attempt to counterattack on the other wing.

13. Try to think out the possibilities of the position several moves in advance. This can be done by studying the board for enemy weaknesses,

so that a series of moves will cause forced moves on his part to defend his position. If he deviates and does not defend correctly, then take advantage of such mistakes.

14. If you are a pawn or two ahead, and find that they can develop into passed pawns, try to exchange the pieces and steer for the end game. The best piece to exchange is the queen, then the rooks, bishops, and knights.

15. Carefully analyze the position in the middle game for end-game prospects. Don't play for a position in the middle game which will not carry through to victory in the end game.

End Game Principles

1. Think of your king as an attacking piece in the end game, and move him into an aggressive position. Sometimes the difference between victory and defeat is the relative positions of the kings at the commencement of the end game. Your king should support your pawns, should support your men, and move in coordination with them. A king is not to be treated as a passive piece.

2. The pawns, which are relatively immobile in the opening and middle game, reach their full potential in the end game. Their terrible threat is that they may be queened. If you have a passed pawn, concentrate on getting it queened. This will put tremendous pressure on your opponent, who may have to sacrifice a piece to prevent the queening, or may have to move his men back to strictly defensive positions in an effort to stop the passed pawn.

3. Because of the power of the pawns, avoid having doubled, isolated, or blockaded pawns. Remember that the fewer the pieces on the board, the more important are the pawns. Once your pawn is passed, the way to keep the threat alive is to push that pawn toward the eighth rank.

4. In rook and pawn endings, try to get your rooks either to the seventh rank, where they are posted with tremendous power, or behind the passed pawns.

5. If you are ahead in material in the end game, try to exchange so that your extra material can roam at will and control the board. But be wary of exchanging pawns, especially if you are only one pawn ahead. It may not be enough to win.

6. If you are behind in material, avoid exchanges which will allow the opponent to control the game. Instead, concentrate on exchanging pawns. If your opponent ends up a bishop ahead or a knight ahead, in knight and king versus king, or bishop and king versus king, he cannot win.

7. Therefore, know the elementary checkmates. Know what pieces are necessary to mate. Also know what the elementary draws are in the end game. In this way, you can steer for a draw with less material, and avoid a draw when you are ahead in material or pawns.

8. Try to move into the end game with both bishops. They have tremendous scope and power when the board is relatively free of material.

9. Thus, in open or semi-open positions, a bishop is superior generally to a knight. If you have a bishop against a knight, avoid covering the squares the bishop travels on with your pawns. Do not limit its mobility.

10. Where there are many pawns on the board, so that the position is closed, a knight may be much superior to a bishop since its mobility is generally not impaired by pawns.

11. If you have a king and pawn versus king ending and your pawn is a rook pawn, you must prevent the opposing king from reaching the queening square, or else it will be a stalemate.

12. Study the basic mates and the principles behind them.

Some Elementary Mates

If one player has a lone king, and the opposing player has, in addition to his king, one knight, or one bishop, the game is automatically a draw, since the player with the extra piece cannot force a win. In all the following examples, Black will have the lone king.

In order to win against a lone king, it is necessary to have either a queen, rook, bishop and knight, or two bishops.

Queen: White first moves his king toward the Black king and then brings his queen into play, forcing the king to the end rank or file, where mate is quite easy.

Rook: Since the rook does not have the mobility of the queen, it is a little more difficult. Again, the white king moves toward the lone king, and then the rook joins in to drive the Black king to the end of the board.

Bishop and Knight: This is quite difficult. The lone king must be driven toward the corner in which the square matches the diagonal on which the bishop travels. The king, bishop, and knight cooperate in this endeavor.

Two bishops: In addition to driving the lone king to the end of the board, he must also be driven into a corner. In this case, the bishops and the king must cooperate.

King and Pawn Endings

Before we examine some of the more basic situations, it is important to define the word "opposition." This means that while the kings face each other with an odd number of squares between them, it is one of the king's turns to move. If it is the White king's turn, the Black king is said to have the opposition. In the following illustration, since it is Black's turn to move, White has the opposition.

Here the following moves win for White:

1.   Ke8
2. e7   Kf7
3. Kf7 and White queens his pawn the next move.

If, in the previous example, it had been White's turn to move, Black would have had the opposition, and it is a draw. The moves would be:

1. e7+   Ke8
2. Ke6   Stalemate

In a situation when the White king has not yet reached the sixth rank and cannot get in front of his pawn, it is a drawn position.

1.   Kf6
2. f5   Kf7
3. Kg5   Kg7
4. f6+   Kf7
5. Kf5   Kf8
6. Ke6   Ke8
7. f7+   Kf8
8. Kf6   Stalemate

Where White's pawn is on the rook's file, it should be a stalemate.

1.		Kg8
2.	Kg6	Kh8
3.	h5	Kg8
4.	h6	Kh8
5.	h7	Stalemate

These are but a few examples of possible end-game situations, which, to cover fully, would require a book of their own. The reader is referred to *Basic Chess Endings,* by Reuben Fine, for a more complete study of the end game and chess endings.

Chess Hustles

Although chess is a game of pure skill, there is gambling on the outcome of matches. The most popular form of gambling is on the results of five-minute matches, in which each player has only five minutes to complete his moves.

When playing five-minute chess, not only does the factor of skill enter into the picture but the other factor of time, which can lead to mind-boggling anxiety in complex positions.

There are two ways to win when playing five-minute chess: Either you checkmate your opponent or he or she runs out of time. In five-minute chess the move is complete when you touch your time button, starting your opponent's clock. While it is your move, you can touch pieces and move them, and then put them back where they were, just as long as you don't press the clock button and thus end your move.

In this form of chess, checks don't have to be announced. If your opponent is checked and doesn't see it, you can checkmate him at once, even though it wasn't announced.

In New York City and in other large cities where chess is popular, chess hustlers play in small coffeehouses or take to the streets in good weather, with the chessboard, pieces, and, of course, the chess clock. They are usually strong players but not of master strength. They have trained themselves exclusively on five-minute chess, however, for this is how they make their living.

When playing against these hustlers, expect them to go into prepared lines of play in openings they are very familiar with. Against very weak players they will be content to overcome the opponent by skill alone, for the general rule in chess is that a more skillful player will beat a less skillful one.

When faced with a player of some skill, however, the chess hustlers have prepared attacks. If possible, they will try the steamrolling tactics of the Giucco Piano or Evans Gambit, which are little seen in tournament chess today, but are dangerous weapons against players who don't know the correct opening moves.

The goal of these hustlers is to take the opponent out of the familiar and into a complex haze, where an attack is launched within a few moves, often directly at the opponent's king. They stay on their own familiar ground when doing this, for these hustlers have all the time in the world to study and play chess, and to concentrate on those positions that give them the best chance to win.

What they also have on their side is the use of time in five-minute chess. In order to win, or, conversely, not to lose, a player can't afford to linger on opening moves. These must be made with lightning speed, and therefore the best way to beat these hustlers is by knowing some standard openings, both with the king's pawn and queen's pawn.

Then, if faced with a peculiar and offbeat opening, apply the opening principles outlined in this book. Develop your pieces and put them on correct squares. If attacked, realize that you can't panic; fend off the attack and you'll find that your opponent has depleted his strength, and now you can counterattack.

But even if you're ahead by a piece or so, these hustlers are tricky. They'll make outrageous moves, forcing you to think. The longer you think, the more time is erased from your clock. Remember, they want to win, and they can beat you, even from inferior positions, if your time runs out. So you must be in a position to move rapidly. When a complex situation presents itself, you can take a little time, and prepare your next few moves.

But if you take time after every move, your flag will fall, indicating that you're out of time and have lost. Then you'll have to pay up. The best advice I can give if you want to play these hustlers is to practice five-minute chess against friends or in a chess club, and familiarize yourself with the pace of the game.

Five-minute chess is a very tense game to play, with the clock forever ticking away those precious seconds. Learn to handle the tension so that you can keep a clear head during the game. With sound knowledge of the openings and tactics you should be able to hold your own against the hustlers if you preserve time, and are not afraid of complex positions or direct attacks at your king.

Finally, don't play passively unless you can win this way on time, since passive play generally loses in all forms of chess. The more aggressively you play, the more threats and attacks you can spin out from your position, the more time the opponent, the hustler, is going to have to take. Even the greatest players overlook positions and make blunders, and blunders are common in five-minute chess. Make your opponent blunder while you keep a calm head. Counterattack if he's started the attack first, but first defend carefully and strengthen your own position. Then you can go after him, and let him sweat out the time he needs to think out correct moves.

Representative Games

The following are games played by some of the most illustrious players in the history of the game. It would be beneficial for the chess novice to replay the games in this collection and to examine collections of games by the great masters. Replaying their games and studying the openings are the first steps toward becoming a strong player.

Game One

This game was played in New York in 1918 between José R. Capablanca, soon to be world champion, and Frank Marshall, for many years the American champion and a player with a great attacking style. This is one of the most famous games in chess history, for Marshall waited for ten years to surprise Capablanca with his eighth move, unleashing an attack of tremendous power that Capablanca, great chess genius that he was, defended against brilliantly.

RUY LOPEZ

WHITE: Capablanca	BLACK: Marshall
1. e4	e4
2. Nf3	Nc6
3. Bb5	a6
4. Ba4	Nf6
5. O-O	Be7
6. Re1	b5
7. Bb3	O-O
8. c3	d4!?

The great surprise!

9. exd4	Nxd4
10. Nxe5	

A dangerous capture.

	Nxe5
11. Rxe5	Nf6

Better is 11. . . . . c6 followed by 12. . . . Bd6

12. Re1

Better is 12. d4 and if 12. . . . Bd6, then 13. Re2

	Bd6
13. h3	Ng4!?

Another bolt from the blue!

14. Qf3!	Qh4
15. d4!	Nxf2!

Marshall's attack is still going according to plan.

16. Re2!?

On 16. Qxf2, Black wins with Bh2+, 17. Kf1 Bg3 because 18. Qxf7?? falls to Rxf7+!

	Bg4
17. hxg4	Bh7+
18. Kf1	Bg3
19. Rxf2	Qh1+
20. Ke2	Bxf2

White now has the better game.

21. Bd2!	Bh4
22. Qh3	Rae1+
23. Kd3	Qf1+
24. Kc2	Bf2
25. Qc3	Qg1
26. Bd5!	c5
27. dxc5	Bxc5
28. b4	Bd6
29. a4	a5

Black has no better moves.

30. axb5	axb4
31. Ra6	bxc3
32. Nxc3	Bb4
33. b6	Bxc3
34. Bxc3	h6
35. b7	Re3

And here Capablanca announced mate in five, beginning with 36. Bxf7 Rxf7 37. b8(Q)+ Re8 38. QxRe+, etc.

Game Two

This game was played between Alexander Alekhine and Aaron Nimzowitsch, the famous chess theorist, in Bled, 1931, as Alekhine approached the zenith of his career. It was the shortest defeat in Nimzowitsch's entire chess career, as the then world champion, Alekhine, demolished him with one of his patented king-side attacks.

FRENCH DEFENSE

WHITE: Alekhine	BLACK: Nimzowitsch
1. e4	e6
2. d4	d5
3. Nc3	Bb4
4. Ne2	dxe4
5. a3	Bxc3
6. Nxc3	f5

Here, Black makes a decisive mistake, since he weakens his dark-colored squares. Better would be 6. . . . Nc6 with equality.

7. f3	exf3
8. Qxf3	Qxd4
9. Qg3	

White now threatens 10. Nb5 or 10. Bf4.

	Nf6
10. Qxg7	Qe5?

Black cannot afford this aggressive move yet. He should also give up the queen's bishop's pawn. The next move allows White to win a tempo.

11. Be2	Rg8
12. Qh6	Rg6
13. Qh4	Bd7
14. Bg5	Bc6
15. O-O-O	Bxg2

Black's game is already helpless.

16. Rae1	Be4
17. Bh5	Nxh5
18. Rd8+	Kf7
19. Qxh5	Resigns

There are no good moves left for Black. 19. . . . Kg7 would lose the queen after 20. Nxe4 fxe4 21. Bh6+

It is quite instructive to see how Alekhine takes advantage of his adversary's mistakes and utilizes the extra tempo for a quick win.

Game Three

This game was played in the Challenge Match, Buenos Aires, 1971, between Robert Fischer of the United States and Tigran Petrosian of the USSR. Petrosian was the former world champion and had to win this match in order to challenge the champion, Boris Spassky. This was the first game of the match, and Fischer had won an unprecedented twelve games in a row in the Challenge Matches prior to this game. He eventually beat Petrosian and then became world champion after defeating Spassky.

SICILIAN DEFENSE/TAIMONOV

WHITE: Fischer	BLACK: Petrosian
1. e4	c5
2. Nf3	e6
3. d4	cxd4
4. Nxd4	Nc6
5. Nb5	

Fischer previously had had tremendous success with this move.

	d6
6. Bf4	e5
7. Be3	Nf6
8. Bg5	Be6
9. Nb1c3	a6
10. Bxf6	gxf6
11. Na3	d5!

An unforeseen move that permits Black to develop rapidly. The sacrifice is only temporary.

12. exd5	Bxa3
13. bxa3	Qa5
14. Qd2	

If 14. dxe6 Qxc3+ 15. Ke2 Nd4+ or 14. dxc6 Qxc3+ 15. Ke2 Bc4+

	O-O-O
15. Bc4	Rhg8
16. Rd1	Bf5
17. Bd3	Bxd3?

Better was 17. . . . e4!

18. Qxd3	Nd4
19. O-O	Kb8
20. Kh1	Qxa3?

Better was 20. . . . f5 21. f4 f6

21. f4!	Rc8
22. Ne4	Qxd3
23. cxd3	Rc2
24. Rd2	Rxd2
25. Nxd2	f5
26. fxe5	Re8
27. Re1	Nc2
28. Re2	

Not Rc1, . . . Nb4

	Nd4
29. Re3	Nc2
30. Rh3!	Rxe5
31. Nf3	Rxd5
32. Rxh7	Rxd3
33. h4	Ne3
34. Rxf7	Rd1+
35. Kh2	Ra1
36. h5	f4?

Necessary here was 36. . . . Rxa2, after which White's winning chances are problematical.

37. Rxf4	Rxa2
38. Re4!	Nxg2

If . . . Rxg2+ 39. Kh3 Re2 40. h6 winning.

39. Kg3

And now the knight is trapped.

	Ra5
40. Ne5	Resigns

The rook cannot stop the passed pawn.

This was a seesaw battle in which Petrosian, although refuting Fischer's opening with his eleventh move, played too passively and was overwhelmed in the end game.

Game Four

This game was played during the World Championship Match between Anatoly Karpov and Gary Kasparov in Moscow, 1985, after the previous match had been stopped by the president of the FIDE with Karpov leading five to three.

This game fully displays the daring play of Kasparov and his ability to slash through to victory with unforeseen combinations in relatively tranquil positions.

NIMZO-INDIAN DEFENSE

WHITE: Kasparov	BLACK: Karpov
1. d4	Nf6
2. e4	e6
3. Nc3	Bb4
4. Nf3	O-O
5. Bg5	c5
6. e3	cxd4
7. exd4	h6
8. Bh4	d5
9. Rc1	dxc4
10. Bxc4	Nc6
11. O-O	Be7

Karpov loses a tempo with this move.

12. Re1	b6
13. a3	Bb7
14. Bg3	

Ba2 may be more accurate here.

	Rc8
15. Ba2	Bd6
16. d5	

Bh4, reestablishing the pin, might be stronger.

	Nxd5
17. Nxd5	Bxg3
18. hxg3	exd5
19. Bxd5	Qf6

The game now appears even.

	Rfd8
20. Qa4	Rfd8
21. Rcd1	Rd7
22. Qg4	Rcd8

Karpov plays complacently, and makes a terrible mistake, for now Kasparov unleashes a beautiful winning combination.

	Rxd7
23. Qxd7!!	Rxd7
24. Re8+	Kh7
25. Be4+	Resigns

25. . . . g6 26. Rxd7 Ba6 27. Bxc6 Qxc6 28. Rxf7 MATE

Karpov felt the game was even when Kasparov began his winning combination. It was this type of brilliant play that finally unseated Karpov from the chess throne.

Five Minute Chess

With the introduction of chess clocks, an interesting form of the game has developed, called five-minute, sometimes seven-minute, chess. Each player has only five minutes to make *all* his moves. As soon as he makes a move, he presses down a lever on his side of the clock, causing the opponent's clock to start moving. A player wins by either mating the other player's king, the other player resigning, or running out of time.

This kind of game is quite exciting, because the time pressure makes for additional strain and tension. Tournaments of rapid chess are held among the highest-ranking players and are quite popular, since an entire tournament can be played in one day.

Correspondence Chess

Another popular method of playing chess. The game is played by mail, a move at a time. Although the game may take months to complete, many games may be played at once against different opponents. There are also correspondence chess tournaments.

Rating Systems

To fully enjoy the game, it is suggested that the reader, once he has learned the game and is playing fairly well, join the United States Chess Federation and receive a membership card. This will entitle him to play in sponsored, official tournaments, and enable him to achieve an official rating.

The rating system is as follows:

Senior Masters	2400 and above
Masters	2200–2399
Experts	2000–2199
Class *A*	1800–1999
Class *B*	1600–1799
Class *C*	1400–1599
Class *D*	1200–1399
Class *E*	Below 1200

The players with ratings above 2400 are generally world class players, rated as International Grandmasters or International Masters.

Certainly, the rating system has done much to spread the popularity of the game in this country, especially among the young. Any member of the USCF can earn a rating.

The highest-rated player in the world today is Robert Fischer. The second highest is the World Champion, Boris Spassky.

A USCF player will find that he can participate not only in local tournaments, but in national ones as well, because of the Swiss system of tournament play, which enables hundreds of players to compete at one time. Under this system, a winner plays a winner in each round, while a loser plays a loser, and so on to the final round, which usually pits two undefeated players. Thus, hundreds can play, although they do not play each other, and the final score determines the players' individual standings. It goes without saying that in the lower standings, there are many ties.

XXI

Backgammon

Introduction

Backgammon is one of the more ancient games in existence, and perhaps the oldest game played with dice. Its origins are buried somewhere in the remote parts of history, but a board that can be used for backgammon was found dating from 3000 B.C. The early Greeks and Romans played a game nearly identical to present-day backgammon, and there are other artifacts in existence which relate to its ancient beginnings.

Parcheesi is continually mentioned in connection with backgammon, since that game, which began in India centuries ago, greatly resembles backgammon. Both games are rather similar in that the object of these games is to *bear off,* or remove checkers from a board. Although in Parcheesi, unlike backgammon, the men start off the board, there are a number of identical features, such as blots, points, and home boards, to suggest a definite link. In fact, in the tenth century the board, which resembled the one used in Parcheesi, was changed to the present backgammon board.

In addition, there are many European, Oriental, and African games similar to backgammon which are played today, making the many variations a truly international game. In 1743, Edmund Hoyle standardized the rules for the modern game, which has changed little since, with the exception of the doubling cube, introduced in the 1920s.

Today, backgammon has become one of the most popular of the gambling games, and backgammon fever has spread throughout the world. It's not only a marvelous game of skill, but it is perhaps the most social of the gambling games, and men and women can easily participate together in private matches and tournaments. While it hasn't yet approached poker in popularity in the United States, it may someday surpass that very American card game.

More and more, backgammon is attracting gamblers who like fast action, and it's not unusual to hear stories of thousands of dollars changing hands in private games. It's a great gambling game at any level, and participants playing for small stakes can get just as much of a thrill as the high rollers.

To be a winning backgammon player requires a combination of skill, luck, and nerve. Skill is the most important, for a good player will beat a mediocre player over the long run. In a short series, anything can happen, because the moves of the men are determined by the throws of the dice, and dice rolls are random in nature; often, lucky rolls can determine a game. In the long run, however, luck cannot overcome skill and nerve.

The game is easy to learn, and the moves can be picked up in just a short while. What is more difficult is understanding the concepts of the game and all the mathematical considerations at every position; backgammon can be almost as complex as a pure game of skill, such as chess. This is not to say that the game cannot be mastered, but it still presents a challenge to even the greatest players.

For many years backgammon was a minor game, with a coterie of admirers, but it began to achieve popularity when the doubling cube was introduced in the 1920s. This cube transformed backgammon into the exciting gambling game it is today, changing it forever.

The doubling cube permitted the payoffs to go beyond the double or triple stakes when a gammon or backgammon was made. Now the stakes could be doubled and redoubled so long as the players felt that they could win the game and had the nerve to back up their judgment. The doubling cube goes up to sixty-four, but that is not the final limit, and it can go way beyond that number if both players keep doubling the stakes.

The doubling cube had another salutary effect, for it speeded up the game by permitting a player far behind to concede if he was doubled. This not only made for faster games, but added a new dimension of skill to backgammon. There is just as much skill in analyzing positions and determining if one is ahead as there is in knowing the correct moves of the men.

In the last fifteen years the game has reached new heights of popularity, and with this new interest, a generation of experts and masters has come along, shaking up the old theories of the game. At one time, safety was all important, but today's game features more risks, balanced with a careful perspective on position.

The players who have mastered these new concepts have found themselves much sought after, as both participants and teachers, and some have made small fortunes from the game, because many addicts of backgammon are wealthy and love to play for large stakes.

The game can be played as a private game with just two participants, or it can be played by three or more players in a form called *chouette*. It has, in the last fifteen years, become a popular tournament game as well. The first great international tournament was held in the Bahamas in 1964, under the sponsorship of Prince Alexis Obolensky. Today, there are many top-notch tournaments scheduled, which attract most of the great players of the game, for there are many thousands of dollars in prize money at stake. Even more money is lost and won in side wagers during these tournaments.

Backgammon seems to be the game of the future. Its combination of skill, nerve, and luck, its gambling features, and its speed of play all contribute to its immense popularity. There is no doubt that this game is one of the fastest and most exciting gambling games ever invented, and one that will continue attracting thousands of new players and adherents.

Equipment

Complete backgammon sets are available in any games or department store, and anyone can get a set containing all the essential equipment at a reasonable price. A beginner might prefer an inexpensive one till he gets more experience at the game, but we suggest a medium-priced set, one that will stand up to a great deal of play.

Most backgammon sets are built into carrying cases so they can be taken anywhere and set up with little inconvenience. As noted, these portable sets can be moderately priced, but some wealthy and professional players get expensive custom-made sets. The average player has no need for such a set, since a good one can be gotten for a modest sum of money, and will give many hours of pleasure in return.

The following basic equipment is necessary:

1. *A backgammon board.*
These vary in size and colors, but they're made in accordance with the

rules of the game, having twenty-four triangles and a bar between the halves of the board.

2. *Thirty checkers (men).*

These men, or discs, or counters, are round and usually made of a hard material, such as plastic or bone, in two contrasting colors. Many come in black and white, but the colors aren't important so long as the players can easily differentiate between them.

3. *Dice and dice cups.*

The game should be played with a dice cup, since the dice can be shaken and thrown more randomly using the cup. The dice should be of a size consistent with the board, neither too large nor too small.

It's better to have two sets of dice and two dice cups, to keep the game moving at a faster pace.

4. *A doubling cube.*

These are made specifically for backgammon and are available in most games stores. Each cube has the numbers *2 4 8 16 32 64* imprinted on its faces.

That's the basic equipment of backgammon. The best way to get all these things is to purchase a complete portable set, but if that can't be done, there's no harm in buying the equipment separately.

The Setup

The board should be set up in the following manner:

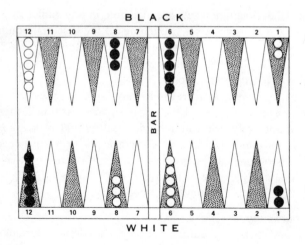

This is the most common setup, although the board may be set up as a left-to-right mirror image of the first illustration:

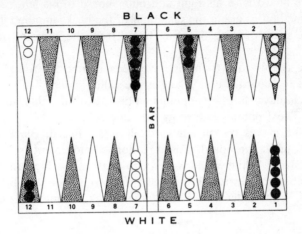

In our discussion of the game, we'll always refer to the setup as shown in the first illustration.

The next illustration shows the setup with the boards labeled and the points numbered. Although backgammon boards used in play don't bear these markings, we will refer to them in the discussion below. In accordance with modern nomenclature, we will use the term "board" throughout, instead of "table." A home board is also called an *inner board;* these terms are interchangeable.

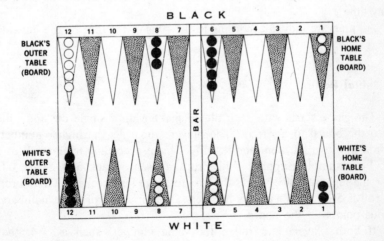

1. Black sits at the top of the backgammon table in the illustration; his home board is to his left, his outer board to his right. He faces White, whose home board is to his right and outer board to his left, so that both players' home boards are in the same half of the backgammon table.

2. The space dividing the outer board from the home board is called the *bar*.

3. The twenty-four triangles have been numbered from 1 to 12 on each side of the board. These triangles are called *points*.

4. Each player has twelve points on his side of the table, six in each of his boards. The 7 point is known as the *bar point*.

5. White moves his men toward his home board; Black moves his men toward his home board. The direction of movement is different for White and Black: White will move his two *back men,* which are on Black's 1 point, counterclockwise through the following boards: Black home, Black outer, White outer into White home. Black will move his men clockwise.

The Object of the Game

Each player endeavors to bring his checkers into his home board by moving them forward (toward the home board); then, once all his men are there, he tries to remove them from the board, or *bear off* his men. The ultimate object of the game is to bear off all one's men. The first player to do this wins the game.

During the course of the game, the players will be moving their checkers in opposite directions, each heading men toward his home board. Men can be moved in only one direction; they cannot be moved backward at any time.

All men are moved according to the rolls of the dice by the individual players.

Initial Roll

The game starts with each player picking up a single die and rolling it into the board to his right. The player who rolls the higher number is the first to move his men, and he moves them according to this roll of the dice. For example, suppose White rolls a 5 and Black a 2. Since White threw the higher number, he is the first to move his checkers. Therefore his first roll is 5-2, and he moves his men a combination of these numbers to various points on the board.

If both players had rolled the same number, such as 4-4, they'd continue to throw the dice. No moves can be made by either player until one player rolls a higher number than the other.

After the initial roll is over and the move made, the players throw both dice from the dice cup, alternating their rolls in the following manner: If White has won the opening roll, he moves his men; then Black rolls the dice and moves; then White rolls again, and so forth. The dice must be thrown into the section of the backgammon table to the player's right. So long as the dice remain on the board, the move is not completed—a player may move checkers, change his mind, and make different moves. However, once the dice are picked up, the moves are deemed completed.

The men are moved in one direction only by each player, and that is forward to their home boards in accordance with the rolls of the dice.

Let's return to the initial roll. White has won the roll and moves first, because he threw a 5 while Black rolled a 2. The first move is therefore 5-2, and White's men can now be moved forward as follows:

1. One man may be moved five points and then two points.
2. One man may be moved two points and then five points.
3. One man may be moved five points and another man two points.

The separate numbers shown on the dice are the important consideration, not their total. Thus, with a roll of 5-2, the important number is not seven, which is their total, but the 5 and the 2. A checker can't simply be moved seven points forward per se. He must be moved either five points and then two points, or two points and then five points.

Let's study another opening roll, this time the 6-3. If White has won the roll by throwing the 6, he can now move his men as follows:

1. One man may be moved six points and then three points.
2. One man may be moved three points and then six points.
3. One man may be moved six points and another man three points.

Doubles

The only exception to the above rule occurs when a player rolls doubles (after the initial roll). A double is a pair on the dice, such as 2-2 or 3-3. When a player rolls a double, he can move his men a total of *double* the numbers shown on the dice. If a player has rolled a 3-3, he can move his checkers double the total of 3-3, which is twelve. After this roll of 3-3, the men can be moved a total of twelve points, or *pips,* each three points at a time as follows:

1. One man may be moved three points, four times in a row.
2. One man may be moved three points three times in a row, and a second man may be moved three points once.

3. One man may be moved three points twice, and another man moved three points twice.

4. One man may be moved three points twice, a second man moved three points once, and a third man moved three points once.

5. Four different men can each be moved three points once.

With doubles you must add the total of the dice and multiply by two to get the maximum number of points the men can be moved. For instance, if 4-4 has been rolled, the total is eight; doubling that makes sixteen; therefore, the men can be moved four points at a time until they've been moved a total of sixteen points.

Cocked Dice

After the dice are thrown, unless both land flat on the board to the player's right with neither resting on a checker, they are deemed to be *cocked,* and the throw must be made again.

Points, Making a Point

Although men are moved according to the roll of the dice, they can't land just anywhere on the board. The rules state that a player's checkers can land only as follows:

1. On a point occupied by the player's own men.

2. On a point that is vacant.

3. On a point occupied by the opponent's single man; this man is called a *blot.*

If a point has two or more men on it, it is called a *made point,* and an opponent's checker cannot land on this made, or *established,* point.

In moving, a man may pass over made points established by an opponent. The important consideration always is the point on which a man must land, not the points in between. For example, if a player has rolled double 5s, and has men on his own 12 point to be moved, it doesn't matter if the opponent has made points on his 11, 10, 9, and 8 points, so long as the 7 point is available for the man to land on.

Blots

When a point is occupied by only one man, the single checker is called a *blot*. A blot may be *hit* by an opponent's man landing on the blot's point. When a man is hit, it is removed from the board and placed on the bar. A player who has a man on the bar cannot make any other moves until that man has been put back on the board by coming into the opponent's home board. If he can't come in with a man on the bar, he cannot make any other moves.

This situation can occur when the opponent has made points in his home board and the roll of the dice would force the man on the bar to land on a made point, which is not legal.

The Bar

After a blot is hit, the player hitting the man picks it up and places it on the bar. In backgammon terminology, the man hit has been sent "to the bar," or "back home," or "off the board." It remains off the board until it can come into the opponent's home board by a throw of the dice.

Reentering from the Bar

After a man is hit and placed on the bar, the player whose man has been hit must attempt to reenter this man on the very next roll of the dice, before moving any other men.

If a player has several men on the bar, he must reenter *all of his men* before he can move any of his other checkers.

If a player has a man on the bar, and his opponent has made all six points in his home board (this is called a *closed board*), then the hit man can't come in, no matter what the player rolls. In this case, the player with the man on the bar skips his turn at rolling the dice, since the roll would be useless.

Primes

Whenever either player has been able to make six points in a row, he is said to have established a *prime*. A prime completely blocks an opponent from moving a checker past it, since the moves are based on single numbers shown on the dice, and no die can have more than a 6 come up. Thus, attempting to bypass a prime is futile, since the man would have to land on a made point.

When a prime has been established in a player's home, or inner, board, the board is called *closed*. Should the opponent have a man on the bar, this man can't reenter against a closed board, and the opponent misses his turn to roll the dice.

Bearing Off

Bearing off is the removal of men from the board after they've all been brought into a player's home board. The first player to bear off all his men wins the game.

If we reexamine the setup, we see that five of each player's men are already placed in the home board prior to play. That leaves each player with ten checkers remaining to be moved around the table and into the inner board, so that bearing off can commence.

Once a man has been borne off, it can no longer enter the board for any reason. However, it's possible for a player to have a man on the board after he's borne off men. This can occur when one of his men, having been a blot, is hit by an opponent's man. If this happens, a player can no longer bear off checkers until that man has been reentered into the opponent's home board and brought around the table into the player's home board.

Once all the player's men are in his home board, they're borne off by rolls of the dice. If this player should roll a 6-4, for instance, he may bear off one man from the 6 point and another from the 4 point. Should he roll doubles, he doubles the value of the roll and bears off men accordingly. For example, if he rolls a 4-4, he can bear off four men from the 4 point or any lower point.

When men are in the home board waiting to be borne off, it's not necessary to roll the exact number to conform with the point these men are on in order to bear them off. For example, if there are men on the 5 and 3 points, a roll of 6-4 is sufficient to bear them off. *The roll has to be equal to, or higher than, the points on which these men are placed in order to bear them off.* This same rule applies when doubles are rolled.

In bearing off, men are moved according to the individual spots on the dice. Thus, if a player has a man on the 6 point, it can be borne off if the roll is 4-2, since the man is moved up four and then two points and thus goes off the board. If this same checker had been on the 5 point, or any lower point, it could also have been borne off by the same roll.

When all the men are in the home board, the player must make use of his entire roll, either to bear his men off or to move them forward.

There may be times when a player prefers to make a point in his home board rather than bear his men off. This situation may develop when an opponent still has men on the bar or has made a point in this player's home board. If a player bears a man off, and as a result leaves a blot, it becomes vulnerable to a hit. Suppose White has blots on his own 6 and 5 points, and several men on his own 3 and 2 points. Black has a man on the bar, and it's White's turn to roll the dice. He throws a 3-2.

In this situation, it would be much better to move the blots on the 6 and 5 points forward, to prevent them from being hit by the opponent's next throw, than to bear men off from the 3 and 2 points.

Scoring the Game—Gambling at Backgammon

Although it can be played without stakes, backgammon is essentially a gambling game. When playing for money, the opponents first agree upon a stake for each individual game before play begins. If the stake is one dollar, and the game is won or lost in the ordinary course of events, the result is that the loser will pay the winner one dollar. However, there are several ways the stake may be increased, due to the initiative of the players and through the rules of the game. The first method we'll discuss is increasing the stake with the use of the doubling cube.

Using the Doubling Cube

At the outset of play, the doubling cube is placed in the middle of the bar, with the *64* facing up. At this time the game is being played for a single unit, whatever that agreed-upon unit is—one dollar, five dollars, or any other stake.

If either player decides that he has a winning edge, he may double the stakes by turning the doubling cube to *2* before it's his turn to roll the dice. Then he moves the cube to his opponent's side of the bar, usually accompanying this move with a verbal statement to the effect that he's doubling.

Now the other player must make an immediate decision before the dice are rolled. He may decide to refuse the double. In that case, he concedes, the game is over, and he pays the original stake of one unit to his opponent.

However, should this same player decide to accept the double, the game goes on, with the participants now playing for two units.

When a player accepts the double, the doubling cube is moved to his part of the bar, and he now *owns the cube*. The game can be redoubled only by the player in possession of the cube.

The game can be doubled and redoubled even beyond the *64* showing on the cube. Theoretically it can go on and on, but this is very unusual.

To summarize doubling:

1. Doubling can be done by a player only before it's his turn to roll the dice.

2. Either player may double when the cube is in the center of the bar, shows *64,* and hasn't yet been used to double.

3. After this first double, any other redouble can be made only by the player owning the cube. Thus, no player can double two times in a row.

4. If a player accepts the double or redouble, the game goes on at that higher stake. If a player refuses a double or redouble, he concedes the game and pays whatever stake he lost prior to the new number's showing on the doubling cube.

Gammons and Backgammons

A *gammon* occurs when the winning player bears off all his men before the other player can bear off *any* of his men. In other words, all the loser's men are still on the board. In this event, the loser must pay double the original stake agreed upon, since a gammon is considered a "double game."

If the doubling cube has been used during the game, and a player was gammoned, then the payoff would be twice the number shown on the doubling cube.

A *backgammon* occurs when the winning player has been able to bear off all his men while his opponent still has one or more men in the winner's home board or on the bar. A backgammon is known as a "triple game,", since the stakes are tripled for the winner. If the doubling cube has been used during the game, the payoff is three times the number shown on the cube.

The optional *Jacoby Rule* is often used by experienced players. It states that if neither player has doubled during the course of the game, gammons and backgammons don't count; the game will still be paid off at the single stake even if a gammon or backgammon occurs.

This rule encourages a speedier game, since if a game hasn't been doubled, the player ahead will not try for a gammon, but will bear off his men as fast as possible.

Automatic Doubles

If agreed upon beforehand, an automatic double occurs when both players toss the same number on their initial roll. Some players agree to keep doubling if they repeatedly throw doubles, until one of them wins the initial roll, but the usual rule limits the automatic double to one throw of the dice.

Sometimes players agree to start a game with the cube at *2, 4,* or even higher, thus making backgammon into a wild gambling game for huge stakes. When this is done, backgammon moves more and more into the gambling sphere and is less a game of skill.

Opening Rolls

The first decision a player faces during the game comes with his opening roll. Therefore, he must know not only the correct moves for every opening roll, but the reasons behind these moves.

Throughout this section, we'll assume that you're White and the opponent is Black, and that you've won the toss and will roll first. Even though, theoretically, doubles can't be made on the very first throw, they will also be discussed as an opening move, because the player must know the correct moves when rolling doubles.

In our discussion we'll cover each possible opening roll of the dice and show strong alternate rolls, when necessary, beginning with the highest non-double roll, 6-5, and working our way down to 2-1. After these rolls are analyzed, we'll study the correct opening moves for doubles.

6-5
Move a man from Black's 1 point to Black's 12 point.

The purpose of the move is to get your back men moving around the board to your home board, and by making this move you've gotten one of the two most difficult men on his way, placing him on your made point, the Black 12 point.

6-4
Move one man from Black's 1 point to Black's 11 point.

Again, your intent is to move your back men forward toward your inner board.

6-3
Move one man from Black's 1 point to Black's 7 point (bar point) and one man from Black's 12 point to White's 10 point.

The alternate move is to move one man from Black's 1 point to Black's 10 point. This moves one back man forward, but the checker is subject to a direct 3 or 2-1 roll of the dice, in which case it'll be hit by one of Black's men on White's 12 point.

6-2

Move a back man from Black's 1 point to Black's 7 point (bar point) and another man from Black's 12 point to White's 11 point.

The alternate choice is moving one back man from Black's 1 point to Black's 9 point. If the man isn't hit, this move will leave only one man remaining in Black's inner board, but this move subjects the moved man to a hit by a direct 4, 3-1, or double-2 roll of the dice.

6-1

Move one man from Black's 12 point and one man from White's 8 point to make White's bar point (7 point).

This makes a strong point on White's side of the board. A 6-1 is a powerful move at the outset of the game.

5-4

Move one man from Black's 12 point to White's 8 point and one man from Black's 12 point to White's 9 point.

Although this move exposes the blot on White's 9 point to being hit, Black would have to roll a 6-2, 5-3, or double 4 to do it. If he doesn't roll any of these numbers, White has taken the first steps to making a point at his own 4, 5, and bar points, all strong, key points.

5-3

Move one man from Black's 12 point to White's 10 point, and one man from Black's 12 point to White's 8 point.

The alternative is to make the 3 point by moving one man from White's 8 point and one man from White's 6 point to White's 3 point. However some experts feel that making this point so deep in White's home board is not that important this early in the game.

5-2

Move two men from Black's 12 point: one to White's 8 point and one to White's 11 point.

This is a relatively safe play and recommended by most experts.

5-1

Move one man from Black's 12 point to White's 8 point, and one man from Black's 1 point to Black's 2 point.

Splitting the two back men is a correct move here, since Black gains little hitting these men so deep in his home board.

4-3

Move two men from Black's 12 point to White's 9 and 10 points.

This move is recommended because both cannot be hit with one roll, and they're in an excellent position to make the key 4, 5, and bar points.

4-2

Move one man from White's 8 point and one man from White's 6 point to the 4 point, to make this point at once.

This is an excellent roll, for it permits White to establish one of his key points immediately.

4-1

Move one man from Black's 12 point to White's 9 point, and one man from Black's 1 point to Black's 2 point.

This isn't a good roll of the dice, but the recommended moves are safer than moving one man from Black's 12 point to White's 9 point and one man from White's 6 point to White's 5 point, where they could be hit either individually or, in some cases, together, by double 4 or double 2.

3-2

Move two men from Black's 12 point to White's 10 and 11 points.

These men have now been moved to White's outer board, with the potential to make points, and only a roll of 9 or 10 by Black will hit them.

3-1

Move one man from White's 8 point and one man from White's 6 point to White's 5 point, making this key point.

This is a great roll, because the 5 point is the best early point to make in White's home board.

2-1

Move one man from Black's 12 point to White's 11 point and one man from Black's 1 point to Black's 2 point.

This move gets one man into White's outer board rather safely, while splitting the two back men.

Doubles as the Opening Move

Although doubles can't be the opening roll, it's still important to study them. A player may lose the opening roll, but if he rolls a double immediately, the way may be clear to move his men according to the recommended strategy.

6-6
Move two men from Black's 1 point to Black's bar point and two men from Black's 12 point to White's bar point, making both bar points with a single throw.

This is a very powerful roll.

5-5
Move two men from Black's 12 point to White's 3 point, making the point.

4-4
Move two men from Black's 1 point to Black's 5 point, making the point, and two men from Black's 12 point to White's 9 point, making this point, too.

3-3
Move two men from White's 8 point to White's 5 point, and two men from White's 6 point to White's 3 point, making both these points.

2-2
Move two men from Black's 12 point to White's 11 point, and two men from White's 6 point to White's 4 point, making both points.

1-1
Move two men from White's 8 point to White's 7 point (bar point), making the point, and two men from White's 6 point to White's 5 point, making this point as well.

This strong roll establishes two powerful points on White's side of the board.

Probabilities in Backgammon

Backgammon can be a very complex game, and sometimes it's hard to know exactly what the correct play is without taking the odds and probabilities into consideration.

In a difficult situation, the player might have to ask himself various questions. Should I leave a blot open to be hit? Suppose I leave a blot open; what are the chances of its being hit? What rolls do I have to make to hit my opponent's man? Is it worth more to hit him or run past him?

The lists of questions can go on and on, but usually, in a game, strategy develops out of the position. Still, in every situation there's a correct move, and often this move is determined by the odds and probabilities. If a blot has to be left open, then which point would the blot be safest at? What are the chances of an opponent's rolling a particular series of numbers to hit that blot?

The more a player knows about the probabilities of the game, the more he knows about the odds involved, the stronger he will be. Knowledge flows naturally into strength, so study the probabilities and odds discussed here, play out practice games using them, and put them to good use when playing for stakes.

Combinations of the Dice

Since the moves in backgammon are determined by the rolls of the dice, it's important to know the various combinations that can be rolled using two dice. In studying these combinations, the individual rolls, rather than the totals, are the important consideration.

Roll	Frequency of Occurrence
Double 1 (1-1)	1
Double 2 (2-2)	1
Double 3 (3-3)	1
Double 4 (4-4)	1
Double 5 (5-5)	1
Double 6 (6-6)	1
1-2, 2-1	2
1-3, 3-1	2
1-4, 4-1	2
1-5, 5-1	2

Roll	Frequency of Occurrence
1-6, 6-1	2
2-3, 3-2	2
2-4, 4-2	2
2-5, 5-2	2
2-6, 6-2	2
3-4, 4-3	2
3-5, 5-3	2
3-6, 6-3	2
4-5, 5-4	2
4-6, 6-4	2
5-6, 6-5	2
Total	36

Chances of Hitting a Blot

This table is divided into two parts, the first part numbered 1–12 and the second part numbered 15–24 for purposes of this table. By rolling doubles, you can hit blots at distant points. A double 4 hits a blot sixteen points away; a double 5, a blot fifteen or twenty points away; and a double 6 can hit a blot eighteen or twenty-four points distant.

Number of Points or Pips Away from Blot	Ways to Hit	Chances of Hitting
1	11	$^{11}/_{36}$ or 31%
2	12	$^{12}/_{36}$ or 33%
3	14	$^{14}/_{36}$ or 39%
4	15	$^{15}/_{36}$ or 42%
5	15	$^{15}/_{36}$ or 42%
6	17	$^{17}/_{36}$ or 47%
7	6	$^{6}/_{36}$ or 17%
8	6	$^{6}/_{36}$ or 17%
9	5	$^{5}/_{36}$ or 14%
10	3	$^{3}/_{36}$ or 8%
11	2	$^{2}/_{36}$ or 6%
12	3	$^{3}/_{36}$ or 8%

When creating a blot one to six points away, the safest blot is one with the lowest number of points, or pips. It's much more difficult to hit a blot one point away than it is to hit one six points away. If a blot is but one point away, a *1* must show on either die for the blot to be hit, but when a blot is six points away, then various combinations on the dice, such as 5-1, 1-5, 2-4, 4-2, or 3-3, can hit it.

Number of Points or Pips Away from Blot	Ways to Hit	Chances of Hitting
15	1	$\frac{1}{36}$ or 3%
16	1	$\frac{1}{36}$ or 3%
18	1	$\frac{1}{36}$ or 3%
20	1	$\frac{1}{36}$ or 3%
24	1	$\frac{1}{36}$ or 3%

Probability of Reentering from the Bar

The following table is important to remember if you've been hit and have one man on the bar. The odds are determined by the points open in the opponent's home board.

Number of Open Points	Ways to Enter	Chance of Entering
1	11	$\frac{11}{36}$ or 31%
2	20	$\frac{20}{36}$ or 56%
3	27	$\frac{27}{36}$ or 75%
4	32	$\frac{32}{36}$ or 89%
5	35	$\frac{35}{36}$ or 97%

Once two points are open, the chances of reentering from the bar are better than even money, and if three points are open, then the chances are three to one, or seventy-five percent, that the man will come in. If four or five points are open, only unlucky rolls keep a man from coming in off the bar.

General Strategic Principles

Although there's an element of luck in backgammon, it's essentially a game of skill. A player versed in the principles of the game may lose a couple of games, or lose for a short period of time to an unskilled player, but in the long run the skilled player will come out way ahead.

Skill is made up of knowledge and instinct. We can't learn instinct, but we should learn as much about the game as we can. The more we know, the better our chances of winning—if we put this knowledge to practical use.

One of the most important things a good backgammon player should have is a sound strategic plan at the outset of play. He should know what his aims and goals are from the opening move to the end game, when he is bearing his men off. And before each and every move he should continually reexamine his priorities as the game and positions change.

Of course, luck can rear its ugly head at times, for it's not always possible to carry out plans if the dice go awry or we get a series of bad rolls. And sometimes our opponent's plans and moves may thwart ours, causing us to alter our own plans drastically.

Backgammon is, after all, a fluid game, and a good player will adjust his game accordingly. He should remember that flexibility, rather than rigidity and safety, is the key to success. A player should be bold and take risks when warranted, but he shouldn't be an out-and-out gambler, hoping for luck to pull him out of a bad situation. He must remain a realist and know what he's doing at all times, keeping his objectives firmly in mind.

Above all, a player shouldn't approach a backgammon game just hoping for the best, without any plan and without taking into consideration the strategic principles of the game. Playing this way is playing to lose. He should play to win, and to win, a player must study the game and plan ahead, making his knowledge work for him.

The following are some of the more important principles of play:

1. Learn all the correct opening moves, and study the alternate opening moves that may be just as valid in some situations.

Unless you've mastered these moves, don't play a game for stakes. I suggest learning the alternate moves as well because you don't always win the opening roll, and your opponent's first move may force you to play a move other than the very best. If you can't play the best move, at least know the next-best move.

2. Try to move your back men (those men in your opponent's home board at his 1 point) forward as soon as you can, when you have a reasonable roll. If possible, make the opponent's 5 point with these men.

3. When moving your back men forward in the early game, you must sometimes split them, leaving them vulnerable to being hit as blots. When splitting these back men, move one checker to the opponent's 2 point and not to his 3 point.

If you split the back men, moving one to the 3 point, an opponent's double 5 will put both men on the bar, at the same time that he makes three points in his inner board. This could be catastrophic to your game.

4. Making an advanced point at the opponent's 5 point should be one

of your top considerations. If that point can't be made, then try for the 4 point, and make that one.

Some weak players endeavor to make the opponent's 2 point and fall into a trap. Their men are still in the opponent's home board, and after a while they are blocked or trapped there, leading to a loss.

5. Try to establish points on your side of the board, and know the order of importance of these points. For example, the most important point you can make is your own 5 point.

Making your own 5 point blocks your opponent's men in your home board, for the 5 point joins the already established 6 and 8 points, leaving only the bar point as an escape route for his back men.

6. The next step is to make your bar point. If you make it early enough, you can trap your opponent's back men by having three consecutive points: the 6, bar, and 8 points. And if you establish the bar point after making the 5 point, you're well on your way to a prime.

7. By making the 5 and bar points early, you're not only setting up a blockade, you're establishing an anchor at these points to allow your other men to come into your home board safely. If a running game (discussed below) results, this is of great importance.

8. The third most important point to establish after the 5 and bar points is the 4 point. If it is made before the 5 point is established, the opponent can still move his back man past your two men covering the 4 point and into your 5 point, a great plus for him, allowing his men to escape and begin running around the board.

9. Sometimes your opening roll will present you with no choice but to establish a weaker point at the outset of play. Suppose you lost the opening toss, and your first roll is a double 5. The best play is to make your 3 point. The 3 point is not the best point to make early in the game, but if, later on, you establish your 4 and 5 points in addition, you've set up a powerful blockade to trap your opponent's back men, and men he may have on the bar.

The trouble with making the 3 point so early in the game is that it's so deep in your own territory that the opponent can easily bypass it with his back men.

10. In the early part of the game, it's not that important to make points at your 3, 2, and 1 points, deep in your home board. They serve little purpose at this time, and you should concentrate on the more important 5, bar, and 4 points.

In the middle game, try to make consecutive points deep in your home board, for then they'll be a powerful blockade against your opponent's men on the bar.

11. Try to make points when you can. This isn't to say that you

should always play it safe, for that isn't the winning way. The way to win is to make the best moves on every roll, wringing every bit of advantage you can out of your men on the board.

In order to make points, it's often necessary to take risks by placing one man as a builder on a point. A *builder* is a man alone (a blot) placed on a point for the purpose of making a point there at the earliest possible opportunity by covering the blot with another man.

12. If you must leave a man to be hit, try to have the blot at least seven points away from being hit, so as to avoid a direct shot. If you can't do this, try to have the blot one or two points away from being hit, rather than five or six points away, so that you can take advantage of the odds against being hit.

If you must expose a man to being hit, split your back men in your opponent's home board, if at all possible. In this case, it might not be to the advantage of your opponent to hit your back men.

13. All things being equal, avoid being hit when you can, and hit your opponent when you can, but only if it is to your advantage to do so.

If he splits his back men, for example, and on an early roll you can make your 5 point, it wouldn't be to your advantage to hit his back man, for making that 5 point might be much more important to your overall game.

14. If you find yourself in a dangerous situation, try to hit an opponent's blot, so that only half his next roll will be useful, since he'll have to waste one number coming in off the bar.

15. Try to block your opponent's forward movement and try to trap his back men. The best way to do this is to make consecutive points. The more points, the more difficult it will be for his men to get by the blocking points.

A five-point blockade is very powerful, and the ideal blockade is with a six-point prime. A prime, which prevents the opponent from passing it, is a powerful plus for you.

16. Primes cannot be kept forever, so when breaking a prime, especially in your home board, it's best to move the outermost men first.

17. When attempting to bring men into your home board, try to waste as few pips as possible. Let's say you have a man on the opponent's 9 point, with a group of your men on your own bar and 8 points. If you roll a 4-3 now, use the 4 to get the man on the opponent's 9 point over to your 12 points, so a direct 6 will bring a man in. In this way, you waste precious few pips.

18. When bringing men into your inner board, it's important to place them on the 4, 5, and 6 points and then to spread your other checkers on the inner points, so that you won't be wasting pips bearing them off.

19. When an opponent has made a point deep in your home board or is on the bar, the best procedure for bearing off safely is to avoid moving your men to your 1 and 2 points. Leave them at points 3 through 6. Then clear your points by bearing off men from the 5 and 6 points. Finally, don't let an unlucky roll of 6-5, for example, cause a blot. To avoid this, try to leave an even number of men on the farthest points in your home board.

20. To conserve your rolls when bearing off, if all the opponent's men are past your home board and there's no more chance for contact, bear off a man rather than moving it forward within the board, if possible.

Types of Backgammon Games

Various kinds of games can develop during the course of play, and the astute player should be prepared to play any of them, either because the opportunity presents itself or because his own rolls or the opponent's position has forced him to steer toward a certain kind of game.

These can be classified as *running game, blocking game,* and *back game.*

Running Game

Backgammon could be defined as a race, in which each player enters into a contest to see who can win by getting his men around and off the board first. However, no game can be merely a race, because the rules and complexities of backgammon make this next to impossible. If it were merely a race, no skill would be involved, and we know that a great deal of skill and strategic planning is necessary to win a backgammon game, especially against an experienced player.

Each player can prevent the other from turning the contest into a simple race. Points can be made and blockades set up. In addition, blots are subject to being hit and put on the bar. All these factors must be taken into consideration during a game. There's no purpose in merely moving men forward as fast as possible if as a result these men will wind up as hit blots on the bar. This strategy would defeat itself, and the player trying to race his men around would find himself far behind instead.

Still, there are games that develop into running games, or races. This happens when both sides break contact, so that neither can hit the other's blots, and then it's merely a race to see who bears off his men first, with the player ahead holding the advantage.

Some running games develop even when there's contact. When there still is contact, the player who is ahead will try to break this contact and bypass the other player's checkers in order to turn the game into a race, in which he'll have the advantage.

On the other hand, if a player is behind and there is contact, his strategy will be to maintain contact in the hope of forcing the other player to leave blots that may be hit.

Once contact is broken and it's an all-out race, a player shouldn't waste any pips bringing his men into the home board. Once there, they should be distributed evenly, so that there won't be pips wasted in bearing these men off.

Blocking Game

This type of game is more of a defensive struggle, in which the player tries to hinder and prevent his opponent's progress.

In a blocking game the player should have as his first strategic consideration the making of points. He should try to set up an anchor in the opponent's 5 point, for if he makes this point, it will not only disrupt the opponent's movement of men but will serve as a base to come in on if his own men are hit.

A player should also attempt to make his own 5, bar, and 4 points, in that order, and, if possible, to make consecutive points, which are very effective blockades. Once gaps are left, the blockade is considerably weakened.

When playing a blocking game, there are risks to be taken in making points, for builders have to be set up, and these blots may be hit by the opponent's men. However, a player should try to minimize these risks by selectively setting up builders that have the least chance of being hit.

Back Game

This is a purely defensive game, resulting from a situation in which one player is far behind his opponent. Instead of trying to establish a running game, in which he will surely lose the race to bear off men, the player behind tries to a) establish points in his opponent's home board and b) hit the opponent's blot at a later stage of the game.

When playing a back game, the player is not concerned about his own blots being hit. When they're hit, he attempts to enter them into his opponent's home board to make even more points and, once they're made, to enter more men to hit the opponent's blots.

When playing the back game, once a couple of points have been made, preferably the opponent's 1 and 3 points or his 1 and 2 points, the player's next strategy is to slow up the game by allowing his other men to be hit. The purpose of this strategy is to prevent all his men from being stuck in his own home board, which would force the player to move his remaining men out of the opponent's home board, breaking up his made points.

To prevent this from happening, the player must spread his men around the board, keeping as many blots as possible open to be hit. The more exposed checkers he has, the better his game.

When playing the back game, there is a risk of being gammoned, of course, but if the back game is played correctly, the opponent can be brought to his knees with some good rolls and a few hits of his blots.

If we reverse this situation, so that an opponent is setting up a back game, a player shouldn't cooperate in this effort by continually hitting the opponent's blots. This is just what the opponent wants him to do. Let the opponent get the rest of his checkers into his own home board, where they'll stew in their own juices.

As mentioned before, the best points to hold in the opponent's home board are the 1 and 3 or 1 and 2 points. If a player can make three consecutive points, such as the 1, 2, and 3 points, it's a tremendously strong back game, but leaves the player with only nine other checkers. Having nine men to move may create more problems, for there are limited moves available, and these men may quickly pile up in the player's home board, defeating his purpose.

In this case, should the player get some unlucky rolls, such as double 5s or double 6s, he'll be in real trouble, destroying his back-game strategies and leaving himself open to a gammon.

Doubling Strategy

Doubling is one of the most important aspects of the game of backgammon, and, all other things being equal, its use often determines whether a player is a winner or a loser. If a player can't make proper use of the doubling cube, if he is too conservative or too wild in its application, his game is going to be in trouble, no matter how well he moves his men.

At the outset of play, the doubling cube is in the center of the bar, placed at *64*. Thereafter, if any player decides to double, he pushes the cube toward his opponent, moving it to number 2. This must be done while the player offering the double is on his roll, but before he has rolled the dice. If the other player refuses the double, then the player offering it has won the game for one unit.

However, should the other player accept the double, then the doubling cube remains on his side of the bar, and from that time on *he owns the cube,* unless he in turn redoubles and moves the cube back to his opponent. Whoever has been doubled or redoubled owns the cube. Owning the cube gives a player an edge, since he can redouble at any time he desires. If his game deteriorates even more, he won't double back, but should his game improve to the point where he has a definite advantage in position, he can redouble with great effectiveness.

Therefore, before a player doubles he should make certain that he has a definite advantage, enough to warrant doubling. Doubling on a whim, or because the position looks right, or because one has a slight edge, may lead to disaster. Backgammon is above all a dynamic game, one in which the tide can turn one way or another with fierce suddenness. Before a player doubles, he must be certain of his advantage, for in doubling he places a potent weapon in his opponent's hands—the doubling cube.

But this is not to say that doubling must be made only when the position is overwhelming. If a player has a healthy lead, he should take the bull by the horns and double. Playing safe in backgammon is usually the sure way to defeat. A player should be bold, but this boldness must come from an appreciation and understanding of the position on the board, not merely from a desire to gamble.

Although a player gives his opponent an edge in giving him possession of the doubling cube, the player's double puts the question right to his opponent and forces him to make an instant decision. If the opponent can't analyze his position correctly at that moment, he may simply pass and concede the game—giving the doubling player an immediate win. But if the opponent decides to accept the double, he leaves himself open to a loss of double the stake. His decision can be quite difficult in some situations.

There is another advantage to be gained by astute doubling. If the doubled opponent finds himself in an inferior position, he'll probably concede the game when the doubling cube is pushed over to his side of the bar. However, if he isn't doubled, he's free rolling, since he has nothing to lose and everything to gain by finishing the game. A series of lucky rolls might put him right back into contention.

There are times when a player's position may be very strong yet he should avoid doubling his opponent. If a player has almost no chance of losing the game, and a very strong chance of gammoning his opponent, he shouldn't double. A double in this case would force the other player to concede for one unit, while a gammon will win two units for the player in the superior position.

The reverse is true when a player is offered a double. If he finds himself in danger of being gammoned, then he must be very careful about accepting the cube. No player wants to pay quadruple the stake when he can get away with only a one-unit loss by refusing the double.

When should a player double or accept a double? The answer can't be given in a short paragraph, because so many factors enter into the game, including the fact that backgammon is a flexible game whose momentum can change rapidly one way or the other.

In deciding on a double, a player must be able to correctly assess his position. He can do this by a pip count, by drawing on his experience, and by understanding the basic concepts of the game. All three are necessary for a proper doubling strategy.

The pip count will be discussed in a later section, and while it's a useful tool in assessing a position, it still is only a tool. Experience counts a great deal, and the more games a player plays, the better he'll be able to look over his position, get a feel for it, and make a correct decision about doubling.

Finally, this decision will come from an understanding of the basic concepts and strategies of the game, as well as the odds and probabilities involved in dice rolls. A player should be able to examine the situation in terms of the important strategic principles. For example, has he made his 5 and bar points? Has he been able to establish an anchor in his opponent's board, preferably at his 5 point? Are his back men trapped? Will he be forced to leave blots on his next roll, and if so, what are the chances of their being hit? And at the end game he'll have to take a pip count and determine who is ahead in the race to bear men off, and by how much. These are but a few of the questions to be asked, for different questions come up in different positions.

The Twenty-five Percent Rule

This rule is useful in other gambling games as well, and is sometimes applied to the concept of surrender in blackjack.

If a player has better than a twenty-five percent chance of winning, he should take the double. If he has less than a twenty-five percent chance of winning, he should refuse it. And if he has exactly a twenty-five percent chance of winning, he should still accept. Let's examine this concept in terms of odds.

Suppose a player has only a twenty-five percent chance of winning. If he accepts the double, the following will occur:

1. He'll lose three games doubled, for a total of six lost units.
2. He'll win one game doubled, for a total of two won units.

The result is a net loss of four units.

However, if the player had refused the double and conceded all four games, he'd still have the same net loss of four units. So he has nothing to lose by accepting the double. If he has better than a twenty-five percent chance of winning, his situation is better, since now he has nothing to lose and could possibly gain in the long run from accepting the doubles.

This method must be treated with caution when a gammon is involved. If a player is in danger of being gammoned, the twenty-five percent rule won't apply, because his losses may be quadrupled when he loses, while if he wins, he'll only double his win. So a player faced with a lost position compounded by a possible gammon should refuse the double. In fact, we already noted that the offering of a double when it's possible to gammon the opponent can be a costly mistake if the other player refuses the double.

Counting Pips

A pip count is a valuable tool for a player to use in assessing his position. By *pip* we mean a distinct unit of movement: the points on the board as vehicles for movement according to the rolls of the dice. For example, if a player has only one man left on the board, on his own 5 point, it will take five pips to bear him off.

The pip count is the difference between the number of pips each of the two players must roll on the dice in order to bear all men off, *without any wasted pips*. A wasted pip is a roll which is higher than necessary to bear a man off, such as a 6 when the man is on the 4 point.

Here's how the pip count is computed: If a player has two men left on his board, on the 4 point and 6 point, his total is ten (adding up the four and the six and multiplying by one man on each). If his opponent also has two men left, one on his bar point and the other on his 6 point, his total is thirteen. The opponent is three points behind the player and the pip count is three.

The player with the lower number of pips is deemed to be ahead of the player with the higher number of pips, since he can bear his men off with fewer numbers showing on the dice. The player with the higher number of pips is behind in the race.

To add up his pips, a player must count each man on his own board and multiply by whatever point that man is on. For example, if a checker is on its home board, on the 5 point, the count is $1 \times 5 = 5$. If two men were on that 5 point, the total would be $2 \times 5 = 10$.

Should a checker be on the opponent's side of the board, the count begins at thirteen for the 12 point and increases to fourteen for the 11 point, fifteen for the 10 point, and so on, since that's how many points away the man is from bearing off.

Let's compare the pip numbers of two players, Player A and **Player B**, and determine the pip count in the following example.

Player A's Men	*Pip Number*
2 men on his own 9 point	$2 \times 9 = 18$
1 man on his own 8 point	$1 \times 8 = 8$
2 men on his bar point	$2 \times 7 = 14$
3 men on his 6 point	$3 \times 6 = 18$
4 men on his 4 point	$4 \times 4 = 16$
2 men on his 3 point	$2 \times 3 = 6$
1 man on his 2 point	$1 \times 2 = 2$
Player A's Total	82

Player B's Men	*Pip Number*
1 man on his opponent's 10 point	$1 \times 15 = 15$
1 man on his opponent's 12 point	$1 \times 13 = 13$
2 men on his own 11 point	$2 \times 11 = 22$
2 men on his own 8 point	$2 \times 8 = 16$
3 men on his own 6 point	$3 \times 6 = 18$
4 men on his own 5 point	$4 \times 5 = 20$
2 men on his own 3 point	$2 \times 3 = 6$
Player B's Total	110

The difference between Player B's total of 110 and Player A's total of 82 is 28. The pip count is twenty-eight, with Player A ahead.

Doubling Strategy Using the Pip Count

Some experts have worked out a formula for doubling based on the pip count. They calculate the number of pips a player needs to bear all his men off and divide this total by the pip count to decide whether the double should be offered or, if offered, accepted.

In shorter races the criterion used is approximately twelve percent to double and approximately fifteen percent to accept the double. In longer races these figures are reduced to approximately ten percent to double and twelve percent to accept the double. Here's how this is computed:

If a player needs fifty pips to bear off his men, counting no wasted pips, and the pip count puts him ahead by six or more, he should double, since six is twelve percent of fifty. If a player is behind by no more than seven pips, he should accept the double. Eight pips, or sixteen percent, may be a borderline case here. With a hundred pips to go, a player should double if he's ahead ten or more pips, and this double should be accepted if the other player is behind no more than twelve pips, with thirteen again being a borderline case.

This method is not scientific and is merely a guide for players. Sometimes a pip count doesn't reflect the true position, especially if all the men are in the home board. If a player has gaps in his home board, and his 3 and 4 points are open, he'll go astray if he bases his calculations strictly on the pip count, because these gaps will waste a lot of pips.

To make a more exact calculation in this case, a player must judge how his men are distributed and figure out how many wasted pips he'll have, by determining how many times 3s and 4s will be rolled before he bears off all his men.

Chouette

A chouette is a form of backgammon which allows more than two players to participate. Three, four, five, or even more may be involved in the game.

Before play begins, each player rolls one die. The player throwing the highest number becomes the *man in the box,* or simply *the box.* He plays against all the others. The person rolling the second-highest number becomes *captain* of the remaining players, all of whom join him as partners against the box.

Then, in order of high rolls, the players with the captain become number one, number two, and so on, down to the player rolling the lowest number on the die. If two players roll the same number, they rethrow the die until one throws a higher number than the other.

These initial rolls of the dice at the outset of play determine the order of play and the positioning of the players throughout the entire session of play, not for just one game. Positions will change as games are played, but there are no more rolls of the dice to determine who is the box or captain.

The captain, when playing against the box, rolls the dice and makes all the moves and all the decisions, including doubling. He may call upon his partners to advise him, but he doesn't have to take their advice. Therefore, his partners are bound by all the captain's decisions but one. This exception occurs when the box offers a double. Then each player may accept or refuse the double for himself, no matter what decision the captain makes.

The winner of each game becomes the man in the box for the next game. If the captain wins, he gets to be the man in the box, player number one becomes the captain, and all other players move up in position. When the box loses, he goes to the bottom of the order, becoming the lowest member of the partnership against the box.

Should the box win his game, he remains in the box, and the captain moves to the bottom of the order among the partners. Then each of his partners moves up the ladder, with player number one becoming the captain. If new players come into the game at a later stage, they go to the bottom of the list and have to work their way up slowly.

In scoring the game, the man in the box plays against each of his opponents separately. Should he win a one-point game, then each of the opponents loses one point to him. If he should lose that one-point game, he loses it to each of the other players. If he's playing against four players and wins, he wins four points; if he loses, he loses four points. In both cases, his opponents either win or lose one point each.

When the man in the box doubles during the course of a game, and the captain rejects the double and concedes the game, if any of the other players decide to accept the double, the game goes on.

In that case, the most senior of the players remaining becomes the captain and plays out the game. Should this new captain win the game, he becomes the man in the box, and the box goes to last position among the partners, while the captain who had rejected the double goes next to last.

When a double is offered by the box, any player may decide to reject it, but he no longer is part of that game and cannot advise the captain on any moves.

Since the box might find himself in a dangerous money situation with doubles and redoubles, his tendency is to double carefully, because he has to pay off a group of players if he loses. On the other hand, the partnership might double more frequently than usual in a chouette, in order to put intense money pressure on the box.

In asking advice of his partners, the captain shouldn't automatically consult them before every move, especially if the roll is fairly obvious and one particular move suggests itself. In difficult moves, he can consult his partners after making his move so long as the dice are left on the board, so that the move isn't completed. In very complex situations, the captain may ask the advice of his partners before making a move.

XXII

Psychology of Winning

Introduction

At one time, the feeling about winning in America was expressed by the platitude, "It doesn't matter whether you win or lose; it's how you play the game." This has, I'm afraid, been replaced by Vince Lombardi's statement: "Winning isn't everything; it's the only thing."

A man who lives by either of these mottos is going to find himself in difficulty. The truth, perhaps, lies somewhere in between. If a man never strives to win, but concentrates on being a good sport, he loses a great deal of magnetism and strength, something associated with that vague term, manhood. On the other hand, the man who tries to win, no matter what the consequences, has distorted winning into something basically foreign to that same concept of manhood.

I know that by disagreeing with the late Lombardi's philosophy, I will irritate a great many people, particularly those whose main occupation is watching TV football games, and possibly I will also irritate those many sports fans who idolized Lombardi. After all, his teams did win, didn't they? Yes, they did. The Green Bay Packers of a certain era won games and won championships. And now, let me ask a question. What difference should that make in our lives?

If winning is so important that one philosophy centers around the fact that it shouldn't even be sought, while another philosophy states that it is the only thing worthwhile, it might be important right now to ask ourselves, what is winning? What does it mean?

The answer, in sports events, is quite simple; just look at the final score and see who won. But that might be *too* simple. If team *A* beats team *B* in football, but in the course of the game two players on team *A* are permanently crippled, is that a win? Perhaps that desperate victory will lead to a string of defeats. In that case, would we say that winning should be the only thing? Another example: If team *A* could only win by sending in a player who has a broken bone, or a torn ligament, or a potentially dangerous injury, by shooting this player up with Novocain or some other pain killer, jeopardizing not only his entire career but possibly permanently crippling him, would we so readily agree that winning is the only thing?

If you still say yes, would *you* go into that game for the greater glory of team *A*? And if you still say yes, what if you were so injured that you were let go right after the close of the season and spent your remaining days in a wheelchair. Would you still agree? And if you still say yes, perhaps it might be better to reexamine your whole concept of what life is really about, don't you think?

If we examine Lombardi's statement a little more closely, what he really was saying was, "In a football game, winning is the only thing." And I don't believe that any coach would apply the same conditions he imposed on his players to his own family. I don't think he would tell a child of his, "Getting the best marks is the only thing," and then shoot up the kid with Novocain and send him off to school with a broken ankle so that he wouldn't miss a class.

Now, at this point a reader might say, yes, all this is rather interesting, etc., but what does it have to do with winning at the games presented in this book? I say that it has everything to do with this book.

Winning has become an important factor in our lives and it has naturally been carried over to games. It is time to ask ourselves what winning a game is all about. How do we feel when we win? And is it necessary to keep an exact score of our wins and losses?

In the actual day-to-day living of life, it is rather difficult to know whether or not we are a success, whether we are "winning." There are no scores kept in most of the aspects of life that confront us. And many of us don't want to know the score. We feel vaguely that we are losing because, perhaps, our life is not exciting, our marriage is not so good, our children have not turned out as well as we hoped, and our work is boring. If we tried to analyze this, we would be moving in the right direction to make our lives better. But it is so depressing to undergo this self-examination that we prefer to look to the outside for our scores, and become winners by osmosis.

How is this done? Simply. We identify with a sports team, and if they win, we win. We identify with many teams and many sports figures, and there is thus a box score every day showing a win for us. If the Knicks and Rangers lost, well the Jets came out ahead, and anyway our alma mater won again this weekend. Always a winning score in our lives.

The tremendous popularity of American sports has a great deal to do with this concept of winning. We want to win, but if we cannot win in our own lives, at least we can identify with a winner; above all, if we can't figure out a score in our own lives, we can find a score somewhere.

What easier way to find a score than in a bowling league or a golf match? Everyone participating knows his handicap. He can be placed somewhere. Statistics then become very important. One of the great loves of Americans is statistics, so that further identification with winners is possible. If the team we follow in pro football didn't have a winning season, at least its halfback is leading in rushing statistics. A sport like soccer, which by its very nature, has no statistics, has never really caught on in this country.

Therefore, a knowledge of what we want to win and how we act and feel as winners is essential to winning in the games discussed in this book. With these games we can't identify with others anymore; we are on our own. We must be prepared, through our own efforts alone, to win.

There are a great many books whose titles begin, *How to win at . . .* or *How to be a Consistent Winner at . . .* or *A Winning System for. . . .* These books have a certain popularity and are read avidly by those who really do want to win at the games or sports mentioned. But these people are usually misled and, in the end, realize that while they looked for the fire of success, they once again tasted the bitter ashes of defeat. They couldn't win because they didn't know what winning implied.

What does it really mean? Based on the example of the crippled football player, we can see that a momentary win may be no win at all, but may result in a permanent loss. Now, a football coach might not risk crippling a player to win just any game, but if it was a Super Bowl game and that player was expendable anyway, he might risk it. And he might win the game. We would call him (the coach) a winner, but in applying that term, we would limit it narrowly to the football game. Because any coach who would do this is obviously a loser in another great area, perhaps much more important than football—courage. Not having the courage to face defeat, he endangered the health of another human being.

This whole concept of winners being losers in the broader sense is involved in most of the major sports, where athletes are conditioned not only to play a game, but to get away with anything they can. It is part of the sport of football, and certainly is involved a great deal in baseball. In baseball, sportsmanship is a dirty word. Take any beanball situation, for example. Or a situation in which a player knows he is out, yet will not admit it. What is particularly galling is that this same practice extends down to Little League ball, where chicanery, cheating, and un-truthfulness are openly encouraged. I would like to know one instance in major league baseball where a player, knowing he was out, corrected an umpire who ruled him safe. The player would probably have been thrown off the team, or fined and ostracized, and yet this game passes for our national pastime.

Extending the theory of winning one step further, we see that a man can be a winner in one or more areas, and yet be a loser in others. A man may rise to the top of a giant corporation, be in command of thou-sands of employees, and have great power, and yet be a failure as a father. Or this corporation head may continue practices which kill a million fish, or pollute great areas. Is he a winner or a loser?

The difficulty with the whole concept of winning is that it is a rather subjective thing. We can look at team scores, we can look at a man's bankbook, at who won the last election, and say that all of these people are winners. But, to paraphrase the Bible, "If a man has won the whole world, but lost his soul, what has he gained?"

All of this is rarely, if ever, discussed in any book on winning at something, especially games. And it is essential to know what concept of winning we are discussing, before going into a discussion of the philoso-phy of winning.

One of the bright aspects of winning at games in this book is that one doesn't have to become a loser at anything else in the process. In fact, winning at games is not much different from winning at various other aspects of life.

For example: Probably most of us know of a man who is a bachelor in his thirties or forties, never married, who goes out on many dates with all types of women. Invariably he comes back from these dates cursing his luck. This woman was too snotty, and this one too timid; this one wasn't his type, and this one came on too strong; and on and on. In essence, he has an excuse for not making out with any of them. It's either their fault or his bad luck.

Having been trained to blame his misfortunes on others and never on himself, this kind of individual never moves ahead at his job or pro-fession either. It's always his bad luck to be stuck in some dreary position, or the boss is jealous of him, or maybe the boss's wife.

This same individual, sitting down at a poker game, starts cursing the cards, blames his bad luck, the bad cards, or the way the other players are betting. He ends the game a loser, still blaming his bad luck.

We also see aggressive players, scared and timid one, cheats, manipu-lators, bluffers, cautious and angry players. It is hard to disguise one's traits in a poker game. It all seems to hang out.

There are basic rules for winning at games involving luck and skill, as there are for getting ahead in one's profession or job and for meeting interesting women. The principles are pretty much the same, strange as it may seem. Card playing takes knowledge, courage, psychology, and skill. What doesn't? In playing cards, there's no need to also bring out destructive impulses, as there is in many sporting events. In fact these traits, in cards, are generally losing ones.

I would like now to itemize some basic rules for winning. These are not the ultimate rules, but have been gathered as a result of studying psychology and studying winners.

Basic Rules for Winning

1. Don't play at a game you stand no chance of winning because of poor odds.

This rule applies to games like keno, bingo, chuck-a-luck, big 6, numbers games, slot machines, and lotteries. Avoid them. Only a rare few ever win anything.

2. If you don't have enough knowledge of a game, don't get involved. If you haven't studied all the ramifications of poker, for example, it would be foolish to play for stakes.

3. If you have enough knowledge of a game, don't play in a crooked game, or one in which you suspect cheating. Hungering after action, or the only game in town, is a sure way of losing.

4. If you are in a game, playing for stakes, and all the other players are superior to you, get out. Games are not a test of manhood. Remember, the panther has a beauty and grace all its own, but when it sees the lion, it retreats a little. This is self-preservation and doesn't demean the panther at all.

5. Know the particular rules of the game you are playing. You may be a great poker player, but if you don't realize that in the particular game you're in, the highest hand is an ace and one-eyed jack, combined with a 7 of hearts and any red deuce, what good is it?

6. If you don't understand the rules of the game, or they seem too complicated, get out of the game.

7. If you are playing well, at your best, but it seems that more than your skill is necessary to win, leave. It may be that the other six participants are all cheats and you are the patsy. Or it may not be your night.

8. Always set a limit to losing. If you get to that limit, quit.

9. Never set a limit to winning. If you have reached a certain level

of winnings, pocket most of it and play with the rest. If you lose this, get out a winner. Always try to quit winners.

10. If you are fatigued or depressed, don't play. A decision made under either circumstance, any psychologist will tell you, tends to be destructive. If you become fatigued or depressed during a game, get out.

11. If you are winning, don't alter your style of play to take a chance. This is the sure sign of a loser.

12. If winning, don't start making foolhardy and high bets to win a great deal quickly. That is the easiest way to lose it all back. If you were playing gin rummy for a dollar a box and were ahead $250 after five hours of play, it would be foolish to raise the stakes to ten dollars a box. One bad streak and you'd be even again or losing. Play the same stakes and retain your winnings.

13. Never blame your losses over a long period of losses on luck or the cards. Always study the game, your opponents, and yourself; somewhere among these three is the reason for your losses.

14. Don't develop a losing psychology during the game. The quickest way to find this out is to see yourself making wild, improbable and foolish bets.

Be confident and play with a confident attitude. Being defeatist will lose for you. If you can't feel confident about the game, don't play.

15. After winning a substantial amount, don't risk it all on one play. Too often, a man may accumulate a great deal of money after an evening of poker, then play double or nothing on a turn of the card. Easy come, easy go is the attitude of a loser.

16. Don't be distracted during a game, and don't drink during a game. Elementary.

17. Play honestly, but play as tough as possible. If an opponent is down to his last few dollars in the game, you have an edge in betting heavily and forcing him to a decision. If you feel sorry for him, or realize that the opponent needs the money to feed the wife and kids, don't play in his game. Unconsciously you'll play to lose, and won't feed *your* wife and kids.

18. Either play for money, or play a friendly game. Don't play for big stakes against friends if it will cost you the friendship. Often, stakes and friends don't mix well over cards. Again, you might unconsciously play to lose.

19. Don't play for stakes with insufficient money. If you are in a dollar-and-two game of poker and you only have twenty-five dollars in reserve, get out of the game. You are playing with "scared money" and you'll have to alter your basic game to preserve your money. Once you do this, you're a loser.

20. Don't allow an opponent to anger or irritate you. You'll then alter your style to get even with him, and take unnecessary chances which will cause you to lose. What if you can't help but get angry? Leave the game.

21. If you feel anxiety or guilt about being in a particular game, stop immediately. For example, a game of dice starts after hours at work, but you have a dinner appointment and know if you participate you're going to be late. The anxiety and guilt you feel will make you a loser.

22. If you have found yourself continually losing and disregarding your skill and knowledge of the game, and feel rather relieved about losing after an initial feeling of guilt, you may be a compulsive gambler. Stop playing for stakes until you have received help.

23. Lastly, the image of yourself that may be well hidden usually comes out in gambling games. If you see traits that brand you as a loser, recognize them and correct them. It will not only make you a winner at the game, but a winner in a much larger sense as well.

Glossary

above the line In bridge, the place on the scoresheet where premiums are scored.

ace 1. The one-spot in a pack of cards. 2. The one-spot on a die. 3. One dollar. 4. The highest card in many card games, such as poker.

ace high In poker, a hand containing five odd cards, the highest of which is the ace.

aces up In poker, a hand of two pairs, the highest pair being aces.

à cheval In roulette, the French term for a split bet. See *split bet*.

Ada from Decatur In craps, a slang term for the 8.

advertise In gin rummy, to discard a card so that the opponent will discard a similar card.

announce 1. Name the trump suit. 2. Show melds.

ante In poker, chips or cash put into the pot before the deal of the cards. Known as sweetening the pot.

auction The period during which bidding takes place in bridge and similar games.

automatic doubles In backgammon, a variation of the rules whereby both players agree to double the stakes for the game if on the opening roll each rolls the same number, such as 5-5.

baccarat The name of a card game in which all 10s and face cards count as zero. Also, the term for a hand valued at zero.

back to back In stud poker, a pair consisting of the hole card and first card shown open. Also called "wired."

back game In backgammon, a game in which one player, who is behind, employs a strategy of making and holding two or more spots in his opponent's home board; thus, while delaying his game, he attempts to hit the opponent's blots in the end game.

backgammon 1. The game of backgammon. 2. A game in which one player has been unable to bear off any men, and also has at least one man in the winner's home board or on the bar. Also known as "triple game."

back in   In poker, to come into the betting after first checking.

back men   In backgammon, the two men who start at the 1 point of the opponent's home board.

backward pawn   In chess, a pawn that cannot advance without being captured by an opposing pawn on the adjacent file.

bait   See *bete*.

banco   In chemin de fer, a term used by a player to show that he will cover the entire bank bet.

banco prime   In chemin de fer, the privilege of the player to the right of the bank to cover the entire bank when more than on player cries *banco*.

banco suivi   In chemin de fer, the call by a player wishing to once again cover the entire bank after losing his previous bet.

Bank, Bank hand   1. In baccarat, the wager in opposition to the Player bet. 2. In chemin de fer, the one who bets against all the other players.

bank craps   A form of craps played on a special layout in which all bets are booked by the house.

bar, on the bar   In backgammon, the strip which separates the inner and outer boards. When a man is hit, it goes on the bar.

bar point   In backgammon, each player's 7 point.

bar 12 (or 2)   In craps, the barring of these numbers as winning numbers for don't-pass and don't-come bettors.

bear off, bearing off   In backgammon, to remove checkers from the home board according to the rolls of the dice. Men can be borne off only when all of the player's men are in his home board. Also called "taking off."

below the line   In bridge, the place on the scoresheet where trick scores are entered.

bet   Any stake placed on the outcome of a deal or game. Also known as "wager."

bet blind   To place a bet without looking at one's cards.

bete   1. A failure to make a contract. 2. The penalty for failure to make a contract.

betting round   A period in card play during which each active player must bet or drop out in turn.

bet the pot   In poker, to bet an amount equal to that in the pot.

bicycle   See *wheel*.

bid   An offer to win a certain amount of points or tricks; to make a bid.

biddable suit   In bridge, a holding that meets the minimum requirements for a bid.

bidder   1. Any player making a bid. 2. The highest bidder, who takes the contract.

bidding   The auction; the period in which bids are made; competing for the contract.

big casino   In casino, the 10 of diamonds.

Big 8   In craps, an even-money bet on the layout that the 8 will be rolled before the 7.

Big 6   In craps, an even-money bet on the layout that the 6 will be rolled before the 7.

blackjack   1. The name of the game. 2. In blackjack, the combination of an ace and 10-value card.

Black Maria   Also called Black Lady, the queen of spades, in hearts.

blind   In poker, the player who must make a bet on the opening round without looking at his cards.

block   In backgammon, made points, which hinder and delay the progress of the opponent's men.

blockade   In backgammon, contiguous points made by a player which hinder and delay the opponent's men.

blocking game   In backgammon, a game in which a player establishes points in order to delay his opponent's progress.

blot   In backgammon, a single man on a point, which is exposed to a hit by an opponent's checker.

bluff   In poker, to attempt to drive the other players out of the game by betting on an inferior hand.

board   1. In poker, the open common exposed cards in a game such as Texas Hold 'Em. 2. The entire backgammon table. 3. One of the four quadrants of the backgammon table, with each player having an inner, or home, board and an outer board. Also called "table."

bonus boxes   In gin rummy, extra boxes awarded for gin, ginning off, underknocking, and game.

book   In bridge, the first six tricks taken in by declarer.

bookmaker, bookie   In sports-event betting, the man who accepts bets from players and gamblers.

box   In gin rummy, a score for winning a deal. In chouette backgammon, the player who is against all the other participants; also called "in the box," "man in the box."

boxcars   In craps, the slang term for a 12.

boxman   In craps, the casino employee in charge of the craps table.

box numbers   In craps, the place bets 4, 5, 6, 8, 9, and 10. Also called "place numbers."

breaking a point   In backgammon, moving men off a made point, turning it into a blot.

breaking a prime   In backgammon, moving men from an already established prime so as to leave either a blot or a gap.

bringing it in   To make the first bet in a round of poker.

bring men in, bear in   In backgammon, the movement of men toward and into the player's home board.

build   In casino, to put together two or more cards so that another card equal in value to their numerical total can take them in.

builder   In backgammon: 1. An extra man on a made point. 2. A blot placed on a point in order to cover it and turn it into a made point.

bull   In poker, the ace.

burn a card   In poker or blackjack, and sometimes in other card games, to remove the top card from the pack unseen to the players and place it out of play.

bury a card   In pinochle, to lay away cards after taking the widow.

business double   In bridge, a double made for the purpose of exacting a penalty. Also called "penalty double."

bust, busting   1. A terrible hand. 2. In blackjack, drawing cards and going over twenty-one. Also called "breaking."

buy   To draw from the widow or stock; as a noun, the cards so received.

call   1. To declare, bid, or pass. 2. In bridge, any pass, double, redouble, or bid. 3. In poker, to see a bet by putting in the same amount of chips as the previous wager.

callman   In baccarat, the dealer who calls and runs the game.

captain   In chouette backgammon, the leader of the team which plays against the man in the box.

capture   In chess, the taking of a piece by an enemy pawn or piece.

card mechanic   A skilled manipulator of cards who uses his skill for cheating purposes.

cards   In casino, winning three points for taking in twenty-seven or more cards.

carré   In roulette, the French term for a corner bet.

case card   The last card of that rank in the deck.

cash   To lead and win tricks with established cards.

castle, castling   In chess, to move the king and rook at the same time, so as to give the king protection.

center   In chess, the third to sixth ranks on the d and e files.

chalk player   In racing, a bettor who wagers only on favorites.

chase   In poker, to stay in against a better hand with the expectation of drawing needed cards.

check   1. In chess, a direct attack on the enemy king. 2. In poker, the equivalent of a pass when it is the player's turn to bet. 3. Another term for *chip*.

check and raise   In poker, when allowed, the raising of a bet after an initial check.

checker   See *man*.

checkmate   In chess, an attack on the king which cannot be repulsed.

chemin de fer   The European version of baccarat.

chip   A token used in place of money for purposes of gambling. Also known as "check."

chouette   A form of backgammon which allows more than two players to participate in the game.

clear   In hearts, having taken in no hearts or minus cards.

clear a suit   To drive out all adverse cards in a particular suit.

closed board   In backgammon, a prime made in a player's home board, closing the board to an opponent's checkers on the bar.

cocked dice   In backgammon or craps, any dice which haven't landed flat and flush on the board or layout.

colonne   In roulette, the French term for a column bet.

column bet   In roulette, a bet on twelve vertical numbers of the layout that is paid off at two to one.

combination bet   In roulette, a wager covering more than one number or choice on the layout, using a single chip or units of chips.

combination shot   In backgammon, a blot that is more than six points away from an opponent's man, so that a combination of numbers on two dice is necessary to hit it.

come bet   In craps, a bet that the dice will win, made only after the initial roll.

come in, enter, reenter   In backgammon, to bring a man off the bar and into the opponent's home board after it has been placed on the bar.

come-out, come-out roll   In craps, the shooter's initial roll before a point has been established.

contact   In backgammon, a position on the board in which each player's men have not yet passed the other player's checkers.

contract   The obligation to win a fixed number of points or tricks.

conventions, bidding conventions   In bridge, artificial bids used in order to give information to a partner.

corner bet   In roulette, a wager on four numbers at one time, using a single chip.

count the pips, count the position   See *pip count*.

coup   In baccarat and chemin de fer, a completed sequence of play, in which bets have been won or lost.

cover, cover a bet   To bet against an event occurring in a gambling game. Also known as "fade a bet."

cover a blot   In backgammon, to put a second man on a blot, making a point.

crap out   In craps, the initial roll of a 2, 3, or 12, losing for the shooter.

craps   1. The name of the game. 2. In craps, the roll of a 2, 3, or 12.

crimp   A method of bending the cards so that a player cutting the cards will do so at a predetermined place.

crossruff   Trumping tricks back and forth between two partners or between declarer and dummy.

croupier   The French term for a dealer.

cube   See *doubling cube*.

cue bid   In bridge, a bid showing control of a suit, either by a void or by an ace.

cup, dice cup   In backgammon, the container used to shake and throw the dice.

cut   1. To divide the pack of cards into two parts after the shuffle, usually done by the player to the dealer's right, or an opponent in a two-handed game. 2. A house charge for operating a game. Also known as "rake."

dead card   A card already played or discarded.

dead hand   A hand that is barred from further participation in the play, usually because of an irregularity.

deadwood   1. In poker, the discarded cards. 2. In rummy, unmatched cards in the hand.

deal   The distribution of cards to the players; one's turn to deal out cards.

dealer   1. The player whose turn it is to deal. 2. An operator of a house game. 3. The banker or operator of a game.

deck   The pack of cards.

declarer   In bridge, the player who plays out the hand for the partnership that won the bid.

deep point   In backgammon, a point far into the player's home board, usually the 1, 2, or 3 point.

defender   In bridge, an opponent of the declarer.

defense   In chess, a prescribed series of opening moves by black in response to white's opening move or moves.

defensive bid   In bridge: 1. A bid made by the opponent of the opening bidder. 2. A bid made to force the opponents to bid higher.

deuce Two-spot in cards or dice.

deuces wild In poker, a game in which the 2s are wild cards.

development In chess, moving pieces off the back rank.

dice Cubes that each contain from one to six spots, with their combinations adding up to thirty-six possible rolls.

direct shot In backgammon, a roll required to hit a blot six or fewer points away.

discard 1. An excess card played from the hand. 2. The play of a card in a suit (other than trump) different from the suit of the card led.

discard pile In rummy, the discarded cards formed into a pile.

discovered check In chess, a direct attack on the enemy's king made possible by moving another piece off the line of attack.

dix In pinochle, the 9 of trumps.

don't-come bet In craps, a bet that the dice will lose, made after the initial roll.

don't-pass line In craps, a bet on the layout that the dice will lose.

door card In stud poker, the first open card dealt.

double 1. In bridge, a call by an opponent that increases the trick values and penalties in the event the preceding bid becomes the contract. 2. In backgammon, to increase the stakes of the game to twice their previous size.

double bete In pinochle, a penalty suffered by a player who elects to play out his hand and loses.

double down In blackjack, a player's option to double his bet after receiving his first two cards.

double game See *gammon*.

double hit In backgammon, to hit two blots with one roll of the dice.

doubled pawns In chess, two pawns of the same color on the same file.

doubles In backgammon, the same number showing on both dice, such as 3-3, allowing the player to move his men four times.

doubleton In bridge, an original holding of two cards in a suit.

doubling cube In backgammon, a cube marked on its faces with the numbers 2, 4, 8, 16, 32, and 64, which shows the stake of the particular game. It is used by the players to double and redouble the stake.

dozens bet In roulette, a wager on any of the three dozens shown on the layout, 1-12, 13-24, 25-36, paid off at two to one.

douzaine The French term for a dozens bet.

draw 1. To receive additional cards from the dealer. 2. To receive cards from the stock to replace discarded cards. 3. To pull cards from the pack to choose the dealer. 4. In chess, a game which neither player won.

drawn game In chess, a game which neither player won.

drop out Withdrew from the current deal; discard one's hand. Also called "folding."

duck In bridge, failing to play higher when able to do so.

dummy In bridge, the declarer's partner, or the exposed hand of declarer's partner.

duplicate board In duplicate bridge, a device, usually of metal, for holding the four separate hands of the players.

early game In backgammon, the first stages of play.

easy way In craps, rolling a 6, 8, or 10 not as a pair.

edge, casino edge   The advantage the casino has over the player. Also called "casino advantage."

eighter from Decatur   The slang term in craps for a roll of 8.

eldest hand   The player at the left of the dealer.

end game   1. In chess, the last part of the game, when pawns and the king play a major role. 2. In backgammon, that stage of the game at which both players are bearing off men.

en passant   In chess, a method of capturing an opponent's pawn after it has moved past a pawn's rank of capture.

en plein   The French term for a straight-up bet in roulette.

en prise   In chess, said of a piece that is open to capture.

en prison **rule**   In roulette, after the spin comes up on 0 or 00, a rule that allows the bet on even-money choices to be imprisoned for an additional spin, without a loss of chips.

enter   See *come in.*

entry   A card that is able to win a trick and thus gain the lead in that hand.

establish   To force out higher cards to make lower cards best.

even-money choice   In roulette, a bet on the high-low, even-odd, or red-black choices.

even-money payoff   Any payoff at one to one.

exchange   In chess, the capture and countercapture of pieces. **Win the exchange**   Capture a piece greater than that lost.

exit   Get out of the lead; compel another hand to win the trick.

exposed card   A card that is inadvertently shown, either during the deal or during play.

exposed man   See *blot.*

face card   A jack, queen, or king.

fade, fade a bet   In craps, to cover part or all of the roller's wager. Also known as "cover a bet."

fader   In craps, the player who has covered part or all of the roller's bet.

false card   A card played to mislead the opponents.

false cut   A cut of the cards which leaves the pack in its original condition.

false openers   In poker, a hand which opened the betting in draw poker but did not meet the requirements necessary to open.

favorite   1. In horse racing, the horse established by the betting public as most likely to win the race. 2. In sports events, the team picked to win by the handicappers or oddsmakers.

field bet   In craps, a bet that on the next roll of dice one of several numbers, usually 2, 3, 4, 9, 10, 11, or 12, will come up.

Fifth Street   In poker, the final round of betting in Texas Hold 'Em; the third round of betting in seven-card stud.

file   In chess, a vertical column of squares.

final   In European roulette, a wager that the last number of a series, such as 4, 14, 24, and 34, will come up next.

finesse   In bridge, an attempt to win a trick with a card that is lower than one held by one of the opponents in the same suit.

first baseman   In casino blackjack, the player who first receives cards and acts upon his hand.

five-cent line   In baseball betting, a price line quoted to big bettors. Also known as "nickel line."

five-numbers bet   In roulette, a disadvantageous wager on the American wheel only of the numbers 0, 00, 1, 2, and 3.

flat bet   In craps, a side bet made among players in a private craps game, either with or against the shooter's roll.

flop   In Texas Hold 'Em, the first three cards constituting the board.

flush   1. In poker, a hand consisting of five cards of one suit, not in sequence. 2. In pinochle, a trump holding of A K Q J 10.

fold   In poker, drop out of play; withdraw from the current round of play.

follow suit   To play a card of the same suit as the lead.

forcing bid   In bridge, a bid that forces a partner to keep the auction open.

fork   In chess, a simultaneous attack on two enemy pieces.

foul hand   In poker, a hand that is compelled to drop out because it contains more or less than the necessary number of cards.

four flush   In poker, four cards of the same suit.

four of a kind   In poker, four cards of the same rank, such as four aces.

Fourth Street   In certain games of stud or Hold 'Em, the four cards each player holds prior to the next round of betting.

free-odds bet   In craps, a bet made in addition to a line or come wager at correct odds on that point number.

full house   In poker, a holding of three of a kind plus a pair. Also known as "full boat."

gambit   In chess, the sacrifice of a pawn or piece for positional advantage or attacking purposes.

game   1. A pastime, in the general sense. 2. A single contest, complete in itself. 3. A variation of a basic game. 4. The number of points necessary to complete and end a game. 5. A fulfillment of a contract. 6. A system of play.

gammon   In backgammon, a game in which the winner is able to bear off all his men before his opponent can bear off any. Also called "double game."

gap   In backgammon, an empty space between made points.

gin   In gin rummy, a hand completely formed of matched sets and sequences and containing no odd cards.

gin off   In gin rummy, to lay off cards so that the hand laying off such cards has no odd cards left.

go bust   In blackjack, going over twenty-one by drawing one too many cards.

go rummy   In rummy, to go out by melding the entire hand in one turn.

grand slam   In bridge, bidding and making all thirteen tricks by the declarer.

grifter   A cheat or confidence man.

hand   1. The cards originally dealt to a player. 2. A holder of the cards. 3. The deal.

handicapper   In horse racing or sports betting, the person who tries to select the probable winner by examining the past performance of the horses or team involved.

handicap race   In horse racing, a race in which there is an attempt to equalize the conditions of the race by assigning different weights to the horses involved.

hardway bet In craps, wagering that the point numbers 6, 8, or 10 will be rolled as pairs, 3-3, 4-4, or 5-5, before they are rolled as nonpairs or a 7 is rolled.

high-low poker A form of poker in which both the low hand and high hand can win, sharing the pot.

high-low split A form of high-low poker, played in casinos, where the cards speak for themselves in determining which hand is high and which low.

high roller The term for a big gambler in a casino. Also known as "premium player."

hit 1. In blackjack, to draw a card. 2. In backgammon, to move a man to an opponent's blot, sending him to the bar.

hit me In blackjack, the term used by bettors to signify that they wish to draw another card.

Hold 'Em See *Texas Hold 'Em*.

hole card 1. In stud poker, a card dealt face down and unseen by the other players. 2. In blackjack, the dealer's down card.

home board In backgammon, that quadrant of the board in which a players 1 to 6 points are located. Also called "inner board" and "inner table."

honors In bridge, the five highest trumps, or the four aces in no trump.

hot In craps, a term used by players to indicate that the dice are passing.

house The entity or operator against which players wager or bet. Also known as the "casino."

Howell settlement In hearts, a method of scoring.

impair The French term for "odd" in roulette.

incorrect pack A deck of cards which has either missing cards or unwanted duplicates.

initial bid 1. First bid made by a side. 2. First bid of a deal.

initial roll See *come-out roll*.

inside straight In poker, four cards in broken sequence which need a fifth card to complete and make a straight. Example: 6 5 X 3 2.

insufficient bid One that is not high enough to supersede the previous bid.

insurance bet In blackjack, an optional wager that the dealer holds a blackjack when his upcard is an ace.

interpose In chess, parrying an attack by an enemy queen, bishop, or rock by placing a piece in the line of attack.

irregularity An inadvertent departure from the correct procedure in a game.

isolated pawn In chess, a pawn that has no other pawn of the same color on either of the adjacent files.

jack One of the face cards, also called the knave.

jackpot 1. A big win in a game like slots. 2. The name of a poker game, in which a pair of jacks or better is required to open the betting.

Jacoby rule In backgammon, a game in which, by agreement of the players, if neither player doubles during the course of play, gammons and backgammons will count as only one betting unit.

J'adoube   In chess, this means "I adjust" when touching one's own piece or pawn.

joker   An extra card furnished with the pack which is sometimes used as a wild card. Also called "bug."

jump bid   In bridge, a forcing bid of two or three over a one bid.

kibitzer   A spectator at a game who may criticize the play or give unwanted advice.

kicker   In poker, an extra card, usually an ace or a king, kept with a pair for a two-card draw.

king   1. The highest-valued face card. 2. In chess, the piece whose capture ends the game.

kitty   1. In pinochle, a pool to which betes are paid, and from which royalties are paid. 2. A percentage taken out of a pot, usually in poker, to pay expenses for the game.

knave   See *jack*.

knight   In chess, a piece which can move over other pieces, also called a horse.

knock   In rummy, to end the play by laying down one's cards.

knock card   In gin rummy, the upcard, which in modern versions of the game determines the points under which a player may knock.

knock off points   In rummy games, to lower the point total by laying down cards on the opponent's matches and sequences.

last   1. In pinochle, the last trick, or the score for taking in the last trick. 2. In casino, the dealer's warning that the last eight cards of the pack are about to be dealt.

lay the odds   In craps, an odds bet against the shooter rolling a point number.

lay off   In rummy, to add cards to the melds or matched sets on the table. Also called "knock off."

layout   The markings, design, or diagram on a table in a gambling game run by a casino or operator.

lead   To play the first card to a trick in any round; as a noun, the card so played.

limit   1. In poker, the maximum amount a player may increase a previous bet. 2. The maximum amount a player may bet on a game, or specific event within that game.

little casino   In casino, the two of spades.

little Joe   In craps, the roll of 4. Also called "little Joe from Kokomo."

long shot   In horse racing or sporting events, a horse or team the betting public feels has little chance of winning.

long suit   In bridge, the holding of more than four cards in a suit; the longest holding in any suit in a hand.

low   The lowest card that can be played, or has been played, to a particular trick.

lowball   A form of poker in which the low hand wins.

maiden race   In horse racing, a race for horses that have never won previously.

major piece In chess, a queen or rook.

major suit In bridge, spades or hearts.

make a point 1. In craps, to roll the point number before the 7. 2. In backgammon, to place at least two men on point so that an opponent cannot touch down or remove a checker.

man A checker, counter, or disk that is used in backgammon, and is moved according to the rolls of the dice.

manque In roulette, the French term for "low."

marriage In pinochle, the meld of the king and queen of the same suit.

mechanic A sleight-of-hand expert who uses his skill to cheat at cards.

mechanic's grip A method of holding a deck of cards so as to facilitate cheating.

meld A combination of cards that have value in scoring, or that reduce the points in a hand.

middle game In chess, the period of the game that immediately follows the opening and precedes the end game.

minor piece In chss, a bishop or knight.

minor suit In bridge, diamonds or clubs.

misdeal Any irregularity that requires a new shuffle and deal.

morning line In horse racing, the track handicapper's early or morning estimate of the probable odds on horses running at the track that day.

move In chess, a play; one's turn to play.

multiple-deck game In blackjack, any game in which more than one deck of cards is used, but it usually refers to at least a four-deck game.

natural 1. A hand formed without the use of a wild card. 2. In craps, the cast of 7 or 11 on the first roll of the dice. 3. In blackjack, the combination of an ace and ten-value card to form a blackjack. 4. In baccarat, the dealing of an eight or nine total on the first two cards.

nickel line See *five-cent line.*

no dice In craps, a call signifying that the roll does not count.

noir In roulette, the French term for black.

no-trump In bridge, a bid to play out the hand without a trump suit.

not vulnerable In bridge, a description of a team that has not won a game toward rubber.

nullo A bid in which the object of play is to avoid winning any tricks.

odds The probability of an event's occurring stated as a ratio.

odds-on favorite In horse racing, a horse whose payoff will be less than even money.

odd trick In bridge, a trick won by a declarer in excess of six.

off the board A term used by a bookie to signify that he will not take any bets on a particular sports event.

one pair In poker, a hand containing two cards of the same rank, together with three unmatched cards.

open 1. Make the first bid, declaration, or move. 2. Make the first lead of a card. 3. In poker, make the first bet on any round of play. 4. Cards that are face up on the table.

open blind A form of California club poker in which the player to the left of the dealer must open the betting, regardless of the value of his cards.

openers   In draw poker, jacks or better, a holding of cards which entitles the player to open the betting.

opening   In chess, the designation for a standard series of moves which occur at the beginning of play, usually under some classification such as Ruy Lopez.

opening bid   In bridge, the first bid of a suit or no-trump.

opening lead   The first lead of a deal.

opening move   In chess, the first move of the game by White.

open poker   Stud poker, in which some cards are dealt face up.

orphelins   In roulette, the French term for "orphans," indicating numbers not covered by *voisins du zero* or *les tiers*.

outer board; outer table   In backgammon, that quadrant of a player's board comprising points 7 (bar) through 12.

overcall   In bridge, a bid that supersedes a previous bid, when made by a defender.

overhand shuffle   A form of shuffling or mixing the cards in which the pack is held in one hand and small groups of cards are removed and dropped into the other hand.

overtrick   In bridge, a trick won by a declarer in excess of his contract.

own the cube   In backgammon, after having been doubled, the player who is now in possession of the cube and can redouble at his option is said to own the cube.

pack   The deck of cards.

paint   A slang term for the face cards.

painted   In hearts, the taking of a heart in a trick.

pair   1. Two cards of the same rank. Example: two 4s. 2. In roulette, the French term for "even."

partner   Another player, with whom one cooperates in the bid and play and shares a common score.

part score   In bridge, a trick score total that is less than game.

pass   1. A declaration that a player does not wish to bid, either on that round or any future round. 2. A withdrawal from the deal. 3. In Black Lady, the exchange of cards before the play of the hands. 4. In craps, a shooter making either a 7 or 11 on the come-out roll or his point after it has been established.

passe   In roulette, the French term for "high."

passed pawn   In chess, a pawn not opposed by an enemy pawn on its own or an adjacent file.

pass line   In craps, an area on the craps layout where bets may be made that the shooter will win.

past performance   In horse racing, the previous race record of a horse.

pat hand   In draw poker, a dealt hand which is not drawn to by a player holding it.

penalty double   See *business double*.

penny ante   A term used to describe an insignificant limit in a game.

perpetual check   In chess, an endless series of checks which causes a game to be drawn.

piece   In chess, chessmen other than the pawns.

pin   In chess, to immobilize an enemy piece by so placing one's own piece that the removal of the pinned piece would cause the opponent's queen to be taken or king to be in check.

pinochle 1. The name of the game. 2. In pinochle, the meld of the queen of spades and the jack of diamonds.

pip In backgammon, each individual point on the board, counted as a unit of movement.

pip count In backgammon, a method of determining the difference between the number of pips necessary to bear off all of one's men without wasted pips and the number of pips the opponent would need to bear off his men.

pit boss A casino employee who supervises a gambling area.

place numbers See *box numbers.*

play 1. Contribute a card to the trick. 2. The card played, or move made. 3. The betting.

point 1. In craps, an initial roll of 4, 5, 6, 8, 9, or 10 which must be repeated before the roll of 7 for the shooter to win. 2. In backgammon, any of the twenty-four triangles on the board; also another term meaning *make a point.*

point count In bridge, the total of high-card points and distributional points held by a player.

pot The total amount of money or chips at stake in any particular deal.

pot limit A betting limit fixed by the size of the pot.

preemptive bid In bridge, a high opening bid made to shut out the competition, also called "shutout bid."

prime In backgammon, the making of six contiguous points anywhere on the board.

psychic bid In bridge, a bid made without supporting strength, the purpose of which is to mislead the opponents.

push A tie or standoff.

rail In craps, the raised edge of the table against which the dice must be thrown.

raise 1. In poker, to increase the bet made by a previous player; as a noun, an amount bet that is more than sufficient to call. 2. In bridge, to bid higher than the partner's previous bid in the same suit or no trump; as a noun, such a bid.

rake The amount of money a house or operator takes from a gambling game as his fee.

rank 1. The position of a card in its suit. 2. The precedence of hands in determining the winner. 3. In chess, a horizontal row of squares.

razz The game of seven-card stud, lowball, as played in a casino.

rebid In bridge, a second bid made by a player in the same suit or no-trump.

redeal A new deal by the same player after an irregularity in dealing.

red-black bet In roulette, an even-money bet that the next spin will come up one of those choices.

redouble 1. In bridge, a bid made by the doubled bidder or his partner, increasing the penalties or the trick values in the event the doubled bid becomes the contract. 2. In backgammon, a doubling of the stakes after a previous double.

reduce In rummy, to lower the point total of the hand by discarding high cards.

reenter See *come in*.

response In bridge, a bid made in reply to a bid by one's partner.

responder In bridge, the player making a bid in reply to a bid by his or her partner, known as the "opener."

revoke To play a card of another suit when able to follow suit; fail to trump or play over a trump when required to do so by the rules of the game.

riffle shuffle To shuffle the cards by splitting the pack and then intermixing the two sections.

right bet In craps, a bet that the dice will pass.

right bettor In craps, a player who bets that the dice will pass, or win.

roll In craps, each individual toss of the dice.

rook In chess, the second-most-powerful piece, also called a "castle."

rouge The French term in roulette for "red."

rough In lowball poker, a term to indicate that the cards below the highest-ranked cards are high, rather than low. Example: 8 7 6 4 3 is a rough 8.

round One complete series of play, in which every participant has the right to bid, bet, or play in turn.

roundhouse In pinochle, a meld of K Q in every suit. Also called "round trip."

royal flush In poker, an ace-high straight flush, which is the highest hand in poker played without wild cards.

royal marriage In pinochle, the meld of the K Q of trumps.

royalties In poker and pinochle, bonus payments to a player who holds certain high cards.

ruff In bridge, to trump the lead of a suit other than trumps.

rubber The winning of two games at rubber bridge by one team.

rules card In baccarat, the card showing the rules for drawing and standing with original hands.

rummy In rummy: 1. A hand containing no unmatched cards. 2. A call made by a player when his hand contains no unmatched cards.

run 1. A sequence of three or more cards in the same suit. 2. In pinochle, a flush.

running game In backgammon, a type of game in which the object is to race men around the board, with the intention of bearing them off first.

sabot In baccarat and chemin de fer, the French term for "shoe."

sacrifice In chess, giving up a pawn or piece to gain positional advantage or a strong attack.

sacrifice bid In bridge, a bid made without the expectation of fulfilling the contract, in order to prevent the opponents from assuming their contract.

safe discard In rummy, the discarding of a card that cannot be used by the opponent.

safe play In backgammon, a play in which a player isn't in danger of having any of his men hit.

salt the deck In 500 rummy, a discard played from a meld so that it can later be picked up by the player discarding it, together with other cards on the discard pile.

schneider In gin rummy, a loss of a complete game without scoring any points. Also called "blitz" or "shutout."

scoop the pot In high-low poker, winning both the high and low hands, thus taking the entire pot.

second dealer A cheat who deals out the second card from a deck rather than the correct top card.

sequence A set or meld of three or more cards of adjacent rank, sometimes required to be of the same suit, such as 9 8 7.

set In bridge, to defeat the contract.

setup In backgammon, the initial arrangement of men on the board at the outset of play.

7 out In craps, the roll of 7 before the point number is repeated.

shoe A card-dealing box used in games like blackjack and baccarat.

showdown In poker, the showing of the hands still in the game after the last bet has been made to determine the winner.

shuffle The mix of the cards prior to the deal.

shuffle up The reshuffling of the cards by a dealer in blackjack.

shutout See *schneider*.

shutout bid See *preemptive bid*.

side bet In craps, bets among the individual players other than the shooter in the private game.

signal In bridge, a legal method of giving a partner information either by a bid or by a play of a card.

singleton In bridge, the holding a single card in a suit.

sixaine The French term for a six-number bet in roulette.

six-numbers bet In roulette, a bet that covers six numbers at one time.

slam bid In bridge, a bid of six or seven in a suit or no-trump.

small slam In bridge, the winning of twelve tricks by the declarer.

smear In pinochle, the playing of a high-point card on a trick won by a partner.

smooth hand In lowball poker, a hand in which the second-highest card is a low one. Example: 8 5 4 2 A is a smooth 8.

smothered mate In chess, a checkmate by a knight where the enemy king is blocked from moving safely by his own pieces.

snake eyes In craps, the slang term for the 2.

soft hand In blackjack, any hand whose total is made up by the ace counting as eleven points. Example: A 6 is a soft seventeen.

split In backgammon, to separate two men previously together on a point.

split bet In roulette, a bet on two numbers with a single chip, paid off at seventeen to one.

split pairs In blackjack, the player's option to separate two cards of the same point value and use each to form a new hand.

spot card Any card other than the face cards.

squeeze play In bridge, an end play which forces the opponents to make adverse discards.

stacked deck In cheating, a deck that has been previously arranged.

stalemate In chess, a drawn game in which only the king can be moved and, while not in check, can only move into check.

stand, stand pat The refusal to draw additional cards to a hand.

stay   In poker, to remain in the game by calling a bet.

steal the ante   In poker, to make a bet on the first round of wagering to force out other players and win the pot immediately, and thus collect the ante.

stickman   In craps, the dealer who calls the game and handles the dice.

stopper   In bridge, a card which can stop the running of a suit by the opponents.

straight-up bet   In roulette, a wager on a single number, which is paid off at thirty-five to one.

suit   Any of the four sets of cards in a pack which are called spades, hearts, diamonds, and clubs.

surrender   In blackjack, a rarely used option which permits the player to lose half his bet only by giving up his original two cards.

sweepstake   In hearts, a method of settlement where the pot is won only by a player who is clear.

table   See *board*.

table stakes   In poker, limiting what a player may bet on a hand to the money he has on the table.

takeout double   In bridge, a double informing one's partner that the bidder has opening strength, or giving other information about the bidder's hand.

taking off   See *bear off*.

tell   An indication in a card game by the holder of the cards as to the value of the cards by inadvertent movements or gestures.

tempo   In chess, time as measured by development.

ten-value cards   In blackjack, the 10, jack, queen, and king, all with a ten-point value.

Texas Hold 'Em   A poker game in which each player receives two cards and uses the five cards on board as community cards. Also called "Hold 'Em."

third baseman   The player in the last seat at a blackjack table.

Third Street   In poker games, the round of betting after each player has three cards.

tiers, les tiers   In roulette, the French term for one third of the wheel.

tourneur   In roulette, the croupier who spins the wheel.

tout   In horse racing, a hanger-on at the track who tries to sell information to bettors.

transversale   In roulette, the French term for the trio bet.

trey   Any three-spot card.

trick   The playing out of cards by the active participants in a game where the highest card or trump played wins in a single round; those cards gathered up by the winner.

trio bet   In roulette, a wager covering three numbers at one time.

triple game   See *backgammon*.

trump   1. A designated suit, each card of which ranks higher than any card in the other suits. 2. To play a trump on the lead of another suit.

trump card   Any card from the trump suit.

turn   A player's opportunity, in proper rotation, to bid, declare, play, etc.

twenty-one   Another name for the game of blackjack.

two pair   In poker, a hand consisting of a pair of one rank, a pair of another rank, and an odd card.

underdog   In betting on sports events, the team not favored to win.

underknock   In gin rummy, a hand that contains fewer points than the knocking hand or the same number of points. Also called "undercut."

under the gun   In poker, having to bet first.

upcard   1. In stud poker, the first open card dealt to the players. Also known as "door card." 2. In gin rummy, the twenty-first card dealt, which is used as the knock card. 3. In rummy, the first card turned up to form the discard pile; also, the top of the discard pile at any time.

vigorish   The percentage taken by an operator of a game or by a bookie as his advantage or cut. Also called "vig."

void   Holding no cards in a particular suit.

voisins   The French term in roulette for a bet on the neighbors of the number previously spun.

voisins du zéro   The neighbors on the wheel of the number 0.

vulnerable   In bridge, said of a side that has won a game toward rubber.

wager   See *bet*.

wheel   1. The device in roulette containing all the numbers and choices that may be bet on. 2. In poker, the lowest possible hand in lowball, a 5 4 3 2 A holding. Also called "bicycle."

widow   Extra cards dealt face down belonging to no player at the outset of the game in pinochle.

wild card   A card that can be designated by the holder to represent any rank and suit.

win the exchange   See *exchange*.

wired   See *back to back*.

wood pusher   In chess, a weak or routine player.

X   A symbol representing an indifferent low card. Example: A Q J x

Yarborough   In bridge, a hand containing no card higher than a 9.

Zugzwang   In chess, a position in which any move by a player will seriously weaken his game.

Index

About the Author

Edwin Silberstang, who is recognized as one of the foremost authorities on gambling, brings to his expertise in this field a novelist's writing skill, a lawyer's precision, and an ex-intelligence officer's concern with significant detail.

He was born in New York City, graduated from the University of Michigan, and spent two years in the U.S. Army Counter Intelligence Corps, then completed law school and practiced law for ten years in New York.

Mr. Silberstang has published five novels, among them *Nightmare of the Dark, Losers Weepers,* and *Snake Eyes,* a novel of Las Vegas. At the present time he resides in New York, and travels frequently to the gambling capitals of the world.